The Ties of the Past

The Gettysburg Diaries of Salome Myers Stewart 1854-1922

Sarah Sites Rodgers

 THOMAS PUBLICATIONS
Gettysburg PA 17325

Copyright © 1996 Sarah Sites Rodgers

Printed and bound in the United States of America

Published by THOMAS PUBLICATIONS
      P.O. Box 3031
      Gettysburg, Pa. 17325

ISBN-0-939631-91-1

Cover design by Ryan C. Stouch

Cover photograph by Michael S. Brouse. Artifacts courtesy of the Adams County Historical Society, the Horse Soldier, Jacqueline and Thomas Sites, and Dean S. Thomas.

For my mother,
Jacqueline Stewart Sites,
for whom the ties of the past are made
manifest in Steve, Sally, Sherry, and Matt.

Curious I halt and silent stand,
Then with light fingers I from the face of the nearest
    the first just lift the blanket;
Who are you elderly man so gaunt and grim, with
    well-gray'd hair, and flesh all sunken about the eyes?
Who are you my dear comrade?

Then to the second I step—and who are you my child and darling?
Who are you sweet boy with cheeks yet blooming?

Then to the third—a face nor child nor old, very calm,
    as of beautiful yellow-white ivory;
Young man I think I know you—I think this face is the face
    of the Christ himself,
Dead and divine and brother of all, and here again he lies.

—Walt Whitman

CONTENTS

FOREWORD

A member of families which had resided in and near Gettysburg for a long time before she was born in 1842, Salome Myers Stewart lived a life of almost fourscore years. During the course of that life she demonstrated in many ways the sturdiness of her character and the abundance of her energy in devotion to the causes in which she deeply believed. There were times when she had to respond to situations not of her own making, such as the one which confronted her in her hometown in the summer of 1863. There were other occasions when she deliberately chose to expend her talents and time on behalf of what she saw as an obvious need, such as teaching the black children of Gettysburg. The contributions of Salome Myers Stewart to the benefit of her contemporaries, both in and beyond Gettysburg, more than warrant a careful, yet sympathetic, treatment of her life.

It is appropriate that Sarah Sites Rodgers, Salome's great-great granddaughter, should undertake such a treatment. Starting with but little knowledge of her forebear, she has worked tirelessly, and effectively, to locate the remaining primary sources of information about her, both in the collections of the Adams County Historical Society and elsewhere. To her credit, she has then taken the time to evaluate with a critical spirit what she has found.

The result of Sarah Sites Rodgers' work is a most commendable contribution to our improved understanding of the impact which a strong-willed and somewhat formidable person can have upon her, or his, time.

Charles H. Glatfelter
March 31, 1995

ACKNOWLEDGEMENTS

Research into the life of my great-great grandmother has probably been the most rewarding experience in my life. With each discovery, each new angle, I found wonderful people who offered their assistance and direction, for no other reason than the best one of all—that they cared deeply for the ongoing story of what took place in Gettysburg during the summer of 1863. There are numerous people to whom I owe thanks in connection with this work. I list them in chronological order in an attempt to include everyone.

I am deeply indebted to Dr. Robert Olwell of the University of Texas, formerly of Mount St. Mary's, who, through his class on the Civil War, got me started on this project. He recognized its value and encouraged me to keep going. His enthusiasm helped to spark my own, and I am forever grateful.

Thanks to Colonel Jacob M. Sheads for the first real connection to Sallie Myers Stewart, for issuing the challenge to "go out there and find Alexander," and for sharing our family tree.

I owe immeasurable gratitude to Dr. Charles H. Glatfelter, director of the Adams County Historical Society, who talked to me at length about Sallie Myers Stewart, and made available the Historical Society's resources throughout this entire project. I could not have conducted this work without his assistance.

I am grateful to Dr. Marie Campbell for a multitude of things too numerous to mention, from suggestions and direction, advice and criticism, to acting as a sounding board whenever I felt overwhelmed. She advised me for many months as I conducted this research.

Thanks also to Dr. Robert Preston, Dr. Curtis Johnson, Dr. Peter Dorsey, and especially to Dr. Carmen Schmersahl for being much more than my teacher these past seven years.

Thanks also to: Dr. Walter L. Powell for his assistance and advice; Elwood W. Christ, who tirelessly hunted down leads and posed wonderful questions for consideration, helped me find records, opened doors and glass cases, and though extremely busy, agreed to read my manuscript; Tim Smith for his enthusiasm, his knowledge of both the 149th Pennsylvania and Henry Stewart, and direction to the file where I found the magical "Alexander letters"; and Betty Myers, who unselfishly shared her information on the Franklin Street School.

To Dean S. Thomas of Thomas Publications, I owe gratitude for time spent helping me take pictures, for patiently listening while I listed all the reasons I couldn't possibly finish the manuscript, and offering much-needed encouragement and support.

To my good friend William A. Frassanito for everything—sharing his wonderful photographs and files, wisdom, and knowledge of Sallie with me. But most of all, for telling me to "write it as though you are writing it for yourself."

To Scott Hann, who truly went out of his way (from New Jersey to Pennsylvania) to share his photographic collection.

Thanks also to my dear friend Lu-Ann Garber, who gave her valuable time to work with me, tracking down information, spending hours reading microfilm, and just being generally helpful.

To my "data friend," Linda Winkler, for her computer expertise, patience, and extraordinary friendship; Janie Huston for hours of encouragement; and to Bill Ridinger, Gregory Coco, Ron Waddell, Ted Streeter, Debbie Antolin, Barb Sanders, Bill Junker, and Bill and Bonnie Portier.

To my "Bucktails" friends for those fascinating conversations on sunny afternoons in November and July at the Gettysburg Battlefield Preservation Association office. Thank you for finding me.

To Tom Sites, otherwise known as Dad, for hours spent proofreading and for all the phone calls asking, "Is Sallie Myers finished yet?"

Finally, I thank Gary, Heather, Anne, Tom, Mom Rodgers, Steve, Evelyn, Sherry, Ken, Matt, Lisa, Skip, Sue, Jennifer, Logan, Erin, Paul, Cameron, the entire Hill clan, and the rest of my family, all forty-three of them. Without their love and affection, this never would have been finished. They have my heart.

The Ties
of the Past

INTRODUCTION

The Salome Myers Stewart Diaries: 1854-1922

Tracing the life story of my great-great-grandmother, Salome "Sallie" Myers Stewart began as a course requirement during my junior year at Mount St. Mary's College. I was assigned to conduct original research on any aspect of the Civil War, which meant I could have spent a few days poring over *New York Times* microfilm, the diaries of Mary Chesnut, or various other first-person accounts already published for the benefit of thousands just like me in search of an "A" from a professor's pen.

From somewhere in my childhood memories, however, fragmented family references to "Grandmother Salome," who had nursed wounded soldiers during the Battle of Gettysburg, formed into a curiosity and a notion to research her story for my project. Curiosities and notions, "curious" things that they are, can quickly turn into obsessions, which is exactly what happened as I sought the life of my great-great-grandmother through her diaries and memoirs about her nursing experience during those great and terrible days of July 1863.

Gettysburg during the time of Sallie Myers' girlhood was a typical northern town of about 2,400 people. Surrounded by farms, it was distinctive in that its location was a convergence of sorts, with roads leading to major cities in all directions from the town center like spokes in a wheel. Only seven miles from the Mason-Dixon Line, Gettysburg's location was, of course, the reason why this crossroads town was eventually to become the site of the most crucial battle of the Civil War. And it was this most crucial battle that changed Sallie Myers' life forever.

Civilians who by sheer circumstance find themselves caught in the midst of wartime catastrophe, with the sights, sounds, and smells of battle and its aftermath, tell a remarkable story of the human capacity for withstanding fear and suffering. They also tell the story of the human capacity for selflessness, heroism, and courage in the face of destruction and devastation. These civilians, innocents caught in the maelstrom of battle, provide a more complete picture of the reality that is war. This reality extends far beyond strategies and tactics, casualties and statistics. It reaches into villages and towns with occupied homes and trampled fields, touching the lives of mothers, fathers, and children. Sparing no one, it leaves behind spirits both broken and reborn through adversity.

The impact of war on the average person is traced through records left behind in forgotten attics, memoirs tucked into back pages of old albums, and diaries and journals stored on top shelves, gathering dust and cobwebs with the passing years. Reconstruction of these records is vital to understanding the civilian experience, and their preservation honors their many contributions to history. Sallie Myers' diaries and memoirs are among those invaluable civilian accounts.

The earliest surviving writing of Sallie Myers is an English composition book owned by historian and author William A. Frassanito. It dates to December 30, 1854, when she was just twelve years old. Described in her own hand as "Number 1," it contains two poems, a few scribbled notations, and a farewell to her younger brother, Peter, who died in 1847. Whether Sallie kept diaries before that time is not known.

The year 1860 marks the beginning of Sallie's continuous diary writings. These writings survive in several ways: through original diaries housed in the Adams County Historical Society for the years 1862, 1864, 1865, and 1906; the 1860 diary privately owned by Sallie's great-granddaughter Jacqueline S. Sites; and typescripts conducted by Sallie's son, Dr. Henry A. Stewart, from her other diaries long ago lost to time. There is virtually no record at all for 1869-1884; there are no diaries extant, and with the exception of a few entries during 1875, no mention of those years is contained in Henry Stewart's typescripts.

Sallie's diaries and memoirs are of dual importance, both to the Gettysburg historian and to the student of nineteenth and early twentieth-century women's culture. They are important to the historian for the record they provide of the Civil War's impact on the average person, as well as the record they provide of the Battle of Gettysburg—particularly Sallie's descriptions of the wounded and the converted battlefield hospitals. They are also important to those who study the lives and private thoughts of women during this period.

Sallie Myers grew to womanhood in a time of great change in America. Politically, the nation was divided over many issues like states' rights, slavery and abolition, and the course of westward expansion. Sectional preferences and splits were redefining the essence of America. Economically, America found itself at the edge of the industrial age. The advent of railroads revolutionized business and trade, and factories and industry began to boom. Socially, the nation was embroiled in a ferment of reform. The status quo in areas like women's and minority rights, temperance, and educational opportunity was being challenged. The long accepted notion of "separate spheres in society" for men and women had been publicly rejected at the Seneca Falls Convention in 1848. Sallie experienced many of these great changes wrought by her time. At age seventy-eight, she voted for the first time.

Sallie's passion for writing extended throughout her life. In addition to her diaries, she wrote extensive memoirs and newspaper articles recounting her experiences as a battlefield nurse. Many of her memoirs, articles, and letters remain on record in the Adams County Historical Society among her private papers.

The task I faced in completing the story of Great-great-grandmother Sallie was twofold: First, the diaries themselves needed to be deciphered and transcribed, an arduous undertaking, for Sallie wrote double and sometimes even triple cross-entries on many pages. These cross-entries were a means of conserving space on relatively expensive paper. In double cross-entries, for example, she wrote in the "normal" direction across the page until it was filled. Then she rotated the paper a quarter turn and wrote again across the lines, going up and down the page. These pages, faded with age, were often difficult to read. As much as possible, the entries are faithfully reproduced, with spelling and punctuation changed only for clarity. Paragraph placement and spacing have been rearranged for readability and continuity. Second, research based on her memoirs and many references needed to be conducted in order to reasonably reconstruct the various aspects of her life.

Presenting the material in a coherent format became the primary objective once the diaries themselves had been deciphered and the research completed. Each section of Sallie's diaries is preceded by an introductory narrative in which passages from the diary itself are included. Thus, the reader is first presented with a segment of Sallie's story, then given the complete diary account. This provides easier access to Sallie's actual writings for that particular section, and references can quickly be identified.

The definitive experience of Sallie Myers' life was the American Civil War, and specifically, the Battle of Gettysburg, which affected the direction her life was to take until she died in 1922. Important, too, and of direct relationship to this definitive experience was the untimely death of her husband after only eleven months of marriage. Decisions resulting from these unforeseen circumstances made Sallie's life exceptional.

Drawn into nursing the wounded of the Battle of Gettysburg, Sallie worked tirelessly night and day for many weeks in the Gettysburg battlefield hospitals. From that nursing experience grew her commitment to preserving the memory of what took place in that small town in the summer of 1863.

Her experience as a young girl living in a border town, with the threat of Rebel invasion a reality, caused her to develop a compassion for the plight of black people in her community that was to carry into the rest of her life. She possessed an acute awareness of the constant threat under which these people lived, and their fear that if an invasion came, they could be sold into slavery.

If Sallie Myers had lived in some other town in America, and not Gettysburg, she probably would have continued her life as just another schoolteacher. She might have eventually married some local gentleman and settled into the routine of married life. Had her husband, Henry F. Stewart, lived a long and healthy life, Sallie most likely would have lived her days as a minister's wife, and possibly faded into obscurity. But these things did not happen. Sallie Myers lived the horror of war firsthand, and several years later became a wife, widow, and mother within the space of a single year. Faced with declining health, she determined to return to Gettysburg in 1870, and raise her small son, Henry, within her family fold.

Sallie Myers never remarried. She lived more than fifty years as a widow, dedicating her life to her son, to the memory of her husband, and to the memory of the battle which raged through her hometown that fateful summer.

Among her private papers is a single quotation which she underlined and saved, folded in the back pocket of one of her diaries. It reads, "I desire no life which will sever the ties of the past." Sallie consciously chose her life's path, one that allowed her the freedom and independence to conduct herself as she chose, reacting to the definitive events of her life with courage and a sense of conviction. Always devoted to the "ties of the past," her life after the war and the death of her husband is forever intertwined with the summer of 1863.

Sallie's life was distinctive in the sense that she survived the horror of war and overcame the many obstacles that life placed in her way. She was not alone in her experiences; she had contemporaries. Other women in Gettysburg who nursed the wounded in converted army hospitals also kept diary accounts or wrote memoirs, like Sallie Broadhead and Tillie Pierce. Countless women have faced widowhood and single motherhood and survived. Yet Sallie Myers experienced all three. She took each hardship life gave her and turned it into personal triumph and achievement. Her experiences left her with an appreciation of life's gifts and blessings, and in her later years she told her son, "Harry, I am glad I had my black bread first."

While tracing the life of my Great-great-grandmother Sallie, I have sometimes found it difficult to remain objective and to avoid reaching beyond the obvious to determine the value of an event in her life. Many times I saw myself in her, for she is, after all, a part of who I am. The journey into her life often resembled the journey into my own, as if through seeking her, I sought myself. Historically, I have striven for accuracy; reflectively, my admiration and love for Sallie Myers surfaces throughout this work. I make no apologies, but I hope I will be forgiven for any mistakes this may have caused.

Sarah Sites "Sally" Rodgers
March 1995

The Role of Henry Stewart in Typescripting Sallie's Diaries

Dr. Henry A. Stewart (1868-1956), the only son of Salome "Sallie" Myers Stewart, conducted typescripts from his mother's diaries. The undertaking was a project of tremendous proportions, and should be recognized as a magnificent attempt to keep his mother's writings alive. Had he not conducted this project, much of Sallie Myers Stewart's writings would be lost. His typescripts cover the period from January 18, 1860, to January 12, 1922, just five days before she died at age 79. The years from 1869 to 1884 are the exception—it seems as though Sallie kept no diaries for those years, except for a few entries in 1875. This is not surprising, for she notes in a later memoir and diary entry that the hardest years of her life were when Henry was young and she worked as a dressmaker, barely making a living for herself and her son. Henry makes no mention of those years in his typescripts. He makes references, however, at several points throughout the typescripts concerning some years when he has no records, and comments that somehow certain diaries have mysteriously disappeared. Whether they simply got misplaced or were actually stolen is unknown. Regardless, Henry Stewart performed an invaluable service in typing the pages of her then existing diaries.

Just how invaluable is evident with the typescripts conducted for the year 1863. The most crucial and historically significant of Sallie Myers' diaries, it was housed along with the other surviving diaries at the Adams County Historical Society. During the late 1960s, however, that particular diary disappeared from the Society and has never been recovered. Had Henry A. Stewart not conducted his typescripts from his mother's diaries, a tremendous element of the Sallie Myers story would be lost.

Accuracy in Henry Stewart's typescripts from the diaries is somewhat problematic. Many diary pages are faded and difficult to decipher, and spelling errors are evident in the typescripts. For this reason, a careful reading of Henry's work is necessary for the historian to properly identify some referenced people and events. For instance, in the 1861 typescript for May 23, Henry wrote: "Summerall's Zouaves paraded today, they made a very fine appearance." Summerall has been typescripted inaccurately; the Zouaves, a home guard unit formed in the spring of 1861, were led by the Rev. Sumwalt, the assistant pastor of the Gettysburg Methodist Episcopal Church.

Henry Stewart was also selective in what he chose to include in the typescripts. Unfortunately, he did not include her diary entries in their entirety, and instead chose to delete bits of information and even entire passages. His finished product contains twenty-eight single-spaced typed pages. Considering that Henry was a general practitioner with a busy practice, a local historian and active member of many Gettysburg area organizations, the Gettysburg area weather recorder, an inventor, a geneologist, and one of the founders and coordinators of The Annie M. Warner Hospital in Gettysburg, it is amazing and admirable that he found the time to work with Sallie's diaries at all.

A comparison made between the existing diaries of Sallie Myers Stewart and the typescripts conducted by her son show that he transcribed those entries he considered historically important and did not include reflective passages to any great extent. Probably the best support for this claim is that the twenty-eight pages of typescripts cover a period of sixty-six years, with the exception of the fifteen years between 1869 and 1884, for a total of fifty-one years. Of these fifty-one years, nine pages of the typescripts are devoted to the years 1861-1865, the period of the Civil War. Therefore, practically one-third of Henry's efforts were devoted to only one-eighth of the years that Sallie kept her personal diaries. From the historian's perspective this is good, for his typescripts contain many references to the war and battle conditions which Sallie experienced.

Occasionally Henry noted his mother's joy at an event, or an insightful comment Sallie may have made about someone or something, but these are brief and to the point, again without any embellishment, inclusion of Sallie's entire remark or feelings on that particular subject. Henry also assumed the role of narrator when he converted her entries onto the typewritten page, using phrases like "she says that" or "she notes" before actual quotation. In other entries, it is apparent that Henry was typescripting verbatim from the diary.

That Henry selectively included certain items in his typescripts does not in any way invalidate what he did. Throughout his project, he remained true to Sallie's writings and only a few times did he insert notations, and then only for clarification. In each instance, Henry carefully made sure the notations were recognizable as his, for he did not change or alter her words. For example, on May 19, 1862, Henry wrote, "mentions death of Nes Baugher, brother of Lee Baugher, one of the teachers (Principal, I think) from wounds ...." The words in parentheses are his. Sallie's diary entry is much longer, but Henry did not alter the facts; he simply shortened her entry tremendously and added his notation that he thought Lee Baugher was the principal. The following is Sallie's actual entry:

> Rose at 6. To school at 8. Home at 11. Went to see Jen. She sent for me for something. To see Rose G. awhile. To the store. Got a dress and stuff for a French jacket for Susie. Home at 12 1/2. To school at 2. Home at 5. Mr. Baugher is not at school today. His brother Nesbitt, a Lieutenant in our army was wounded seven times while engaged in the battle at Pittsburg Landing. I think it was in that battle. His father went to see him as soon as the news reached Gettysburg. He left him about a week ago and then the physicians thought he was in a fair way to recover, but poor fellow! he died from the effect of his wounds on last Friday. His remains will be sent home as soon as possible. I pity his family so much. His only sister Allie had just gone to New York on a visit and she has been sent for. What a sad time, when his remains arrive. Went out to see Carrie. I am not going to take any more music lessons until vacation which will be in two weeks. To see Ellie Aughinbaugh on business. Sade Rupp and I were walking. Home at 9 1/2.

Henry did not invent anything. He simply omitted a huge amount of text. The following examples from Henry's typescripts and Sallie's diaries are offered. On December 15, 1864, Sallie wrote,

Morning. Finished Jennie's dress. Afternoon. Busy. Evening. Went up street. Received a letter from Sue & one from Andrew's sister Margaret. Wrote to Susie. To prayer meeting. Mr. Gantry led. To Aunt Lizzie's. It is feared that Cousin Dave is dead, a prisoner starved to death. God grant that it is false. Poor Aunt! She is almost heartbroken. She seems to have nothing but trouble.

Henry's typescript of the same day is as follows: "To Aunt Lizzie—It is feared that Cousin Dave is dead—a prisoner starved to death." Nothing is altered; the facts are correctly given, but what is removed is the personal reflection and sad lament that Sallie's entry contains.

An even better example of just how much Henry removed Sallie's emotions and reflections from his typescripts is the following:

May 31, 1862. Morning. Very busy. Did all the sweeping. Mother was working in the garden. Afternoon. Sewing at an apron for myself and trimmed Susy's bonnet. Evening. Raining. Very disagreeable. Jen was up. I was real glad to see her. Went over to Mr. Powell's after she went home. Spent a pleasant hour with May. Home at 10. Feel miserably, but I seldom feel any other way now. I do hope it will not last long. I suppose time will help me. It sometimes does wonders.

Henry chose not to include this day at all in his typescripts. He recorded the May 30 entry which was one full page and an additional page cross-entered in Sallie's diary with the words "school closed," and then jumped ahead to record June 5.

Although Henry's contribution to Sallie's history was certainly selective and focused almost entirely on what he considered to be of historical significance, if it were not for his typescripting work, there would be no record at all for many years of Sallie's life. Therefore, while it seems justified to criticize Henry for leaving Sallie's private thoughts and emotions out of the existing records, it is still important to recognize the value of the service he performed in recording Sallie's life for posterity. It is because of Henry's work that certain aspects of Sallie's life can be pinpointed and researched, and that a reasonable reconstruction of her life can be achieved.

The Diaries

The Salome "Sallie" Myers Stewart diaries, letters and memoirs cover the period from 1854-1922. Unfortunately, most of Sallie's diaries have disappeared over the years. At her death, her personal papers and diaries were passed on to her son, Henry. And when he died in 1956, his personal records and papers, including his mother's writings, were under the direction of the Adams County National Bank, as executor of his estate. For unknown reasons, some of Henry's personal property was sold, while other items were donated to the Adams County Historical Society. Thus, a few of Sallie's diaries are housed there, while others must have been sold either privately or at public auction. The emergence of Sallie's 1860 diary in 1995 at a public auction clearly shows that Henry's personal collection was not kept intact. Other records that have surfaced piecemeal over the years indicate that his collection was, in fact, scattered to the four winds and no satisfactory explanation for this exists. Enough remains, however, to closely document a life of almost eighty years.

Sallie's early life is reconstructed on the following pages primarily through her diaries that are still in existence, supplemented by Henry's typescripts and her later memoirs. Her later life is reconstructed through other writings and memoirs, the typescripts, and one surviving later diary for the year 1906. The early diaries are reproduced in their entirety in this book; the 1906 diary is used only as a reference for portions of Sallie's story. Enough references are contained therein to provide impetus for further research, such as descriptions of Sallie's settlement work with Cornelia Hancock. Otherwise, the diary contains mostly weather references and daily activities.

The Civil War, and especially the Battle of Gettysburg, is an important part of the early Salome "Sallie" Myers Stewart diaries. Many references to the war are contained there, and they record names and everyday events which bring the war years alive from the perspective of a young girl who happened to live in a time and place defined by turmoil, upheaval, and uncertainty.

Of perhaps greater significance is the picture the diaries present of a young woman in conflict with the world around her. Sallie's diaries record for posterity the struggles and personal conflicts of a young woman of strong character who, under the constraints of her time, was forced to live a life of conformity. Sallie perceived herself as someone plagued with troubles and adversity, but who was compelled to keep her problems to herself. The world as she understood it provided little outlet for expressing her feelings or living her life free of the social restrictions placed upon her. She privately rebelled against her mother, who ruled with an iron hand, and secretly longed for her father (whom she idolized) to return home from the war, feeling that he was the only person she could trust to understand her troubles.

Those who have explored women's diaries discuss the motivation behind diary writing as the crucial element to understanding the writer. In Sallie's early diaries, there is little evidence that her motivation for writing was eventual publication. Rather, her diaries serve as the one relatively safe place where she could speak her mind and wrestle with her conscience. As she wrote in March 1862, "no one shall ever see it while I live, and perhaps not after I am gone." Further evidence of this can be seen in the following passage: "... I will have to suffer and be strong though no one shall ever know what has passed between us this evening unless someone should get this diary which is very unlikely. I would burn it first."

Sallie's early writings disclose many private aspects of her personality which she kept hidden away from others by placing them within the pages of her diaries. She wrote passionate lamentations about her self-perceived inability to live as a true Christian; she wrote of secret longings for Thomas Snyder, the early love in her life, and she recorded her hopes and fears for herself and others. Sallie spoke of her diary as being "like a friend in which I can confide without fear of being betrayed" (January 10, 1862). The "betrayal" she wrote about is evidence of the conflict typical in nineteenth century women, that of ideal womanhood versus women's real desires, thoughts, and ideas. Sallie's conflict emerges from the struggle over how she must outwardly conduct herself as opposed to her private reactions to the social constraints placed on her.

Sallie's diaries were, in essence, the outlet for her conflicts. On those pages, she could speak frankly of her dislike for church sermons, the preacher, and her inability to keep her mind on religious matters. She could express her basic distrust of local gossips and know-it-all relatives as well as the resentment she felt toward her mother who, she believed, unfairly controlled her life.

Despite Sallie's speaking of her diary as "a friend in which I can confide," she made frequent references to feelings that she could convey to no one, not even her diary. Fear of discovery sometimes restrained her from writing about problems she felt were too private. This fear was not without reason. Several times during the year 1862, when Sallie and her mother disagreed over her romance with Thomas Snyder, she referred to her mother's knowledge of details she could have attained only through eavesdropping and reading Sallie's diary. This intrusion into her private world forced Sallie to retreat to allusions in her diary which only she could decipher. Sallie's comments on September 8, 1862, reveal her resentment over an invasion of her privacy when she acknowledges that perhaps her mother has read her diary:

> She says she knows things and has heard things which lead her to believe that I am deceiving her. There is an old adage, "Listeners never hear any good of themselves." I suppose she has got my diary and read it for I had it in a drawer which is unlocked. In the future I shall keep it with me...She says I am trying to make them believe that I do not care anything about Snyder. It is nobody's business whether I like him or not and no one is going to know from me. I have resolved to give him up and we have met as strangers. I will continue to do so, but that is all I shall do.

Sallie alternated between two distinct writing styles: a somewhat disjointed, trivial-entry style for entries about work, teaching, chores, sibling responsibilities, church-going, and other daily events; and a narrative voice whenever she expanded on personal reflections, her deepest feelings and emotions. This alternation is not unusual, considering that Sallie was writing for herself rather than others. The use of the trivial-entry style combined with narrative form gives insight into what Sallie considered to be important when she wrote. The trivial-entry used for daily events simply recorded them; the narrative for self-exploration served as her means of self-discovery.

Writing in this manner removes the temptation for glorified details, unnecessary description, and overblown reaction to events as they occur. What is revealed, then, is truth without pressure to convince the reader, and truth without embellishment. This enhances the cultural importance of her early writings, for it is important when examining the autobiographical writings of women to construct the honest personal viewpoint. Regardless of societal demands that restricted women's outward activities and required an almost unilateral acquiescence to norms, women's thoughts were still uniquely their own. It is in writings like Sallie's that the construction of truth against the background of cultural influence can be discovered.

The sense that Sallie perceived herself as alone in the world pervades her diaries. She identified herself as separate, apart from her family and friends, existing in a world where she was the different entity. She lamented often on her troubles, and wondered if she was the only person who felt things as she did. The conflict appears in her relationship to her social experience, her feminine role, her religion, and her personal identity. For all outward appearances, however, Sallie functioned well in her environment. She lived an active, normal life, helping with the care of her family, teaching, and socializing with friends.

Only in her diaries can we get a glimpse of the young woman who battled with her conscience, aware of the futility of her efforts; a woman who secretly wished for her burdens to ease and her life to become less care-ridden. Her diaries allow a look into her other self that she kept hidden from everyone she knew, and her public self which others saw.

Despite the beginning struggles against long-standing gender roles, nineteenth-century American women were still primarily defined by their culture as nurturers. They were seen as mothers, nurses, and comforters, experts in all areas of domestic life. Social activity was tied to the home and church. Traditionally the weaker sex, women looked to men and the male-dominated society for a definition of their roles in life.

Sallie's view of herself embraces the traditional roles of women yet struggles to break free of them, for she yearned to be independent. Working as a schoolteacher, she earned her own salary which she willingly contributed to household expenses, except for the small amount she needed for personal items. Her strong need for independence is evident in the following entry dated January 2, 1862: "Got my salary for December (10.00). Paid some debts and had ten cents left. Feel free as an uncaged bird. I can now say, 'I owe no man (or woman either) anything.'"

Sallie's writings reveal that the relationship with the significant others in her life was often one of discord. The diaries are filled with her own ideas and thoughts, by nature diametrically opposed to those of others and in opposition to cultural expectations. She sometimes hated housework, although she did a lot of it. She disagreed with her mother's demands but outwardly conceded to them. She also disagreed with her friends' activities like dancing and card playing, which went against her religious principles.

Sallie fulfilled the traditional role of nurse and comforter when she was called upon to tend the soldiers in the converted army hospitals. She did not do so, however, without a struggle. She was surprised at her ability to overcome her terrible aversion to the sight of blood. Yet her experiences ultimately caused her to wish for the rest of her life that she had enlisted as a nurse rather than stayed at home where her many family responsibilities weighed heavily upon her.

Sallie's sense of identity as a Christian caused her much anxiety and produced some of her most eloquent narratives. She despaired that she would never be able to live up to her convictions; her perceived lack of faith and feelings of failure were expressed privately in her diaries. She sought to find herself, to come to terms with her religious world. Examined in the cultural context of her society, her perceptions can be traced to a shift in religious emphasis that occurred in the nineteenth century. Methodist in origin, this shift marked a change from the believer bound by laws of determinism left over from Calvinist doctrine, to an emphasis on personal religious experience. The faithful Christian in Sallie's world needed to be personally filled with the Holy Spirit by her own volition and will, rather than be guided by concrete laws set in place which took personal responsibility out of her hands. Thus, failure was also personal. Sallie's self-perceived failures were her own, the responsibility for them on her shoulders.

In later writings, as shown in her 1906 diary, her conflicts seem to be resolved. Her focus was her family, routine events, and her memories of the past. The search for identity, the rebelliousness of young womanhood, the feelings of alienation and loneliness, and the spiritual angst had vanished. None of the earnest soul-searching, self-doubt, and troubled outpourings of emotion so freely expressed in her early, formative years, is found. In their place are the writings of a woman who has established a life and gained the respect of her peers. When she died, Salome Myers Stewart, after a long life of hard work, adversity, and self-sacrifice, had attained peace and contentment.

Sallie's diaries tell the story of one young woman. Her story is one among many, constructed from her own thoughts and opinions, no more or less honest than any other. History is, after all, only the interpretations of individuals who must, in their own fashion, make a determination about what they perceive as important enough to commit to paper. Sallie began the opening page of each new diary with the following inscription:

Let love and truth indite—
Whatever here I write.

Elizabeth Salome (Sallie) Myers, 1842-1922. c. 1860. (ACHS)

1

THE EARLY YEARS:
"I WAS A SCHOOLTEACHER"

Elizabeth Salome "Sallie" Myers was born June 24, 1842, in Gettysburg, the daughter of Hannah Margaret Sheads and Peter Appel Myers. The Myers and Sheads families were firmly entrenched in Gettysburg and Adams County, tracing back to the beginnings of the town. Both maternal and paternal great-grandparents settled in Pennsylvania after initial immigration from Europe to Frederick County, Maryland, in the early 1700s.[1]

Sallie's maternal ancestry traces back to her great-grandfather, John Troxell, Sr., born May 3, 1760, the son of Daniel Troxell who immigrated to America from Switzerland. It was John Troxell, Sr., who was said to have "built the first house in Gettysburg after the town was laid out."[2] He is described on his tombstone in Evergreen Cemetery as the first settler in Gettysburg. His daughter Salome (1784-1860) married Peter Sheads (1741-1848) of Gettysburg. They had eleven children, including Hannah Margaret, who was born January 6, 1818.

Sallie's paternal great-grandfather was Sebastian Moyer, born April 30, 1747, who immigrated with his father, Johannes, to Philadelphia from Rotterdam in 1749.[3] The Moyer (later Myers) family settled in Frederick County, Maryland. Sebastian later married Charlotte Appel from Thurmont, Maryland, and located his family permanently in Gettysburg during its early days as a town.

Their son, John Moyer, was born in 1788 and married Maria Elizabeth Gilbert in 1811. Maria died in 1826, followed by John in 1828. They left their son Peter an orphan at age twelve.[4]

Peter Appel Myers and Hannah Margaret Sheads married on September 8, 1837.[5] They had two sons and five daughters: John Jefferson, Salome, Virginia, Peter, Susannah, Isabell, and Ella Grace. Six of them survived infancy and reached adulthood. Their youngest son, Peter, died in 1847 at not quite three years of age. Peter Myers' occupation as a cabinetmaker sufficed to support eight people, but the family did not own a home of their own.[6] Peter held a position of respect in Gettysburg, for he served as a borough Justice of the Peace and Judge of Elections.[7]

John Troxell, 1760-1855.
(ACHS)

Salome Troxell Sheads, 1784-1860.
(ACHS)

Peter Sheads, 1871-1848.
(ACHS)

Hannah Margaret Sheads Myers,
1818-1881. (ACHS)

Peter Appel Myers, 1818-1872
(ACHS)

John Jefferson Myers,
1839-1883

Susannah Myers (seated left), sister
of Sallie Myers. With Miss Alice
(Allie) Powers, seated right, and
Susan Shields, standing. (ACHS)

Sallie Myers' childhood was typical of her era, much like any other young girl's life in the mid 1800s. She spent her days going to school, helping her mother at home, studying the piano, and attending the Gettysburg Methodist Episcopal Church, where she often described the sermons as "just tolerable."[8] As the eldest daughter, the care of her siblings often fell on her shoulders. She played games with her sisters Sue, Jennie, Belle, and Grace, and doted on her only living brother, Jefferson. The death of her little brother Peter affected her greatly, though she was only five years old when he died.

Sallie received her education in the Gettysburg public schools and attended the High Street School when it opened. By the time she was 17 years old in 1859, Sallie had received her first "Provisional Certificate"[9] and began to teach in Room #7, in the southeast corner of the first floor in that same High Street School.[10] She was the "5th Assistant" to the principal. Under the system that was in use then, the principal was the teacher; directly under him were a number of assistants, ranked numerically, with the "1st Assistant" the next highest position after the teacher. Thus, a number of relatively young people could go into teaching immediately upon completion of their public school education and a successful examination. Many of her students were only a few years her junior when she taught them.[11]

Sallie did not seem daunted by this fact. She applied discipline according to the standards of the day and seemed to have her classroom under control. In a note written to another teacher, she described just what was necessary to handle one particularly difficult young man:

> Oh, goodie, what a question. Just ask the young gent if I ever applied the rod of correction to his royal hide. Did you ever whip him? If you did not, just try it & see if he don't shake his head & scold, for which I always had to whip him the second time.
>
> Sallie[12]

Sallie occasionally composed poetry for *The Star and Banner*, a Gettysburg newspaper. As was fashionable in her day, she often submitted her work under a *nom de plume*, one of which was "Rosa Alba," meaning the white rose.[13] *The Star and Banner* for June 27, 1859, published one of her poems entitled, "There Are No Tears In Heaven," written when she was seventeen years old. The language is flowery and the tone sentimental, a style typical of the era. Religious themes formed the basis for her poetry, with particular emphasis on the afterlife and the rewards of Heaven.

In 1860 Sallie celebrated her eighteenth birthday and was earning a teacher's salary of $18 a month. This was also the year that her diary writing began in earnest. The entries include pupil attendance records at her school, church activities, and her intentions to study geometry, algebra, and arithmetic during her summer vacation. She also noted her two-year anniversary of officially joining the Methodist church in her entry dated May 16.

The 1860 diary depicts scenes of ordinary small-town American life. Friends, teaching, and family life are discussed at length, often with vivid descriptions of

everyday events. Threaded throughout the early months of 1860 are tragic references to friends and relatives who were taken sick and died. The illness and
subsequent death of her friend, Ada White, is poignantly described as Sallie
repeatedly visited her sick-bed, reading to her, singing hymns, and sometimes
just holding her hand on cold winter night visits. When Ada died on February
16, Sallie recorded a sad family tale in her diary:

> Ada White died this morning about half past 9 Oclock. From all I can
> learn, she was resigned to God's will. I never had an opportunity to
> converse with her excepting a few words which passed between us on
> last Sunday morning. Ada is the seventh one, of a family of eight, who
> have all died within four years. Her sister Annie died last Spring. She
> was one of my dearest friends. I often think of her but not with sorrow,
> for I know that one day we will meet to part no more forever. Dear
> Annie....[14]

Neatly folded into the back pocket of her 1860 diary is fifteen-year-old
Annie Elizabeth White's obituary, with the date June 1859 inscribed in Sallie's
hand. Also folded there is a newspaper clipping of a poem titled "Our Dead," the
first stanza of which reads,

> Day by day, the circle lessens
> Round our hearthstone—
> Day by day, the number strengthens
> On the everlasting shore....

Sallie's deep faith in God and belief in the rewards of Heaven are evident
throughout the diary of 1860, and her devotion usually sustained her, giving her
strength through many of her trials. Sometimes, however, she sank into a deep
melancholy over the loss of those she loved. Her maternal grandmother, Salome
Troxell Sheads (1784-1860), described by Sallie as "the oldest inhabitant of the
place" passed away on April 3 and Sallie attended the funeral on April 5:

> She lies in her coffin as peacefully as though she were sleeping. She
> is sleeping, but it is the long sleep of death which knows no waking.
> She, who was ever ready to sympathyze with us in our sorrows, lies all
> unconscious of the tears which are shed around her... Have just returned
> from grandmother's funeral... Struggle as I would I could not keep back
> the tears. One by one my relations and friends are being carried to
> Evergreen Cemetery and laid beneath the clods of that lovely place. I
> know not who will be next. It may be myself. Four of the companions
> of my childhood are already there, and one dearly loved friend of my
> girlhood lies there....[15]

The melancholy that overwhelmed Sallie after the death of both her friend
and her grandmother caused her to contemplate her trials and troubles. She saw
herself as alone and unable to confide in anyone, for she felt that no one truly
understood her. A passage written on April 10 explored these feelings of alienation:

I was sitting at my window a long time this evening as it was getting dark, thinking over "matters and things," and came to the conclusion that I have my share of the trouble and sorrow of this life. If only I had some friend into whose ear I could pour my griefs perhaps I would feel relieved, but, alas! that blessed privilege is denied me...But as I am a thoughtless and light-hearted girl, those to whom I could open my heart, only laugh and say, "they don't see what I have to trouble me."

Sadness and tragedy notwithstanding, Sallie found much in her life to enjoy. Her diary is filled with notations of clear blue skies, beautiful moonlight nights, and lovely days: "I do not know when we have had such a night. It is magnificent! The ground is covered with snow, and I suppose the sleighing is good."[16] She enjoyed long walks through the streets of Gettysburg and into the surrounding countryside with friends and family.

Politically, Sallie's family was Whig, and later, Republican,[17] although most of the people in Gettysburg at that time were Democrats. The political party opposition within the town was sufficient to produce heated debates in local newspapers. Gettysburg had three major papers in circulation during the 1850s and 1860s, each one strongly partisan. *The Compiler*, heavily Democratic under owner Henry J. Stahle, opposed John T. McIlhenny's *The Star and Banner* and Robert Goodloe Harper's *The Sentinel*, both heavily Whig. Events surrounding the Presidential election of 1860 were reported from them with considerable mudslinging and innuendo.[18] Sallie's diary entry for October 9, 1860, noted the gubernatorial elections, and she described a "good deal of fighting" going on downtown. She wrote that her father, the judge of elections, was still "not home yet" on the following day.

A somewhat controversial addition to the Gettysburg political scene during the fall of 1860 was the formation of a Wide Awakes club on October 1.[19] Consisting of Republican activists whose main objective was to excite the local population and get them to vote in the 1860 election, such Wide Awake clubs formed in several other communities throughout Adams County as well. The Wide Awakes frequently held torchlight processions through the streets of Gettysburg.[20] Their activity proved to be a source of some of the heated political debate in Gettysburg newspapers, for the October 6 issue of *The Compiler* has its Democratic editor openly criticizing the Wide Awakes, relating them to the Know Nothings of the 1850s. He warned his readers to "keep their eyes on these suspicious Wide Awake clubs." *The Sentinel* responded quickly on October 10 by describing the club as "an active, energetic band united to pull down the rotten fabric at Washington, and place there an honest administration in the person of Abraham Lincoln, of Illinois."[21]

Townspeople took notice of the demonstrations and torchlight parades of the Wide Awakes. Abraham Lincoln's election to the Presidency caused much rejoicing in Gettysburg, and on November 6 Sallie covered half a page in her diary with the notation "Hurray for Lincoln and Hamlin!...Everyone is rejoicing over the great triumph the Republican Party has achieved." The Wide Awakes then participated in what Sallie described on November 15 as,

> A grand Republican jollification...There was a nice torch-light procession. The Wide Awakes were out. Came home about 8 1/2 Oclock. We did not illuminate. Father and mother are both opposed to it, and so am I.

Although Sallie's family supported the Republican Wide Awakes, and enjoyed the celebration, they apparently opposed the community "illumination" encouraged by the organization as they processed through the streets.

🍂 🍂 🍂

The year 1861 marked a change in Sallie's diary. Accompanied by remarks about family members and items concerning her teaching, entries concerning the Civil War began. In May, the first glimpse of the war appeared, when she recorded that "Summerall's [Sumwalt's][22] Zouaves paraded today [and] they made a very fine appearance."[23] No hint of real worry or anxiety is found, however, until her entry of June 20 which contains the words, "Mr. [Leander] Welsh, a member of the volunteers that went from here is dead." These volunteers, a local militia unit known as the Independent Blues, had marched out of Gettysburg in answer to President Lincoln's initial call for 75,000 men after the firing on Fort Sumter. Formed as Company E of the 2nd Pennsylvania Volunteer Infantry, they were commanded by Captain Charles H. Buehler.[24]

On July 22 Sallie anxiously wrote about her brother Jefferson, who on June 8 had enlisted in the 1st Pennsylvania Reserves, Company K, and was encamped in Harrisburg, Pennsylvania[25]: "Cousin John Myers saw Jefferson today in Harrisburg. Am almost wild to hear from him." Sallie's beloved father enlisted as well, joining the 87th Pennsylvania Volunteer Infantry on September 2, 1861.[26] Sallie's sadness at her father's departure was mixed with concern for his health, for Peter Myers was 45 years old when he joined the army: "Father went. Somehow I think he will not stay, for he will not stand a medical exam. He was very anxious to go and we said nothing either way. It was very hard to see him go but I really can't express my opinion." Closing the entry for that day, Sallie listed many other members of her family who had gone off to fight for the Union Army. "Uncles Isaac Sheads, Lewis Myers, John Sheads, and William Culp. Cousins Dave Sheads and two distant cousins John Sheads and William Sheads also went. Wonder where father and brother are tonight. God be with them."[27]

There is a sense in the diaries, however, that her life still continued as usual, for on August 2 she wrote happily of her promotion to second assistant to the principal at her school. "I was promoted from 5th Assistant to Miss Whitehead's place. When I heard the joyful news I had to come home and tell Mother. My heart is brimful and overflowing with happiness."

On March 31, 1862, the Myers family moved into a new house. What is presently 55 West High Street was then occupied by Sallie's Uncle Lewis Myers and his family. Sallie described the move to the house on West High Street with excitement, yet sadness, at the prospect of leaving her old home behind:

It seems so queer to think we are going to move. I hate to leave the old house. I doubt very much if I ever spend as pleasant hours again as I spent in the "little front room." I certainly shall not spend any pleasanter hours. Oh! the "blest days of yore" and more particularly "the friends of my girlhood's early days."[28]

The location of the old house from which the Myers family moved is unknown. No documentation has been found to describe just where Sallie spent her "blest days of yore."

Sallie took music lessons from her cousin Carrie Sheads, who owned and administered the Oak Ridge Seminary for Young Ladies, located a short distance west of Gettysburg on the Chambersburg Pike.[29] Carrie Sheads' family tragedy is well known to Gettysburg historians: her four brothers, Elias, David, Jacob and Robert, were all Union soldiers, and all four either died in the war or died shortly thereafter as a result of their service.[30] Carrie's mother and one sister, Louise, are said to have died early deaths from the hard work and sheer worry associated with nursing soldiers in their home, combined with the heartbreak of their sons' and brothers' deaths.[31]

Carrie and Sallie had a "falling out" over some critical comments which Carrie made in August 1862. Sallie's diary entry for August 18 spoke of her outrage at Carrie's remarks about public school teachers. Since she herself taught in the public schools, Sallie took the remarks to heart and considered her high morals and standards maligned. In this particular diary entry, Sallie recalled

Home of Carrie Sheads, principal of the Oak Ridge Seminary for Young Ladies, and first cousin to Sallie Myers.

walking home with her friend Beckie Belch from Ann Culp's house, when they encountered Carrie along the way:

> Met Cousin Carrie for the first time since June 25th. On that afternoon she used what I consider very insulting language to Beckie and me, because we happened to be teachers in the Public School...She said, "Quiet, sensible girls that could behave themselves were rejected [as teachers] and flirts and upstarts were retained."

Sallie wrote rather indignantly that this visit to Cousin Carrie "... shall be the last." Her wounded pride healed quickly, however, for by September Sallie was again taking music lessons from Cousin Carrie Sheads.[32]

Sallie's high moral standards are often reflected upon in her diary entries. Among her files at the Historical Society is a handwritten note from a girlfriend, inviting her to join a gathering of friends for a social evening with the Porter Guards, the 10th New York Cavalry, which was encamped in Gettysburg from Christmas 1861 to March 1862.[33] Having received deployment orders to Havre de Grace, Maryland, the Porter Guards joined with the young people of Gettysburg for a social gathering that night. The invitation reads:

> Miss Sallie,
> I am going to have company tonight and if convenient I would like to have your company as the Porter Guards are out here. There will be no dancing, but as for cards, you know there can't be a party without playing Old Maid. So if you are not afraid of having your good morals corrupted, I would like to see your smiling face.[34]

Her diary mentions another social evening which ended badly. On February 4, 1862, she wrote, rather self-righteously:

> ...we went to spend the evening at Aunt Salome Culp's. Met a crowd. Expected to spend a pleasant evening, but unknown to me a fiddler was employed and they got to dancing. That was against my principles, and Jennie Gilbert and I left in disgust. They were cross that we left but we were determined. Feel sorry for this evening's performance, but it was no fault of mine.

Sallie was escorted home from this morally offensive outing by a young soldier named Ed Casey,[35] whose name occurs quite frequently in her writings. She made many good friends in the Porter Guards, particularly Ed Casey, who temporarily romanced her while encamped in Gettysburg and continued a correspondence with her after the regiment moved on to Maryland.

Apparently Sallie's friendship with several of the Porter Guards caused a bit of local gossip, for she commented acidly on this in her diary entry of March 18:

> O. S. Jones was here once or twice and as he was a pretty hard one people talked about it. I could not help him being here and stopped it as soon as I could. Mr. Casey came here a good deal and the "dear public"

Pvt. Edwin Casey, 10th New York Cavalry (Porter Guards).
(William A. Frassanito collection)

Thomas E. Snyder. c. 1880. (ACHS)

had to talk about that too. I didn't care for that as long as they kept to the truth which they did not do.

Regardless of gossip, Sallie's association with the soldiers in the 10th New York was pleasant. Gettysburg itself seemed to have received them warmly, for when they left, *The Compiler* wrote, "During their stay here, by their gentlemanly deportment, the Porter Guards made friends of all, who regret their leaving. Many pleasant associations have been formed, which will not soon be forgotten."[36]

The real love of her young life, however, was one Thomas E. Snyder, whose name appears on numerous pages of the 1860 diary with the words "Snyder came home with me." Born on February 14, 1834, Snyder was twenty-six years old in 1860 and was employed as a tailor.[37] He was also in love, and kept frequent company with, seventeen-year-old Sallie. Active in the Methodist Episcopal Church congregation where the Peter Myers family attended services, Snyder sometimes led prayer meetings and evening worship.[38] Mentions of Thomas Snyder continue well into the diary of 1862, when problems surfaced with the relationship.

By 1862 Sallie's romance with Snyder took place under her mother's objections for reasons unexplained in the diary. Sallie spoke eloquently and painfully of her love for Snyder and the turmoil she faced while trying to see him despite her mother scoldings. She mentioned frequently that he was ill; she feared he had consumption and would not recover. Descriptions of his cough and his sickly countenance pour onto the pages of her diary, and Sallie was very frightened that he would soon die. She pitied him and prayed for him, yet she knew that she must give him up, that inevitably he would be taken from her by God.[39] She wrote wistfully of a return to the "good old days when life was not so hard."[40]

Snyder tried to convince her that they belonged together. On May 22, 1862, she described a verse from Corinthians which he wrote her: "And I will very gladly spend and be spent for you; though the more abundantly I love you, the less I be loved." They met secretly to talk, and Sallie wrote, "We stayed rather late and I expect a scolding....Oh, dear me! What shall I do? I cannot pray for I know not what to pray for. Oh, God, direct me in the right path!"

Sallie privately rebelled against her mother's objections and secretly longed for her father whom she idolized to return home from the war. She described him as the only person she could trust to understand her troubles caused by her relationship with Snyder. She finally ended her relationship with Thomas Snyder in late 1862, but not without a struggle. Quite a number of pages contain emotional references to the love she felt for him, but could never again express anywhere but in the diary. Mention of Snyder dwindles in the 1864 diary, for by that time he was replaced as the object of Sallie's affections by Henry F. Stewart, a disabled Civil War veteran and Presbyterian theology student from New Brighton, Pennsylvania.[41]

Summer and fall of 1862 brought increased worries about her father's health. Forty-five years old when he enlisted in 1861, Peter Myers had difficulty withstanding the life of a soldier. He developed both varicose veins and chronic rheumatism in his legs, which caused his absence from the company muster rolls for the months of May and June 1862. That July, Peter was sent to the General Hospital in York, Pennsylvania, returning home briefly in August before reporting once again to York for further medical examination.[42] On August 16 Sallie fearfully wrote in her diary, "Father had a letter from Lieut. T. C. Norris of Co. F. 87th Penn. Vol. He is to go to York to the hospital and there be examined by a physician. If unfit for duty he will be discharged. I wish he could stay at home."

Sallie's concern for her father's health proved accurate, and her wish for his return was granted. Upon completion of his medical examination, on October 18, Peter Myers was pronounced unfit for duty and discharged from the army hospital in York, Pennsylvania. Sallie's beloved father was at home once more.[43]

An astounding number of Sallie's family members fought in the Civil War. An article written for the 40th anniversary of the Battle of Gettysburg, July 1903, contains the following passage about Sallie and her family: "The family came from patriotic stock, her father, her only brother, five uncles, and eight first cousins being in the Union Army during the Civil War."[44]

Just as interesting is what the article fails to mention. Sallie also had two first cousins, George Sheads and Robert Sheads, who fought in the war for the Confederate Army. Both joined the Little Fork Rangers, a cavalry unit from Culpepper County, Virginia, in May 1861. George was discharged in 1862, re-enlisted in the 6th Virginia Cavalry, and died in 1890 at the age of 61. Robert, less fortunate than his brother, died of pneumonia while home on leave in September 1861, at age 21.[45] Thus, Sallie's family, like so many others during this time, was split into opposing sides of the conflict, and possibly faced off against each other on the battlefield.

The 1862 diary entries mix descriptions of her personal affairs with references to the war, and various relatives coming home on leave. She also wrote that her teaching was disrupted due to the war, for the High Street school closed its doors temporarily when three companies of soldiers were quartered in the building.[46]

The death of Nesbitt Baugher, brother of Levi Baugher who was then principal of the High Street School, from wounds at the Battle of Pittsburg Landing (Shiloh) was noted on May 19, and on June 5 Sallie reported that Fred Huber, a member of the 23rd Pennsylvania Volunteer Infantry and a "son of Dr. Huber," was killed near Richmond in the Battle of Fair Oaks. Commenting on his body being brought home for burial, Sallie wrote, "The War is coming home to us at last."[47]

The remainder of the summer of 1862 is filled with teacher examination results ("very good, #1 in everything"), news of her father's medical problems and concern for his convalescence and full recovery, notes on the death of cousin Melchoir Sheads, and her study of Latin and astronomy.

In the fall of 1862 her diary became more focused on war news. On September 6 she described the threat that some cavalry (Loudon Rangers) from Loudon County, Virginia, were coming to Gettysburg. "Quite an exciting time, wagons everywhere and streets crowded but I feel quite calm and self-possessed. Hope it will last." And on September 13 she maintained her calm with the following: "It was reported and believed that a party of Rebels were coming to Gettysburg and our town companies were to go out to meet them. A false report, however."

***Present-day Peter Myers home on W. High Street, where Myers family moved
in 1862, and lived through the war years.***

Such reports that the Rebels were coming became a common entry in her
diary from this point on. Living only seven miles from the Mason-Dixon Line, it
was quite commonplace to hear rumors of Rebels advancing into the North, and
the citizens of Gettysburg understood that the constant fear of Rebel invasion
was a fact of life. In October two entries reported such rumors. On the 11th she
noted, "Great excitement. The Rebels are in Chambersburg and up on the mountain
stealing horses, etc. A regiment of [soldiers] came from Frederick." And on the
13th, Sallie excitedly wrote:

> Dismissed school in a hurry as several parents sent for their children.
> The Rebels were reported coming in force. Two Regiments went out to
> meet them, and took their artillery to Mr. Shultz' Hill. Report was false,
> they are up along the mountain.

General J.E.B. Stuart's cavalry raid of early October, although concentrated
in Chambersburg in nearby Franklin County, caused Gettysburg great concern,
for the soldiers rode through the communities of Cashtown and Fairfield, only a
few miles from Gettysburg. Taking horses, materials, and even prisoners like
John D. Paxton, the postmaster of Fairfield, Stuart's forces came much too close
for comfort to the people of Gettysburg.[48]

The 1862 entries continue through the end of the year in a similar vein.
They contain descriptions of social events, friendships, chores, family fun—as
well as disagreements—and war. Sallie detailed long walks on quiet evenings,
and conversations with friends like Harriet Shillen, Ada McMillan, Beckie Belch,
or Jennie Gilbert. She recorded attending soirees at Cousin Carrie's house, lively
parties, and gatherings around town. She also described pleasant encounters with

Snyder and not-so-pleasant ones with her mother. Music lessons with Cousin Carrie are intertwined with news of violent death at Fair Oaks, of cousins and uncles going to war, of wondering "where Father and Brother are tonight." When her father finally returned home with a medical discharge, she fearfully wrote, "Poor father. I wish he was well. I am afraid he will be a cripple for life. He has lost the use of one of his legs. I hope home & good nursing will restore him."[49]

The year 1862 drew to a close on a somewhat idyllic note. Sallie's school closed for the holidays on December 19, and the Myers family celebrated Christmas. Sallie and brother Jefferson "bought presents for the children, candy, nuts, etc. We are going to have a Christmas tree."[50]

Typical, yet anything but typical, was the life Sallie Myers lived during the early years of the Civil War. Beneath the surface of her normal existence was the terrible reality that this was an era which could not possibly be described as ordinary, for America was embroiled in its most bitter conflict. Although the conflict touched Sallie's life, its impact in the beginning was slight, the effect fleeting. As the weeks and months continued, and the new year progressed, the impact would become greater, and the effect more lasting. Little did Sallie Myers foresee, however, as the year 1862 drew to a close, of the conflict that was yet to come.

Sallie Myers, c. 1862. (ACHS)

DIARY 1854-62

The earliest extant writings of Sallie Myers are contained in a Parker's English composition book dated 1854, from the personal collection of author William A. Frassanito. These early writings consist of a few variations of quoted verse, two poems, and a farewell notation to her brother Peter who died in 1847. The quoted verses and the farewell notation are both dated 1854, when Sallie was just 12 years old. The poem written on the front inside page, "The pearl of great price," is undated. "A Home in Heaven," found on the back inside page of the composition book, is dated January 18, 1859.

Whether the two poems are original or simply copied from another source is not known. Sallie did write poetry throughout her life, however, and Sallie's signature is at the end of both. The religious nature of the poems is typical of Sallie's writings, and gives early evidence of the deep spiritual commitment that pervades Sallie's entire life.

All notations, inscriptions, and poems are reproduced as written, with punctuation and layout unchanged. Inscribed inside the front page of the English Composition book is the following:

To my brother
"Farewell! a word that must be and hath been—
A word that makes us linger—yet, farewell!"

Sallie E. Myers
December 30th, 1854
Gettysburg, Penna.
Number 1.

The facing page contains a similar attempt at these poetic lines:

"Farewell! a word that must and hath been—
A sound which makes us linger—yet; farewell.

Say not—Good Night—but in some brighter clime
Bid me, Good Morning

E. S. Myers
Gettysburg, Adams County
Pennsylvania
December 30th, 1854

Below is the undated poem signed by Sallie.

The pearl of great price

The pearl that worldlings covet,
   Is not the pearl for me;
Its beauty fades as quickly
   as sunshine on the sea;
But there's a pearl sought by the wise,
Tis called the pearl of greatest price:
      Though few its value see,
      Oh! that's the pearl for me.
The crown that decks the monarch,
   Is not the crown for me;
It dazzles but a moment,
    Its brightness soon will flee;
But there's a crown prepared above
For all who walk in humble love,
      Forever bright twill be—
      Oh! that's the crown for me.
The road that many travel,
   Is not the road for me:
It leads to death and sorrow,
    In it I would not be.
Yet there's a road that leads to God,
It's marked by Christ's most precious blood:
      The passage here is free—
      Oh! that's the road for me.
The hope that sinners cherish,
   Is not the hope for me;
Most surely they will perish,
    Unless from sin made free.
But there's a hope which rests in God,
And leads the soul to keep his word:
      And sinful pleasures flee—
      Oh! that's the hope for me.

S. E. Myers

The date inscribed at the bottom of this poem is January 18, 1859, indicating that Sallie wrote this when she was 16 years old.

A Home in Heaven

A home in Heaven! what a joyful thought
As the poor man toils in his weary lot!
His heart opprest, and with anguish driven
From his home below, to his home in Heaven.

A home in Heaven! as the sufferer lies
On his bed of pain, and uplifts his eyes
To that bright home; what a joy is given,
With the blessed thought of a home in Heaven.

A home in Heaven! when our pleasures fade,
And our wealth and fame in the dust are laid;
And strength decays, and our health is riven,
We are happy still with our home in Heaven.

A home in Heaven! when the faint heart bleeds,
By the Spirit's stroke, for its evil deeds;
Oh! then what bliss in that heart forgiven,
Does the hope inspire of a home in Heaven.

A home in Heaven! when our friends are fled
To the cheerless gloom of the mouldering dead;
We wait in hope on the promise given;
We will meet up there in our home in Heaven.

A home in Heaven! when the wheel is broke,
And the golden bowl by the terror-stroke;
When life's bright sun sinks in death's dark eve'n
We will then fly up to our home in Heaven.

Our home in Heaven! oh, the glorious home,
And the Spirit, joined with the bride, says "come"!,
Come, seek his face, and your sins forgiven,
And rejoice in hope of your home in Heaven.

Composed by   Sallie E. Myers

January 18, 1859
              Gettysburg Adams County
              Pennsylvania

Sallie also wrote a poem titled "There Are No Tears In Heaven" for *The Star and Banner*, dated June 27, 1859. Published in the July 8, 1859, edition, Sallie used the *nom de plume* "Rosa Alba" or the "White Rose," instead of her real name.

There Are No Tears in Heaven
by Rosa Alba

How sweet when earthly pleasures fade,
    And earthly ties are riven,
To know, that though our friends are laid,
Within the cold grave's silent shade,
    "There are no tears in Heaven."

When by our worldly cares oppressed,
      And by rude tempests driven
From earthly hopes, we find a rest
In that bright region of the blest,
      And troubles end in Heaven.

"Eye hath not seen, ear hath not heard"
      The joys which God has given,
To those who serve their blessed Lord
On earth, when at his holy word,
      They went to live in Heaven.

There all is peace, and love, and joy,
      And crowns of life are given;
There earthly cares cannot annoy,
All, all is bliss without alloy,
      For Jesus reigns in Heaven.

Oh! that we all when life is o'er
      May reach that blessed Heaven
Where friends shall meet to part no more,
And through eternity adore
      The Lord of earth and Heaven.

Another of Sallie's poems from this time period exists among her personal papers contained in the Adams County Historical Society. Written March 10, 1860, for her friend Ada McMillan, the poem describes the pleasures of home and friendship.

Home Again

Home again, home again,
      From a foreign shore;
And O! it fills my soul with joy,
      To meet my friends once more.
Here I dropped the parting tear,
      To brave the ocean's foam;
But now I'm once again with those
      Who kindly greet me home.

(Chorus) Home again, home again,
      From a foreign shore;
And oh! it fills my soul with joy,
      To meet my friends once more.

Happy hearts, happy hearts,
      With mine have laughed in glee;
But oh! the friends I loved in youth,
      Seem pleasantest to me.

And if my guide should be the fate
    Which bids me longer roam,
Yet death alone can break the tie
    Which binds my heart to home. (Chorus)

Music soft, music sweet
    Lingers 'round the place;
And oh! I feel that childhood's charm
    That Time cannot efface.
Oh! give me but my homestead roof,
    I'll ask no palace dome;
For I can lead a happy life
    With those I love at home. (Chorus)

Written for Miss Ada McMillan.
    By her friend,
        Sallie
Saturday Evening, March 10, 1860.

🍒   🍒   🍒

A note on the 1860 diary:

Before March 1995, the only record in existence for Sallie Myers' 1860 diary was the typescripted manuscript prepared by her son, Dr. Henry A. Stewart. New records, documents, and photographs on Sallie Myers have emerged occasionally during the previous decades, but not one of her other diaries has surfaced in the past forty years, since the time when the Adams County Historical Society acquired much of the Stewart family records. But on March 30, 1995, the 1860 diary for Salome Myers Stewart, to the amazement of my family and the historical community of Gettysburg, suddenly appeared. On that day, a tiny notice appeared in *The Gettysburg Times* advertising a consignment sale held by the Mason-Dixon Auction Service in Emmitsburg, Maryland. It described an "1860 Civil War era diary from Gettysburg."

My father, Thomas E. Sites, an enthusiast for auctions and old estate sales, quickly contacted me when he read the notice in the paper. Intimately familiar with my project, he wondered if perhaps this just might be one of Sallie Myers' diaries. Intrigued but skeptical, I admitted that this might be worth checking, but privately I was sure that the chances were pretty slim. Dad previewed the diary that day, and saw some references that sounded similar to the Sallie Myers story. That evening, on Dad's advice, I drove to the auction house and asked to view the diary. When I opened the book to the front inside page, I read, in what I instantly recognized as my great-great-grandmother's own hand, the words, "Let love and truth indite—Whatever here I write," the very same words she used to open every diary she kept.

The excitement generated when indeed, this "1860 Civil War era diary" turned out to be none other than Sallie Myers' I cannot adequately describe. The tiny book had been in the possession of a family from Hanover, Pennsylvania, since the 1950s. Why this diary had not been donated to the Historical Society is unknown. But it laid dormant for over forty years until it was sold as part of this Hanover resident's estate.

The 1860 diary is now owned by my mother, Jacqueline Stewart Sites. One hundred and thirty-five years after Sallie Myers wrote on its pages, her great-granddaughter brought it back into the family—and I have been able to include it in this book. Some might call this a matter of chance and unusual circumstance. I prefer to think that Sallie's diary finally made its way back home through a series of events too personal for coincidence.

⸻ *1860* ⸻⸻⸻⸻⸻⸻⸻⸻⸻

"Let love and truth indite
Whatever here I write."

Sunday, January 1.

Rose at 7 O'clock this morning and after assisting mother at her household duties, I went to Sabbath School. Two of my scholars were absent but we had a very interesting time. There were not many at prayer-meeting but I enjoyed it very much. Class meeting seemed like the very "Gate of Heaven" to my soul. This evening Mr. Cadden preached a very interesting sermon from the parable of the barren fig-tree. Mr. S. came home with me.

Monday, January 2.

Had no school to-day as the building was too cold. Called to see several of my Sabbath School Scholars and was very kindly received. Went to the Temple this evening. There were not many there and it was dismissed early. Snyder came home with me. It has been a very cold and windy day. A great deal of snow on the ground and excellent sleighing.

Tuesday, January 3.

Went to school this morning very much depressed in mind, but this evening I feel better. Called to see Ada White this afternoon after school and found her with considerable fever. After reading awhile to her I left her. She seems calm and looks just as her sister Annie did, before she died. Her eyes are very bright, and her face almost as white as the pillow upon which her head is resting. It has been cold and cloudy all day.

Wednesday, January 4.

Rose this morning with a severe head-ache, in consequence of which I have felt dull all day. To-day has been a cold, windy, and to me, very disagreeable day.

Thursday, January 5.

Called to see Ada White this evening but did not read to her, as she seemed too weak to bear it. She has a high fever, and I think she is getting worse. Went to prayer-meeting and enjoyed it tolerably. I would have enjoyed it more, had I not found myself unable to keep my thoughts fixed on those things which alone should engage me at such times. Mr. S. came home with me. To-day father is fourty-four years old.

Friday, January 6

Heard that Ada White was worse, but had not time to go to see her. Mother is fourty-two years old to-day. To-morrow our fourth Quarterly Meeting begins. The air has been very sharp and piercing all day.

Saturday, January 7.

Went to church this morning at 11 Oclock, and listened to a very interesting sermon on the nature, excercise, and results of faith, by Mr. Monroe, a preacher sent by our Presiding Elder, who could not attend. His text this evening was, "Guide me by thy counsel, and afterward receive me to glory," and from it he preached an excellent and very instructive sermon. The weather has been very unpleasant, but the good I received from Mr. Monroe's sermons amply repaid the trouble I had to get to hear him. I think he is an excellent preacher. Snyder came home with me.

Sunday, January 8.

Went to love-feast at 9 Oclock but did not enjoy it very much as I have had a severe head-ache ever since I arose. Mr. Monroe preached again this morning, and after preaching, the sacrament of the Lord's Supper was administered. I think I have never been as much benefitted by that means of grace as I was then. The evening sermon by Mr. Monroe was excellent. The church was crowded and the audience was very attentive. The roads are muddy and the air damp and unwholesome. S. came home with me.

Monday, January 9.

Went to school, as usual to-day, and this evening went to church. Mr. Dill preached and after he was done Mr. Cadden exhorted. I enjoyed the sermon and the other exercises tolerably well, but I have felt unusually sober all day. I think there is a prospect of having a revival. My prayer is, "Oh! Lord revive thy work." Mr. Snyder came home with me.

Tuesday, January 10.

Went to preaching this evening. Mr. Cadden preached but as I caught a severe cold by going to and from school to-day and yesterday, I did not listen to the sermon with as much interest as I would have liked to have done. S. came home with me.

Wednesday, January 11.

The weather has been very disagreeable to one who is obliged to go out, as it has been raining all day. Mr. Dill preached an interesting sermon this evening, from the 3rd verse of the 37th Psalm. "Trust in the Lord, and do good; so shall thou dwell in the land, and verily, thou shall be fed."

Thursday, January 12.

The sky is clear this evening but it has been snowing and raining all day. The walking is better than it has been for the last week. Mr. Cadden was unwell and Mr. Dill preached from the 126th verse of the 119th Psalm. "It is time for thee, Lord to work, for they have made avid thy law." The prospects are brightening for a revival, and the meeting was very interesting. One young lady presented herself at the Altar of Prayer. May God, for Christ's sake continue to revive his work. Snyder came home with me.

Friday, January 13.

Went to church this evening. Mr. Cadden preached, but I did not enjoy it much on account of my throat being sore. I received a letter from Mattie Durboraw, one of two twin-sisters with whom I have been acquainted about a year, and I also received one from Lucy Ellis a young lady of Oxford who acquaintance I formed while attending the Teachers Institute, which met in that place the second week of last December. Both letters were very welcome. S. came home with me.

Saturday, January 14.

Have been very unwell all day. I have had a severe head-ache and very sore throat and my throat seems to be getting worse. Last night it commenced snowing before 9 Oclock, and it has been raining all day. I am afraid I will be unable to attend church and Sunday School to-morrow, if the weather continues so unfavorable.

Sunday, January 15.

Feel better this morning, and as the weather is considerably improved I went to school. None of my scholars were there for various reasons, so I took my place as a scholar in the class to which I belonged before I took charge of my own class. I felt very badly in prayer-meeting and left before it was over, but I enjoyed class very much. School was dismissed earlier than usual this afternoon, and I went to Union prayer-meeting. Took tea with Eliza Welty. Mr. Dill preached at the usual time to a crowded house. This has been a very pleasant day. Snyder came home with me.

Monday, January 16.

Rose this morning before 6 Oclock and have felt very well all day with the exception of my throat which is a little sore yet. Lizzie Durboraw and Mattie Geiselman took tea with me this evening and after it was over we called on Ellen Snyder and went from there to church. There were not very many there, but as there is a fair now going on, it is not at all strange. Our meeting was discontinued this evening having lasted over a week and resulting in the conversion of two souls. The sky has been clear all day but this evening it looks very much for snow. S. came home with me.

Tuesday, January 17.

Went to school this morning at the usual time. This evening I finished some lines which Mrs. Schively, a lady who lives in Millerstown [Fairfield], requested me to write on the death of her two little boys who died some ago, of Putrid sore throat. I have been knitting very busily every spare moment I can get, at a pair of woolen undersleeves which I am very anxious to finish. This has been a very pleasant day, if we leave out the mud which is plenty every place.

Wednesday, January 18.

Rose this morning about half past 6 Oclock. We have a very pleasant time at school. Two of the furnaces are broken and none of the teachers are teaching except Miss Thompson and myself. We have the whole building and yard to ourselves, and I think I get along better with my school than I ever did, because there are not so many schools to annoy me. I have eighty-six names on the roll, with an average attendance of sixty-six scholars.

Thursday, January 19.

Over-slept myself this morning, which was caused by sitting up late last night. I was very busily engaged in knitting at my undersleeves, and before I was aware of it the clock struck 11. Went to prayer-meeting this evening. There were more there than there usually is. Mr. Dill led. I did not enjoy it very much as several other things of importance engaged my attention.

Friday, January 20.

Had a very pleasant time at school both this morning and afternoon. Dismissed at 3 Oclock, as it is Friday afternoon and we have been along all week. Spent a part of the evening at Aunt Salome's, with my work. This has been a delightful day, almost as warm as summer, I thought. I hope it may continue.

Saturday, January 21.

Overslept myself again this morning and as a natural consequence I have not felt right all day. Mother and I went to see Ada White this afternoon. She seemed very glad to see us but was too weak to talk much. She does not seem to be getting any better. This has been such a pleasant day, that we thought we would take a walk, as it is seldom we can get out to-gether. We went to see the new Court House, and to see Charles White, Ada's brother who is very poorly.

Sunday, January 22.

Went to Sabbath School this morning, but did not get there in time, for which I am sorry. Three of my scholars were absent. Mr. Dill preached a very interesting sermon from the 16th verse of the 6th chapter of Jeremiah. This evening after preaching Mr. Dill spoke of continuing the meeting and it had been stopped under very unfavorable circumstances. There were no objections made, and he appointed preaching for to-morrow evening. Snyder came home with me.

Monday, January 23.

Rose this morning with a dull head-ache, but it has gradually worn off and this evening I feel very well. Went to preaching at 6 1/2 Oclock. Mr. Dill preached an excellent sermon from the 13th verse of the 28th chapter of Proverbs. After preaching I went to the Temple and was there about a half an hour, and then came home. Had some notion of going to the colored church, but as it was rather late I gave it up. Perhaps I will go to-morrow night if nothing prevents me from doing so. S. came with me home.

Tuesday, January 24.

Rose at 6 Oclock this morning. Father sat up last night with Charles White. He is very low and cannot possibly recover. I caught a severe cold this evening, but it was by my own imprudence. Beckie Belch, was down, and as she has been away for several weeks we had more than usual to tell each other, and talk about. I went out with her, in my bare-head, and as it was cold and damp it was natural that I should feel the effects of it. I would like to have gone to the colored church, but could not.

Wednesday, January 25.

The weather for the last few days has been delightful. The sky has been clear, and the sun very warm, so that it seems almost like summer, but this morning the sky was cloudy and it looks a little for rain. This morning I heard that Charles White is dead. I trust he died the death of a christian and I have every reason to believe that he did. Ginnie Powers spent the evening with me, and we had a very pleasant time. The beauty of the night added to my enjoyment, as I was out a little while. Snyder came down and we took Ginnie home about 9 Oclock. Had a pleasant walk.

Thursday, January 26.

Went to prayer-meeting this evening, but did not enjoy myself.

O why should gloomy thought arise
    And darkness fill my mind?
Why should my bosom heave with sighs,
    And yet no refuge find?
Have I not heard of Gilead's balm-
    The great Physician there?

> Who can my every fear disarm,
> > And save me from despair?

Would that I could adopt the language of another beautiful verse.

> I lift my streaming eyes to heaven
> > The great atonement see;
> And all my sins are now forgiven,
> > Believing, I am free.

Friday, January 27.

I have felt unusually dull all day. I do not know the reason, unless it be that I have been thinking a great deal about death, and the Judgement. I feel more than ever my unworthiness, and my need of God's help, for of myself I am unable to do a good deed, or think a good thought. Oh! God, "guide me by thy counsel," while in the world, "and keep me from all sin," and "afterward receive me to glory," for Christ's sake. Amen.

Saturday, January 28.

Feel very tired this evening, as I have been doing more housework to-day than I generally do. I wrote two letters this evening, one to Lucy Ellis and one to Mattie Durboraw. This has been a cold and windy day, tolerably clear, but now it is cloudy. I hope it will soon clear again.

Sunday, January 29.

Went to school this morning, and had a very interesting time. Enjoyed prayer-meeting tolerably well. I have been thinking a great deal about Ada White to-day. I went to see her this morning and she seems to be getting worse. Her brother John died last night and I think probably that had a bad effect upon her. I enjoyed class this morning a great deal better than prayer-meeting. Mr. Cadden preached a very good sermon to-night, but I did not listen very attentively. Snyder came home with me.

Monday, January 30.

This has been a delightful day, at least I thought so. The sky is clear and it is very warm for this season of the year. Called to see one of my day scholars this morning after school, and I have since heard that she is dead. After school this evening I went to see Ada White. She felt better, but looks very pale, and is very weak. Went to the Temple this evening. We had a very interesting time. Returned home about 9 Oclock.

Tuesday, January 31.

There has been quite a change in the weather since yesterday. The sky is cloudy, the wind blowing, and it is snowing and altogether it is about as disagreeable as it can well be. This afternoon our Sabbath School attended the funeral of one of the scholars. I am afraid that going to the Cemetery was not good for me, for the ground was very damp, the wind was blowing, and part of the time it was raining. Mr. Wilson Longwell took charge of my school while I was absent.

Wednesday, February 1.

This has been a lovely day, clear, but cold as it has been this winter. To night the moon is shining, and the stars twinkling very pleasantly. Cousin Annie Sheads spent the evening with me, and I went part of the way with her when she went home. I do not know when we have had such a night. It is magnificent! The ground is covered with snow, and I suppose the sleighing is good. Called to see Ada White this evening. She was a little better than she has been.

Thursday, February 2.

This has been a very cold day, and very cloudy. This evening it is clear, and oh! such a lovely night! It does me good to be out. Coming from prayer-meeting, I was thinking how good God is to give us so many things to add to our enjoyment. Although it was very cold, yet I staid out as long as I could without doing myself injury, and then I went in the house very reluctantly, for I love dearly to look at the stars and moon.

Friday, February 3.

Feel very tired this evening, and did not work much. Rose with a slight headache this morning, but that was caused by sleeping too much. I retired last night immediately after coming from prayer-meeting, which was over about 8 Oclock. This is a very pleasant night, almost as light as day, but it is very cold. Snyder spent the evening with me.

Saturday, February 4.

10 Oclock—Almost another week has rolled into eternity, to be known no more until it rises up before us in that great day for which all other days were created. What a solemn thought that each week, each day, each hour, and each moment of time brings us nearer, and bears us rapidly on to that dread day. Oh! Lord help me to live so that I may meet thee with joy, when thou shall come to make thy jewels up.

Sunday, February 5.

The sky has been cloudy all day, and this evening we had some snow. This morning Mr. Cadden preached a very interesting sermon from the 14th verse of the 33rd Chapter of Exodus—"And he said my presence shall go with thee and I will give you rest." This evening his text was the 9th verse of the 10th chapter of John. Perhaps it is the last time we shall hear him preach as Conference meets on the 29th of this month. I enjoyed class very well to-day. S. came home with me.

Monday, February 6.

Rose this morning about half past 6 Oclock. It has been raining all morning which with the snow and mud already on the ground makes the walking anything but pleasant. I received a very welcome present yesterday in the shape of the miniature of a friend of mine, Miss Eliza Welty. Went to the Temple and by going got the tooth ache, which is not very pleasant company.

Tuesday, February 7.

Rose this morning with a very severe sick head-ache. I could scarcely see across the room, but I went to school at the usual time. I remained there about a half an hour, and found it would not do. Mr. Baugher very kindly permitted one of his scholars to teach for me and I came home and lay down until 12 Oclock. I went to school this afternoon and have felt very well all afternoon and evening.

Wednesday, February 8.

Have been sewing very busily all evening, and feel almost too tired to write in my diary, but as I have commenced it, I want to try and persevere until the end of the year, if my life be spared. This has been a delightful day, but the roads are tolerably muddy. I rose earlier than my usual time, but do not regret it as I have felt better to-day than I have for some time. I must stop now, or I cannot get up as early as I wish, so Good night, my "dear little diary." (?) [Sallie often included question marks in her entries.]

Thursday, February 9.

Rose about 7 Oclock this morning, which was not quite as early as I wanted to, but I overslept myself. Went to prayer-meeting this evening and enjoyed it very much, more than I have for some time. The wind is blowing so much that I could scarcely get home, but it is a warm wind, not at all unpleasant, if it were a little milder.

Friday, February 10.

This has been one of the coldest days we have had this winter. The wind has been blowing all day, and last night it blew so hard that it shook the house. When I went to school this morning the thermometer was down to freezing point in one of the rooms, and we had no school until this afternoon. I intended to spend the evening with Mattie Geiselman, but as it was so cold and windy I concluded to stay at home.

Saturday, February 11.

Have been working harder than usual to-day as mother was unable to do any-thing except some sewing. I baked for the first time for more than a year, and I had almost forgotten how. Went up street this evening to the store and called to see Ada White. She is very low. She requested us to sing for her. Several young ladies were there and we sang for her, about an hour. I called to see one of my Sabbath School scholars, who has been sick, but is now getting better.

Sunday, February 12.

Rose about half past 6 Oclock this morning but did not get to S.S. as mother was unable to get up & I was obliged to stay at home. I went to prayer-meeting, but we had no class and I went to see Ada White. We thought she was dying but she still lingers, but she is very weak. She requested us to sing for her and we sang "We are passing away" and "Oh! sing to me of heaven." She seemed to enjoy it and tried to help us but could not. After we sang Mr. Finefrock prayed. It was a very solemn time. I do not think there was a dry eye in the room. I was fanning her and I asked her if Jesus was precious. She could not speak but inclined her head forward. I told her to trust in the Lord that he would not forsake her. She said she did. I went to see how she was after church. She seemed to be just the same. I would like to have staid but could not as mother is not well. Mr. Dill preached a very interesting sermon from the 24th and 25th verses of Jude. This has been a very pleasant day. It seemed like spring. Snyder came from church with me.

Monday, February 13.

Went to school this morning at the usual time. Mother is a great deal better and I went to the Temple. We had not a regular meeting, but a Temperance Speech by Mr. Guss. We were permitted to invite our friends. I invited Mattie G. Beckie B. and Eliza W. Eliza and Becky did not go, Beckie starts for Baltimore to-morrow morning and had not time. It rained a little this morning. I received an invitation to attend a wedding next Thursday morning at 8 Oclock. It is to be private.

Tuesday, February 14.

This has been a very pleasant day, very warm, but not a very wholesome air. It is rather damp. Mother is not so well this evening but she is no worse than she was yesterday. Called to see Ada White after school this afternoon. She is weaker than she was but was resting better than she had for some time. I went up to Mattie Geiselman's with my work this evening, but did not do much as we were talking about a certain event which will transpire soon. Snyder is twenty-six years old to-day, he would not come down and let me pull his ears for him.

Wednesday, February 15.

We have had a very fine snow to-day. It has been snowing steadily all day, but has stopped now. Mother seems to be better to-day. I was afraid she was going to have a serious time with her throat, but the symptoms are more favorable now, for which I am very thankful. Several of the scholars of my day-school have been removed and I have now seventy two names on the roll, with an average attendance of fifty scholars.

Thursday, February 16.

Went to Mattie Geiselman's wedding this morning. She was married by Mr. Dill, to Mr. D. Webster Robison, of Millerstown [Fairfield]. The wedding was private, there being no invited guest but myself present. They will remove to Millerstown in April. Ada White died this morning about half past 9 Oclock. From all I can learn, she was resigned to God's will. I never had an opportunity to converse with her excepting a few words which passed between us on last Sunday morning. Ada is the seventh one, of a family of eight who have all died within four years. Her sister Annie died last Spring. She was one of my dearest friends. I often think of her but not with sorrow, for I know that one day we will meet to part no more forever. Dear Annie. She has only gone before, and is now singing the song of redeeming love in that "sun bright clime, Undimmed by sorrow unhurt by time." O, Lord keep me faithful, and after death give me a resting place at the right hand in heaven.

Friday, February 17.

Clear and pleasant. Went to school at 9 Oclock and again at half past 1 Oclock. Was at Aunt Salome's a few minutes before I commenced to sew. Received a letter from Mattie Durboraw. Mother seems to be getting better, but is still far from being well. Mr. Thomas E. Snyder, came down and we spent a very pleasant evening.

Saturday, February 18.

Cold and windy. The snow has been falling steadily all day until this afternoon, about 4 Oclock, and this evening there are some signs of clearing. Purchased for my Sabbath School class book which cost $1.00. Feel very tired as mother was rather worse to-day and in addition to the usual Saturday work, I baked. Hope to-morrow will be clear.

Sunday, February 19.

Rose about 7 Oclock this morning. Was late at S.S. Went to church. Mr. Dill preached a very good sermon. Went to School at 2 Oclock. My scholars were very much pleased with their books. Mother seems to be better to-day. Alice Diehl went to preaching with me this evening. Mr. Dill preached. This sermon closed his labors with us for the present Conference Year. Have felt very badly all day. I feel as though every thing is not right, and I am afraid it is not, for I never feel so without cause. To-day sister Bell is seven years old. I bought her a small book with which she was very much pleased. I answered Mattie Durboraw's letter last night. It was rather soon, but I felt in a humor for writing and did not know when I would have another opportunity. After church Snyder and I took Alice home, from there to my home.

Monday, February 20.

Clear and cold. Had no school this morning as the building was very uncomfortable. Mother is better to-day. Went up to spend the evening with Ginnie Powers but was called home, as there was company came for me. Did not sew any, as I neglected preparing my any work. The company that came was Mr. Snyder and a younger brother, Amos—Spent a very pleasant evening.

Tuesday, February 21.

This has been a pleasant day over-head. I have felt very much cast down all day. I have given way to my temper several times, and it has made me perfectly miserable. I have tried to overcome it, but I am afraid the efforts have been made too much by relying on my own strength. I am determined from this time forward to try by God's help, to overcome it. Oh! that he may ever be with me, that he may give me grace to help in this time of need, for the sake of him who ever liveth to make intercession for me.

Wednesday, February 22.

Have not seen the sun to-day. It has been raining steadily all day, until this evening. The weather has not been so very unpleasant for a long time. We had school, but a great many persons kept it as a holiday. I trust I have made some progress to-day in overcoming temper, but not I, it is God working in me, Oh! that he may continue to work until the last remains of sin are all subdued. In him will I put my trust.

Thursday, February 23.

Sun shining, and very pleasant. To-day is Sister Grace's birthday. She is three years old. I bought her a doll, and dressed it for her, with which she was delighted. We had no prayer-meeting, as there was a lecture before the Bible Society of Penna. College. I was very much disappointed, for I did not know it until I was all ready to go. Have not been as watchful to-day as I should, but feel more than ever determined to be a better christian, by the help of God.

Friday, February 24.

This has been a very pleasant day, but this evening it is cold. Have not been very well to-day, I have had a dull head-ache. I fear I have not made any progress to-day. "Create in me a clean heart, O Lord, and renew a right spirit within me." S. spent the evening with me.

Saturday, February 25.

Cold and cloudy. Have been very well, and have worked hard to-day. Mother is a great deal better than she has been. To-morrow, God willing, I expect to enjoy the priveleges of another Sabbath. Oh! that I may improve it as I ought, and may it
"Prove a foretaste clear
Of that Sweet rest above"

Sunday, February 26.

Clear and pleasant. Went to Sunday School at 9 Oclock. Alice Diehl went with me. Rev. W. Guinn led prayer-meeting. I did not enjoy it very much, as my mind was rather out of order for Sunday. The cares of the week engrossed my attention to the exclusion of all else. Had an adjourned missionary this afternoon. Mr. Guinn led prayer-meeting again this evening. I went and enjoyed it more than I have for some time. I was enabled to rejoice in the God of my salvation. S. came home with me.

Monday, February 27.

Went to school this morning at the usual time. Had some difficulty in fixing my mind on my school. Met with a lady to-day with whom I have not been on very friendly terms. The meeting was anything but pleasant, but I hope and have every reason to think that it will do something toward restoring good feeling. The present state of affairs is anything but agreeable. Went to the Temple this evening. Had a very pleasant time—S. came with me.

Tuesday, February 28.

This has been a pleasant day, very warm but cloudy. This evening it is clear and very pleasant. The moon is shining brightly. Went to a degree meeting held at Mr. Samuel Weaver's residence. Went to see the lady whom I met yesterday, and had a long conversation with her. Keller Culp, One of my scholars was thrown from a horse this noon, and his arm was broken very badly. Went to see him after school this evening.

Wednesday, February 29.

Warm and cloudy. Feel very much cast down this evening, caused by giving way to my temper to-day. To-day Sister Susie is twelve years old. Gave her, as a present, a hymn-book—like those used by Methodist congregations.

Thursday, March 1.

Warm and very pleasant. Went to see Keller Culp after school this afternoon. His arm is very much inflamed. It is broken in several places. He was very glad to see me, and had asked for me during the day. Went to prayer-meeting, and enjoyed it very much. This is a very pleasant, warm, and tolerably clear evening. Had a pleasant walk from prayer-meeting. S. came home with me.

Friday, March 2.

Warm and tolerably clear. Went to see Keller Culp before school this afternoon. He seems easier, but I do not think he is any better. Went down to Cousin Annie Sheads' for tea, after school, and staid until about 7 Oclock. Feel very much depressed in mind this evening, and have felt so during the day.

Saturday, March 3.

Cloudy, but warm—Had some rain to-day. Went up street this evening. Made several calls—Returned home about 8 Oclock.

Sunday, March 4.

Rose this morning very much depressed in mind and have been unable to overcome it. Had no class to-day. Did not enjoy either Sunday School or Prayer-meeting. Our preachers have not yet returned from Conference. Mr. McMillan led prayer-meeting this morning Mr. Thomas E. Snyder this evening. Snyder came with me home.

Monday, March 5.

Went to school this morning but as Mr. Baugher and Mr. Little are both sick we have no school until next Monday Morning. Went with Beckie Belch to get our miniatures taken. I gave her mine and she gave me hers. She expects to start for Missouri this week to stay a year or two. Returning from the Temple this evening met Miss Ada, Miss Laura, and Mr. Oscar McMillan, Miss Jennie Buckingham, Mr. Joe Wills, and Mr. William Heltzel on their way to the colored church. There was no meeting there, and they all came back with me and Mr. Snyder and spent a short time at our house.

Tuesday, March 6.

Very pleasant. Have been very unwell all day. Very hoarse, a bad cold and severe head-ache. Added to this I am very much depressed in mind more so I think than I ever have been. Tried to sew but could not and as it was very pleasant I took Grace and went over to see Mrs. Lashell.

Wednesday, March 7.

Feel better to-day, than I did yesterday. Wrote in Beckie Belch's Album. Went up to Ginnie Powers's to spend the evening, and staid until about 9 1/2 Oclock. Ginnie and Mr. Free came down with me. Spent a tolerably pleasant evening.

Thursday, March 8.

Wrote in Lizzie Trainer's Album, and in Mrs. Drumm's. Went out to Mr. Hanaway and to Mr. McMillan's. Spent a very pleasant afternoon, Stayed until prayer-meeting time. Took Selma's Album home. Mr. Warren led prayer-meeting. Did not enjoy it much. Met Mr. S. as I was going from the church and had company home. Had some notion of going to the colored church but it was raining and the walking was bad.

Friday, March 9.

The weather has been very changing to-day. Part of the time the sun was shining, and several times we had a considerable snow-storm. My temper still causes me to pass many sad hours. I sometimes think I cannot overcome it, but I am still trying, by God's help to subdue it. "When I seem most upon my guard, It takes me by surprise." The stars are shining. The sky is getting clear.

Saturday, March 10.

Cold and windy. I intended to go up street this afternoon, to see my Sabbath School Scholars, but as it was so disagreeable out, I concluded to stay at home. Am afraid I shall have the company I had last night, which was very unpleasant, viz, a severe tooth-ache.

Sunday, March 11.

Rose about 7 Oclock this morning. Mother was not able to get up, and as I had the work to do, I did not get to Sunday School. Did not enjoy prayer-meeting at all. Went to Sunday School this afternoon. Had a S.S. Prayer-meeting which I enjoyed very much. Went to preaching. Mr. Dill preached his first sermon for the present Conference Year. The sermon did not benefit me much as I could not fix my mind upon it. Ada Mc, Jennie B., Mr. Mills, Mr. Thad Welty, Mr. Snyder, and I went to the colored church after our preaching.

Monday, March 12.

Went to school this morning at the usual time. It has been tolerably cold to-day, and this evening it is very cold and windy. Went to the Temple this evening. Snyder came home with me. Have just finished reading the Water cure Journal—which a friend of mine very kindly lent me. They are very interesting to me.

Tuesday, March 13.

Overslept myself this morning. Went to school to-day as usual. Took a walk this evening after school out to the Cemetery. Never enjoyed a walk more in my life. The air was fresh, the sun shining, the sky clear, the birds singing, and all nature, as it were, rejoicing. Ada Mc called for me this evening to go to the Sewing Society. Went but there was no meeting. Ada and Mr. Mills came home with me, about 9 Oclock. Spent a very pleasant evening.

Wednesday, March 14.

Clear and very pleasant. Did not feel as well as usual this morning but this afternoon and evening feel very well. Took a walk to the York Bridge this evening after school, Enjoyed it a great deal, but not as much as the one yesterday evening. Sewed until about 9 1/2 Oclock this evening. S. was here this evening. This has been a delightful day, as pleasant as we have had for some time. Read the Water-cure Journal for March. Liked it very much.

Thursday, March 15.

Clear and very pleasant. Wrote two letters to-day. Went to prayer-meeting this evening. Enjoyed it very much. Mr. Drum led. He and Selma start for Wrightsville to-morrow morning, where they have been stationed by the Conference. Mother is very sick again with quinsy. Am afraid she will have a more severe spell than she had before.

Friday, March 16.

Rose at half past 6 Oclock this morning. Mother was unable to get up. When I went to school this morning I consulted Miss Thompson and Miss McCurdy about dismissing my school until this afternoon. They thought it best for me to dismiss and I did so, and went home to bake. Went to school this afternoon. Mother seems to be a little better this evening. This has been a very pleasant day. Snyder was here this evening.

Saturday, March 17.

Rose at six Oclock this morning, and have been working hard all day. Went up to Mr. Rupp's after supper, and Sade, Lou, and I went down street. Sade has been in Pittsburg for nearly a year and has just returned home. Went to the store and called to see Jennie Buckingham. Thought this morning that it would rain, but it has cleared off very pleasant. Read in the Water cure Journals. They are interesting to me.

Sunday, March 18.

Went to Sunday School as usual this morning and this afternoon. Rev. A. E. Taylor preached in Mr. Dill's place both morning and evening. Have not been to class for more than a month. Grandmother is very low, and we cannot meet at Uncle Robert's as she is living with them. Took a walk to the cemetery this evening after school with Jennie Buckingham. Enjoyed it very much. Snyder came with me from church.

Monday, March 19.

Very disagreeable. Raining and cool. Mother is getting better, I am very glad, for when she is sick nothing goes right. Sewed steadily from 7 until half past 9 Oclock. Read a book which Ginnie Powers lent me, called, Little Maggie's trials and triumphs. It is very interesting showing what a child can do who has the love of God in her heart.

Tuesday, March 20.

Tolerably clear and very windy. Have had a dull head-ache all day but feel better this evening. Intended to go to the Sewing Society this evening, but it was so cold and windy that I concluded to stay at home. Very glad I did not go, as Snyder came and spent the evening, or rather a part of it, with me. He read aloud from the Templar's Magazines. I think they are interesting.

Wednesday, March 21.

Cold and windy. Sky clear. Dismissed school this afternoon, at half past 3 Oclock, as the building was very uncomfortable. Went up street to the store after supper, and to see Maggie Buckingham. Almost blew away on the street. It was so very windy. Sewed until half past 10 Oclock.

Thursday, March 22.

Very cold and windy. Went to prayer-meeting this evening. Mr. Sumwalt, our single preacher for this year, commenced leading, and Mr. Dill finished. Did not enjoy it very much. Snyder came home with me. Dismissed school at 3 Oclock this afternoon as the building was uncomfortable.

Saturday, March 24.

Cold and windy. Have been very busy all day. Went up to the store this evening. Have been reading all evening in a book entitled, "Alone" by Marian Harland. Have heard so much about it that I was anxious to read it. It is well written but did not interest me very much.

Sunday, March 25.

Went to Sabbath School this morning at 9 Oclock. To prayer-meeting at 10 1/2 Oclock. Mr. Snyder led. Did not remain until it was over, as I felt very badly. Did not go to class. Went to S. School at 2 Oclock. Went to preaching this evening. Mr. Sumwalt preached a sermon that pleased and interested me very much. Have been very much depressed in mind all day, but do not feel so badly to-night. Mr. Snyder came with me from church.

Monday, March 26.

Overslept myself this morning. Went to school at 9 Oclock and again at half past one. Mr. Baugher came up to school this afternoon. He has been sick for two or three weeks but is now getting better, but unable to teach. Took supper with Annie S. Went to the Temple this evening. Did not get there until half an hour after the time. Snyder came home with me. Mattie Robison and I went down street after school this evening.

Tuesday, March 27.

This has been a delightful day, clear and tolerably warm. Went to school as usual this morning and afternoon. Read a book this evening called Gilbert Gresham. Sade Rupp lent it to me. Mattie Robison came down a few minutes this evening. She is going to Fairfield next week. I went up a little way with her. Met Mr. Snyder and his brother Amos. Had a short conversation with them. Mr. Snyder came down with me but did not stay as he and Amos were going to the colored church.

Wednesday, March 28.

Sun shining. Very pleasant and clear all day. This evening the moon and stars are very bright. Mr. Snyder came for me to go to the colored church but I did not go. Went up to Aunt Salome's with my work, and she and I went down street. Went to see cousin Annie Sheads a few minutes with Aunt. This is a delightful evening.

Thursday, March 29.

Clear and very pleasant. Went to Prayer-meeting this evening. Brother Sumwalt led, and we had a very interesting meeting, I enjoyed it very much. This is a delightful evening. Was at Mattie Robison's a few minutes after prayer meeting, or rather at her mother's. Snyder and I took Mattie from prayer-meeting.

Sunday, April 1.

Had no services of any kind at our church to-day as there was a Quarterly Meeting at Rock Chapel. Went to the German Reformed S. School this morning, and to their infant School. Was very much pleased with both of them. Heard Mr. Bucher preach at 10 Oclock. He preached a very interesting sermon. Went with Alice Powers to the Lutheran S. School and also to the infant school. The small school is a very pleasant one. I like it better than the large one. Went to the Catholic church after school, but was too late. Went to hear Mr. Heiser preach this evening. His text was "The harvest is past, the summer is ended and we are not saved." His sermon was interesting, but rather long, I thought. Sade Rupp lent me a book called "The blind girl of Wittenberg." I read it to-day and found it very interesting.

Monday, April 2.

This is a day of general uproar and confusion. Helped Aunt Salome to move and took dinner with her. After dinner went to see Aunt Lizzie and Aunt Agnes who are also moving. Went to the Temple this evening at 8 Oclock. S. came home with me. Spent a very pleasant day but feel considerably tired this evening. I am thankful that "moving day" only comes once a year.

Tuesday, April 3.

Very pleasant and clear sometimes. Had no school yesterday on account of moving. Had 65 scholars this morning and 63 this afternoon. Grandmother is a great deal worse. I am afraid that she will not live long. She had a very severe spell. She had a stroke of palsy and suffers a great deal. 8 Oclock mother told me to go and see Grandmother if I wanted to see her alive. I went but she did not speak. She has not spoken since noon. I would like to have staid but mother and father were there, and I had to come home. 11 Oclock P.M. Grandmother is dead. She died about an hour ago. She was the oldest inhabitant of the place, respected by all who knew her. I can hardly realize that she has gone to her long home. Peace to her ashes.

Wednesday, April 4.

Have been very busy all day. Mother is so distressed about Grandmother's death that it makes my heart ache to be near her. Received a letter from Mattie Durboraw this morning.

Thursday, April 5.

10 Oclock A.M. Clear and very pleasant. Had no school to-day or yesterday on account of Grandmother's death. I went to see her this morning and took Grace and the other children along. She lies in her coffin as peacefully as though she were sleeping. She is sleeping, but it is the long sleep of death which knows no waking. She, who was ever ready to sympathyze with us in our sorrows, lies all unconscious of the tears which are shed around her. She knows nothing of the grief of hearts which are well nigh to breaking. 4 Oclock P.M. Have just returned from grandmother's funeral. It was a mournful time. Struggle as I would, I could not keep back the tears. One by one my relations and friends are being carried to Evergreen Cemetery and laid beneath the clods of that lovely place. I know not who will be next, it may be myself. Four of the companions of my childhood are already there, and one dearly loved friend of my girlhood lies there. And while standing there, I thought of the morning when they and I shall rise from our graves and a prayer went up that we all might have a part in the great resurrection. Oh! God help me each day and each hour to live in thy fear, that when the messenger comes I may calmly yield my spirit up, and sink to sleep, resting on the bosom of him who has promised to support me in that trying hour.

Friday, April 6.

Clear and pleasant. Went to school this morning, and afternoon at the usual time. Had 48 scholars this morning and 45 this afternoon.

Saturday, April 7.

Have been working hard all day. Received a letter from Cousin Lizzie Myers of Centreville, Wayne Co. Indiana. She was on a visit to Baltimore last fall and winter and spent three weeks with me. Went up street this evening, and made several calls.

Sunday, April 8.

9 Oclock, at Sunday School. 10 1/2 Oclock at Prayer-meeting. Mr. McMillan led. Enjoyed it tolerably. Did not go to class as I had a dull head-ache. 2 Oclock, at S.S. Had a missionary meeting and S.S. prayer-meeting. Went to preaching at 7 Oclock. Mr. Dill Preached a very interesting sermon on the suffering and death of Christ—S. came home with me. The sky has been cloudy all day and we have had a little rain to-day.

Monday, April 9.

Had fifty-three scholars this morning and the same number this afternoon. Cloudy and very unpleasant. Mr. Snyder and I went to the Temple this evening, but was too late as we met the members returning as I was going down. Returned home about 8 Oclock after a very disagreeable walk. 11 Oclock P.M. Feel very badly this evening. "Oh! that I had the wings of a dove that I might fly away and be at rest."

Tuesday, April 10.

58 scholars this morning and the same this afternoon. The weather is very unpleasant and has been since Sunday. It has been raining all day. I was sitting at my window a long time this evening as it was getting dark, thinking over "matters and things" and came to the conclusion that I have my share of the trouble and sorrow of this life. If only I had some friend into whose ear I could pour all my griefs perhaps I would feel relieved, but alas! that blessed privelege is denied me. I have often thought that if I were not naturally inclined to look on the bright side of everything that I could not endure some of my trials. But as I am a thoughtless and light-hearted girl, those to whom I could open my heart only laugh and say, "they don't see what I have to trouble me." Well, they don't see, and I am very thankful they don't see my heart. By and by I'll get home, where there is no trouble or sorrow to mar our peace.

Wednesday, April 11.

58 scholars this morning and 60 this afternoon. The sky was cloudy the early part of the day, but now it is clearing off and is very pleasant. Mother and I went up street this evening to see about a mourning bonnett. Aunt Salome and cousins Jane and Mary Myers were down this evening. Snyder was here when mother and I got home. A memorable day & night in consequence of misunderstanding.

Thursday, April 12.

59 scholars this morning and 53 this afternoon. Clear and very pleasant until this evening when it rained a little. Went to Prayer meeting this evening. Brother Sumwalt led. Enjoyed it tolerably. S. came home with me. Lizzie Durboraw was in town to-day. She was to see me awhile, at school. Had a very pleasant conversation with her. She only staid about a half an hour as she was to go home with her father to-day.

Friday, April 13.

56 scholars this morning and 55 this afternoon. Clear and pleasant. This evening, mother and I called on our neighbors who moved across the street from us this spring.

Saturday, April 14.

Thought this morning we would have rain but it has cleared this evening. Went to preaching this evening. Mr. Dill preached, but as I had a very bad tooth-ache I could not pay very much attention to the sermon. After church, Mr. Dill detained the members and spoke about enlarging or rebuilding the church which is entirely too small for us. Going home met Snyder, and he came with me.

Sunday, April 15.

Went to love-feast this morning. Enjoyed it very well, just before it closed, Mr. Dill preached an interesting sermon and after it, he administered the sacrament of the Lord's supper. Went to Sunday School this afternoon. This evening I went to church expecting to hear Mr. Dill, but heard Mr. Paxton preach a very interesting sermon, from the text, "This man receiveth sinners." He is a local preacher formerly a resident of this place but now living in Chambersburg.

Monday, April 16.

55 scholars this morning and 52 this afternoon. Cloudy and cool. We have had some rain to-day. Was at Aunt Salome's for tea this evening and called to see Mrs. Dill.

Tuesday, April 17.

47 scholars this morning and 45 this afternoon. This has been a delightful day, warm and pleasant. Met with a lady from Baltimore, Miss Sarah Robison, an old schoolmate of mine whom I have not seen for several years. Ginnie Gilbert called to see me this evening and she and I went up street a little while. Ellie Aughinbaugh was here an hour or two this evening. Went to the store after supper and bought a dress for myself and Susie, a shaker for myself and hats for Ginnie and Bell.

Wednesday, April 18.

45 scholars this morning and the same number this afternoon. Warm and very pleasant. Went down to Aunt Lizzie's this evening.

Thursday, April 19.

47 scholars this morning, and 42 this afternoon. Went to prayer-meeting this evening. Enjoyed it tolerably. Mr. Dill began leading and Mr. Sumwalt exhorted and closed. Mr. Snyder came with me home.

Friday, April 20.

50 scholars this morning, and the same this afternoon. Miss Powers and I took our schools a walk this afternoon. We had one hundred and eight scholars altogether. Went over to Ellie Aughinbaugh's this evening. We were sitting in the door until almost 9 Oclock, it was so very pleasant. Answered Mattie Durboraw's letter to-day but it was too late for the mail and cannot go until Monday.

Saturday, April 21.

Rose at 6 Oclock this morning with such a severe head-ache that I could not stay up, and so I lay down until 11 Oclock when I awoke no better, but rather worse than when I lay down. I was very agreeably surprised this afternoon by a visit from Mattie Durboraw. She came about three Oclock accompanied by Miss Coshun and is going to stay until to-morrow. We went to the Cemetery this evening and I think I took cold for after I came home I had the tooth-ache so badly that I was almost crazy. These attacks of tooth-ache do not come like angel's visits, as I heartily wish they would.

I gave Mattie her letter instead of sending it through the Office. And she is reading it while I am writing.

Sunday, April 22.

Rose this morning about 7 Oclock. Mattie and I went to Sunday School. We had no preaching and Mattie & Miss Coshun went to hear Mr. McElwine preach, They wanted me to go along but I did not and am very glad that I stayed for I enjoyed prayer-meeting so very much. Mr. Snyder led and it was indeed a "foretaste clear Of that sweet rest above." I have not enjoyed any means of grace so much for a long time. Mr. Sumwalt preached an interesting sermon this evening from the 12th verse of the 6th chapter of St. Mark, "And they went out and preached that men should repent." Snyder came with me from church. Mattie Durboraw went home this morning. It went hard to see her go but a promise to write soon made it a little less painful. She does not live far from town but I see her so seldom that when she does come, I do not like to see her go. I like her very much and expect to visit her after my school is done, if I live and am well.

Monday, April 23.

52 scholars this morning and 54 this afternoon. Went to the Temple this evening, and was just in time. Had a very pleasant time. This was the evening for nominating

officers for the next term. It was almost 10 Oclock when I got home (or rather when we got home)

Tuesday, April 24.

51 scholars this morning and 48 this afternoon. Very cold weather for this time of year. This evening mother and I went to see Aunt Agnes, Aunt Lizzie and Mrs. Sweeney. We found Mrs. Sweeney very cheerful. She seems better this evening but has been very poorly. She is very much troubled with Asthma. This is a lovely night, both moon-light and star-light.

Wednesday, April 25.

43 scholars this morning and 48 this afternoon. Very cold and windy. Lizzie Durboraw came up this evening about 5 Oclock. I was very glad to see her, but was not expecting her until to-morrow. We went up street to the store and to see Mrs. Dill. Aunt Lizzie and Uncle George were here this evening a long time. Heard a serenade this evening but it was too cold to stand out and listen, so we did not hear as much as we wished.

Thursday, April 26.

41 scholars this morning and 46 this afternoon. Went to prayer meeting this evening. Did not enjoy it at all. Mr. Sumwalt led. Lizzie Durboraw staid with me all night and went home to-day. She wanted to stay until to-morrow but could not as she had promised to be home to-day. This is a beautiful moon-light night, but rather cold. Snyder brought me from prayer-meeting.

Friday, April 27.

46 scholars this morning and 47 this afternoon. Went up street this evening a short time with Ada McMillan.

Sunday, April 29.

Overslept myself this morning and was late at Sunday School. This morning was Mr. Sumwalt's appointment for preaching but he was called away to attend a funeral and was not back in time. We had a very good prayer meeting. Mr. Snyder led. Went to Sunday School this afternoon. Mr. Sumwalt preached this evening to a very large and attentive congregation. His text was the last clause of the 26th verse of the 11th chapter of the Acts of the Apostles. "And the disciples were called Christians first in Antioch." S. came home with me.

Monday, April 30.

54 scholars this morning and 56 this afternoon. Went to see Mrs. Eyster this evening about going to school this summer during vacation. Went to a Temperance Meeting this evening at 7 oclock. Revs. Sumwalt, Heiser, Bucher and Mr. Guss addressed the meeting. It was very interesting but I did not relish it as I have been in the house all day and was tired. This is a magnificent, moon-light night. S. came home with me.

Tuesday, May 1.

48 scholars this morning and 54 this afternoon. Very disagreeable. It has been cloudy and cool all day and this evening it is raining. Rose at half past 6 Oclock this morning and enjoyed the morning air a great deal.

Wednesday, May 2.

48 scholars this morning and 41 this afternoon. Very unpleasant all day but this evening it has stopped raining and looks a little like clearing off. Hope it will for to-morrow evening will be prayer-meeting evening.

Thursday, May 3.

47 scholars this morning and 49 this afternoon. Went to prayer meeting this evening. Did not enjoy it all. Mr. Sumwalt led. S. came with me. Bought a Geometry, and Arithmetic and an Algebra. I intend studying with Mrs. Eyster this summer during vacation which will be in June and July and perhaps I will go to school longer.

Friday, May 4.

47 scholars this morning, and 45 this afternoon. Spent a very pleasant evening. Ellie Aughinbaugh was over and stayed the whole evening. Mr. Snyder brought me 4 numbers of the Templar's Magazines to read. I read aloud to Ellie while she was working at my bonnett. They are very interesting. This is a delightful night. The moon is bright, the sky clear and the air warm and pleasant.

Saturday, May 5.

Have been sewing very busily all day, and feel very tired. Ellie A. and I went up street this evening a little while. This is a splendid night although I have been too busy to enjoy it much.

Sunday, May 6.

Went to Sunday School and church as usual to-day. Have been very much depressed both in body and mind all day, but feel better this evening. Took a walk to the colored church to listen to them singing, after we came from church. Very pleasant and warm. Read a S.S. book to-day which Ellie A. lent me, called, "Vara, or the child of adoption."

Monday, May 7.

47 scholars this morning; 46 this afternoon. Very warm and oppressive all day but this evening it is cool and pleasant. Went to the Temple this evening. There was a public installation of the officers for the next Term. Rev. Mr. Bucher made some remarks also. Bro. Guss and Rev. Weaver. Read the March number of the Templar's Magazine. Snyder brought me home.

Tuesday, May 8.

47 scholars this morning; 44 this afternoon. Wrote a long letter to cousin Lizzie Myers to-day or rather finished writing it. I commenced it yesterday. It is very warm to-day. Went over to see Ginnie Gilbert a while this evening. Mary Belch was down this evening. Did not get to my sewing until 9 Oclock, and sewed busily until 10 Oclock.

Wednesday, May 9.

51 scholars this morning; 45 this afternoon. Very disagreeable. Cloudy and raining all day. Mr. Sumwalt preached at the colored church this evening. Ellie A. and I wanted to go, but it was too wet and the sky was very cloudy and looked like we would have rain. Sewed until 10 Oclock.

Thursday, May 10.

48 scholars this morning; 44 this afternoon. Could not go to prayer-meeting as it was too wet. It has been raining all day and this evening it fell in torrents. I was very much disappointed as I wanted to go, but I sewed the whole evening until 10 Oclock.

Friday, May 11.

29 scholars this morning; 34 this afternoon. The weather is very unpleasant and has been since Wednesday evening. Sewed until 11 Oclock this evening.

Saturday, May 12.

Raining almost all day. Went up to the store this evening. Feel very much depressed in mind and have for several days.

Sunday, May 13.

To-day is worthy of particular notice. reconciliation. Went to Sunday School this morning. Expected to hear a sermon this morning but was disappointed. Mr. McMillan led prayer-meeting and I enjoyed it more than I have for some time. Had a very interesting Class. There was only eight there but I enjoyed it very much. Went to S.S. this afternoon. Mr. Sumwalt preached a very interesting sermon this evening. The house was crowded and a great many went away that could not get in. Snyder came home with me.

Monday, May 14.

54 scholars this morning; 52 this afternoon. Did not go to the Temple this evening as mother wished to go to class. Heard that Lizzie Durboraw is very ill with Putrid Sore Throat. Had a little rain to-day but I think it is very pleasant. It is just two years this evening since I received the assurance that my sins were pardoned and I have this day renewed the covenant I then made. Oh God, give me grace to keep it.

Tuesday, May 15.

57 scholars this morning; 51 this afternoon. Warm and pleasant. Kate Foster and I went out to Mr. McMillan's this evening. It was a very pleasant walk out, but coming home it was rather cool. Mr. Snyder spent the evening with me.

Wednesday, May 16.

45 scholars this morning; 47 this afternoon. Received a letter from Mattie and Lizzie Durboraw this morning. Mother and I went up street this evening to the store and called on Aunt Mary Sheads, Mrs. King, and Mrs. Troxel. Ellie A. and I took a walk after we came home. Read some in the Water-cure Journal. To-day, it is two years since I united myself with the Church of God.

Thursday, May 17.

37 scholars this morning; 43 this afternoon. Mother and I went out to Mr. Hanaway's this evening. Had a very pleasant walk. Went to prayer-meeting and enjoyed it very much. Mr. Sumwalt led. S. came home with me.

Friday, May 18.

43 scholars this morning; 43 this afternoon. Went over to Ellie Aughinbaugh's this evening and was there until 8 Oclock and then came home and sewed until 10 Oclock.

Sunday, May 20.

Went to Sunday School this morning. Went to prayer-meeting, but did not enjoy it much on account of a very unpleasant conversation I had after Sunday School with an acquaintance of mine. Had a delightful time at class. There was not very many there but I enjoyed it very much. It was like a "little heaven below" Ellie A. and I took a walk this evening about a mile from town and took our books along to read. This is a delightful evening, clear and warm. Mr. Sumwalt's text this evening was the first clause of the first verse of the 53rd Psalm. It was a splendid sermon. I could have listened to him all night. He was very much indisposed. Snyder came with me from church.

Monday, May 21.

42 scholars this morning; 44 this afternoon. Went to spend the evening with Ginnie Buckingham but as the sky was very cloudy and for several other reasons, did

not stay but spent the evening at home. Mr. Elias Redding, an old friend of mine was here this evening. We had quite a storm this evening. It rained very heavily for a short time.

Tuesday, May 22.

45 scholars this morning; 43 this afternoon. Went over to see Ginnie Gilbert this evening and went down street with her. Snyder was here. Feel very much depressed this evening. I am not making the progress in the divine life which it is my privelege and duty to make. "Preserve me O God for in thee do I put my trust."

Wednesday, May 23.

46 scholars this morning 40 this afternoon. Warm and pleasant. This is a delightful evening, both moon-light and star-light. Sewed until 10 Oclock.

Thursday, May 24.

41 scholars this morning; 42 this afternoon. Instead of prayer-meeting this evening an Indian preached in our church. He preached a good sermon but I would rather have had prayer-meeting. I think I would have enjoyed it more. S. came home with me.

Friday, May 25.

36 scholars this morning; 35 this afternoon. Elder Collins preached in McConaughy's Hall this evening. Mother and I went, but did not stay. Went over to Aunt Salome's. Have been very much interested in a book by Dr. Hodgson on Predestination which Mr. Snyder lent me. It is in three discourses and when I commenced the first, I became so interested in it, that I did not stop until I had read it all.

Saturday, May 26.

Have been sewing very busily all day. Made a dress for Grace and finished one for myself. Went up street this evening. Cousin Annie Sheads and Mr. Thad Welty came down this evening and stayed about an hour. Snyder came while they were here.

Sunday, May 27.

Went to Sunday School this morning as usual. Ellie Aughinbaugh went along and staid for preaching. Rev. Edward Kinsey preached a very interesting sermon from the first clause of the 14th verse of the 14th chapter of Job. "If a man die shall he live again." He is an excellent preacher and is preaching in Hanover this year. He and Mr. Sumwalt exchanged for to-day. Did not go to class as mother was sick. Went to Sunday school this afternoon. Ellie and I were going to take a walk but it rained and we could not go. Mr. Kinsey's text this evening was the first clause of the 3rd verse of the 2nd chapter of Hebrews. "How shall we escape if we neglect so great salvation." Snyder came from church with me.

Monday, May 28.

37 scholars this morning; 36 this afternoon. Cousin Annie Sheads was here this evening and we took a walk. Went to the Temple this evening at 8 Oclock. This is a delightful night. Clear and moon-light. Snyder came home with me.

Wednesday, May 30.

37 scholars this morning; 36 this afternoon. Wrote in Miss Harriet Shillen's Album to-day. Went to our church to-night to hear a Quaker preach. Was very much pleased. there was a good congregation when the weather is taken into consideration. It has been cloudy all day & some rain. S. came with me from church.

Thursday, May 31.

35 scholars this morning. Mr. McCreary, the President of the Board of Directors, came up this morning to school, examined my first reading and spelling class, and dismissed the school until the 1st of August. Went to prayer-meeting this evening but did not enjoy it any. S. came home with me.

Friday, June 1.

Have been very busy all day. Had to iron and bake to-day as we are going to have a Sabbath School pic-nic to-morrow. Went up to see Mrs. Eyster to-day about starting to school on Monday. Went to the store this evening, and made several calls. Finished Mattie Durboraw's letter and wrote one to Lizzie Durboraw.

Saturday, June 2.

Rose about 6 1/2 Oclock this morning. Went to the church at 7 Oclock and we started for Spangler's Springs about 8 Oclock. Got there safely and spent a delightful day, just as we were about starting for home we missed Ginnie, and were very much alarmed. It was about 6 Oclock I suppose, when we missed her. We hunted all over the woods and could not find her. They all went home but Maggie Buckingham, Julia Weygandt, Mr. Guinn, Mr. Snyder and myself, and we waited until word would come from town whether she had got home or not. About 8 Oclock father came out and told us that she was home. She had wandered off while trying to find us, and Mr. Buehler met her and brought her with him to town. It was a dreadful load off our minds for we feared she had fallen into the creek. We started home in good spirits, considering our fright, and reached town pretty tired.

Sunday, June 3.

Did not feel very well when I rose this morning. Went to Sunday School. Had a very interesting time with my class. Went to prayer-meeting. Enjoyed it very much. Had a glorious time at class. This is the regular afternoon for the meeting of the Missionary Society of our Sabbath School. Mr. Dill preached to-night but I could not fix my mind upon the sermon, was, of course, not benefitted by it. It rained considerably this afternoon and evening. S. came with me from preaching.

Monday, June 4.

Rose about half past 7 this morning. Went to school at 9 Oclock. Mrs. Eyster was away from home and we had no school this morning, and as she felt very tired and her little son was unwell we had none this afternoon. Had a dreadful hail-storm this afternoon. I never saw hail like in my life. I saw some as large as a good-sized walnut and I heard that there were some larger ones found. This was the regular "Degree Night" of our Temple, but I did not go and I suppose there was no meeting as the weather was bad. Snyder spent the evening with me.

Tuesday, June 5.

Rose late this morning, and as a natural consequence, do not feel as well as usual. Went to school to-day and like it very much. I am studying Arithmetic, Algebra, Astronomy, Geometry, Natural Philosophy. Have exercises in, writing, composition, and parsing in Pollok's Course of Time. I may take some other studies, but it is probable that I will not, as I think of going for two months only. Had some rain to-day, but it has been pleasant. S. spent the evening here.

Wednesday, June 6.

Rose this morning at half past 5 Oclock. Helped mother to wash before I went to school. Went to school as usual. Ellie Aughinbaugh was over a while this evening. Mary Belch was down about two hours. This is a very pleasant and warm.

Thursday, June 7.

Recited my first Geometry lesson, Like it very much. Went to prayer-meeting. Did not enjoy it at all. Snyder came with me home.

Friday, June 8.

Wrote a composition to-day. Could not fix upon a subject, and so I wrote a soliloquy on Essay Writing. Did not read it before the school. Mrs. Eyster excused me as it was the first time. Went down to see Maggie Buckingham after school this evening.

Saturday, June 9.

Very cold all day for this time of year. Went up street this evening to the store. Showed Callie McMillan how to crochet a shawl of Shetland Wool. Mr. Wills came with her and they stayed until about half past 8 Oclock.

Sunday, June 10.

Rose late this morning. Went to Sunday School as usual this morning and afternoon. Did not go to class. Ellie Aughinbaugh and I took a walk, about a half a mile out the Emmitsburg road. Mr. Dill preached this evening. Went from church home. Snyder came with me.

Monday, June 11.

Went to school as usual to-day. Went to the Temple this evening at 8 Oclock. Had a very interesting time. Went from the Temple home. Snyder came with me. Had a pleasant walk. Received a letter from Cousin Lizzie Myers this morning. Bought ribbon for a bonnett this evening.

Tuesday, June 12.

Rose late this morning. Have not been very well to-day. Went to school as usual. Did not stay until school was out this afternoon. After supper I went and lay down, and slept a short time. Had a queer kind of a pain in my side. Jennie Buckingham stopped a few moments at the door on her way home. I went a long part of the way. It is just one year to-day since Annie White died. I have been thinking a great about her to-day. Hope I shall meet her in heaven, and by the grace of God I will.

Wednesday, June 13.

Very warm and pleasant. Sewed at my dress after I came from school, until 7 Oclock, and then dressed. Mr. Snyder was here this evening. He is going to Philadelphia next Monday morning, to stay for some time. This is a delightful evening. Feel very much depressed in mind and have felt so all week.

Thursday, June 14.

Went to school to-day as usual. After school this afternoon I sewed at my dress until half past 7 Oclock, and wrote my composition. The subject was, "Time does not linger." Went to prayer-meeting this evening. Mr. Dill led. Did not enjoy it at all. Mr. Drum was at prayer-meeting. He and his wife and the baby are here. They are going home to-morrow. Snyder came home with me.

Friday, June 15.

Went to school as usual to-day. Read my composition this afternoon. Mrs. Eyster said it was very good. Mother and I took a walk after supper. Went over to see Ellie Aughinbaugh, and Ginnie Gilbert, this evening. Cousin Annie Sheads was here a few moments.

Saturday, June 16.

Have been sewing very busily this evening at my dress. Sewed until 7 Oclock this evening and then dressed. Expected company this evening but was disappointed and took up so much time to dress that I did not get my dress done.

Sunday, June 17.

Rose at 8 Oclock this morning. Went to Sunday School and from there to prayer-meeting. Mr. Snyder led. Enjoyed it very much. We had no class and I went to Mr. Jesse Culp's. Mr. Snyder led it. Did not enjoy it at all. Went to Sunday School this afternoon. Mattie Robison went with me. Went to preaching at 6 Oclock. Mattie came down for me and we took a walk. Mr. Sumwalt preached an interesting but short sermon. Mr. Snyder came down after church. Ginnie, Susie, Bell, and Grace all gave him good bye and kissed him. They feel loth to part with him. He stands very high in their estimation. After the children went to bed. He & I went down to see Maggie B & Sallie B. Mr. Snyder wished to bid them Good bye. Came home about 9 Oclock and bade him Good bye myself. Do not know when I shall see him again.

Monday, June 18.

Rose before 5 Oclock this morning and have felt very well all day. Went to school but came home about 10 Oclock and did not go back again. Finished my dress. Mother, Jefferson, Ginnie, Bell, and I went out to the Cemetery after supper. Went to Aunt Salome's when we came back. Went down to Mr. Minnigh's, and afterwards took a walk with Annie McCleary. Came home about 9 Oclock. Mr. S ... started for Philadelphia this morning.

Tuesday, June 19.

Rose this morning (Oh! for shame, that I must make this humiliating confession to my diary) at 15 minutes after 8 Oclock. I note in my diary when I arise early and of course I must do so when I indulge in the sinful practice of lying in bed after I have slept as much as nature requires. Went to school as usual to-day. Have felt dull and no wonder! I ought to suffer for it both bodily & mentally.

Wednesday, June 20.

Rose a little earlier this morning, I was up at 6 1/2 Oclock. I must really try to form the habit of early rising, next Sunday is my birthday. That will be a good time to begin (if it only does not stop there). I must try to have an hour or two to myself in the morning, which I never can have if I rise at 8 and go to school at 9. Besides I want red cheeks, I'll never have them if I lie in bed after sunrise. I mean natural ones, not those made by red cotton flannel. I am going to try and be up to-morrow morning, so early that I need not be ashamed to put it in my diary.

Thursday, June 21.

Rose at half past 6 Oclock this morning. That is not early enough, but it is better than 8 Oclock. Went to Prayer-meeting this evening, Mr. Sumwalt led. Enjoyed it very much. 9 Oclock. Feel very sleepy and so I will stop writing and retire for to-night.

Friday, June 22.

Rose at 7 Oclock this morning. Went to school as usual. Wrote a composition this morning, or rather finished it, for I commenced it yesterday. I took for a subject, "An hour in Evergreen Cemetery." Mrs. Eyster said it was very good, but rather long. I could have made it longer but was compelled to stop. Mary Belch was down this evening with Miss Lizzie Hooper, a lady who is staying with her for a short time. Went up street with them. Came home about 9 Oclock.

Saturday, June 23.

Rose at 6 1/2 Oclock this morning. Have been ironing all morning and until 2 Oclock. Went to the store this evening. Ellie A. and I went up street a few minutes, and coming home we stopped at Mrs. Harriet Shillen's. She was playing her piano. We stayed until after 10 Oclock. She played several beautiful pieces for us. Came home about 10 1/2 Oclock.

Sunday, June 24.

Went to S.S. this morning. Went to preaching. Mr. Sumwalt preached. His text was the 9th verse of the 7th ch. of Hosea. "Grey hairs are here & there upon him, yet he knoweth not." Went to class. Mr. Sumwalt led. Enjoyed it very much. Went to S.S. this afternoon. Went to preaching at 6 Oclock. Mr. Sumwalt preached a very interesting sermon from the last clause of the 30th verse of the 16th chapter of Acts. "What must I do to be saved?" Went from church home. To-day is my birth-day. I am eighteen years old. Where will I be on my nineteenth birthday?

Monday, June 25.

Went to school as usual to-day. I like my students more and more every day. I love my Geometry and Algebra. but oh! the abominable Arithmetic. I never did like it, but I am getting along very well in it. Went to the temple this evening. Had a very pleasant time. Going home I missed my accustomed escort. Wonder where he is to-night. Returned home about 10 Oclock.

Tuesday, June 26.

Went to school as usual to-day. It has been very warm all day, and this evening. Mr. Seitz was down this evening. While I was knitting my cloud last winter, he bet me a treat of oysters that I would not have it done for a month. I finished it in two weeks. It never suited and this evening he came to pay with this difference. It was ice-cream instead of oysters. Came home about 9 1/2 Oclock.

Wednesday, June 27.

Went to school as usual to-day. Have been sewing very busily all day, at a dress for Grace. 9 Oclock—Feel very sleepy and will retire for to-night. So good night my dear little diary.

Thursday, June 28.

It has been very warm all day. This evening it is a little cooler. Went to prayer-meeting this evening. Did not enjoy it very much. Did not go to school this morning. Mother was not very well, and I stayed at home to wash. I feel very tired, as I do not often do such heavy work, not because I cannot, but it does not suit, as I have been teaching and going to school for the last ten months.

Friday, June 29.

Did not get to school until 10 Oclock this morning. I baked some cakes for the children. They are going to have missionary fair to-night and to-morrow night. Wrote a composition this morning. Took for a subject, "When shall we meet again?" Read it this afternoon before the school. Mrs. Eyster read it and said it did not need correction. Had the Fair this evening, and such a confusion it made. I am glad it is over for to-night I am very tired.

Saturday, June 30.

Rose late this morning. This fair is putting me all out of sorts. I cannot get anything done for myself. It has been very warm all day. Ciphered for about two hours this afternoon, in my Arithmetic, and a short time in Algebra. I like my studies a great deal better than when I commenced them. 11 Oclock. Am so tired I can scarcely walk. The fair is over, and the house is quiet once more, and I will retire for to-night.

Sunday, July 1.

Rose late this morning. It has been raining very heavily all morning until a while before noon it stopped, and this evening it is clear. Although it was pouring down, I went to sunday School. None of my scholars were there I suppose on account of the weather. I taught a class of little girls who could not yet read and I was delighted with them. When I commenced teaching S.S. I wanted a small class, but it did not suit. Mr. Culp led prayer-meeting. Had no class. Our S.S. went to Union S.S. held in the Presbyterian Church. The services were very interesting, but I would rather have been at our own. Mr. Dill preached this evening. This is a splendid night. Clear, moonlight, and warm.

Monday, July 2.

Did not go to school to-day as mother was not very well, and was unable to wash. I did the greater part of the washing and was done by 12 Oclock, and everything cleaned up, and dinner ready. Wrote to Cousin Lizzie Myers this afternoon. Went up street this evening, to the shoe-store and to the Post Office. Went to Aunt Agnes' and staid until 9 Oclock. It has been very warm to-day. This evening we had a little rain. Ciphered all afternoon, in Algebra and Arithmetic. Was three hours at one sum in Algebra, and did not get it then. I cannot imagine why.

Tuesday, July 3.

Very warm and sultry all day. Ironed this morning, and this afternoon sewed the facing on a dress for myself. Went up street this evening to Miss Harriet Shillen's to see about making a new dress. It is not so warm this evening but very pleasant. It is moonlight.

Wednesday, July 4.

Rose late this morning. Our social Temple had a Temperance pic-nic to-day but I did not go, as mother was not well, The Hiawatha Temple of Honor, Cadets of Honor also went with them. Went up street this evening, and came home about 8 Oclock. Have been sewing very busily all day at my new dress.

Thursday, July 5.

As yesterday was the fourth we had no school, and have none to-day or to-morrow. Sewed all day at my dress. After supper went over to Aunt Salome's and staid until prayer-meeting time. Mr. Dill led prayer-meeting. Did not enjoy it at all. Coming home I passed Mr. Shillen's and saw Harriet sitting by herself sewing. Thought she looked lonesome & went in and stayed awhile. Had a very pleasant talk with her. Came home about 6 Oclock.

Friday, July 6.

Sewed all day at my dress. This evening, I went to the store and to see Rose Wertz. While there Mr. Benner and Mr. Pierce came, and I staid longer than I intended to stay. Rose and I had quite an interesting conversation. Came home about 10 Oclock.

Saturday, July 7.

Rose a little earlier than usual this morning. Our second Quarterly meeting began to-day. Mr. Kinsey of Hanover preached at 11 Oclock. There were very few present. Brother Kinsey did not seem to like it. He said "He did not mean to task his physical powers to preach to a handful, and he wanted us to keep our heads up and our eyes and ears open to hear what he did say." I don't think he did "tax his physical powers" but he preached a very good sermon. His text was the first clause of the 7th verse of the 7th chapter of Matthew. "Ask and it shall be given you." His text this evening was the first clause of the 44th verse of the 24th chapter of Matthew "Therefore be ye also ready." I hope we will have a good congregation to-morrow, for then we will have a good sermon. Went to see Annie S. after church, about something particular. Came home about 10 Oclock.

Sunday, July 8.

Rose at 6 Oclock. Went to love feast at 8 1/2. Enjoyed it very much. I think it was because I spoke last night. Brother R. told us to examine our hearts. I did so this morning in love feast. I dedicated myself anew to his service, and was blessed in the act. Oh! that God may give me grace to keep my good resolutions. Mr. K. preached an excellent sermon at 10 1/2 Oclock. He preached almost an hour, his text was the 26th verse of the 24th chapter of Luke. "Ought not Christ to have suffered these things, and to enter into his glory?" I was very much benefitted by the sermon. After preaching the sacrament of the Lord's Supper was administered. I did not get home until after 1 Oclock. Saw Mattie and Lizzie Durboraw. Had a pleasant talk with them. They went home this afternoon. It has been so long since I saw them last. I could hardly get away from them. Had no S.S. or Prayer-meeting this afternoon, and I went out to Mr. McMillan's about 2 Oclock to see Mattie Plank. Had something of importance to talk about. Did not get home until after 6 Oclock. Mr. Cregh preached this evening at 8 Oclock. The church was crowded. His text was the [unclear text]

Monday, July 9.

Rose at 6 Oclock this morning. Went to school as usual to-day. Had company to-day for dinner. This evening I read from half past 7 Oclock. I am reading a book entitled "Objections to Cahamsin" by Dr. Foster, lent me by a friend of mine. It is very interesting. Went to the Temple at 8 Oclock. Had a very pleasant time. A. S. brought me the "Templar's Magazine" for July. I was very glad to get it.

Tuesday, July 10.

Rose at 5 Oclock. Went to school as usual to-day. Have had a very disagreeable head-ache to-day. Do not know what is the cause of it. Read this evening, "The life and adventures of Daniel Boone" from our school Library. Read some of Lord Byron's writings this evening. I have all his works in a large volume. I borrowed it from Mrs. Stahle. It is a real treat to read his productions. I mean an intellectual treat. I was reading about two hours.

Wednesday, July 11.

Rose at 5 Oclock. Did not join the family, until 6 Oclock. Went to school as usual. Had the head-ache all day. Read from half past 8 Oclock until 11 Oclock. Read Byron's life which is prefixed to the volume of his works. It is intensely interesting. I am afraid I spend too much time reading them.

Thursday, July 12.

Went to school as usual to-day. Had a little rain to-day. Ada Mc came for me to go to prayer-meeting this evening. Mr. Dill led. Did not enjoy it very much. Commenced my composition to-day. The subject is "What I would love."

Friday, July 13.

Did not go to school this morning. Stayed at home to wash, as mother was not able to do it herself. Went to school this afternoon. Read my composition. Mrs. Eyster said it was very good. Went to see Maggie B. on some business this evening. Went down to Aunt Agnes' this evening. Did not get home until after 10 Oclock.

Saturday, July 14.

Ironed this morning but did not finish until this afternoon. Altered the trimming on my dark bonnet after supper. Read in Byron until late. Feel very tired. I have been busy all day.

Sunday, July 15.

Went to S.S. this morning. Went to prayer-meeting. Mr. Hoy led. Did not enjoy it very much. Did not go to class. Went to S.S. this afternoon. Had a very short session, I thought. Mr. Sumwalt preached at 6 Oclock this evening. I did not listen as attentively to the first part of the sermon as I should have done. I could not fix my mind upon it. Worldly affairs, and the trials of life have weighed upon my mind ever since I arose.

Monday, July 16.

Awoke at 5 Oclock, but did not get up immediately and then fell asleep and slept until 8 Oclock. Have felt unwell all day. Had a dull head-ache, but that can easily be accounted for. Went to the store. Rose Wertz was here this evening but I was not at home. Mary Belch and Miss Hannah Hooper were here when I came home. They stayed about an hour. Read in Bryon this afternoon.

Tuesday, July 17.

Rose before 5 Oclock this morning. Mother has an abscess, I think, on her hand and cannot do anything. I baked this morning. Have been busy all afternoon fixing my knit shawl. I am making it larger. Went up to Aunt Pollie's awhile this evening. Saw a very bright star in the south east and did not know its name. Have noticed it several evenings, and this evening I got my atlas. I think it is Fomalhaut in the southern Fish.

Wednesday, July 18.

Rose about half past 4 Oclock this morning. Washed a week's wash and was done washing by 10 Oclock. Retired last night, so anxious about getting awake this morning in time to wash, that I awoke about 2 Oclock. Went up to school this afternoon and to see Aunt Agnes. Ada Mc brought me the Templar's Magazine and I took it to Mrs. Sanders. Came home about 9 Oclock. The sun was eclipsed this morning. I forgot it until after 7 Oclock, and then had to smoke glass before I could see it. I think it must have been almost over when I saw it. It was about half past 7 Oclock when I looked and then the sun was about one third darkened. It gradually decreased from that time. I intended to have glass ready and watch it throughout the eclipse but I forgot it. I was so busy washing that I could hardly spare the time. Kate Foster lent me a book this evening called "The Great Supper." It has been very warm all day, but this evening it is cool and pleasant. I think we will have rain.

Thursday, July 19.

Rose about half past 5 Oclock. Did the work and then began ironing. Finished ironing by 12 Oclock. It was about 8 Oclock when I commenced. Received an official letter from Mr. D. A. Buehler this evening informing me of my re-election to the station of teacher of School No. 2 at a salary of $18 per month. He is secretary of the School Directors of Gettysburg. The salaries of all connected with the school excepting the Principal have been reduced from two to five dollars. Mine was $20 last session. It is now $18. Was late at prayer meeting. Mr. Dill led. Mr. Sumwalt closed. Did not enjoy it at all. Was at Aunt Pollie's after prayer meeting.

Friday, July 20.

Rose at 4 1/2 Oclock this morning. Have been working hard all day. Went over to Aunt Salome's a few moments this evening. Came home about 8 Oclock. Finished reading "Objections to Cahamsin." It is very interesting, and I think, very clear. To-day has been the warmest day we have had this summer, at least it seemed so to me.

Saturday, July 21.

Rose at half past 6 Oclock. Baked some this morning. Have been busy all day working at my knit shawl. Went down to Aunt Lizzie's this evening and to see Rose Wertz. Came home about 9 Oclock. Kate Foster sent me a book this evening called "The Great Supper" an illustration and defense of the leading doctrines of grace by Fairchild. It has been very warm to-day.

Sunday, July 22.

Slept late this morning. Had a severe head-ache, and did not get up until half past 8 Oclock. Did not go out at all this morning. Went to Sunday School this afternoon, and to preaching at 6 Oclock. Mr. Sumwalt preached a splendid sermon. I could have listened to him an hour longer. His text was the 29th and 28th verses of the 5th chapter of John. He proved from the Bible and from nature that there would be a resurrection of all men both good and bad. He described the condition of all men on the judgement day, and he also gave us a description and an idea of how vast a multitude would be there. His sermon was very interesting. I like 6 Oclock preaching. The hour seems so calm and almost holy. It was almost impossible for me to think of anything but heaven, but I succeeded in fixing my mind upon the sermon at last, and I am very glad I did.

Monday, July 23.

Rural Hill. [Durboraw farm near Two Taverns, Pa.] Rose this morning about 6 Oclock. Got ready for a visit to Mr. Durboraw's. Father brought me down. We started about 1 1/2 Oclock were about two hours on the road. Had a delightful ride. Ginnie and Bell came along for a ride. Met a large company there. Miss Sarah and Fannie Coshun, Miss Mary and Maggie Young, Miss Sarah and Martha Conover, and a lady whose name I have forgotten. Went to hear an Indian preach, the same one who preached in Gettysburg some time ago. Spent a delightful day. Coming from preaching I was with Mattie and Lizzie Durboraw. Saw the moon set. Had a very pleasant walk but a much pleasanter conversation.

Tuesday, July 24.

Rose about 4 Oclock this morning. Mattie and Lizzie and Mary and Margaret Young and I went to Mr. Coshun's. Miss Sarah and Fannie Coshun and Miss Ann Wintrode were there. Spent a delightful day. Lizzie went home after dinner but the rest of us staid until after supper, Mattie and I had a very pleasant walk. I have not walked in the country for a long time and I enjoyed it so very much. The moon was shining. Got home about 8 Oclock.

Wednesday, July 25.

Spent a delightful day at Rural Hill. Maggie was washing. I helped her a little, when she was nearly done. Fixed a dress for Mattie, and a bonnet for Lizzie. Read the Ladies Repository.

Thursday, July 26.

Rose this morning about 6 Oclock. Helped Maggie to iron awhile, but had to stop, as I got the headache. After dinner, the twins and I started for Mr. Conover's, We had a very warm walk. Met Sarah and Mattie Conover, Maggie Young, and Fannie Coshun. Was very glad to see them. Was introduced to Mr. and Mrs. Conover, and their other daughters Mary, Maggie, Amanda, Phebe, and Clara. One of their daughters is away from home. Spent a pleasant day among them, they are all so lively and entertaining. Took a walk in the woods. Stayed until after supper, and Fannie Coshun came along home with us. Feel very tired. It is almost 9 Oclock. We just got home a few moments ago.

Friday, July 27.

Good old Gettysburg. Got home unexpectedly this evening. I wrote to father last Tuesday, not to come for me until Monday but he did not get the letter, and came for me to-day. Went to Mr. Joseph Coshun's this morning with Maggie Durburaw and Fannie Coshun. Had a very nice time. Started home about 3 Oclock, and just as I got to Rural Hill, father drove up the lane. He brought Susie and Grace along. They all stayed for supper, and about 6 Oclock we started for home. I was glad to get home but very much disappointed as I expected to stay until Monday. It went hard to give the girls good bye but I had to do it. Was very glad to meet an old friend of mine. Mr. Snyder came back yesterday evening and he was down this evening. It seemed like old times to spend an evening with him, he has been away nearly six weeks.

Saturday, July 28.

Rose late this morning, and then had the head-ache. Went down to see Rose Wertz, and from there to Aunt Lizzie's. Read awhile this evening. Feel very badly, and have been very much depressed in mind all day.

Sunday, July 29.

Rose late this morning. Went to Sunday School, but did not stay for prayer-meeting. Went to S. School this afternoon. Mr. Dill preached this evening, but I did not feel very well, and could not take much interest in the sermon. Snyder came with me from church.

Monday, July 30.

Rose about 6 Oclock. Washed from 7 Oclock until 12 Oclock. Felt very tired when done. Went over to Aunt Salome's this afternoon. Lizzie Rupp was down a while this evening. Went down to Aunt Agnes' and from there to the Temple. Left the Temple in no very agreeable humor. Snyder came with me. This is a lovely night. Clear, warm, and moon-light. How I do enjoy it.

Tuesday, July 31.

Rose at 5 1/2 Oclock this morning. Ironed all morning and after dinner until 1 Oclock. Went down to Aunt Agnes' to help her to sew this afternoon and evening. Had a pleasant time. Mr. Snyder came down for me about 8 1/2 Oclock. This is a lovely evening. Warm, clear, and moonlight.

Wednesday, August 1.

Commenced school to-day. Had 68 scholars this morning and 62 this afternoon. Have been very unwell all day. This evening Mary Powers and I took a walk. Came home about 9 Oclock. This is a splendid night. I do not remember when we have had so many beautiful nights before. It is tolerably cool but the moon is so bright I am afraid.

Thursday, August 2.

63 scholars this morning, 63 this afternoon. Feel very unwell to-day, and did all day yesterday. Do not know what is the cause of it. Added to this I am depressed and troubled mentally and altogether am about as miserable as I well can be. Went to prayer-meeting this evening. Coming home I met Sarah and Fannie Coshun. Had a short conversation with them. Got home about 9 1/2 Oclock. Snyder came with me.

Friday, August 3.

54 scholars this morning, 58 this afternoon. Feel unwell this evening. Am glad school is over for this week. Sent twenty-six of my best scholars to Miss Thompson and got twenty-four from Miss Bentley. Was at Miss Harriet Shillen's a few moments. Came home, and read in Byron until I got sleepy. Read his "prayer of Nature." Was very much pleased with it.

Saturday, August 4.

Lizzie Rupp and I went to see Kate Minnigh this evening. Were there about an hour. Took a walk. Came home about 8 1/2 Oclock. Took Byron's works home and in its place got "Rising in the world" by T.S. Arthur and "Ernest Bracebridge or school-boy days" by Kingston. It has been very warm to-day. Average attendance of my scholars since Wednesday morning 60 1/2. Snyder spent the evening with me.

Sunday, August 5.

Went to Sunday School this morning. Went to preaching. Prof. Jacobs preached. Had no class this afternoon. Had a missionary meeting. Went to preaching this afternoon. Prof. Muhlenburg preached. Came home after preaching, and read until 9 1/2 Oclock. Very warm and sultry all day.

Monday, August 6.

60 scholars this morning, 59 this afternoon. This evening was the regular Degree Night for the Temple. Alice Powers and I went down but there was no meeting. Came home about 8 Oclock. Snyder came down a few minutes after I got home. Warm and clear.

Tuesday, August 7.

58 scholars this morning, and 57 this afternoon. Went to the store this evening. Bought thirty yards of muslin and a lawn dress for myself. Went up to see Lizzie Rupp this evening. We took a walk. While I was away Ginnie Powers and Annie Sheads came. Returned home about 8 Oclock, and took a walk with A. S. Went down to Aunt Lizzie's, and stayed until 9 Oclock. Warm and sultry all day.

Wednesday, August 8.

59 scholars this morning; 57 this afternoon. Thought we would have some rain to day but had only a few drops. Went up to Foster's this evening but they were not at home and I went to see A. S. Thad Welty came home with me, about 9 Oclock. Saw a splendid rainbow this evening. It extended almost to the zenith. Very warm to-day.

Thursday, August 9.

58 scholars this morning, 57 this afternoon. Wrote in Ann Maria Rupp's Album to-day and took it home this evening. Went to prayer-meeting & was very agreeably disappointed by hearing a sermon by Mr. Monroe the same minister who was sent here by our Presiding Elder, last January. His text was "Praying always with much prayer." The sermon was splendid. H. M. came home with me.

Friday, August 10.

When I arose this morning I had a severe head-ache, and my right cheek was dreadfully swelled. The swelling was caused by the tooth-ache. Went to school but did not stay. Mr. Baugher very kindly heard my classes. I came home and lay down until dinner. My head is better this evening but my cheek is swelling more I think. It is not very pleasant to be sick, especially when one, like myself, is not used to it.

Saturday, August 11.

Rose this morning feeling better, but with a swelled face, notwithstanding which

I ironed until dinner time. Sewed at my dress this afternoon. While sewing Ellen Snyder called to see me. She lives in Cashtown, and is in G. for a few days. She intends going to Mr. D's to-morrow. She was here nearly two hours. We had a very interesting conversation about things in general and particular. Felt a great deal better this evening. Lizzie Rupp was down. Went home with her and we went to Harriet Shillen's and heard some nice music, some that was sentimental and some that was not. The air is very cool this evening. My face is a great deal better than it was, but I am afraid I will not get out to-morrow. Won't that be dreadful. Oh! dear!

Sunday, August 12.

Rose this morning feeling very unwell. Did not go out at all to-day, until this evening. Went to hear Mr. Sumwalt preach at 6 Oclock. His text was the 5th and 6th verses of the 10th chapter of Revelation, "And the angel which I saw stand upon the sea, and upon the earth lifted up his hand to heaven, and swore by him that liveth forever and ever, who created heaven, and the things that therein are, and the earth and the things that therein are, and the sea, and the things that are therein, that there should be time no longer;" He told us what time should be no longer, when time should be no longer and why time should be no longer. The sermon went splendid. I think it was the best I ever heard. Mr. S. preach. It was very short though for it was past 7 Oclock when I was coming from church. Ginnie Powers and I took a walk after I came home. This evening is pleasant, but cool.

Monday, August 13.

46 scholars this morning; 46 this afternoon. Went to school this morning through the rain, and a muddy walk I had. It has been raining all day, until this evening. There was a lovely rainbow about sunset. Went up to see Kate Foster, and Hattie Williams and took Kate's book home. It commenced raining before I got home. It was about 8 Oclock when I came home. Sewed at my dress until 11 Oclock and finished it.

Tuesday, August 14.

55 scholars this morning; 55 this afternoon. This has been a delightful day, neither warm nor cold but just pleasant. I enjoyed it so much after a day like yesterday. Helped mother wash at noon. School begins at 8 Oclock in the morning and at 2 Oclock in the afternoon. Sewed this evening at a white skirt for myself. These evenings are so pleasant, & nice to sew. They are getting longer too. Ginnie Powers and Lizzie Rupp spent the evening here. We had a lovely time. I enjoyed it a great deal. I have just folded my clothes ready for ironing to-morrow, and now it is after 10 Oclock. I suppose it is time to retire, as I am pretty tired and want to get up early to-morrow. Truly,

> "My days though few have passed below
> In much of joy, but more of woe"

Would that I were fit for a home in Heaven. How gladly would I leave this world of care and sin, at my father's word.

Wednesday, August 15.

50 scholars this morning; 49 this afternoon. Rose at 6 Oclock this morning. Helped mother until school time. After school this evening, sewed until 7 Oclock. Went up to Lizzie R. and took a walk with her. Finished reading "The Cry of the last minstrel" by Sir Walter Scott, and commenced "Marmion" by the same writer. Was very much pleased with both. I borrowed a volume of his poems from Mary Powers. They are very interesting and beautiful.

Thursday, August 16.

53 scholars this morning 53 this afternoon. Finished reading Scott's "Marmion." Like it very much. Went to Prayer-meeting, Mr. Thomas Warren led. Did not enjoy it at all but that was all my fault. I am getting along in my school, better than I ever did before. The average attendance last week was 58 1/8. I have 63 names on my roll. I like to teach better and better every day and I would not give it up now, for any other occupation in which I could engage.

Friday, August 17.

63 scholars this morning; 50 this afternoon. Went to school as usual to-day. The average attendance of my scholars this week was 57. Lizzie Rupp and I took a walk out the Emmitsburg road this evening. Read the "Lady of the Lake." It is very beautiful. I was almost persuaded to read it again but had not time. Took Scotts Poems home, and got Bryant's poems from Lizzie Rupp. Mr. S. was down a while this evening. He did not stay very long. He has been unwell for more than a week but is getting better now. Feel very much depressed in mind and have felt so all day. Feel worse this evening than I have for months. Oh! Lord help me to bear all my trials,

> "How dark this world would be
> If when deceived and wounded here
> I could not fly to thee"

Help me to cast all my cares on thee, and never let me forget that thou art the Rock on which I build.

Saturday, August 18.

Rose at 5 1/2 Oclock this morning. Baked and help mother do the house-work. Finished my skirt. Very glad it is done for I have had a great deal of trouble with it. After my work was done I was in the parlor & singing away "for dear life" as they say out of father's old note-book when some one pounded against the door, and a manly, well-known voice called out "be quiet, in there." I was not certain who it was until, a few moments after there was a knock at the door and when I answered it Mr. S. was there. He came in and was here about an hour. Was at Aunt Salome's for supper this afternoon. Went to see Ellen Snyder. Mother & I went up street this evening. Those families who have gas fixtures in their dwellings, had gas light tonight for the first time. There were some boys in Centre Square, and they had a large bonfire, and seemed to be enjoying it. Some of the merchants I think, must have missed their store boxes this morning.

Sunday, August 19.

Slept late this morning. Went to S.S. this morning. Got three numbers of the "S.S. Teacher's journal," a monthly for which I subscribed last week. Expected to hear Mr. Sumwalt preach but did not. Mr. Wolf, a stranger preached. Mr. Sumwalt closed and spoke a while. Did not go to class. Had a S.S. prayer-meeting this afternoon. Enjoyed it a great deal. Mr. Sumwalt preached this evening. Did not like his sermon at all. To me, it was a strange mixture of the sublime and the ridiculous. His text was the 1st and 3rd verses of the 14th chapter of John. His text was a very good one, a great deal too good for the sermon that followed it. After church, Lizzie Rupp and I took a walk. Came home about 7 1/2 Oclock. Read my S.S. Journals. The Journal is a new monthly, started last June for the express benefit, as its name indicates, of S.S. teachers, Superintendents, and Bible classes. I like them very much.

Monday, August 20.

Rose at 5 1/2 Oclock this morning. 50 scholars this morning, 51 this afternoon. Got three numbers of the "Laws of Life" this evening for which I sent early in the month. Was up at Powers's a few moments. S. was here awhile this evening. Was reading in the "Laws of life." I like the journal very much as far as I have read. The weather has been very pleasant. Got a letter from A. S. Answered it immediately.

Tuesday, August 21.

Rose at 6 Oclock this morning. 47 scholars this morning; 48 this afternoon. Helped mother wash after school this morning. Had some rain this evening but not enough to hurt any thing. Read in The Laws of life awhile. Folded the clothes.

Wednesday, August 22.

Rose at 7 Oclock this morning. 47 scholars this morning 49 this afternoon. Sewed this evening until 8 Oclock, and then went up to see Lizzie Rupp a few moments. Lizzie and I went to Mr. Powers's, and were there awhile. Ginnie Powers and I took a walk.

Thursday, August 23.

47 scholars this morning 43 this afternoon. Rose at 5 Oclock this morning and kneaded the bread. Got the August no. of "Laws of Life" a Circular of "Our Home" "Christianity and the Health Reform" by Dr. Jackson, "The American Costume for Women" by Harriet V. Austin M.D. out of the Post Office today. Mr. Dill preached this evening. There were very few there. His sermon was very good. His text was the 8th, 9th, and 10th verses of the 35th chapter of the prophecy of Isaiah. S. came home with me.

Friday, August 24.

48 scholars this morning 50 this afternoon. Average attendance this week 48 5/10. Sent the Ledger, to A.S. for Aunt L. and the Star and Banner to Fannie C. Ginnie Powers and I went to the Post Office. I got a good long letter from Cousin Lizzie M. Was over at Aunt Salome's. Took Mr. Flemming some lines which I wrote on the death of his two little daughters who died, one last Jan. and one in March. He was very much pleased with them.

Saturday, August 25.

Made Susie a dress to day. Mary P. Lizzie R. and myself went down street a while. Came home about 8 1/2 Oclock. The Gas Lamps at the principle corners in G. were lit awhile this evening. They are very nice. Mr. S. was down awhile this evening.

Sunday, August 26.

Went to Sunday School this morning at 9 oclock. Went to Prayer-meeting at 10 1/2 Oclock. Enjoyed it very much. Mr. Snyder led. Had no class. Went to Sunday School at 2 Oclock. Had a very nice session. I do not know when I enjoyed S.S. as much as to-day. Mr. Dill preached at 7 1/2 Oclock. I forget the text. I could not fix my mind upon the sermon. This is a lovely day and this evening is beautiful, grand. How I love such calm peaceful evenings when the moon shines so sweetly down on our beautiful earth, for the world is beautiful, and, if so beautiful now, what must it have been before sin entered it, to deform it, and bring misery and death upon its inhabitants.

Monday, August 27.

49 scholars this morning 50 this afternoon. Wrote a long letter to Cousin Lizzie to-day. How I love her. It will soon be a year since I enjoyed those three weeks in her society. Truly, "Time does not linger." Went to the Temple this evening. Made a resolution, which I think is good for me, and I am going to try hard to keep it. S.

came with me home. This is another lovely evening. Oh! but I do enjoy them so. I am sorry when the time comes to retire.

Tuesday, August 28.

51 scholars this morning, 47 this afternoon. Rose at 5 1/2 Oclock. Saw a splendid scene which was no more nor less than the eastern horizon, a short time after sunrise. It was magnificent. Purple and gold, and the clear blue arch of heaven between. Finished one week's wash which I commenced yesterday evening. This morning it became cloudy and before noon it was raining. It has been raining all afternoon. The walking is very unpleasant, the roads and pavements which are nearly all newly made are very muddy & sandy. Received a present from Mr. A. W. F. this evening viz, a large package of envelopes & letter paper of different sizes and kinds. I wrote some lines last week for him, on the death of his two little daughters who died, one last January and one last March. He was very much pleased with them. Went up to spend the evening with Lizzie, but met several other young ladies going, and I did not get my talk out with her. Lu and Bell Bushey, Lucy and Kate Minnigh, Allie Powers and my self were there. Spent a delightful evening. Came home about 10 Oclock. The roads are muddy, but the sky is getting clear. I am very glad it is clearing.

Wednesday, August 29.

53 scholars this morning; 52 this afternoon. Mrs. F. sent me an invitation to come and take supper with her. Mary P. was there, but she was called home to entertain some company. Went to Aunt Salome's a little while. Came home about 7 Oclock and went down to Rose W. and to Aunt Lizzie's. Called on Miss F. Spent a very pleasant evening. This is a lovely night. Clear and moonlight. It is just cool enough to be pleasant. Came home about 10 Oclock.

Thursday, August 30.

50 scholars this morning; 48 this afternoon. Went to prayer-meeting this evening. Mr. Dill led. Enjoyed it tolerably well. T. S. came home with me. This is a delightful night. The moon is full, the sky clear, and it is almost as light as day. Spent a very pleasant evening. Laughed more than I have for some time. Received an invitation to attend a S.S. pic-nic, but will not accept it, as I am otherways engaged and do not care about going.

Friday, August 31.

48 scholars this morning; 46 this afternoon. Average attendance this week. Julia W. was here this evening, she wanted me to go along with her out to G. B's but I could not go. Went up street with Lizzie R. Mary P. wished us to come and spend the evening with her. She is going to Pinetown to-morrow to teach school three months. There was about a dozen girls there and several gentlemen. Lizzie and I stayed until 10 Oclock. T. S. came home with me. This is a delightful night, so calm. Got a good long letter from Mattie D. and one enclosed in it from Lizzie. They were both very welcome as are all letters from friends whom I love so much as them.

Saturday, September 1.

Sewed to-day. This evening mother, Aunt Mary and I went down to see the cars coming in, and to see the Gas Works. Lizzie R. and I took a walk this evening and went to the store. Ginnie Powers and Mollie Vanarsdel a lady who lives near Hunterstown, were here a long time this evening. Had a very nice time. This is a lovely night, but it is rather cool for this season of the year. Feel very tired.

Sunday, September 2.

Went to S.S. this morning. Mr. Dill preached at 10 1/2 Oclock. Went to class. Enjoyed it. Went to S.S. this afternoon. It was Missionary Afternoon. Sung several of our prettiest hymns. Had one of the nicest session that I think we ever had. If not nicer, fully as nice and heavenly, as any I ever enjoyed. Lizzie R. and I took a walk this evening. Mother went with me to church. Mr. Dill preached a very interesting sermon. His text was the following verse "And Enoch walked with God, and he was not, for God took him." I thought his sermon was very good, and the text was one from which I never before heard a sermon preached. S. came home with me. I feel badly this evening. Grace is sick and so are Susie and Jennie, but Grace is the worst. She looks pale and thin. I do hope she will not have a spell of sickness like that which she had last fall, but I will try to say "Thy will be done."

Monday, September 3.

Got 13 new scholars this morning. Had 66 present this morning; 67 this afternoon. A very fine day. This was Degree Night at the temple but I did not go. I began the washing after school and washed until 7 Oclock. Father has been sick all day, and is rather worse this evening. Commenced a letter to Mattie Durboraw, and wrote one to Cousin A.S. for her mother. Feel pretty tired this evening, and think I shall retire early.

Tuesday, September 4.

63 scholars this morning; 63 this afternoon. This has been a very pleasant day. Got a letter from A.S. this evening. Father is worse this evening. He has been confined to his bed all day. Oh! I hope he will soon be well. It does not seem right to come home and find him, lying weak and sick in bed. Have been reading awhile this evening but do not feel interested in anything. There is a heavy burden resting on my mind, which added to the sickness of Father and Grace seems almost too heavy to be borne. But I will try to bear it, hoping for a better "day coming." Oh! Lord help me in this trying hour. Show me the path of duty and give me grace to walk therein. Amen and amen!

Wednesday, September 5.

64 scholars this morning; 65 this afternoon. Went down to Aunt Lizzie's awhile this evening. Father is better this evening. Thank God! T.S. was down a while this evening to see him. He did not stay long as he had a S.S. Report to make out. Went up for a bucket of water. I.F. was at Powers's. He went with me for the water and brought it home for me. Stayed about half an hour. He is going home to stay next Saturday morning.

Thursday, September 6.

62 scholars this morning 55 this afternoon. Went to Prayer-meeting this evening. Was late. Had a S.S. Meeting after Prayer-meeting. It did not interest me very much. Father does not seem any better, he is a great deal weaker. Met an old friend of mine after Prayer-meeting, Henry Buckingham. He is now living in York, but is home on a visit. He is Jennie Buckingham's brother. It is rather cool this evening but pleasant. Snyder came down after prayer-meeting.

Friday, September 7.

58 scholars this morning; 60 this afternoon. Father is a great deal better. Spent a very pleasant evening. Lizzie Rupp and I took a walk this evening and after we came back Ginnie P. and Mr. Free came down and they staid until nearly 10 Oclock. Mr. Free and Ginnie had made an engagement to spend the evening with me but Lizzie I did not expect. She was none the less welcome. Feel more like myself this evening than I have for some time.

Saturday, September 8.

Have been working hard all day. It Rained very heavily this afternoon. John L. was here to see us this afternoon. Went up street this evening and went to Powers's a while after I came home. Went up to Aunt's for some eggs, and coming home I met John R. He came down with me. We had a very interesting conversation about our Gas Works. He explained a great deal to me that I did not understand before. Average attendance of my scholars this week. 62. Father is a great deal better to-day. He is still very weak, but is slowly convalescing.

Sunday, September 9.

Went to Sunday School this morning. Mr. Schick and Mr. John Culp our new Superintendents were there. Had a very nice session. Went to Prayer-Meeting. Mr. McMillan led. I enjoyed it very much. Enjoyed class a great deal. Went to Sunday School this afternoon. Had a S.S. Prayer Meeting. Very interesting. Ginnie Powers came down this evening and we took a long walk. She went to church with me. Mr. Sumwalt preached. His text was "As for me and my house, we will serve the Lord." The sermon was good, but very short I thought. Father is better. I am so glad. Snyder brought me the "Water Cure Journal," "The Templar's Magazine" and the first volume of Cowper's poems. This has been a beautiful day. Cool and pleasant. Just such a day as I love. I could sing this morning,

"O the sabbath morning beautiful and bright
Joyfully I hail its golden light" &c.

Monday, September 10.

58 scholars this morning; 57 this afternoon. Went to school as usual to-day. It was very cool this morning. Commenced washing after school this afternoon. Washed until 7 1/2 Oclock. Mary Jane Slentz was here, a long time and went up street with me when I went to the Temple. Was late there but could not help it. T.S. came home with me and brought me the 2nd and 3rd volumes of Cowper's Poems. This is a very pleasant night. Had the tooth-ache a little while after I came home.

Tuesday, September 11.

60 scholars this morning 60 this afternoon. Lizzie Rupp wants me to go along with her to the Lutheran S.S. pic-nic to-morrow, but I will not go, as I can not leave my school, and would not, if I could. It has been very cool to-day. Read the Templars Magazine for September, and a part of the Water cure Journal for this month. Like them both very much.

Wednesday, September 12.

42 scholars this morning; 45 this afternoon. I feel very badly this evening. Have a very severe cold, which has settled in my head, the effects of washing late last Monday evening in the yard. Read awhile this evening. It is very cool now, and to-day it was windy. I suppose our schools will attend a Panorama of Dr. Keane's Arctic Expedition to-morrow afternoon. I have heard it is a splendid affair, and well worth the money. It will be worth mine for teachers get free Tickets. I am very anxious for to-morrow. I want to see it so much. I anticipate a pleasant time.

Thursday, September 13.

59 scholars this morning. Had no school this afternoon. My scholars, about twenty of them, myself and the other teachers and scholars, went to the Panorama. I was very much pleased. Some of the scenes were too magnificent for description. We had a storm at sea, which was so natural especially the thunder and rain, that some of the children cried, and one or two went home. Altogether it was a magnificent affair, well worth the price of admission which for teachers was nothing. Came

home about 4 Oclock feeling very tired, and my cold none the better for coming out of a warm close room into the cool air. Went to prayer-meeting. Was late. Mr. Dill led. After prayer-meeting there was some talk of starting a Bible class. All interested are to meet on to-morrow night one week at the church. I hope we will be successful in starting a good one, for I am not the only one that feels the necessity of attending one. Snyder came home with me.

Friday, September 14.

56 scholars this morning; 55 this afternoon. Answered Mattie and Lizzie Durboraw's letters. Received one from cousin Annie S. After school this evening Mattie Bently and I took a walk down the rail-road. We went on until we heard the cars coming, and then came back. Feel tired but I am sure the walk was good for me. Going and returning we walked about two miles. It is cool this evening.

Saturday, September 15.

Helped mother at the house work to-day. Heard of a dreadful accident this evening. Mathew Little a boy about 10 years old was run over by the wheel of a wagon owned by Mr. Hanaway of this place. The wagon was heavily loaded with wood, and the wheel passed over his body, injuring him so greatly that he did not live half an hour after the accident. Lizzie Rupp and I took a walk and called on Miss Mary Rupp of Hanover. Came home about 9 Oclock. I cannot get done thinking about Mattie Little. He was one of my scholars last session. I had a great deal of trouble with him at first, but he grew to be as obedient as any of my scholars and was one of the kindest-hearted and most affectionate scholars in my room. This session he was transferred to Miss Thompson and now, where is he? Alas he is now an inhabitant of the spirit-land. Poor, motherless boy. He has at length found a home "in that sunbright clime."

Sunday, September 16.

Went to Sunday School this morning & afternoon. Mr. Sumwalt preached a very interesting sermon, or rather commenced it, for he did not finish it until this evening, from the text "There is a sin unto death." This morning I listened very attentively but this evening I was so tired that I could not fix my mind upon it and of course was not benefitted by it a great deal. Went to Mattie Little's funeral at [unclear text] Oclock with Lizzie Rupp. It was very large. Mr. Sumwalt and Mr. Keiser spoke. Yesterday evening the people of Gettysburg, myself included, were shocked at hearing of poor Mattie's dreadful and sudden death, and this afternoon, we were more shocked if possible, by hearing of the death of Mrs. Herbst, an old and esteemed resident of G. who committed suicide this afternoon by hanging herself in the stable connected with her residence. Her own daughter found her hanging and her own son cut her down. She was partially insane, it is supposed when she committed the dreadful act, and she has been melancholy for some time. How dreadful, How shocking! Her family truly are bereaved and her spirit, where is it? Oh! it is a theme on which I dare not, cannot dwell. Lord, have mercy upon me! S. came with me from church.

Monday, September 17.

50 scholars this morning, 52 this afternoon. Received a letter from Beckie Belch this morning. A good, long interesting letter. Washed this evening. Cousin A.S. was down. She came home very unexpectedly yesterday evening.

Tuesday, September 18.

52 scholars this morning 51 this afternoon. Have no school until Friday Morning. Lizzie Durboraw came to town to day and is here this evening. We went down street intending to go and hear a lecture in Christ's Church. The commencement

exercise of Penna. College will be held this week. We did not go to hear the address but instead went to see Aunt Agnes. Came home about 8 Oclock and did some sewing.

Wednesday, September 19.

Went with Lizzie this morning to hear the Junior Class speak. Went at 9 Oclock and we were in until after 12 Oclock. Lizzie and I went up street this afternoon. This morning Mattie Durboraw, and her cousin Miss Lizzie Sprecker of Franklin County came. They took supper with us. Lizzie went home this afternoon but she is coming up to-morrow morning. Lizzie S. Mattie and I took a walk after supper. They went to hear the address but I did not care about hearing it. Lizzie Rupp and I took a walk and then went to see Miss Harriet Shillen. Spent a very pleasant evening. Came home about 9 Oclock. Feel very tired and sleepy.

Thursday, September 20.

Lizzie Rupp, Lizzie Sprecker, Martha Durboraw and I went to hear the seniors speak this morning. We went at 8 Oclock and did not get out until 1 1/2. Lizzie Durboraw came to town again this morning and took dinner with me. We went up street after dinner to the store and then she started home with her brother. Jennie Buckingham and I took a walk. Went down for Eliza Welty when I went to prayer-meeting. Did not enjoy it very much. William Dill led. Mr. Sumwalt and Mr. Earnshaw were there. Mr. Earnshaw was our junior preacher several years ago. He is going to preach for us next Sabbath morning and night. I am anxious to hear him. Had a very disagreeable walk from Prayer-meeting. It was raining hard all the time, and was very windy but I got home safely for all. N.B. Had a good escort.

Friday, September 21.

58 scholars this morning. 49 this afternoon. Mattie Bentley and I took a walk down the rail-road after school this evening. Had a pleasant walk but it was rather cool. Folded my clothes this evening, and then went to Bible Class. I was too late, but I suppose as the old saying runs, "Better late than never." Snyder came home with me.

Saturday, September 22.

Worked hard to-day. Ironed & helped mother do the usual house-work. Did some sewing this afternoon. Lizzie Rupp, and her cousin Miss Mary Rupp of Hanover, were here this evening. I went up street with them. We took a walk, and then went home with Mary. After we took her home, Lizzie & I went down to Rose Wertz's and were there a good while. Had a very pleasant time. As we came home we passed Mattie Bentley's home and we stopped there a few minutes. Came home about 9 Oclock.

Sunday, September 23.

Went to Sunday School this morning, and to preaching at 10 1/2 Oclock. Mr. Earnshaw preached a very good sermon this morning. Did not go to class. Went to S. School this afternoon. Coming from school I passed Mr. McElwee's church and took a notion to go in. He preached an interesting sermon. His text was "Jesus." Mr. Earnshaw preached again this evening. Snyder came with me.

Monday, September 24.

56 scholars this morning. 58 this afternoon. Commenced washing after school this afternoon. Ginnie Gilbert came over about 7 Oclock, and staid awhile, and then we went to the "Temple." Came home about 8 1/2 Oclock. Went up to Aunt Mary's

for mother and as I came home I stopped a while with A.S. Came home a second time, about 10 Oclock. G.P., G.G., S.T., T.S., J.H., C.G., A.F., and myself were the only ones at T. This is a very pleasant night, a little cool.

Tuesday, September 25.

54 scholars this morning. 56 this afternoon. Went up to Mr. Rupp's this evening. Lizzie & I took a walk and she came down with me. Cousin A.S. was here when we came home.

Wednesday, September 26.

56 scholars this morning 52 this afternoon. Mat Bentley and I took a short walk after school. Lizzie R ... spent the evening here. This is a pleasant evening moonlight, but rather cool.

Thursday, September 27.

56 scholars this morning, 53 this afternoon. It rained hard this afternoon. Went for Eliza Welty this evening and we went to the Church but there was no Prayer-Meeting. Went with Eliza home and stayed awhile. Came home about 9 Oclock. This is a dull evening. Cool and cloudy.

Friday, September 28.

55 scholars this morning, 60 this afternoon. Went to school as usual to-day. Feel very tired. Helped father shake carpets this evening after school. There was a Democratic Mass Meeting this evening in Gettysburg. I would like to have heard the speeches (not from any great love for the party or its principles) but it was too cold and damp to stand out. Ginnie Powers and Lizzie Rupp came for me to go down street, but I declined going. Cousin A.S. spent the greater part of the evening here. She went home about 9 Oclock. This is a lovely night, calm, bright; clear but rather cool.

Saturday, September 29.

Have been working all day. Ironed and baked. Eliza Welty was here for supper and she is going to stay all night. Eliza and I went up street to the store and to see Mrs. Eyster. Came home about 8 Oclock. Very pleasant, bright moonlight. Snyder spent the evening, and we had some "fine fun." It was so pleasant and we wanted to take Snyder home, but he "giv us the mittere." Only just think of it.

Sunday, September 30.

Rose at 7 Oclock this morning. Eliza Welty and I went to Sunday School at nine. Went to Preaching. Mr. Dill preached. Had no class. Went to Sunday School at two. Went for Eliza this evening and we went to church. Mr. Dill preached. It rained awhile this evening. S. and I took Ellie home.

Monday, October 1.

49 scholars this morning. 50 this afternoon. Answered Beckie Belch's letter to-day. Wrote a long letter to her. It has been very disagreeable all day. Raining and cool. Sewed this evening until 9 Oclock.

Tuesday, October 2.

55 scholars this morning. 60 this afternoon. It cleared off beautifully this morning and is warm and pleasant now. Miss Emma Pittenturf of Heidlersburg and Ginnie Powers spent the evening with me. Lizzie Rupp came down about half past eight. We all took a walk. Came home about half past nine. This is a beautiful night. Clear and moonlight.

Wednesday, October 3.

58 scholars this morning, 57 this afternoon. Very pleasant. Helped mother wash this morning, before I went to school. Mat B. and I took a walk after school this evening. Mr. S. was here this evening. He brought me the Templar's Magazine. It is warm this evening, but cloudy.

Thursday, October 4.

57 scholars this morning, 58 this afternoon. Went to Prayer-meeting this evening. T.S. led. There was not many there, but it was a disagreeable evening. S. and I took Eliza home and stayed there awhile after prayer-meeting.

Friday, October 5.

59 scholars this morning, 54 this afternoon. Bought myself a new dress this evening. Mat Bently and I had got dresses off the same piece at Fahnestock's. Eliza spent the evening with me. We had a pleasant evening. At least I enjoyed it. She is going to teach school the 1st of next month at Centre Mills in this county. Went part of the way with Ellie when she went home.

Saturday, October 6.

Rose at six. Have been very busy all day. Mother has a carbuncle on her leg and cannot stir about much. I had the greater part of the work to do. I baked and ironed. Finished about 5 Oclock. Eliza and I went to the P.O. I got a letter from Mattie & Lizzie Durboraw. Two good long letters. Eliza and I took a walk and I went home with her and stayed until 8 Oclock. Spent a pleasant evening.

Sunday, October 7.

Went to Sunday School this morning. Went to Prayer-Meeting. Did not enjoy it very much. Had no class. Rose Wertz and I took a walk. Had the sick headache severely at noon. Slept an hour and felt better when I awoke. Went to Sunday School again this afternoon. Ginnie Gilbert and I took a walk after S.S. Had a pleasant walk. Went for Eliza and we went to church together. Mr. Sumwalt preached. His text was, "It is appointed unto men once to die." His sermon was good but very short, I thought. Snyder and I took Ellie home.

Monday, October 8.

44 scholars this morning, 53 this afternoon. Went to the store to-day. Got Plaid Flannel sacques for Ginnie, Bell & Grace and Persian delaine dresses for them. A shawl for mother and several other things. Lizzie Rupp and I went down to Mary Wolf's for the pattern for the children's sacques. Got home about 8 Oclock. Sewed until 10 Oclock. Have had a slight head-ache to-day. I do not know what is the cause of it.

Tuesday, October 9.

56 scholars this morning, 54 this afternoon. Miss Harriet Shillen was here a short time this evening. Mattie Bentley and Lizzie Rupp spent the evening with me. Snyder and I went home with them about 9 Oclock. This is "Election Day." There has been a good deal of fighting to-day.

Wednesday, October 10.

2 Oclock, A.M. Father has not come home yet. He is "Judge of the Election." I thought I would try and stay up until he came home but I am too tired and sleepy besides having the sick head-ache, so I will have to retire. 9 Oclock P.M. Have been sewing very busily all evening, and as I got no sleep last night I must retire earlier than usual. 55 scholars this morning, 51 this afternoon.

Thursday, October 11.

55 scholars this morning, 51 this afternoon. Had a shower of rain this morning about eight. Mother, Aunt Emily Sheads & Aunt Lizzie Myers spent the day at Mr. Hahn's about 3 1/2 miles from town. They went in the cars. Mother got back about 7 Oclock and it was then too late for me to go to prayer-meeting. I was very much disappointed.

Friday, October 12.

55 scholars this morning, 55 this afternoon. Have been very busy all week making flannel sacques for Ginnie and Bell. Mat and Mr. J.T. ... spent the evening with me. It is very cool this evening. Mr. Drum and his wife and little daughter are in town. Mr. Drum led prayer-meeting last night. I am so sorry I could not be there. It is the first time I have missed it for a long time.

Saturday, October 13.

There was a very heavy frost this morning. Feel tired this evening. Eliza was expecting me to stay all night with her, but I did not get done in time to go, and had to give it up. I have been so very busy all week. To-morrow is the blessed sabbath. Thank God for one day of rest in the seven.

Sunday, October 14.

Went to S.S. this morning. Went to Preaching at 10 1/2. Brother Drum preached. His text was the [unclear text]. His sermon was splendid. I love to listen to Mr. Drum. Expected to hear him his evening but was disappointed. Harris Clippinger preached. He is an old acquaintance, and an old resident of Gettysburg. I was disappointed and his sermon did not interest me very much. Two years ago, the 14th of last May on, Friday night, Mr. Drum preached from the text, "blessed are they that mourn for they shall be comforted." That night I sought and found my Savior, and never while I live shall I forget that night, that sermon, or Brother Drum. God bless him and his little family with the richest of his blessings. Snyder came home with me.

Monday, October 15.

56 scholars this morning, 56 this afternoon. Dismissed my school at recess this morning. It was too cold. After supper, I went up to Mr. Powers's awhile. Ginnie came down with me and brought her work along. Mr. J.T. came down 8 Oclock and Snyder a little later. Spent a very pleasant evening. If nothing prevent, I expect to go out to see Mr. & Mrs. Drum to-morrow evening.

Tuesday, October 16.

56 scholars this morning. 57 this afternoon. Eliza and I went out to Mr. McMillan's this evening. Saw Mr. and Mrs. Drum. Spent a very pleasant evening. Had a nice walk home. Eliza is going to the country on next Thursday. Her parents are going to move on their farm. They have lived in town nearly two years. I will miss her a great deal, especially on Sunday and Thursday evening. I almost forgot, Snyder was there too and we took Ellie home.

Wednesday, October 17.

58 scholars this morning, 56 this afternoon. Was down to Eliza's this evening with mother. Was down to see Rose Wertz a few minutes after school. She and Will Guinn were at our house yesterday evening after I left. They intended spending the evening here. I am so sorry I was not at home. I guess Eliza will go to the country to-morrow if it does not rain.

Thursday, October 18.

51 scholars this morning, 52 this afternoon. Went to Prayer meeting this evening. Mr. Dill led and Mr. Drum closed. He and his family start for Wrightsville to-

morrow morning and I had to say "Good bye," but I said it reluctantly if that be my consolation. Eliza went to-day. I miss her a great deal in prayer-meeting.

Friday, October 19.

53 scholars this morning, 52 this afternoon. Very disagreeable all day. The "Wide-Awakes" were out this evening but I did not go up street at all. I was not out of the house all evening. It was so wet and I was not very much interested, so I staid at home and sewed. Got a letter from Fannie Coshun to-day. An agreeable surprise.

Saturday, October 20.

Have been very busy all day, sewing at a dress for Susie. Fixed a dress for myself this evening. Did not go up street as I was too busy.

Sunday, October 21.

Went to Sunday School this morning. Mr. John Culp led prayer-meeting. Had no class. Went to Sunday School this afternoon. Had no preaching this evening. Our preachers are attending a Quarterly Meeting at Littlestown. Went to the Lutheran church with Ginnie P. Expected to hear Mr. Heiser preach but did not. Harrie Clippinger preached in his place.

Monday, October 22.

53 scholars this morning, 50 this afternoon. This was the evening for our Temple to meet but I did not go. I could not find time. Was over to Ginnie Gilbert's a short time after supper. Lizzie Rupp spent the evening. It is not nine yet but I feel very tired. I was up early this morning. I have been getting up earlier than usual for the last few weeks.

Tuesday, October 23.

54 scholars this morning, 53 this afternoon. Ginnie Powers and I spent the evening with Mattie Bentley. Spent a very pleasant evening. Came home about 8 1/2 Oclock. S. was here this evening. He came while I was away. Cloudy and cool all day.

Wednesday, October 24.

51 scholars this morning, 54 this afternoon. This has been a delightful day. It reminds me of two lines from Bryant's "Death of the flowers." "And now when comes the calm, mild day, As still such days will come" &c. I think the poem is very beautiful. I have been sewing all evening and feel tired. Got the "Cambria Tribune" out of the office to-day from Johnstown. I suppose it is from Fannie G. C.

Thursday, October 25.

53 scholars this morning, 54 this afternoon. Very pleasant day. Ginnie Powers wanted me to spend the evening with her. Several of our aquaintances were there, but as it was prayer-meeting evening I declined the invitation. Did not enjoy prayer-meeting very much but I am by no means sorry I went. S. came with me home.

Friday, October 26.

58 scholars this morning, 47 this afternoon. Rose this morning feeling very badly. Had a dull head-ache and my throat was a little sore. Went to Ginnie Gilbert's according to a previous engagement. Did not enjoy myself as well as I expected which I suppose was owing to a slight indisposition. My throat is a little better this evening for which I am thankful. Mother is not very well.

Saturday, October 27.

Went to preaching this evening. Mr. Dill's text was "Nevertheless we made our prayer to our God." Came home and went with mother up to see Aunt Lavinia. She has rheumatism. Mr. M.C. was with cousin Annie.

Sunday, October 28.

Went to love-feast this morning at 8 1/2 Oclock. Enjoyed it very much. Mr. Dill led, and also preached a very good sermon at 10 1/2. After preaching the Sacrament of the Lord's supper was administered. Went to Sunday School this afternoon. Mr. Dill preached to night. His sermon last night and the two to-day interested me more than he generally does. Got a good long interesting letter from Beckie Belch to-day. Snyder came with me from church.

Monday, October 29.

52 scholars this morning, 53 this afternoon. Went to church this evening. Mr. Dill preached a very good sermon from the text "Turn you to the strong hold ye prisoners of hope &c" A lady who was at the altar last night went forward to-night and was blest. Enjoyed the meeting very much. It seemed to my soul like "a little heaven below."

Tuesday, October 30.

49 scholars this morning, 53 this afternoon. It has been raining all day. I could not go to church this evening it was too unpleasant. Sewed awhile. I am so sorry I could not go. Got a good long letter from Eliza Welty. She is teaching at Centre Mills about nine miles from here. I was so glad to hear from her.

Wednesday, October 31.

49 scholars this morning, 53 this afternoon. Did not get to church to-night. The weather is too bad for me to go out at night. It is bad enough to be out in the day time. I feel disappointed for I was expecting to go.

Thursday, November 1.

Went to General Class this evening. Did not enjoy it at all. S. came home with me. Mr. Dill led. The weather is not so bad this evening.

Sunday, November 4.

Went to Sunday School this morning and afternoon. Went to prayer meeting at 10 1/2 Oclock. Did not enjoy it very much. Mr. Sumwalt preached this evening a very interesting sermon. Subject—the Millenium. I have forgotten the text. This is a very pretty night. Coming home I met S. He came with me.

Monday, November 5.

Rose Wertz and Will Guinn were here this evening. Spent a very pleasant evening. Do not feel very well and have not been right well for about two weeks.

Tuesday, November 6.

Election Day. Have been very unwell all day. I don't think I will be foolish enough to stay up until the "wee sma hours" to-night as I did four weeks ago—The night of the Governor's election. I wonder where I will be, and what my circumstances in life will be when another President will be elected. Snyder spent the evening here.

Wednesday, November 7.

Hurrah!, for Lincoln & Hamlin.

Every one is rejoicing over the great triumph which, it is said the Republican Party has achieved. (I mean of course all the Republicans and those who supported Lincoln) The poor democrats—but I will wait until I am sure of our victory before I boast of it. For once I am prudent. Wonderful it is worth recording, that I have once thought before I spoke (or rather wrote).

Thursday, November 8.

Went to prayer meeting this evening. Bro. Clippinger led. Snyder brought me home.

Saturday, November 10.

Have been very unwell all week. It has been very unpleasant this week. Went up street a short time this evening.

Sunday, November 11.

Went to S.S. this morning and afternoon. Did not stay for preaching as I felt very unwell. We had no services to-night. I went with Lizzie Rupp to their church. Mr. Dill delivered an address before the Female Bible Society. Snyder came home with us.

Monday, November 12.

Went to the Temple this evening. Snyder came home with me. Came home about nine. Cousin A.S. was here. This is a lovely night. The Wide-awakes were out to-night.

Tuesday, November 13.

Very pleasant. Cool and clear. Mother has been very ill all day. She could not be out of bed. I promised Aunt Emily to quilt for her this evening. I expected to go about six but did not get there until half past eight. Got home a little after nine. This is a lovely night. Clear and star-light. Snyder got there about 5 minutes after I did.

Thursday, November 15.

Had no school this afternoon as there was a grand Republican Jollification this afternoon & evening. I washed this afternoon. Commenced at one and was done by half after four. Went to prayer-meeting. There was only eight there. Mr. Dill led. I enjoyed it more than I have for some time. "We" went down street after it was out. Ada and Laura McMillan went along. The houses looked well—some of them, but I did not enjoy myself very much running around. It was too cold and damp, besides I was thinking of other and better things. There was a nice torch-light procession. The Wide Awakes were out. Came home about 8 1/2 Oclock. We did not illuminate. Father and mother are both opposed to it, and so am I.

Friday, November 16.

This has been a very pretty day. We have had unusually fine weather this week. Wrote in Mollie Vanorsdel's Album to-day. Got a good long letter from Eliza this evening.

Saturday, November 17.

To-day has been a very disagreeable one, out of the house. Although I spent a very pleasant one. The sky has been cloudy, and a very fine rain has been falling. Finished a dress for Susie. Feel very tired, and am going to retire soon. Hope to-morrow will be pleasant.

Sunday, November 18.

Went to S. S. this morning and afternoon. Went to prayer-meeting this morning. Mr. John Culp led. I enjoyed it very much. Had no class. Went to see A.S. a little while before church. Mr. Dill preached this evening. S. came with me home. This has not been a very pleasant day. Cool and cloudy. I am very anxious for the weather to settle.

Monday, November 19.

Went to school as usual to-day. Wrote to Beckie Belch to-day. I did not sew as much this evening as I expected. I did not feel like it, and so did not do it.

Tuesday, November 20.

Cold and windy all day. Went over to Ginnie Gilbert's with my work this evening. Came home about 8 Oclock. It is very cold and windy this evening. I would not be astonished if we would have snow.

Wednesday, November 21.

Very cold and windy all day. Went to school as usual. Spent the evening with Cousin A.S. Stayed until after eight Oclock. Rose Wertz and Mary Belch were there a little while. I do not feel very well this evening. Wonder what is the cause of these languid don't-care-kind-of-feelings, that sometimes come over me.

Thursday, November 22.

This has been a tolerably pleasant day. This evening I went down for Rose Wertz before prayer-meeting. It was very pleasant then but it has clouded, and the present appearance of the sky, gives me every reason to believe that we will have snow before to-morrow morning. I did not enjoy prayer-meeting at all. I got there too late to hear the first prayer. Mr. S. led & came with me home.

Friday, November 23.

Had a fine snow last night, not a very deep one though but it is enough to let us know that "Winter bright winter" will soon be here. It is not so cold to-day.

Saturday, November 24.

Have been sewing all day. Finished dresses for Ginnie, Bell and Grace. Fixed my shaker with winter beginning. Eliza Welty came home this afternoon. She and Nancy White were down this evening. I went up street this evening with them but did not stay long. It was too cold and windy. Last night I thought the house would blow over. I was as much frightened that I got up in the middle of the night. I suppose it was for our clock had stopped at 11 1/2. It was so windy that it blew our garret window out and broke the glass. I do hope it will not be so windy to-night.

Sunday, November 25.

Was late at Sunday School this morning. I was so busily engaged in reading the 1st chapter of Genesis that I did not "note the march of time," Mr. Hoy a minister from Philadelphia preached in Mr. Dill's place. Went to S.S. this afternoon. Did not go to class. Mr. Dill preached this evening. His text was "Kiss the son, lest he be angry &c." Went with A.S. Snyder and I took her home from church.

Monday, November 26.

Very cold. Went to School this morning. The whole school dismissed as it was too cold in the building. This afternoon they all dismissed but myself. I was in until 15 minutes of five. 4 1/2 is the regular time. Had a very interesting session. Ginnie Gilbert came over for me this evening and we went to the Temple. Every appearance of snow. 11 1/2, The ground covered with snow, and snow still falling. Snyder came from the Temple with us.

Tuesday, November 27.

Cloudy, wet, rainy, muddy, damp, cool, disagreeable, and—well I believe that is all. Such a time as I have had going to school and coming home—It is enough to give me chills to think of it. But with a splendid pair of overshoes (very good but not very nice-looking) and a tolerably short dress I navigated pretty well, I mean in comparison with some others I saw.

Wednesday, November 28.

This morning the sky cleared beautifully, splendidly, gloriously. I stood at my school window this morning at recess and watched the clouds moving towards the zenith and leaving the western skies calm and clear. The clouds moved on toward the east gradually and majestically until at last the whole dome of heaven hung "clear calm and blue." To-night is a sweet night. Oh! how my heart swells with gratitude toward God for all his goodness and kindness towards me & all his fallen creatures, manifested by placing us in a world so beautiful. Would that I had the pen of a ready writer that I could express all the feelings that well up within me, and struggle for utterance but alas! they struggle in vain. Snyder spent the evening here. Got a letter from Lizzie and Mattie D. and a very welcome one too.

Thursday, November 29.

Thanksgiving Day. Spent it, or rather the best part of it, at the wash tub. Went to prayer-meeting this evening. Did not enjoy it very much. Mr. Thomas Warren led. There was very few there. I believe there was a Union Thanksgiving sermon preached in Mr. McElwee's church, the United Presbyterian. Perhaps that accounts for an unusually small number at prayer-meeting. Feel very tired. This has been a very pleasant day overhead. The ground is damp and very muddy, but sky is clear. The air is pretty cool, especially in the evening. Snyder came with me home.

Friday, November 30.

Went to Mr. John Culp's this evening to help to organize a Bible Class or rather to join it. It is to meet at Henry Clippinger's next Friday night. I hope this attempt will be more successful than the last.

Saturday, December 1.

Have been ironing, baking, sewing, and doing a little of all kinds of work to-day. Went up to the store to-day and over to Aunt Salome's before supper. Went to see Cousin A.S. after supper. Rose Wertz was there. Stayed until about 7 Oclock. Snyder was here when I came home.

Sunday, December 2.

Have not been out of the house all day. I have been very sick all day. Had sick head-ache and pain in my stomach. It seems like such a long day, and it is a long time since I have been as sick as I was to-day. Feel considerably better this evening.

Monday, December 3.

Very sick all day. Could not go to school and from present appearances will not be able to go for two or three days, perhaps more but I will hope for the best. Rose W. and A.S. were here this evening. 9 Oclock. I feel a great deal worse than I did to-day. My head aches and I am very feverish and sometimes chilly. Snyder came down awhile but his little namesake, Eddie Warren, is sick and he did not stay long.

Thursday, December 6.

Have not been to school all week until this morning. I ought to have stayed in the house to-day but I went to school. Did not go to prayer-meeting.

Friday, December 7.

Could not go to school this morning but I went this afternoon. I have not been as sick for a year as I have been this week, but I am getting a little better.

Saturday, December 8.

Have been sewing all day. Sewed more than I ought to have done but I wanted to get Ginnie's dress done for to-morrow.

Sunday, December 9.

Went to Sunday School this morning but did not stay for church. Went to School this afternoon. Went to church this evening. Mr. Sumwalt preached. His text was "The wicked shall be turned into hell." His sermon was excellent, but as usual, very short. This has been a bad day. Snow on the ground and a tolerably warm sun and air.

Monday, December 10.

Very wet and disagreeable all day. This was the regular evening for our Temple to meet, but I did not go as I have not been well and it is so damp and cold.

Tuesday, December 11.

It is getting clear but cold. Have had a dull head-ache all day which going to school has not made any better. I suppose my school will be examined and close for one month, on next Thursday morning.

Wednesday, December 12.

Cold and tolerably clear. Lizzie Rupp and I went up to Aunt Emily's to help at a quilt for the sewing society connected with our church. Rose W. Mrs. Clippinger, Mrs. Bowen, Mrs. Kendlehart, Lizzie and myself were there. Came home about 9 Oclock. Snyder was here while I was away, I am sorry I was not here, for he has not been here for sometime. Mr. Warren's little Eddie has had Typhoid Fever.

Thursday, December 13.

Three of our school directors, Mr. Carson, Mr. Buehler, & Mr. Welty were in my school this morning. I examined my school in spelling and reading. They were very much pleased. Aunt Emily & Mrs. Earnshaw were there. Washed this afternoon. Went to prayer-meeting this evening. Mr. Dill led. Enjoyed it very much. This morning my school was dismissed until the 14th of January. Three cheers for vacation. Snyder came with me from P.M.

Friday, December 14.

Went to the store this morning. Bought the material for cloaks for Ginnie and Bell. I do not feel well at all this evening. My head aches and my throat is sore. Went for Ginnie Powers and we went to Bible class. It met at Mr. Schick's residence. There were thirteen persons there. Will Guinn came home with me. N.B. Rose was not there. Very cold.

Saturday, December 15.

Snowed this morning from 9 until twelve. Sewed this afternoon at Bell's cloak. Went to the store. Sewed until 10 Oclock and finished Bell's cloak.

Sunday, December 16.

Went to S.S. this morning. Went to prayer-meeting. Mr. Culp led. Did not enjoy it very much. Did not go to class. Went to S.S. this afternoon. Went to preaching. Harrie Clippinger preached in Mr. Dill's place. Mr. Dill is sick I believe. Snyder came with me from church.

Monday, December 17.

Have been busy all day. Sewed at Jennie's cloak, and commenced a dress for myself. T.S. was here this evening. After he left I answered Mattie and Lizzie Durboraw's letters and now it is almost 11 Oclock, and to-morrow is Wash-day. Oh! dear.

Tuesday, December 18.

Washed to-day. Did not get done until 2 Oclock. Went down to Rose Wertz's with my sewing. W.G. and T.S. came down. Went to the post office, came home about 8 1/2 Oclock, Feel very tired. Got the Laws of Life this morning.

Wednesday, December 19.

A fine continuous rain all day. Finished Jennie's cloak this morning, and sewed at my dress this afternoon and evening. Folded the clothes ready for ironing to-morrow. Wrote to Eliza Welty this evening. I feel very tired and sleepy.

Thursday, December 20.

Ironed this morning. Sewed at my dress all afternoon. Went up to Mr. Warren's to see how Eddie was. Did not go in. I had not time. Went down to see Rose W. before I went to Prayer-meeting. Mr. Snyder led. I enjoyed it more than I have for a long time. I felt more of "the awe that dares not move, And all the silent heaven of love," than I ever did before. Snyder came home with me but I did not ask him to come in. His little pet is very low. Snyder thinks he will die soon. He would feel his death as much as anyone. I hope he may be able to say, "God's will be done." Got a letter from Beckie Belch to-day.

Friday, December 21.

Sewed all day at my dress. Went to Bible-class this evening. Eddie Warren died this morning. He has been sick for more than six weeks and suffered a great deal. He was a great favorite with a friend of mine. Poor Eddie! he is better off than we.

Saturday, December 22.

Busy all day. Went to the store this morning. Mother and I went to the funeral this afternoon at 2 Oclock. Eddie looked lovely, lying in his coffin so peacefully. The funeral was not large but every one seemed to feel the deep solemnity of the occasion. Ginnie Buckingham & Henry Test of York were here this evening. Went to Aunt Salome's to see my two Aunts Mary, one of whom has been sick and to see Cousin A.S.

Sunday, December 23.

Went to Sunday School this morning. Went to preaching. Mr. Dill preached his text was "Keep thy heart with all diligence for out of it are the issues of life." Had no class. Went to School this afternoon. Eliza Welty came home yesterday and she was with me for supper and is going to stay all night. William Dill preached to-night in his father's place. Snyder came home with us. He does not seem like "Snyder" since Eddie is dead. Poor fellow.

Monday, December 24.

Ellie and I went up street this morning to the store and several other places. Ellie was here for dinner. About 3 Oclock she went home. Thad Warren took her out in a buggy. Eliza wanted me to go along but I could not. Helped mother bake all afternoon. Ginnie G. ... came over about 6 and stayed until 7 and then we went to the Temple. Came home about 8 Oclock. Ginnie and I are going to the Catholic Church to-morrow morning at 5 Oclock. I will not go to bed at all to-night. I think I have some writing which I have been requested to do, and as I am going to church at 5, I think I may as well stay up. Snyder spent a great part of the evening here.

Tuesday, December 25.

7 Oclock A.M. Have just come from the Catholic Church. I wrote until 2 Oclock this morning then went to sleep and slept until about half past 3. I heard splendid music this morning, too sweet and solemn to describe, besides I am hungry and want my breakfast. 10 Oclock P.M. Stayed at home all day until about 5 Oclock. Went down to Aunt Agnes' and stayed until after 6. Came up street with her and went to see Cousin A.S. She is not very well. Came home about 7 Oclock.

Snyder was here when I came home. This has been a dull Christmas to me. Mrs. Warren wants me to write some lines on Eddie's death. I am going to do it, and thinking of the circumstances of his death has made me feel very sad. Poor little Eddie! He was almost well, the doctor thought him entirely out of danger, but just a week before he died he took a relapse and now he is sleeping in the cold grave. His curly head has a hard pillow, but his spirit we know is in the mansion of joy. He was an interesting child. Truly God's ways are not as our ways, "His will be done."

Wednesday, December 26.

Sewed all morning. Went up to see Lizzie R. after dinner and we went to the store, milliner shop and to see Mrs. Warren. This evening Lizzie and I went over to Aunt Salome's with our work. Spent a pleasant evening. Came home about 8 1/2 Oclock. Feel very badly this evening. I wish I were a better christian. At times I am almost discouraged. Oh! Lord strengthen me for every temptation.

Thursday, December 27.

Sewed to-day at my dress. Made a pair of under-sleeves. Wrote some to-day. Went to prayer-meeting. Was late. Mr. Dill led. Enjoyed it very much. Finished my dress after prayer-meeting. Snyder came home with me. This is a lovely night. It reminds me of some nights which I enjoyed last winter. How time flies. And am I improving it as I should? I fear not. Lord help me, for I am weak and ignorant!

Friday, December 28.

Sewed at my calico dress to-day. Washed a few things and ironed them. Went up street this evening to the P.O. Got a letter from Lizzie Durboraw. Lizzie R. Sade R. and Alice P. were down before I went to Bible-class. Lizzie stayed until after I came home. Did not take any interest in anything that was said or done at Bible class. I might as well have stayed at home. S. came home with me. 13 years ago to-day I lost a dear little brother. God help me to live that I may meet that loved one in heaven. I was a mere child when he died, yet I remember him well enough to love him.

Saturday, December 29.

Helped mother with the work this morning. Sewed at my dress a while this afternoon. Went up street after dinner. Finished the lines I wrote on Eddie Warren's death. I wrote them at his mother's request. Gave them to the Editor of the Star. Was at Aunt Salome's a little while. Went to see Rose Wertz, Aunt Lizzie and Cousin A.S. Came home about 9 Oclock.

Sunday, December 30.

Snowing steadily all day. Went to school this morning. To prayer-meeting. Mr. Clippinger led. Had no class. Went to School this afternoon. Mr. Schick gave two prizes to the two scholars who recited the most verses in three months. Dora Fleming, one of my scholars took the first and sister Susie the 2nd. Gave my class Christmas presents. Gave Amanda Warren a red morocco Bible for coming the most regularly since July. Gave the rest smaller books. Mr. Sumwalt preached this evening. Text—2nd Peter, 3rd chapter, 17th, 18th and 19th. A very good sermon—in my estimation. Snyder came with me home. Feel very badly this evening. Had a regular fit of the "Blues" all last week and began this week with them. Cause—cannot commit it to paper.

Monday, December 31.

Sewed at my dress to-day and finished it this evening. Helped mother wash a little. Cousin A.S. was here this evening. Went up street with her. 9 Oclock. I am now going to watch meeting. By the time I return the year 1860 will have passed into Eternity. Eternity—Eternity—Solemn thought—Oh Lord how much I need thy grace to keep me in the right way.

1861

From typescripts by Dr. Henry A. Stewart.

Thursday, May 23.

Summerall's Zouaves paraded today. They made a very fine appearance.

Thursday, June 20.

First mention of the war found—"Mr. Welch, a member of the Volunteers that went from here is dead—"

Monday, July 22.

Finished Jefferson's letter but news came today that his regiment had left West Chester for Charleston, Va. Cousin John Myers saw Jefferson today in Harrisburg. Am almost wild to hear from him.

Friday, August 2.

Today Miss Whiteside, formerly 2nd Ass't was promoted to 1st Ass't (Miss Mary's position) and I was promoted from 5th Ass't to Miss Whiteside's place. When I heard the joyful news I had to come home and tell mother. My heart is brimful & overflowing with happiness.

Tuesday, September 3.

Father went. Somehow I have an idea that he will not stay, for I think he will not stand a Medical exam. He was very anxious to go & we said nothing either way. It was very hard to see him go but I really can't express my opinion. Uncles Isaac Sheads, Lewis Myers, John Sheads & William Culp, Cousin Dave Sheads & two distant cousins John Sheads & William Sheads also went. Wonder where father and brother are tonight. God be with them.

Friday, September 6.

News of father & Jefferson.

Friday, November 8.

Jefferson—certificate of disability—be home as soon as he gets his discharge.

Thursday, December 26.

810 soldiers came last night. They are cavalry and are to spend the winter here.

1862

*"Let love and truth indite—
whatever here I write—"*

January 1st, 1862

Wednesday, January 1.

A.M. Returned from Watch meeting. Enjoyed it very much. Mr. Stevenson's text was "Time is short." Had prayer meeting and General Class. God help me keep the covenant I have made with him. 9 1/2 P.M. Rose late as I felt rather sleepy. At home all day. Afternoon. Snyder was here. Evening. Went up to Mr. Schick's store. Stopped at Aunt Mary Sheads' on the road home and also at Shillen's. Home at 9. John came with me. Cold and windy. Feel sad I have not been as careful today as I thought I would be. I am afraid I trusted too much in my own strength. Oh that I could trust in my Father with a child-like faith. God help me. I want to be a Christian.

Thursday, January 2.

Morning. Went to the store. Got my salary for December ($10.00) Paid some debts and had 10 cts. left. Feel as free as an uncaged bird. I can now say "I owe no man (or woman either) anything." Home at 11. Afternoon. At home sewing. Evening. Went to prayer meeting. Mr. T. Warren led. Enjoyed it tolerably. Jeff came home with me. I found it a great difficulty to fix my mind upon those things which should have engaged my attention. I was not altogether unbenefitted. Jennie is sick. She has a bad cold and complains of a pain in her side and breast. She coughs a great deal. She looks so pale and weak I am really alarmed about her.

Friday, January 3.

Morning. Went to the store for mother. Home at 10. Sewed at my wrapper. Afternoon. At home sewing. Finished my wrapper. Evening. Harriet and Kate Shillen, Sallie Steffy, Louisa Rupp, Lizzie Frazer and I spent the evening at Mrs. Bamer's. There was a kind of a musical entertainment there. Some of the members of the band belonging to the "N.Y. 10th" were there. Spent a delightful time. Mrs. Bamer played on the piano and Harriet sang. Home at 10 1/2. A Mr. Clark was there. He played and sang. I never heard a gentleman sing so well. His friend "Tom" came home with Harriet and me. He is also a member of the Band. I do not know his last name, neither do I care.

Saturday, January 4.

Morning. At home. Sewing at a dress for Grace. Afternoon. Went up street to the store for mother, and made some calls. Called to see Ellie Aughinbaugh, Harriet Shillen, Lizzie Rupp, Aunt Pollie Myers and then home at 8. Sewed at Grace's dress. Evening. Went to the Doctor for Jennie. She is no better I think. Got some medicine. To see Rose G. awhile. She is improving fast. Had a good long talk with her. Ellie A. and I went up street. Home at 6 1/2. Finished Grace's dress. Sewed until 10 1/2.

Sunday, January 5.

To S.S. at 9. Home at 10 1/2. Mother and Susie went to church. Mr. King, a member of the "New York 10th" (I think he is assistant Quartermaster) preached. He will preach next Sunday night. Thought I would go to class, and started about 11 3/4 but there was no class. Home at 12 1/2. Afternoon. To S.S. at 2. A soldier opened and Snyder presided at the Missionary Meeting and closed. Home at 3 1/2. Ellie Aughinbaugh was with me at Sunday School. Evening. Jeff and I went to church. Mr. Sumwalt preached. We took Ann Culp home as we had business with Aunt Salome. Stopped at Aunt Lizzie Myers' on the road home. Jennie seems better. Very cold, moonlight. Feel miserably and have felt so all day. I never spent a Sunday with as little benefit to my soul. Father is 46 years old today.

Monday, January 6.

Morning. Mother is 44 years old today. Made the skirt of a dress for Jennie and commenced one for Bell. Jennie is better. Afternoon. Went down to Aunt Salome Culp's with my sewing. Commenced a pair of drawers for Jennie. Evening. Went to see Ginnie Powers. She is getting better. Home at 6. Cold. We have fine sleighing now. Sewing all evening. Finished Bell's skirt and Jennie's drawers. Feel pretty tired but I have been working harder than usual for a poor (?) delicate (?) soul like me. Mother had a letter from father today. He is well and expects to come home as soon as they are paid. Cousin David Myers came at noon from the company of which father is a member. Mother is 44 years old today.

Tuesday, January 7.

Cold. Sewing all day. Jennie is better. Mr. Lyttle was here to see her. Evening. Went down to Aunt Lizzie's and to see Rose Guinn and then spent the evening at Aunt Salome's recording lot arrangements. Miss Maggie Benner, Miss McIlvane of Oxford were there also Cousins Lizzie, Lou and Carrie Sheads. Cousins Ann and Mary Slentz, Cousins Mary, Lizzie, and Jane Myers. Spent a tolerably pleasant evening. Home about 10 1/2. Jeff came with me. This is a lovely night. Calm, clear and the sweet moon shining brightly down upon the pure white snow. Oh! if earth be so beautiful what must heaven be!

Wednesday, January 8.

Morning. Washing. Finished at 12. Afternoon. Sewing awhile. Evening. Went to the store to see Ginnie Powers, Harriet Shillen and Ellie Aughinbaugh and then spent the evening with Mrs. Sechrist and Mrs. Grumbine, Lieut. Mitchell, Mr. Hayes. Ellie Aughinbaugh & Ann McCreary went with me to the door. Had some fine fun snowballing with a large company. Sade, Lou and Lizzie Rupp, Mr. and Mrs. Fisher and Mrs. Baker. Orderly Sergeant Jones, and Privates Edmonds, Casey, Burke and Sanders. Spent a pleasant but rather a noisy evening. Home at 10. Mr. Sanders came with me. Had a slippery walk as it had rained during the evening, and it had frozen and the pavements were like glass. Snyder was here while I was away. I am both glad and sorry that I was not at home. He does not seem like the Snyder I used to know and I can say with the poet "It does not ease my heart to know that change resides in me." Perhaps it is but a passing cloud. If such be the case the cloud is a heavy one and very long passing.

Thursday, January 9.

Morning. Sewing. Afternoon. Went up to Aunt Pollie Myers' with my work. Evening. Went to prayer meeting. Mr. Sumwalt and Mr. Stevenson both officiated. I did not enjoy it at all. I could not fix my mind on any one subject for ten minutes at a time. I feel so strangely of late.

> "My thoughts are vain my heart is hard
> My temper apt to rise
> When I seem most upon my guard
> It takes me by surprise"

I thought I would be a better Christian this year, and I am sure if there is any change at all, it is for the worse instead of the better. I am ashamed to make any good resolutions any more. I wonder if any one else has trials like me. Every one else seems to get along so well that I often think my trials are peculiarly my own.

Friday, January 10.

Morning. Helped mother to bake. Afternoon. Sewing at a cloth circular for Grace. Finished it. Folded the clothes. Evening. Jennie Gilbert spent the evening here. Spent it very pleasantly. Had a sociable quiet chat. I have been thinking of Snyder a great deal this evening. I always do when I sit in this room in the evening. It reminds me of "the good olden time" when we spent such pleasant evenings together. Poor Snyder. I do not think he will live long and I never expect to spend such evenings again, or to find a friend like him. God bless him and prepare me for any trial which may be in store for me. It may seem foolish for me to write thus of him but I unconsciously yield to this weakness, and indeed it is a comfort for me to do so. My diary seems like a friend in which I can confide without fear of being betrayed. O! may God be with him and bless him with the choicest blessings. I will have to reconcile myself to parting with him. His looks tell that, but God alone knows the agony of my heart at the base idea of such an occurrence. Oh God help me. Give me grace in this my hour of need. How much I need the grace to contend with the trials and temptations which are ever around me.

Saturday, January 11.

Morning. Helped mother at the work. Afternoon. Ironing. Snyder was here. He has been worse all week. He looks very badly. His cough is worse. It commenced hailing while he was here and he had to go home. I hated to see him go. It seemed almost like he was never to come here again and it may be true, for he looks as though, to quote an old saying "he had one foot in the grave." May God help my dear friend. Little did we think three years ago, that this would be the end of our friendship. Truly "Man proposed, God disposes." Evening. At home, reading. Very disagreeable. Raining and very muddy. Feel miserably. Got a letter from Mattie Durboraw.

Sunday, January 12.

To S.S. at 9. To prayer meeting at 10 1/2. Had General Class after prayer meeting. Enjoyed it tolerably. Several of the others spoke. Afternoon. To S.S. at 2, Ada Mc came home with me for supper. Evening. Ada and I went to church. Mr. J.B. King preached. He is a congregationalist and is Quartermaster Sergeant. His text was "Prepare ye the way of the Lord." The church was crowded. Home at 8. Mr. Casey came home with me.

Monday, January 13.

Morning. Cut carpet rags until 11 1/2 and until my fingers were blistered. Afternoon. Got my likeness taken for one of my Sunday School scholars—Dora Fleming. This is her birthday. She is seven-teen. I did not give them Christmas presents and so I will give them birthday presents. Home at 7. Cousin Ann Sheads and Ann Culp spent the afternoon and evening here. Spent a very pleasant evening. Harriet Shillen was here awhile. Knit at Susie's cloud.

Tuesday, January 14.

Morning at home. Busy. Afternoon. Wrote to father. Evening. Spent the evening with Jennie Gilbert. Mr. Jones came for me to go down and he also came home with me. Mr. Jones, Mr. Casey, Mr. Metcalf (I think) Mr. Sanders, and Mr. Bush were there. Lizzie, Lou and Sade Rupp and myself were there. Spent a tolerable pleasant evening. Home about 10. Feel badly. I wish I knew how Snyder is getting along. I may as well "out with it" as the old saying runs.

Wednesday, January 15.

Sewing all day. Evening. Had company. Harriet Shillen, Lizzie Frazer, Jennie Gilbert, Lizzie, Lou, and Sade Rupp. Messrs., Jones, Bush, Edmunds, Casey, Sanders, Downs, Metcalf and Carey. Spent a tolerable pleasant evening. They stayed too late, it being after 11, when, Jones, Casey and Edmunds left.

Thursday, January 16.

Morning. At home sewing. Afternoon. Went to the store for mother. Went to see Ann Culp, Slentz's girls, Aunt Lizzie and Jennie Gilbert. Evening. Went to prayer meeting. Mr. Stevenson led. Mr. McMillan exhorted. Jeff came home with me. Jennie Gilbert and I took a walk before I went to prayer meeting.

Friday, January 17.

Sewing all day at a dress for Grace. Got a letter from my dear father and one from Fannie Coshun. Evening. Went to the store for mother, or rather for Grace. Mrs. Jane Grumbine and I went to help Mrs. Fisher to iron. Mr. O'Carr came home with us. Mr. Jones was here while I was gone. I am very glad I was not at home. Heard that school will not commence until the 1st of February. I was glad to hear from papa. It is the 1st letter I have received from him since he has been gone.

Saturday, January 18.

Morning. Finished Grace's dress and commenced an apron for her. Afternoon. Ironed until 2 1/2. Mr. Downs was here a long time. He is a member of Company G. Capt. Carpenter. Evening. Went to the store to see Aunt Agnes. Home at 6 1/2. Read the "Song of the Lost Minstrel." Very disagreeable.

Sunday, January 19.

To S.S. at 9. To preaching at 10 1/2. Mr. Stevenson preached. Had no class. Mr. Culp is sick. Afternoon. To S.S. at 2. Evening. Went to church. Mr. Stevenson preached. I did not enjoy the sermon at all. It was long and I could not fix my mind upon it. Jeff came home with me. Very disagreeable. Damp and wet. Heard today that Snyder is sick again. I should not wonder if he were. Poor fellow!

Monday, January 20.

Very disagreeable all day. Raining, snow on the ground, and muddy. Wrote to father. Uncle Isaac Sheads from father's company was here. Finished Grace's apron and helped mother sew awhile. Got supper. Evening. At home sewing. I feel so sad and lonely and worse than all, I feel very much discouraged and cast down in my endeavors to be a Christian. It seems almost useless for me to try any longer. I am no ornament to the church rather a reproach. And yet if I give up what will become of me. I have made good resolutions and broken them until I am ashamed of myself. I am afraid to try again. Oh! if I could be a Christian and know and feel that I was on my way to heaven, I think I could be happy in any situation, but Oh! miserable me! I was happy once, but in some way unknown to me I have lost my evidence and I have been trying to regain it for some time but it seems to be impossible. I have had so much trouble lately that I have suffered my thoughts to be drawn off the purpose, or what should be my sole desire and aim in this world. Will this struggle never cease? Must I go mourning all my days with only an occasional gleam of light? Why cannot I have the glorious light of the "Sun of Righteousness" ever shining into my soul? I long for it. My inmost soul desires it.

Tuesday, January 21.

At home all day. Very disagreeable. Feel miserable. This cloudy rainy weather makes me feel badly, and other things help considerable. School was to have commenced yesterday but the soldiers (three companies) are quartered in the building and it was post-poned until the 3rd of February.

Wednesday, January 22.

Morning. At home sewing. Afternoon. Mother and I went to see Mrs. Baker. Evening. Uncle John Sheads was here. He brought us a letter from father. Very disagreeable.

Thursday, January 23.

Morning. Washing. Finished at 12. Afternoon. Sewing. Evening. Sprinkled the clothes. Jennie Gilbert was here. Went to prayer meeting. Mr. Stevenson led. Did not enjoy it very much. Mr. O'Carr came home with me. He belongs to Company B Captain Jarvis.

Friday, January 24.

Ironed until 1 o'clock. Went down to Jennie Gilbert's to spend the afternoon. Did some sewing for her. Evening. Very disagreeable. Raining, hailing, snowing, or something of the kind. Jennie and I went up street. We went to Slentz's and Aunt Salome's and Aunt Lizzie's. Spent a pleasant evening. Had a good deal of quiet fun.

Saturday, January 25.

Morning. Last night was very disagreeable and as Jennie wanted me to stay all night so I stayed. Got home about 7. Worked hard. Went to the store for mother. Afternoon. Snyder was here. He looks badly. He says he does not expect to get well. He is hardly able to get along. I can hardly realize that he is so changed. He is not at all like he used to be and it is no wonder. Poor fellow! Evening. Jennie Gilbert was here. She brought me a head-dress she had made for me. Very windy.

Sunday, January 26.

To S.S. at 9. To preaching at 10 1/2. Mr. Stevenson preached a missionary sermon. McMillan came home with me for dinner. Afternoon. To S.S. at 2. Evening. Went to church. Mr. Sumwalt preached. His text was "If a man die shall he live again." The sermon was splendid.

Monday, January 27.

Morning at home sewing. Afternoon. Mother and I went up street to see Aunt Mary, Aunt Agnes and Aunt Lavinia Sheads. I went to see Jennie Gilbert and then Rose Guinn and I went to see the dress parade. Evening. Wrote to Mattie Durboraw. Sergeant O'Carr, Mr. Bush and Jennie Gilbert came up and we went to Rupp's to spend the evening. Lidie Powers, Fannie Dutterra, Sergeant Jones, Mr. Wilcox, Mr. Casey, Mr. Minor and Mr. Carey were there, also John Rupp and John Tipton. Spent a tolerable pleasant evening. O'Carr came home with me.

Tuesday, January 28.

Morning. Sewing. Afternoon. Father came home. God bless him. Mr. Downs and Mr. Casey were here all afternoon. Downs stayed for supper but Casey went to the dress-parade. Mr. Downs is not well. He and I washed the dishes. Mr. Casey came to see Grace. Evening. Mr. Downs and I went to spend the evening at Aunt Polly Myers's. The misses Rupp were there, Harriet Shillen and Lydia Powers. Messers. Bush, Carey, Casey, Jones, Wilcox, Minor, and O'Carr. Did not enjoy myself very much. Mr. Downs came home with me.

Wednesday, January 29.

Morning. Washing. Afternoon. Sewing. Jennie G. came down for me to go to the store with her. We went up street and had a good long talk. Evening. According to arrangement, Mr. Casey called and we went up to spend the evening at Shillen's. Harriet played and sang beautifully for us. Came home about 9. This evening seemed like old times—to have father home. Spent a pleasant evening but feel badly. It is so damp and disagreeable.

Thursday, January 30.

Morning. At home sewing. Afternoon. Sewing. Went over to see Mrs. Grumbine and Mrs. Sechrist awhile. Evening. Went to prayer meeting. Mr. Sumwalt and Mr. Stevenson led. Enjoyed it tolerably. Mr. Casey came home with me. Had a real sociable chat. He seems like an old friend. His name is Ed, he [unclear text]! He is a member of Company B. Capt. Jarvis.

Friday, January 31.

Morning. Finished washing. This is the first clear day we have had this week.

Downs was here until dinner time. Afternoon. Went down to Mrs. Guinn's to spend the afternoon. They have gone to housekeeping. Evening. Jennie Gilbert and I went up street and called at Rupp's. Home about 7. Feel very tired.

Saturday, February 1.

Morning. Snowing. Helped mother at the work. Mr. Casey came down about 10 1/2 and stayed until dinner-time. Afternoon. Mother and I went up street to see the flag presented to the Porter Guards. Went down to see Cousin Carrie Sheads about taking music lessons. Home at 4. Downs and Jennie Gilbert were here for supper. Evening. Mr. Casey came up and we went down to Cousin Annie Shead's to spend the evening. Julia Weygandt was there awhile. Mr. Corwin of Company A. was there. Spent a pleasant evening. Home about 9 1/2.

Sunday, February 2.

To S.S. at 9. To preaching at 10 1/2. Mr. Sumwalt preached. Home at 10. Eliza W. is in the western part of this state, visiting a sister. Aunt Hannah Welty (Eliza's mother) was here for dinner. Afternoon. To S.S. at 2. Home at 5 1/2. Ada M'Millan came with me for supper. Evening. Ada and I went to church. Mr. Sumwalt preached his last sermon for this conference year, though it is his last appointment he may preach again. Mr. Casey came home with me. Mr. Sumwalt's sermon was elegant. The last seems to be the best always. It was tolerably affecting.

Monday, February 3.

Morning. Washing. Could not put the clothes out. It is snowing. Afternoon. Sewing at an apron for Grace. Finished it. Mr. Casey was here. Evening. Mr. Casey came up and we went down to spend the evening at Uncle Elias Sheads's, Cousins Lizzie, Carrie, Lou, and Dave were also, & two ladies who are visiting there, Miss Maggie Benner and Miss Juliet Shearer. Spent a pleasant evening. Carrie sang and played for us. I am going to commence to take music lessons from Cousin Carrie. Home about 10. Snowing. Very ugly walking.

Tuesday, February 4.

Morning. Took my first music lesson at 7 1/2. Like it very much. Afternoon. Snyder was here. He seems better today. It is pleasanter than it has been for some time. Mr. Casey was here. Evening. Mr. Casey came for me and we went to spend the evening at Aunt Salome Culp's. Met a crowd. Cousins Ann and Mary Slentz, Ann Culp, Cousins Lou, Lizzie, Carrie & Dave Sheads, Maggie Benner, Juliet Shearer, Sade, Louisa and Lizzie Rupp & Jennie Gilbert. Mr. Carey, Mr. Jones, Mr. O'Carr, Mr. White, Mr. Cameron, Mr. Rogers, Mr. Sherman, Mr. Lenox, Mr. Casey & Lydie Powers. Expected to spend a pleasant evening, but unknown to me a fiddler was employed and they got to dancing. That was against my principles, and Jennie Gilbert and I left in disgust. They were cross that we left but we were determined. Mr. Casey came with us as far as Jennie's & he would have me stay there the evening. He did not care much about going back but we insisted. He said he would call for me and he came about 9 1/2, and left the rest there plus Mr. Bush and another fiddler. Got home about 10. Have had a miserable head-ache all evening. Feel sorry for this evening's performance but it was no fault of mine. Downs and Wade were here while I was away.

Wednesday, February 5.

Morning. Finished washing. Commenced washing last Monday but the weather has been so bad. Afternoon. Mr. Casey came to give me "Good-bye." They were very unexpectedly ordered to their barracks this morning. Sewing at an apron for Jennie. Evening. Jennie Gilbert was here. We went up street together. Stopped to see Harriet awhile. This is a beautiful night. Clear and moon-light.

Thursday, February 6.

Went down to have my music lesson at 7. Like it very much. Mr. Casey came in while I was there and came up street with me. Very disagreeable. Afternoon. Went to the store. Snyder was here. Had a long talk with him. How one's feelings change! Had anyone predicted, one year ago, the change which has taken place in my feelings towards him I should not only have discredited it but very likely would have been offended. It is better thus. I am certain. Snyder seems better. Evening. Went to see Jennie Gilbert awhile from there to prayer meeting. Mr. Stevenson led. Enjoyed it tolerably. Home at 8. Very disagreeable.

Friday, February 7.

Morning. Clear and pleasant. Got a letter from Mattie and Lizzie Durboraw. Fixed a dress for myself. Afternoon. Went to the store for Aunt Pollie Myers. Mother and I went down to Uncle Elias Sheads'. I went to practice. Cousin Carrie had no school this afternoon. Home at 5. Evening. Jennie Gilbert was here. We went to the post-office together. Home at 7. Aunt Pollie was here awhile. Feel very sad. It seems as though I have more little trials than any one I know. So many little troubles to vex me. Harriet S. ... says "they are only the splinters of the cross."

Saturday, February 8.

Went down to get my music lesson (an hour) and to practice awhile. Commenced at 7 1/2 and kept at it pretty regularly until 12. Had no idea it was so late and I was very much interested in my employment. Afternoon. Commenced to make sun-bonnetts for Jennie and Bell. Snyder was here. Feel badly. The weather is so unpleasant that one cannot help feeling a little uncomfortable. Evening. Went up street to the office and to see Jennie G. We took a long walk and had a long talk. Home at 6 1/2.

Sunday, February 9.

To S.S. at 9. To prayer-meeting at 10 1/2. To S.S. at 2. Had a S.S. prayer-meeting. Enjoyed it tolerably. Felt very sad all the while. Stopped at the Catholic Church on my way home to hear the music. Home at 4. Clear and very pleasant though cold. Evening. Went to preaching. Mr. Stevenson preached. His text was "the spirit helpeth our infirmities." The sermon was good, what I heard of it. I was so worried about some things that my mind wandered very often. Mr. Casey came home with me. This is a glorious night. Clear, cold and moonlight.

Monday, February 10.

Rose at 6 1/2. Went to school at 9, but we adjourned until 2. Home at 9 1/2. Helped mother wash and finished Bell's bonnet. Afternoon. Went for Beckie and we went to school. It seems a little strange yet a great deal like old times. Evening. Went down to Uncle's to practice. Started home about 6. Met Ellie S amd we took a walk while the mail was being distributed. Home at 7. Learned my music lesson. Very pleasant. Moon-light. Cold.

Tuesday, February 11.

Took my music lesson at 7 1/2. At school all day. Afternoon. Snowing. Beckie Belch and I went down street. Evening. Snowing. Sewed at Jennie's bonnet until my thread gave out. Jennie G. and Mr. Casey were here awhile. Jennie had to go home early. Mr. Casey is picket tonight. Studied my music lesson about an hour and a half.

Wednesday, February 12.

At school all day. Evening. Went down to Cousin Carrie's to practice. Home at 6. Jennie G. was here, and Lizzie Rupp spent the greater part of the evening with me. Wrote in Jennie Buckingham's album. Wrote about two hours. Had my class-book to arrange. Studied my music lesson. Got part of dutch almanac for a valentine.

Thursday, February 13.

Morning. Took my lesson at 7 1/2. Practiced till school-time. Afternoon. At school. Got a valentine. Evening. Went to see Jennie Gilbert before prayer-meeting time. To prayer-meeting. Mr. Stevenson led. Enjoyed it tolerably. Home at 8.

Friday, February 14.

At school all day. Very disagreeable. Cloudy, windy and cool. Snyder is twenty-eight years old today. Evening. Mr. Casey was here, and Jennie Gilbert came while he was here to go to church with me. I did not go. Mother said I had better stay at home.This has only allowed him to stay until 8. We went with Jennie up to Mr. Aughinbaugh's. Her mother was there waiting on her. Home at 8. Tolerably pleasant but cool. Moonlight.

Saturday, February 15.

Morning. Took my lesson at 7. Home at 9. Finished the children's aprons. Snowing. Afternoon. Snowing. Went to see Jennie G. and from there to Cousin Carrie's to practice. While there the Porter Guards passed. Saw ever so many that I know. It kept us busy "bobbing our heads." Evening. Mother and I went to church. Mr. Stevenson preached a very good sermon. Home at 8 1/2. Very cold.

Sunday, February 16.

To love-feast at 8 1/2. Did not speak and of course did not enjoy myself very much. To preaching at 10 1/2. Mr. Stevenson preached. After preaching the sacrament of the Lord's Supper was administered. Afternoon. Jennie Gilbert came for me and we went to Union S.S. in St. James Lutheran Church (the one Jennie attends) We went to hear Mr. M'Elwee preach at 3. Home at 4 1/2. Very cold. Snyder was here while I was away. Evening. Jennie G. and I went to church. Mr. Stevenson preached. Mr. Casey came home with me.

Monday, February 17.

At school all day. Raining and hailing. Very disagreeable. Evening. Went to see Jennie G. awhile. She came up and went to church with mother and me. Mr. Sumwalt preached. Home at 8 1/2. Very damp.

Tuesday, February 18.

At school all day. Afternoon. Clear. Went down to practice after school. Evening. Mr. Downs was here. He went with me to church but did not come home with me. He had to go to camp at 7 1/2 and then back to town at 9 to the police. Mr. Stevenson preached a good sermon. Home at 8 1/2. Damp and cold. Clear. Did not take my lesson this morning. I had the head-ache and the walking was very bad.

Wednesday, February 19.

At school all day. Took my music lesson this morning instead of yesterday morning. Evening. Very unpleasant. Raining. Had a fine snow but it is all slush. Ciphered awhile. Read part of the "Life of Jacob Gruber." Bell is 9 years old to-day.

Thursday, February 20.

Went down to practice at 7 1/2. At school all day. Evening. Went to prayer meeting at 7. Mr. Stevenson commenced and Mr. Sumwalt exhorted and closed. Home at 8 1/2. Stopped to see Harriet awhile but she was away spending the evening.

Friday, February 21.

At school all day. Evening. Went down to practice after school, from there to see Jennie Gilbert. Home at 6. Mr. Casey was here. Sade Rupp and Jen Gilbert spent the evening here. Mr. Casey's pass only extended until 8. Spent a very pleasant evening, (with one or two exceptions). Jen is nineteen years old today.

Saturday, February 22.

Took my lesson at 7 1/2. Home at 9 1/2. Helped mother at the work. After-noon. Jennie Gilbert and I went up street. The Porter Guards were in town and had some kind of demonstration in honor of the birthday of "The father of his country." Jen came home with me for supper. Mr. Downs was here. Jen went to choir meeting at 7. Mr. Downs spent the evening here. Cloudy and disagreeable.

Sunday, February 23.

Grace is 5 years old to-day. To S.S. at 9. To prayer-meeting at 10 1/2. Enjoyed it tolerably. Mr. Hoy led. He is a preacher and an agent for some society, forget what. Had no class. Home at 11 1/2. Afternoon. Ellie A. came down to go to S.S. with me. We went to vespers after S.S. Evening. Snyder was here until church-time. Mother and I went to preaching. Mr. Hoy preached. Very damp and disagreeable. Raining.

Monday, February 24.

At school all day. Mr. Casey was here at noon awhile. Evening. Went to see Jen and Rose. Down to Cousin Carrie's to practice. Johnnie Baker is dead. He died this morning of Inflammation of the Lungs. Poor child. He suffered so much. Jane Grumbine and I sat up with him awhile until the others came. Home at 10. Copied a piece of music.

Tuesday, February 25.

At school all day. Very pleasant. Clear and cold. Evening. Jennie Gilbert came up and we went up to Mr. Rupp's awhile. We were all going to Quaker meeting in our church, and Jen and I came down home to get ready. Mr. Casey was here when we came, and we did not go. I spent a pleasant evening, but "Ed" had to go at 8. The Colonel will not give any longer passes than from 5 to 8, unless on extraordinary occasions. Jennie, and her sister Annie spent the remainder of the evening here and Susie and I went part of the way home with them. Practiced awhile after school this afternoon.

Wednesday, February 26.

At school all day. Cloudy. Snowing awhile. Evening. Raining. Went down street to the Dentist's and to cousin Carrie for some music. Met two soldiers (of Comp. G.) Home at 6 1/2. Snyder spent the evening here. I copied four or five pieces of music. Feel very tired. Little Johnnie Baker was buried this afternoon at 2 o'clock. It is a long time since Snyder spent an evening with me. I know he has been sick, but for all that I cannot help thinking he has changed. I mean in his feeling toward me. I am pretty certain of it and I have been trying to overcome my affection for him. I am succeeding very well. It lasts as long as his health keeps tolerable good, but when I think of him sick and suffering I would do anything to be with him. Oh! how foolish I am, but that is the truth and no one will know it unless some one gets this book.

Thursday, February 27.

At school all day. Very cold and windy. Evening. Went to see Jennie Gilbert and then down to practice awhile. Mother and I went to prayer meeting. Enjoyed it tolerably. Snyder led. Took a music lesson this morning.

Friday, February 28.

At school all day. Have worked harder than usual this week. Miss Whiteside, our 1st assistant, has the mumps and has not been at school this week. Took my lesson this morning. Evening. Mr. Downs was here until his pass, or rather the time for which it was written expired except enough for him to go to barracks, a distance of one mile and a half. If they are not there when their time is up they are put in the guard-house.

Saturday, March 1.

Morning. Very busy. Mother and I went to Mr. Speight's and had our likeness taken. Afternoon. Mr. and Mrs. Aughinbaugh and Mattie—cousins Lou and Carrie Sheads and Maggie Benner, Brother Jefferson, Mother, Jen Gilbert and I went to the barracks about 3 o'clock. Saw battalion drill and dress parade. Started home about 5. Jen and I had a pleasant walk and talk. Evening. Feel very tired. Harriet S. and Mrs. Bamer called. Mr. Casey was here as long as his pass allowed him to be. Ellie A. was here. Feel sick, tired and sleepy.

Sunday, March 2.

Morning. Did not go to S.S. Jennie and Bell are taking the mumps. Did most of the morning work. Mother went over to see little Mary Townsley. She is very ill. To prayer meeting at 10. Mr. M'Millan led. Enjoyed it very much. Home at 11 3/4. Went to see Mary Townsley. She is not any better. Afternoon. To S.S. at 2. Home at 4. Went to see Mary Townsley. Snyder was here till churchtime. Went to preaching at 7. Mr. Stevenson preached from Jude 21st. Home at 8 1/4. Mr. Downs came home with me. Went to see Mary Townsley. Cloudy, damp and disagreeable.

Monday, March 3.

Very disagreeable. Raining cold and damp. At school all day. Afternoon. Got my salary for February. (20.00) Evening. Went down to practice. Home at 6. To see Mary Townsley. She seems a little better. Ciphered until 9, with Susy in her Algebra. Found it quite interesting. Feel to a certain extent sad. I have been trying more than usual today to be a Christian and feel like continuing to try. Oh that I may have help from above to enable me to be a better Christian. It is the sincere desire of my heart.

Tuesday, March 4.

Took my music lesson at 7 1/2. To school at 9. There were 4 panes of glass broken in my recitation room and it was so windy and cold that I could not teach. Went down to practice while they were being replaced. Afternoon. To school at 1 1/2. Practiced from 4 1/2 until 6. Home at 6 1/2. Jennie Gilbert was here. Went to see Mary Townsley. She died a few moments after I left, about 9 o'clock. Poor Mary. She is at rest. She said two or three times that she wanted to die and be at rest. She wanted to see her mother. Her mother died several years ago.

Wednesday, March 5.

At school all day. Took my music lesson at 7 1/2. Evening. At home sewing. Went to the store for some calico. Commenced a dress for mother. Cool and cloudy. Feel badly. Feel sad and discouraged. Mr. Snyder spent the evening with me. We had a conversation very interesting to us the purpose of which I cannot state here.

Thursday, March 6.

At school all day. Afternoon. Mr. Casey was down but I was not at home. He left his likeness for me. Evening. Went to prayer meeting at 7. Home at 8 1/2. Stopped with Harriet awhile. Mr. Casey was here. He came about 9 o'clock. The

Regiment leaves Gettysburg to-morrow for Perryville, Md. He has not been very well since he was here last. We had a real pleasant visit and I suppose it will be the last. I am sorry they are going in some respects and in some respects I am glad. Ed does not like to go. He does not like a soldier's life but he is one of Uncle Sam's boys, and Uncle lets them see a good deal of the country. I hope Ed will find as good friends in Perryville as he found here.

Friday, March 7.

At school all day. The Porter Guards started at noon. Evening. Jennie Gilbert was here. Went down to practice. Home at 6. Filled out cards for our scholars, and did some other writing.

Saturday, March 8.

Took my lesson at 8. Practiced until 9 1/2. To see Rose Guinn a few minutes and to see Jen. Her little brother is very ill. Afternoon. Went to Mr. Speights' room to get my likeness taken but he was so busy that I had to wait. Lou, Lizzie and Mattie Durboraw there. They were getting their's taken. They wanted me to go along but I could not go. Practiced until 5 about an hour and a half. Home at 6. Stopped to see Harriet. Went to see Ellie A. Jen sent for me to come and stay all night. Cousin Annie was here. Snyder was here while I was away. Sorry I was not at home.

Sunday, March 9.

Stayed with Jen all night. Her brother is better. Home at 7. To S.S. at 9. To prayer meeting at 10 1/2. Snyder led. Enjoyed it tolerable. Ada M'Millan came with me for dinner. To S.S. at 2. Evening. Wrote to Fannie Coshun and commenced a letter to Mattie Durboraw. Snyder was here until church time. To prayer meeting at 7. Mr. M'Millan led. Enjoyed it tolerable. Felt so sleepy that I could not enjoy it much.

Monday, March 10.

At school all day. Evening. Ellie A. went along with me to practice. We stayed until 7. Carrie played and sang for us. Raining. Home at 7 1/2.

Tuesday, March 11.

Took my lesson at 7 1/2. To school at 9. Afternoon. Got my likeness taken for Mary Myers, one of my S.S. scholars. To-morrow is her birthday. Evening. Went down to practice. Home at 6. Got a letter from Ed (Mr. Casey) real interesting and very welcome too. Snyder spent the evening here. Spent a very pleasant evening. Clear and very pleasant. Moon-light.

Wednesday, March 12.

At school all day. Very pleasant. Clear, warm, just like a spring day. Evening. Jen Gilbert and I took a walk. Stopped to see Harriet, Lizzie Rupp and Ginnie Powers. Home at 8. Answered Mr. Casey's letter.

Thursday, March 13.

At school all day. Not so pleasant as yesterday. Cloudy and cool. Evening. Went down to practice, and took a lesson instead of this morning. Home at 6. Aunt Hannah was here. Jen came up and we walked until time for prayer meeting. Went at 7. A stranger led. Did not enjoy it much. Home at 8. Drizzling. Disagreeable.

Friday, March 14.

Took a music lesson at 7 1/2. At school all day. Evening. Went down to practice. Home at 6 1/2. Mr. Snyder spent the evening here. Spent a pleasant evening. It is just a week since the Porter Guards left Gettysburg. I am beginning to miss them or rather Ed, for I knew him better than any other one in the Regiment. May God be with him wherever he goes.

Saturday, March 15.

Morning. Sewing. Made a sun-bonnet for Susie. Very disagreeable. Raining all day. Afternoon. Mother got a letter from Father. He is well, and they expect to be moved shortly. I had one from Ed. It was very unexpected, but nonetheless welcome. Evening. At home writing. Very disagreeable.

Sunday, March 16.

To S.S. at 9. To preaching at 10 1/2. Mr. Drum preached a very good sermon. Afternoon. To S.S. at 2. Evening. Answered Mr. Casey's letter, or rather finished it. Cold and windy. Feel very badly. Have had the head-ache all day and my throat feels so queerly. Snyder was here until church-time. Went to preaching, though if any one but Mr. Drum had preached I should have stayed at home and retired early. His sermon was good. Home at 8.

Monday, March 17.

To school at 9. Home at 11. I am afraid I am taking the mumps, and so I came home. I will soon know for certain. Hope not. Afternoon. Feel miserably. Wrote to father and Mattie and Lizzie Durboraw. Have a dreadful head-ache and a very disagreeable feeling in my throat. Cold and windy. I do wish this war was over and father was at home once more. He would not get away on an expedition like it soon again, if I could help it. But I must be resigned to what I can not prevent. Such resignation!

Tuesday, March 18.

At home all day. Jen was here to see me at noon. Evening. Miss Whiteside, Mrs. Martin and Lizzie M'Cright were there to see me. Snyder spent the evening with me. We had a long conversation about our own affairs. For some time past, five or six months, I have thought he was so much changed. I knew his conduct was changed and of course thought his feelings were. That made a change in my actions and gradually a change in my feelings. He came as a friend he said, and I thought it very strange. Knowing, or at least thinking he had changed, I thought the best thing for me to do was not to think as much of him as formerly. I succeeded in overcoming my feelings, though not without some hard struggles. Of course, the change in my feelings was visible in my actions, and Snyder spoke of it not for awhile after he noticed it. He was very much hurt at some things I said and did which did seem strange to him though they were unintentional on my part. O.S. Jones was here once or twice and as he was a pretty hard one people talked about it. I could not help him being here and stopped it as soon as I could. Mr. Casey came here a good deal and the "dear public" had to talk about that too. I didn't care for that as long as they kept to the truth which they did not do. But this is a digression. Snyder says he has not changed in his feelings though his sickness made some change in his actions. I was considerably "taken down" when he told me. That was the subject of our conversation on the evening of March 4th. I may and probably will have more to write on the subject in the future.

Wednesday, March 19.

At home all day, sewing as much as I could, which was not very much. Evening. Ellie Aughinbaugh was here a long time. Feel badly. This is a very disagreeable evening.

Thursday, March 20.

Morning at home. Sewing. Afternoon. Went to school. Got a letter from Ed. I think from the date it must have been delayed. Home at 4. Answered Ed's letter. I could not go to prayer meeting, it is too damp and is raining. Ed says my letter did him so much good that he answered it soon, so he would get another one right speedily. If I had waited until to-morrow he would not get it until next week. Very damp and disagreeable. I miss prayer-meeting already.

Friday, March 21.

Snowing. At school all day. Evening. At home. Jen G. was here. Snyder spent the evening here. We had a very serious conversation. It has made me feel very badly. He asked me if I was "changed yet" and if I wanted to "discontinue keeping his company." I did not answer him to-night—for I could not. He said he would not insist upon an answer to-night. He told me to consult my feelings alone. Not to think of his feelings, or what he will think of it, but to consult my feelings alone. I feel very much worried. I am changed, yet, I was very much surprised when he told me he had not changed. I respect him and value his friendship highly. I have succeeded in overcoming my feelings, and do not think as much, in one way as I once did of him. It was hard for me to do it, and it will take some time to get back to the old "standpoint," if I ever can get back. I thought I ought to do it, and when I came to that conclusion I set to work immediately. I had many a hard struggle and a long one, and just when I am congratulating myself upon my success, I must be worried in this way. I am real sorry. I do not think I ought to keep his company and mother thinks so too, though I will consult my own feelings. I would not have written this in my diary, but some things which I wrote a long time ago required some explanation but no one shall ever see it while I live, and perhaps not after I am gone. I will do nothing rashly, and I have been praying for guidance, and I have no doubt I will get it— Nothing but trouble in this world.

Saturday, March 22.

Morning at home sewing. Afternoon. Went up street on business. To see Rose Guinn, Jennie Gilbert, Ann Culp, and Aunt Lizzie Myers. Home at 6 1/2. Evening. At home. Feel badly. Got a letter from father. A very welcome one too.

Sunday, March 23.

To S.S. at 9. Thought we would not have prayer meeting. Heard that Ellie A. was sick and went to see her. We had prayer meeting and Snyder led. I am so sorry I did not stay, for I wanted to have prayer meeting so much. Mother says they had a good one. I could cry because I missed it. Afternoon. To S.S. at 2. Felt miserably all afternoon. Home at 4. Grace and I stopped at the Catholic Church awhile. Disagreeable. Cloudy and cool. Evening. Snyder was here. I did not go to prayer-meeting. I did not feel like going though I had other and better reasons for staying at home. Spent a tolerable pleasant evening. Susie and Jennie went to prayer-meeting. Mr. M'Millan led. Feel a little sorry that I did not go, but I guess it is all right.

Monday, March 24.

At school all day. Morning. Helped mother wash awhile before school. Evening. Went down street on business and to see Cousin Annie Sheads. Stayed until 6. Annie came up street with me. Ann Maria Rupp was here, and spent the evening with us. Spent a pleasant evening. Annie was here for me to go up street but I could not. Cold. Annie is going to Baltimore to-morrow, and will stop in Lutherville. Her father, Uncle John, is there. I wish I was going along. Got a letter from Ed. Jen went to the Country this afternoon to stay a week or two.

Tuesday, March 25.

At school all day. Evening. Answered Ed's letter. Rose Guinn was here. We went up street and took a walk. Home at 7. Lizzie Rupp and Snyder spent the evening here. Snyder and I took Lizzie home about 9. After we came back we had a very serious chat. I answered his questions. I told him that I respected him, if possible more than ever, and valued his friendship highly but my feelings were changed, and I could not help it. If I had known all the time that he felt the same affection for me, there would be none of this trouble. I am real sorry. I told him that I did not think it would be right for me to keep his company as I once did. I have prayed over it and thought seriously of it and still think the same. Strange to say. He still thinks as much of me as ever, and he says that if I ever regret what I have told him, I must let him know, that he will be glad to hear it. Poor Snyder! I never in my life did any thing which went so hard, but I think I am doing right and cannot think otherwise. I may rue it and it would be like me if I would but "Time will tell." Everything looks dark now but I will try to do my duty and perhaps I may yet enjoy myself as I once did. But if I should not, I will have to "suffer and be strong" though no one shall ever know what has passed between us this evening unless someone should get this diary which is very unlikely. I would burn it first.

Wednesday, March 26.

At school all day. Evening. Got a letter from Jennie Gilbert and answered it immediately as she requested me to do so. Went to the post-office, and as the cars were not in, I thought I would go to see Rose awhile. While there Will came home and brought Thad Warren along. The cars did not come in until 8 so I stayed although I had no idea of doing so when I went. Spent a tolerably pleasant evening. Home at 9. Thad, of course, came with me. He was telling me some of his troubles. Poor fellow! Every one has their difficulties and I think that I particularly have my share. I only ask grace to bear them as I should. This has been a glorious day.

Thursday, March 27.

Very pleasant. At school all day. We have been moving some things to-day. We are to move on the first of April in to the house in which Uncle Lewis Myers now lives. Evening. Mother and I went to prayer-meeting. Mr. Warren led, enjoyed it tolerable. Home at 8. Feel miserably and have felt badly all day.

Friday, March 28.

At school all day, helping between times to move. Did several errands. Evening. At home. This has been a delightful day. Snyder spent the evening here. Spent a pleasant evening.

Saturday, March 29.

Very disagreeable. Afternoon. Snowing. Moving some things. Moved the bed occupied by Susy and me. Evening. Got my Teacher's Journal. Feel "awful" tired. Finished mother's dress, fixed her band and mended a dress for myself.

Sunday, March 30.

To Sunday School at 9. To preaching at 10 1/2. Our preacher in charge, Mr. Berkstresser preached. The text was—"I will therefore that men pray everywhere, lifting up holy hands, without wrath and doubting." The sermon was good, I think Bro. B. is a fine-looking man. Home at 12. Very disagreeable. Cloudy & cool. Sleeting awhile. Afternoon. To S.S. at 2. Snyder was Superintendent in Mr. Schick's absence. Had quite a storm. Lightning, thunder, rain, hail, and snow, all in one day. Home at 3 1/2. Evening. Snyder was here until church-time. Went to preaching at 7. Mr. Berkstresser preached. His text was "Her ways are ways of pleasantness and all her paths are peace." A very good, but rather a long sermon. Home at 8 1/2.

Monday, March 31.

At school all day. Moving between times. Evening. Feel very tired. Went to see Mr. Rupp's. They are to move to-morrow, and I am sorry for they are a pleasant family. Sade and I took a long walk. Home at 7. Snyder was down. It seems so queer to think we are going to move. I hate to leave the old house. I doubt very much if I ever spend as pleasant hours again as I spent in the "little front room." I certainly shall not spend any pleasanter hours. Oh! the "blest days of yore" and more particularly "the friends of my girlhood's early days."

Tuesday, April 1.

Moving day. Morning. Moving. Jen Gilbert got home from the country this morning and came right away up to help us. Beckie Belch was here and so was Rose Guinn. Snyder helped us. We had not much to do as we have been moving for the last week. I like our new home very much. Got a letter from Ed this afternoon. They have moved to Havre de Grace. Evening. Jen stayed. We took a walk. Feel very tired. We have had a good deal of fun to-day. Snyder and I took her home about 9 o'clock. Very pleasant.

Wednesday, April 2.

At school all day. Evening. Started to go out to take a music lesson (Uncle's have moved off 3/4 of a mile from town) but felt as badly that I could not walk so far, so I stopped to see Ann Culp awhile and went to see Rose Guinn a few minutes. Home at 7. Reading the Press.

Thursday, April 3.

At school all day. Very pleasant. Evening. Went to see Sade Rupp and the rest of the girls in their new home. Sade is not well. She has a bad cold and so have I. I feel miserably. My breast is so sore I can hardly talk. Jen was up before prayer-meeting time. Went to prayer-meeting. Mr. B. led. Enjoyed it tolerably. I could not sing. After it was over I went down to see Jen and she came along up with me to write a letter. Finished Ed's letter. This is a glorious night. So calm and bright—

> "The peaceful moon she sits above
> Encircled with a zone of love
> A zone of dim and tender light"

That will do for once I guess. Got a letter from Lizzie and Mattie Durboraw this evening.

Friday, April 4.

At school all day. Sade Rupp was here for supper. She stayed part of the evening. Lou and Lizzie were here. Harriet Shillen was here awhile. After they left went down to Jen's and we took a walk. Had a very pleasant walk. Very pleasant, Clear & moonlight. Home at 7. Snyder spent the evening here. Spent a very pleasant evening. A good deal like old times. Snyder's health is improving considerably and how thankful I am. And who knows but it is in answer to my prayer, for if I have prayed for one thing more than another, it is that his health may be restored. At all events I feel encouraged to pray on.

Saturday, April 5.

Working hard all day and feel very tired this evening. Went to see Jen. She was not at home, so I called on Ellie Aughinbaugh. They have moved and live next door to Jen. El and I took a long walk, tired as I was. Very pleasant. Home at 8.

Sunday, April 6.

Rose late. Did not go to Sunday School. Grace and I went to prayer-meeting. Enjoyed it tolerably. Mr. Osborne (a bible agent & a local preacher) led. Had no class. Home at 7 1/2. Afternoon. To S.S. at 2. Home at 3 1/2. Jen G. ... was here when I came home. She stayed for supper. We took a walk our old way; out Washington street, home at 5 1/2. Snyder was here until church time. To preaching at 7. Mr. Burkstresser's text was "The days of our years are three score years and ten; and if by reason of strength they be fourscore years, yet is their strength labor and Sorrows; for it is soon cut off and we fly away." The sermon was good but rather long. This is a glorious night. Clear and moonlight, neither warm nor cold. How I enjoy such nights, especially when I feel in a good humor with myself and everybody else, as I do now.

Monday, April 7.

At school all day. Very disagreeable. Cloudy and cool. Evening. Took a music lesson after school. Stopped to see Jen on the way home. She came up to the office with me. Met Snyder, he came home with me about 7 1/2. Cut a sun-bonnet for Mrs. Speights. Snowing. It looks very much like winter. Feel tired.

Tuesday, April 8.

At school all day. Morning, raining, sleeting and snowing. Evening. Snowing. Went up street on an errand and went to see Jen Gilbert. Home at 7. Snyder spent the evening, very much like old times, though I did not enjoy it so much. It seems queer to me when I think of it and the queerest part is, that I do not think so much of him as ever after all that has been said by him. I respect him more than ever, and have more confidence in him than I ever had and that was always a great deal. He is the same old friend whom I know and loved "in the happy days gone by." All the difference is, I am not the same "old Sallie," though that is only true in one respect. I do not love him now. What if I should get to thinking as much as ever of him again? Would not that be strange? If I ever do, my love will be tenfold stronger, deeper, purer, truer, and (shall I say it?) sweeter than it ever was. God bless my dear friend Snyder, for he is dear to me as a friend, as he ever was and I "should not wonder" if he is a dearer friend than ever, now I know how true he is and how scarce true friends are.

Wednesday, April 9.

Snowing all day, and this evening, from the appearance of the sky and ground one who did not know would think it was the middle of winter instead of the 9th of April. Still snowing. Went over to Mr. Shillen's intending to stay a few minutes and stayed until 8 1/2. Feel badly. I wonder if everyone gets "blues" or "horrors" as badly and as often as I do. The misery is, I can't tell exactly what is the cause of it. It is not very hard to guess though.

Thursday, April 10.

Very pleasant all day over-head. At school as usual. Evening. Sade Rupp and I were walking awhile. To prayer-meeting at 7 1/2. Mr. Berkstresser led. I enjoyed it just tolerably. At one time I thought I would enjoy it very much and thoughts of other things intruded and I did not feel so again. I feel so strangely. I cannot describe my feelings. I desire more than ever to be a true Christian & yet I find it so hard to fix my mind on religious subjects for any length of time. The cares of the world have more to do with it, I am afraid, than I am willing to own. I almost wish I could undo and unsay everything that has been said and done by me during this past twelve months. But I must battle with life and it is not as I wish it to be. I feel like being a better Christian but am almost ashamed to say it for I have said it so often and never perservered. Oh! Lord, help, "I am weak but thou art mighty. Guide me through life and afterward receive me to glory."

Friday, April 11.

At school all day. Evening. Sade Rupp and Jen Gilbert were here this evening. We all took a walk this is such a pleasant evening. Clear, warm & moonlight. How I could enjoy them if I had nothing to worry me, but— Oh well, what is the use in moralyzing or rather sentimentalizing over that which cannot be helped now, though it could have been at one time. Got home at 8. Snyder was here. He spent the evening here. Taking all things into consideration, if I could have my choice I believe I would rather feel as I felt, or rather have the trouble I had one year ago, than be worried and perplexed as I am now.

Saturday, April 12.

Morning. Delightful. At home helping do the housework. Afternoon. Jen and I went up street. I got a pair of fine shoes. We called on Mr. Rupp's family. Very pleasant. Jen and I took a long walk. Home at 4. Evening. Mother and I called on Mrs. Speights but she was not at home. Jen was here before time for choir-meeting. Lidie Powers and Sade Rupp were at the door a few minutes, also Harriet S. Had quite a conversation at the door with Snyder. He did not come in but it was pleasant at the door. It was delightful, such a pleasant moon-light. The moon is always pleasant, but then everybody knows that sometimes it is a good deal pleasanter than others. At least it is to me. Jen came up a few moments after prayer-meeting and brought Mr. Healkecker & Nat Martin, Mr. Vanderstoot and Ann, Mr. Rupp and Mr. C. Danner and Sade Rupp along. Quite a crowd.

Sunday, April 13.

Very pleasant. Morning cloudy. To S.S. at 7. To preaching at 10 1/2. Mr. Berkstresser. His text was "For bodily excess profiteth little: but godliness is profitable unto all things, having promise of the life that now is, and of that which is to come." To class after church, enjoyed it tolerably. We have not had class this year and I have been to class but once this year. To-day is twice. Afternoon. clear. To S.S. at 2. After S.S. Ada Mc and I started for the Cemetery and we met Snyder who accepted an invitation to go along. We went inside of the gate but it was too wet to go in. Home at 4. Had a pleasant walk. Ada, Harriet and I took a short walk, out Washington street. Evening. cloudy and raining a little. Mother, Ada and I went to church. Mr. Berkstresser preached. His text was "Best ye, beloved, building up yourselves on your most holy faith, praying in the Holy Ghost, keep yourselves in the love of God, looking for the mercy of our Lord Jesus Christ and eternal life." Dr. Baugher, Mr. Baugher's Father, closed. Home at 8 1/2. Raining.

Monday, April 14.

Morning. Rose at 6 1/2. Helped mother with the work. To school at 8 1/2. Home at 11 1/2. Sewing. Fixing a dress for myself. Cloudy, raining a while. Afternoon. Pleasant. To school at 2. Home at 5. Went out to Cousin Carrie's to get a lesson but she was not at home, so I practiced until 6 1/2. Stopped to see Jen. Home at 7. Mother and I went to see Mrs. Speights. While there Jen came for me and we went up street a few minutes. Home at 7 1/2. Warm but cloudy. Snyder spent the evening here. Sewed awhile. Feel tired and feel badly. Have the "blues."

Tuesday, April 15.

Cloudy, raining every "whipstitch." At school all day. Evening. Jen and I went down to Mr. Rupp's to spend the evening. Lidie Powers, Maggie Raimer, Martha Martin, Mr. E. Vanderstoot, Mr. J. Tipton, and Mr. C. Danner were there. Enjoyed nothing but some music, which Mr. Danner and Mr. Tipton favored us with. Home at 9 1/2. Jen and Mr. Danner came home with me. Cloudy. Very disagreeable. I wish I had stayed at home this evening. I did not feel much like going but as I had made an engagement I thought I must keep it.

Wednesday, April 16.

At school all day. Very pleasant, cloudy and clear, by times. Evening, clear. Very pleasant. Went down to Mr. Speights Gallery and had my likeness taken. Jen and I went down street and were walking awhile. Home at 8. Mother and Susie went away to spend the evening and I stayed home to keep house. Snyder spent the evening here. Did not spend a very pleasant evening. The children were troublesome. This is a glorious night. Clear and moonlight. It had been cloudy, but when I went to the door with Mr. Snyder, the moon was shining and the sky was clear. A few of the stars of the first magnitude were shining. The rest could be seen, for the heavens of the lovely "Queen of night" were too bright. I feel a little worried, but not very much. I am just in a humor to take everything coolly. I am glad I feel so, for if I allow myself to be worried at every thing which happens, (and which at one time should have completely unsettled me) I would go "mourning all my days," but as that will do no good to myself or those concerned, I think the better course is to put on a cheerful countenance and try to be contented. I suppose I can if I try. I always could do what I really tried to do.

Thursday, April 17.

Very pleasant. At school all day. Evening. Beckie Belch and I went to the store after school. Home at 6. Got a letter from father. A very welcome one too. Went to prayer-meeting at 7. Mr. Hardin, our Presiding elder, was there and led. He has come to attend Quarterly Meeting. Some years since, he was the junior preacher on Gettysburg Circuit. I enjoyed the meeting tolerably. I find so much trouble in keeping my thoughts fixed on Religious subjects for any length of time, but I am determined to persevere

> O! that in me the sacred fire
> Might now begin to glow
> Burn up the cross of base desire
> And make the mountains flow.
> O that it now from heaven might fall
> And all my sins consume
> Come Holy Ghost for thee I call
> Spirit of burning come
> Rending fire go through my heart
> Illuminate my soul
> Scatter thy life through every part
> And sanctify the whole"

To all of the sentiments and particularly the last stanza, my heart says Amen and amen.

Friday, April 18.

At school all day. Very warm. Afternoon. Had a refreshing shower which has made the air very pleasant. Evening, raining awhile. Ann Culp and I went to preaching. Mr. Hardin preached an excellent sermon. His text was "Then had the churches rest throughout all Judaea and Galilee and Samaria, and were edified and walking in the fear of the Lord, and in the comfort of the Holy Ghost, were multiplied." Home at 9. Stopped & had a long talk with Harriet about religion &c. She was busy working. Home at 10 1/2.

Saturday, April 19.

Morning. Rose at 6 with such a miserable headache that I had to lie down again until 8. Felt a little better and helped mother do the work. Our Quarterly Meeting commenced to-day. Went to the store and then to preaching at 10. Mr. Harden preached a splendid sermon. His text was "Of ye know these things, happy are ye if ye do them." His sermon encouraged me some, but oh! how weak I am, and what an unprofitable servant! Oh Lord, help to live nearer to thee. I am only safe when near thy side— Home at 11 1/2. Afternoon. Went over to Harriet's with my work. Fixing a spring dress. Evening. Sewing. Maggie Kuntz and Ellie Aughinbaugh were here. Ellie and I took a walk. Jen Gilbert came up and we went down street, met Sade R. and we all took a walk until 7 1/2. They went to choir meeting and I went to preaching. Mr. Hardin preached a good sermon, I suppose, for I was so tired and sick and worried that I could not pay as much attention to it as I should have done, and as I would like to have done. His text was "Likewise I say unto you, There is joy in the presence of the angel of God over one sinner that repenteth." Home at 9. Sewing awhile. Still have the headache. Hope it will be well by tomorrow.

Sunday, April 20.

Rose at 8. To lovefeast at 9. Did not enjoy it very much, but I feel somewhat encouraged to persevere in my efforts to gain a home in heaven. Did not speak. Sorry I did not. To preaching at 10 1/2. Mr. Hardin preached. His text was "Let us hear the conclusion of the whole matter: Fear God, and keep his commandments; for this is the whole duty of man." Oh! what an elegant sermon. So deep and yet so simple that the youngest believer might comprehend it. After preaching the sacrament of the Lord's Supper was administered. I enjoyed it very much and have dedicated myself anew to God. Oh that he may help me to keep my covenant. Raining. Ada and Laura M'Millan came home with me for dinner. Afternoon. Cloudy and cool. Ada and Laura and I stayed at home all afternoon, but feel condemned. I have been so trifling in my conversation. Snyder was here until time for church. Jen Gilbert was here awhile. Alas! for my good resolutions. Evening. Ada, Laura, sister Jennie and I went to church. Just in time to get a seat. The church was crowded. Mr. Hardin preached. His text was "And she called the name of the Lord that spake unto her, Thou God seest me." Home at 9. Snyder was at church, but of course he did not come home with me. He stopped at the door a few moments on his way home. Very disagreeable.

Monday, April 21.

Raining all day. At school as usual. After school this afternoon I went out to Carrie's for a music lesson through all the rain. Home at 7 1/2. Raining very hard. Almost a flood. Sewed at a dress for myself until 10 1/2. Feel tired.

Tuesday, April 22.

Clear and tolerably pleasant. At school all day. Afternoon. Got a letter from Ed. It is three weeks to-day since I have heard from him. He wants me to answer immediately to let him know something it does not suit to put on paper. I do not know whether I will answer soon or not. I think I will, under the circumstances. After school went out to practice. Practiced until 7 1/2. Snyder came out for me. Carrie sang and played for us. Spent a pleasant evening. Home at 9 1/2. Jeff played a trick on us. On the night of the 3rd of April, Jen and I played a trick on him & to-night he came home early and locked me and Snyder in the kitchen. We could not think what he was about until after it was done but we were a match for him. Snyder had a key which opened the back kitchen door. We went into the cellar from the yard and up to the door which opens from the pantry into the cellar. That was latched but we got it open at last and came up first-best after all. Cold.

Wednesday, April 23.

At school all day. Evening. Intended going out to get a music lesson after school this afternoon but it was so windy that I thought I had better stay at home. Harriet Shillen was here at noon. Spent the evening with her. Fixing a shaker for her. She has so many dresses to make now, and she needs her shaker so I am trimming it for her. Spent a very pleasant evening. Home at 10. Very windy and disagreeable. Cold.

Thursday, April 24.

Cloudy and cool. At school all day. Sewing at noon. Evening, at home, writing until prayer-meeting time. I answered Ed's letter, after thinking about it a good while. I wrote him a long letter and I guess a satisfactory one, I am anxious to get an answer. Georgia Wade was here, or rather Mrs. M'Clellan, for she was married last Tuesday one week, to Louis M'Clellan. Went to prayer meeting at 7 1/2. Mr. Berkstresser led. Enjoyed it tolerably. Home at 9.

Friday, April 25.

At school all day. Unpleasant. Windy and cloudy. Evening. After school this afternoon I went out to have a music lesson. Mr. Baugher went out nearly all the way with me. Had a pleasant walk and conversation. Home at 8. Stopped to see Jen. We came up street to-gether and walked awhile, but I was not well, and came home early.

Saturday, April 26.

Morning, at home busy. Helping mother. Afternoon. Went up street. Got my salary for March. Bought a parasol and some other things. Went out for a music lesson, but Carrie was sleeping and as she had a severe headache I did not waken her, but practiced an hour. Home at 4.

Rural Hill. I had written this far when I was agreeably surprised by a visit from Mattie and Lizzie Durboraw with two gentlemen. They stayed for supper, and after supper I came to Rural Hill, with Mattie and Mr. David Eckert, Lizzie and Mr. George Hartman following in their own buggie. Had a very pleasant evening with Maggie, Mrs. Durboraw and the rest of the family. Clear but cool.

Sunday, April 27.

Morning at Rural Hill reading. Afternoon. We all went to preaching at the school house. Mr. Berkstresser preached at 2 1/2. His text was [unclear text]. Evening. Gettysburg. After preaching, Mr. George Hartman and Lizzie brought me to Gettysburg. Had a delightful ride. We came up the Bonaughtown [Bonneauville] road. I came that road about 2 1/2 years since, with Mrs. Sanders, Jeff and Mr. Snyder. I could not help thinking of the changes which have occurred since then. Got home at 5 1/2 and George & Lizzie stayed for supper. They started about 6 1/2 for home. Snyder was here until church time. Ally Powers was here a few minutes. Jen G. came to go with me to church. Allie, Jen and I went at 7 1/4. Mr. Berkstresser preached. His text was "For what is a man profited if he shall gain the whole world and lose his own soul? or what shall a man give in exchange for his soul?" Feel very tired. Home at 9. Pleasant.

Monday, April 28.

At school. Very pleasant. Mother and I went up street at noon, and bought a carpet and a set of chairs. Afternoon. At school. Evening. Went out to get a music lesson at 5 1/2. Home at 7 1/2. Snyder spent the evening here. Cut a pattern for sleaves, and fixed the trimming on it, for Mattie and Lizzie. Feel tired.

Tuesday, April 29.

At school all day. Morning, raining. Afternoon. Went out to Carrie's after school to practice. Practiced awhile but felt too badly to stay long. Came in town about 7. Stopped to see Jen and we went up street. Met Sade Rupp and Lidie Powers. We walked around awhile. Home at 8. Feel too tired to work. May Powers and Ally Powers were here a good while. Feel miserably but why I feel so, I cannot nor will not commit to paper. Wrote to Mattie and Lizzie about their dresses—a sort of a business letter.

Wednesday, April 30.

Morning. As I was going to school, met Mr. Snyder. He started to Carlisle, with a gentleman who is going to consult a physician. He will only be away a day or two. At school all day. Evening. Went out to get a music lesson. Practiced awhile. Home at 7. Ada M'Millan was here when I came home. She stayed awhile and then we went up to the office. Got a letter from Mattie D. We walked awhile, and then it got dark, and Ada had to go home. Home at 8. Feel very tired. Cloudy.

Thursday, May 1.

Aunt Salome sent for me last night to stay with her. She was alone, and sick. Got home at 6. At school all day. Sewing at the carpet between times. Raining. Evening. Mother and I went to prayer-meeting but there was none. We came home about 8. Sewed at the carpet. Feel tired.

Friday, May 2.

At school all day. Finished the carpet this morning and at noon we tacked it down. Bought a dress and several other things this evening. Working at my bonnett. Fixing it for spring. Wrote to Mattie & Lizzie. A lady who lives near there is going down tomorrow and will take a letter down and also the things which I bought for their dresses. Very pleasant. Clear. Sny[der and] Jen Gilbert, came up and we took a long walk. Home at 6. Snyder spent the evening here. Did not spend a pleasant evening. For some time past mother has not liked to see Snyder coming here and scolded me every time he came for letting him stay late. I have not time, nor the inclination to write very much about it. I will only write that mother wrote to Father about it, and I do not know nor care what she wrote but this I know. He told mother to tell me that I must stop keeping Snyder's company, (How can I stop what I am not doing?) that he is astonished at me, etc. etc. I told him and he said it was nothing more than he expected, so he was not surprised. I care only on his account, I am perfectly satisfied, only I hate anyone to meddle in my affairs, especially such affairs. I will write more in the future.

Saturday, May 3.

Morning. Very busy helping with the work. Finished trimming my bonnett. Afternoon. Went up street to see Rose G. and Aunt Lizzie Myers, and then went out and got a music lesson. Practiced awhile. Came in town about 7. Stopped for Jen and we took a walk. Home at 8. Reading in book which Cousin Carrie lent me. The Hills of the Shatess [unclear text] by the author of the Wide Wide World. Like it tolerably so far, but think from reading the Wide Wide World that it will be very interesting. Clear and moonlight. In looking over my diary for yesterday I find these words. "I care only on his account—I am perfectly satisfied." That is not so. It was written when under the influence of feelings in which I should not indulge. I hope God will forgive me, and I mean to try to be more humble, but oh! my proud heart! — I care on my own account and his also. Perhaps the motive is selfish, I am all selfishness, wickedness and ingratitude. I almost wish I had never been born, or else that I could die and go where there is no sorrow. But I must prepare for it and if this is to help me, God alone knows the fiery ordeal through which I must pass and I feel I am passing through it now.

Sunday, May 4.

Mr. Berkstresser was here. To S.S. at 9. Laura M' and I took a walk after school. Osea is here from Harney's company looking very well. To prayer-meeting at 10 1/2. Did not enjoy it. Mr. Berkstresser led. Home at 12. Wrote to father. Afternoon. To S.S. at 2. Ally Powers and I took a walk after S.S. Home at 6. Evening. Snyder was here for the last time. He brought a book home that I had lent him. He stayed until church time. Went to preaching. Mr. Berkstresser preached. His text was "By faith Moses, when he was come to years, refused to be called the son of Pharaoh's daughter, choosing rather to suffer affliction with the people of God, than to enjoy the pleasures of sin for a season; esteeming the rewards of Christ greater riches than the treasures in Egypt, for he had respect unto the recompense of the great reward." Jennie Speights went with me and came home with me. Heard very little of the sermon. Felt too miserably to pay much attention. I could not help thinking of the hour I spent with Snyder. I cannot describe it, and would not if I could. He says I will have a friend in him as long as he lives. God bless him. Poor fellow! It is on my own and not only on his account that I care so much. I not only care much but very, very much.

Monday, May 5.

Morning. To school at 8. Home at 11. Feel miserably. Sewing awhile at noon. Afternoon. To school at 2. Wrote some poetry for S. which he requested me to do and sent it to him. Evening. Went out to practice. Stopped for Jen and we took a walk. Met Sade R., Lidie & Ally P. and we all took a walk. Got the journal and a letter from Mattie D. Home at 8 1/2. Feel tired and sad. Reading awhile. I wish I could claim the promise that "all things work together for good" etc., but alas, alas! I feel that I am not worthy. O God look in mercy upon me, and forgive me.

> Oh! drive these dark clouds from my sky
> Thy soul cheering presence restore
> O take me to thee upon high
> Where winter snow clouds are no more.

Amen to all especially the last two lines.

Tuesday, May 6.

At school all day. Sewing at noon. Went out and took a music lesson. Practiced awhile. Home at 7 1/2. Beckie Belch was here at noon. Went to see Harriet on an errand. Jen was up for me and came over to Harriet's for me. We took a walk and called to see Mr. Rupp's family. No one was there but Lizzie. Home at 9. Reading awhile in "Hills of the Shatess [unclear text]."

Wednesday, May 7.

At school all day. Sewing and reading at noon. Evening. Sewing awhile. Finished the "Hills of the Shatess [unclear text]." Find it very interesting. Especially the latter part about Winthrop and Elizabeth. Went to see Harriet a few minutes and to see Mr. Powers' girls. Thought I would stay until it was time to light the lamp and sew and stayed until 9. Feel miserably. I am just beginning to realize that I am done spending any evenings with Snyder. I wonder how all this will end! I would like to know and yet I am almost afraid. I am perfectly miserable. I neither enjoy religion or anything else. I do hope it will not last long. I can not bear it. I mean the feeling of desolation. I cannot write all I feel, and would not if I could.

Thursday, May 8.

At school all day. Went to see Rose Guinn at noon awhile. Started out to Mr. M'Millan's after school this afternoon. Got out about 5 1/2. They were just getting ready for supper. Met some one there of whom I was thinking all the way out. After supper we all took a walk over into the woods. Had a pleasant walk, but would not stay long as it was prayer-meeting evening. We started for G[ettysburg] about 7 o'clock. Had a pleasant walk but were late at prayer-meeting. Ada and I had a pleasant walk together in the woods. Our conversation was serious—about our troubles and Ada's especially. Poor Ada, and she thought Poor Sallie. So it is. Home at 8 1/2. Very pleasant but I did not enjoy the beauty of the night or prayer-meeting either. Oh! God, forgive me for my many & oft-repeated transgressions. Help me to be a better Christian and then I can hope for improvement in other respects.

Friday, May 9.

Morning. To school at 8. Filled out the cards for April. Home at 11. Wrote a note to Snyder asking his advice about something. He told me that whenever I felt like asking him anything or telling him anything I should write to him, that he would be glad to do anything for me. I did so. I think it is not wrong though I may be mistaken. If I am, I must suffer, for no one knows it but myself and if it be a sin I sin ignorantly. Very warm. Mother is not well, neither am I though Mother is worse than I am. Ironed my clothes after dinner. Afternoon. Got a letter from Ed. A real interesting one too. He is not well. The "sciatic nerve" of his hip is affected & the Dr. says he will not be able to do much this summer. He will try and go home when they are paid. The Dr. offered him a discharge and he would not accept it. The matter to which I referred on April 22nd is all right. He says he was a little surprised at me but when he read my letter he made up his mind that I was what I professed to be and he values my friendship more than ever. He says he was hardly able to write sooner and begs to be excused. Of course I will excuse him but when I write I can beg to be excused also. I am sorry he is sick. Poor fellow. Home at 6. Sewing awhile. Very pleasant. Evening. Got a letter from father and never was a letter more welcome. Jen Gilbert was here a few minutes. She was going away to spend the evening. Harriet S. and I took a long walk. Very warm & pleasant—moonlight.

Saturday, May 10.

Morning. Very busy. Snyder gave me an answer to my note. Afternoon. Feel sick. Mother got a letter from father. They have been paid & he sent some money home, and I had several errands to do for mother, though I was hardly able to go up street. Evening. While fixing Grace's hat, Kate Shillen came in, and after she went Jen G. came and of course we took a walk. Home at 8 and cleverly seated at my work when Harriet came for me to take a walk. The evening was pleasant, clear & moonlight, so I went. My throat is a little sore, I hope it will not last long. Finished Grace's hat about 10 1/2. Feel very tired.

Sunday, May 11.

Morning. Feel badly. My head aches & my throat is sore. Wrote an answer to Snyder's kind and welcome note of yesterday. To S.S. at 9. Ada and I took a walk. To preaching. Mr. Berkstresser preached. His text was "Come unto me, all ye that labor and are heavy laden, and I will give you rest." The closing remarks almost brought tears. I felt so badly that I would not stay until it was over, so while they were singing the last hymn I left. Clear and very warm. Home at 11 3/4. Afternoon. To S.S. at 2. Home at 3. Left as soon as I could. Wrote to Mattie & Lizzie, Mattie Robison is going down to-morrow and will take it along. Evening. Very pleasant.

Clear and warm. Snyder was at the window a few minutes. He is not well. Went to church. Mr. Berkstresser preached. His text was "If ye then, being evil, know how to give good gifts unto your children, how much more shall your heavenly Father give the Holy Spirit to them that ask him." Wrote to father.

Monday, May 12.

Awoke early but fell asleep and overslept myself. Rose at 7. To school at 8. Home at 11. Cut the skirt of my dress and got the facing for my dress. Snyder gave me an answer to my note. A very kind one, but it made me cry. To school at 2. Home at 5. Went out to Carrie's to have a lesson. Practiced awhile. Home at 7 1/2. Thought I would sew but it was so pleasant I did not. Harriet and I were running around. Real sorry I did not sew. Very pleasant. Moonlight.

Tuesday, May 13.

Rose at 6. Carried twelve buckets of water for mother. She is washing. Did a very tedious and tiresome job—Scalloped the top of the facing of my dress. Commenced seaming up the skirt when the bell rang. To school at 8. Home at 11. Finished seaming up my skirt and sewed the facing on. Afternoon. Went over to Harriet's and cut the lining for my sleeves. To the store in a hurry. To school at 2. Very warm. Home at 5. Intended going out to practice but did not. Took my work and went over to Harriet's. Cut my sleeves, and Harriet and I fit the body of my dress. Worked all evening. Had quite a storm. Raining. Home at 10. Feel tired.

Wednesday, May 14.

Rose at 6 1/2. Worked at my dress until school time. Cloudy & cool. Raining awhile. To school at 8. Home at 11. Went to the store for trimming for my dress. Home at 12. Ellie Aughinbaugh was here. Afternoon. Working at my dress. To school at 2. Home at 5. Sewing. Evening. Went over to Harriet's and cut the body of my dress while they went to church. Went to see Cousin Annie Sheads. She came home yesterday. She came along up with me. Sewing at my dress. Finished one sleeve, all but the trimming. There is a great deal of work about them. Sewed until 11. Feel very tired. Cloudy and cool.

Thursday, May 15.

Rose at 6 1/4. Finished the other sleeve of my dress before breakfast. I am anxious to get my dress done before Sunday. It is Shepherd's plaid, black & white barred. Clear. Very pleasant. To school at 8. Home at 11. Worked on my dress until school time. To school at 2. Home at 5. Worked at my dress until prayer-meeting time. To prayer-meeting at 7 1/2. Mr. Warren led. Did not enjoy it very much. Have a severe headache. Cloudy and raining awhile. Cool.

Friday, May 16.

Rose at 6. Worked at my dress until school time. To school at 8. Home at 10. Could not stay. Came home, and lay down awhile. To school at 2. Home at 5. Put the trimming on one sleeve. Took a short walk and met somebody and took a longer walk. Got a scolding when I came home. Went over to Harriet's and sewed at my dress until 9. Home at 10. Pleasant.

Saturday, May 17.

Rose at 6. Worked at my dress. Helped awhile at the work. Afternoon. Finished my dress. I like it very much. Started out to Mr. M'Millan's about 5. Met Snyder there but did not know he was to be there. I was not sorry. We took a walk over in the woods. Had a real pleasant walk. Started home about 9. I told mother that I would not be likely to come home tonight, and so when we got home the doors were all locked. I did not want to disturb her so I waited until Jefferson came which was after 11. Caught cold, and got a scolding in the bargain because I met Snyder. She says it was an arrangement but she is mistaken. Feel badly.

Sunday, May 18.

Rose at 9 and did not get to Sunday School. I could not get up any sooner. I was sleepy and tired. To prayer-meeting at 10 1/2. Mr. M'Millan led. Did not enjoy it any. Had a miserable head-ache, no wonder! We had no class but I stayed in church for Mr. Guinn's class. Snyder led part and then Mr. John Brinkerhoff closed. Enjoyed it tolerably. Home at 12. Afternoon. To Sunday school at 3. We stopped at the Catholic Church on the road home. Home at 4 1/2. Jen Gilbert was here and we took a walk to the cemetery. Met Snyder, by a previous arrangement—of course (?). Had a pleasant walk. Home at 6 1/2. Wrote to Ed. To church at 7 1/2. Mr. Morgan of Littlestown preached. His text was "Pray." He is preaching instead of Mr. Brown who was appointed by the Conference but whom our members refused to receive. His sermon was good but I did not enjoy it very much. Home at 9.

Monday, May 19.

Rose at 6 1/2. To school at 8. Home at 11. Went to see Jen. She sent for me for something. To see Rose awhile. To the store. Got a dress and stuff for a French jacket for Susie. Home at 12 1/2. To school at 2. Home at 5. Mr. Baugher is not at school today. His brother Nesbitt, a Lieutenant in our army, was wounded seven times while engaged in the battle at Pittsburg Landing. I think it was in that battle. His father went to see him as soon as the news reached Gettysburg. He left him about a week ago and then his physicians thought he was in a fair way to recover, but poor fellow! He died from the effect of his wounds, on last Friday. His remains will be sent home as soon as possible. I pity his family so much. His only sister Allie had just gone to New York on a visit and she has been sent for. What a sad time, then his remains arrive. Went out to see Carrie. I am not going to take any more music lessons until vacation which will be in two weeks. To see Ellie Aughinbaugh on business, Sade Rupp and I were walking. Home at 9 1/2.

Tuesday, May 20.

Slept late. To school at 8. Home at 11. Working at Susie's dress. Beckie Belch was here at noon. We went up street. To school at 2. Home at 5. Working at Susie's dress. Mrs. Speights sent for me to show her something about her dress. Home at 9. Feel very tired and also very badly. I cannot write down the cause of my miserable feelings. I already miss a friend who was always ready to sympathize with me and advise me.— Mother still thinks I met Snyder last Saturday evening by arrangement. That is something I shall never do. I think, at least I will never make a practice of it. I have more respect for myself than to meet any one any place else than at home when they dare not come there. Dare not! The very idea of such a thing provokes me and how much more the reality. I think it is too bad under the circumstances, and makes me feel as I never felt before. My feelings are anything but invisible. I suppose it will yield to time as things have done before. Poor consolation at present.

Wednesday, May 21.

Raining. Rose at 6. Wrote a letter to Mrs. Louisa Kuhn of Baltimore, (who visited Gettysburg last summer and is an old friend of mother's) for Uncle George Myers to take along. I forgot it until just before I rose. He starts to the city this morning. Wrote it and took it down to him just in time. Had a miserable walk. To school at 8. Home at 11. Working at Susie's dress. To school at 2. Lieut. Baugher's remains arrived in the afternoon train and out of respect to Mr. Baugher school was dismissed. Met Harriet Shillen and we went out to see him about 4 o'clock. I had no idea a human being could look as he did. I have not gotten over it yet. Poor fellow! Home at 4 1/2. Cut out all of Susie's dress, and sewed at it. Harriet wanted me to bring my sewing over there. I did so. Sewed until 10. Very pleasant.

Thursday, May 22.

To school at 8. Home at 11. Working at Susie's dress. Went up street to see Ellie A. about Susie's bonnet, and hats for Jennie and Bell. Very warm. To school at 2. Home at 5. Went several errands. To prayer meeting at 8. Mr. Snyder began to lead and then Mr. Berkstresser came in and closed. Have a dreadful cold. Did not enjoy it much. Home at 9. Harriet wanted me to come over and sew with her. I went home to get my sewing and as I was coming to the door Snyder passed. He stopped to talk awhile. Had decidedly an interesting conversation. More so to ourselves than it would be to anyone else. We were talking of texts, and about a piece of prose which I had copied for him on the subject of "Love" by Harriet Fry. Just before he went away he said, "Well, Sallie, I am going to give you a text and the next time you see me tell me whether you believe it as far as I am concerned."

"I will if I can." said I. "Where is it?"

"You will find it," he replied, "in 2nd Corinthians, 12th Chapter, 15th verse."

"Perhaps you are mistaken," said I, "but will I know the verse if I see the right one?"

"Yes," he answered, "you will." & with a good night we parted. Sewed until 10 1/2. Home at 11.

Friday, May 23.

To school at 8. Home at 11. Working at Susie's dress. To school at 2. Home at 5. Evening. Went to Mrs. Speight's and she helped me at Susie's dress. Home at 9 1/2. Went over to Harriet's and sewed until 11. Feel very tired. Cool but pleasant.

Saturday, May 24.

Morning. Sewing at Sue's dress. Afternoon. Pleasant. Finished that dress at last. Turned hats for Jennie and Bell. Altered the trimming on Grace's hat. Evening. Went down to Uncle George's for a pair of garters which Lou Kuhn bought for me in Baltimore. Met Jen. Walked awhile. Home at 8. This morning I asked mother if Snyder might come over this evening. She did not like it very much but did not say "no." I told him to come and then she scolded me for telling him. How would he have known it without me telling him? Spent a pleasant evening. The most pleasant one I have spent for some weeks. We had a serious conversation but it was the kind which benefits those engaged in it. He stayed rather late and I expect a scolding but we have no clock going. Oh! dear me! What shall I do? I cannot pray for I do not know what to pray for. I suppose Oh God! direct me in the right path!

Sunday, May 25.

According to expectations, got a scolding and of course was benefitted by it. To S.S. at 9. To preaching at 10 1/2. Mr. Morgan preached. His text was, And he said unto Jesus, Lord, remember me when thou comest unto thy kingdom. And Jesus said unto him, Verily I say unto thee, Today shalt thou be with me in paradise. To class. Did not enjoy it at all. Went from a sense of duty, not from any inclination. Oh! dear me. Will it always last? Afternoon. Beckie Belch went with me to S.S. Home at 3. Very pleasant. Went over to Aunt Salome's a few minutes. Harriet S. and I went to the cemetery. Had a delightful walk. To preaching at 7 1/2. Mr. Morgan preached. His text was "Turn you at my reproof: behold I will pour out my spirit unto you, I will make known my words unto you." Home at 9. Cool. Oh! I feel so miserably. I cannot describe my feelings. I miss Snyder so much. I am accustomed to making him my confidante, and although at one time, he did not visit me very often, yet when he was there (with a few exceptions) he was always ready to sympathize with me, and advise me. We spent a nice evening last night. I feel that I have wronged him, and yet he is still the same dear friend. He is indeed a brother, and now that I am deprived of the pleasure of spending my time with him (a part of it, I mean) I can appreciate the privilege, even at the risk of a scolding, if possible, I prize him more highly as a friend, and have stronger confidence in him than ever. God bless him! Amen!

Monday, May 26.

Rose at 6 1/2. Could not get time to sew but was busy all the time. Clear and pleasant, but cool. To school at 8. Feel miserably. Home at 11. Sewing. Finished fixing one dress and commenced fixing another. Very pleasant. Wrote a letter to Carlton and Porter renewing my subscription for the Teacher's Journal. To school at 2. Home at 5. Finished my dress. Ginnie Powers and I took a walk. Cousin Annie Sheads was here. Cool. Feel very tired. Had no sewing ready and did not sew.

Tuesday, May 27.

To school at 8. Home at 11. Commenced altering my new dress. It was too long in front. To school at 2. Home at 5. Finished fixing my dress and began Susy's French Jacket. May Powers was here with her work awhile. Ginnie Powers and Sade Rupp were here. We were enjoying ourselves finely. Cousin Lou, and Miss Mina Crise, (one of Carrie's scholars from Baltimore) were here. Very pleasant. Jen Gilbert was here but she could not stay long. Ginnie Powers and I took a walk. Home at 9. Had a long talk about the war, at the door with Snyder, and got a scolding when I went in. I had made up my mind what plan I am going to pursue and am going to persevere, mo matter how hard it goes, or what those who are concerned may think. I am tired of this way of living. I am unhappy any how, and may as well suffer in one way as another. Every time I am with Snyder I get a scolding and that makes me unhappy so, although it will be hard, I will avoid meeting him any place, and see if that will do any good. He will think strangely of it, no doubt, but I will trust to affection for me, and to his knowledge of the circumstances of the case, and I think I need have no fear of losing the esteem of the best friend I have. I almost wish I thought as much of him as I did at one time, but as it is, I do not. It seems strange to me and the more I think of it the stranger it seems. How will it all end.

Wednesday, May 28.

Rose at 6 1/2. Worked at Susy's jacket until 7 3/4. To school at 8. Warm and pleasant. Cloudy. Home at 11. Ironed my clothes. Worked at Susy's Jacket until school time. To school at 2. Home at 5. Working at Susy's Jacket. Cousin Annie Sheads came for me and I went down with my work. Went to see Aunt Agnes a few minutes. They live in the same house. Mattie P. was there. Sewed until 9 1/2. Home at 10. Cool. A lovely night. Clear and starlight but precious little I enjoy it.

Thursday, May 29.

Working at Susy's Jacket until school time. Very pleasant. Clear and cool. To school at 8. Home at 11. Finished Susy's Jacket. To school at 2. Home at 5. Sewing. To prayer meeting at 8. Mr. Berkstresser led and Mr. Drum exhorted. Home at 9. Father's company has been moved to Baltimore. Feel badly. Had this evening a strong temptation to break the resolution I recorded on last Sunday night but I resisted, successfully though it went very hard.

Friday, May 30.

To school at 8. Had an examination. The directors were there and some visitors. Did not dismiss until 12. Mr. B. Miss W. and myself had a very pleasant chat after the rest left. I feel sad always at the close of school, though I am glad in one way. Afternoon. Raining awhile. Fixed a dress for Grace and fixed my shaker. Went to the store for some stuff for a coat for myself. Evening. Intended going to Cousin Carrie's semi-monthly soiree but did not. Went to see Jen. She had gone and I did not stay very long. Home at 8. While looking out of one of the parlor windows (between 8 and 9) I saw Snyder coming so near that I was afraid I could not leave the window without him seeing me. I stayed and he stopped and talked until 10. I felt a little sorry afterwards that I had not gone in but—well I will try and be more careful. We had an interesting conversation notwithstanding the rain and fears of taking cold, and also the certainty of getting a scolding. I was anxious to have a conversation with him whether it was right or not, I do not know. Judging from the scolding, it was wrong.

Saturday, May 31.

Morning. Very busy. Did all the sweeping. Mother was working in the garden. Afternoon. Sewing at an apron for myself and trimmed Susy's summer bonnet. Evening, raining. Very disagreeable. Jen came up. I was real glad to see her. Went over to Mr. Powers's after she went home. Spent a pleasant hour with May. Home at 10. Feel miserably but I seldom feel any other way now. I do hope it will not last long. I suppose time will help me. It sometimes does wonders.

Sunday, June 1.

To S.S. at 9. To prayer meeting at 10 1/2. Had no class. Cool. Afternoon. To S.S. at 2. Left before it was over. Feel so badly. Evening reading. Jen came up to go to church with me. We went at 7 1/2. Mr. Morgan was there and as he had preached twice already, he did not feel able to preach. He was just commencing prayer meeting when Mr. Drum came and preached for him. His text was "But we preach of Christ crucified." His sermon was very good. Home at 9. Feel very badly.

Monday, June 2.

Rose at 6. Washing. Finished at 1 1/2. Had a large wash. Afternoon. Sewing. Made an apron for myself. Evening. Beckie Belch came for me to go out to Mr. M'Millan's with her. We went. Home at 7. Sewing awhile. Ginnie P. Sade R. and I took a walk. Got my Teacher's Journal and read it. Gave it to Snyder to read. I am the only subscriber in Gettysburg and he has been reading it since I take it. Had a long talk with him. Pleasant. Feel badly.

Tuesday, June 3.

Rose at 5 1/2. Ironed awhile. Went out to practice at 8. Home at 11 1/2. Very warm. Got my salary for April. Paid some debts. Home at 12. Finished ironing my clothes. Afternoon. Went over to Harriet's to cut out my coat. Worked at it until 7 1/2. Jen G. and her sister-in-law called this afternoon. Very warm but a shower refreshed us considerably. Evening. Helped Harriet at a hearth rug she is making for their fair which will be in August I suppose. Raining. Mrs. Speights was there. Spent a tolerably pleasant evening. Home at 9 1/2. Feel tired, sleepy and—miserable.

Wednesday, June 4.

Rose at 5. Helped awhile with the work. Sewing at my coat. Raining. I intended going out to take a music lesson but it was raining so very hard that I did not.

Afternoon. Still raining. Sewing at my coat. Went up street for some material for it. Evening. Raining very hard. Sewed until 9. Feel miserably. I do think I have more troubles and temptations than any one I know, and also less grace to bear them. The bitterest drop in my cup of misery, is the knowledge of the fact that I in a great degree have been the cause of it. Others are concerned but that is no consolation to me.

Thursday, June 5.

Rose at 4 3/4. Made the fire which I have not done for a long long time. Working at my coat. Cloudy & cool. Very disagreeable. Afternoon. Finished my coat. Like it very much. Evening. Cloudy. Mrs. Speights went with me to prayer meeting. Mr. T. Warren led. Did not enjoy it much. Stopped and sewed awhile at the rug for Harriet. Home at 10 1/2. Feel badly, that is about all I can write about it. Heard today that Fred Huber (a son of Dr. Huber) and Ed Wert were killed in the battle of Richmond. Poor fellows or rather their poor bereaved friends.

Friday, June 6.

Rose at 5 1/2. Commenced getting breakfast, made the fire etc. Saw Mr. Free, of York County whom I have not seen for nearly two years. He is going home this morning. Went out to Carrie's to get a music lesson at 7 1/2. Practiced until 12. Was very much interested in my lessons which was a song and accompaniment—"Cling to the rock boy cling." Home at 1 1/2. Did some sewing for Harriet. Evening. Ginnie Powers and I went down to Mr. Rupp's awhile. Mrs. Rupp's father, Mr. Gillespie was buried this morning. Jen G. was here. She, Ginnie and I took a walk. Home at 10. Very pleasant, moonlight.

Saturday, June 7.

Rose at 6 1/4. Helped with the work. Cleaned the front part of the house. Afternoon. Went to the store. Grace and I went out to Carrie's to practice. It was very pleasant and warm when we started but while it began to rain. Met Matt—something I forget what. Home at 8. Feel very tired. Had a temptation this evening which was peculiarly trying and the worst of it is, I yielded to it partially.

Sunday, June 8.

Rose at 7 1/2. Awoke early but did not arise. I will not do it again especially on Sunday morning. To S.S. at 9. To prayer meeting at 10 1/2. Mr Snyder led. Did not enjoy it very much. Cool and pleasant. Had no class. Home at 12. Afternoon. To S.S. at 2. To see Jen a few minutes. Home at 4. Evening. Very pleasant. Clear. There is no preaching anywhere but in St. James Church. There is to be a lecture delivered on the state of the Country. I am not going. Snyder spent the evening here. Spent a very pleasant evening with one exception. Very pleasant. Clear and moonlight. One year ago today brother left home to join the army. I am so glad he is home now.

Monday, June 9.

Rose at 5 1/2. Got the material for a bonnett. Ellie A. is going to make it for me. Went out to Carrie's to practice. Very pleasant. Clear. Home at 12. Afternoon. At home working for Susy. Evening. At home reading. Rose Guinn was here. We took a walk. Home at 8. Aunt Lizzie Myers was here. Harriet and I went in to Mr. Speights awhile. Home at 10. Very pleasant. Clear and moonlight.

Tuesday, June 10.

Rose at 6. Went out to practice at 7 1/2. Home at 12. Afternoon. Very disagreeable. Raining and cool. Working at Susy's dress. Evening. Worked awhile at Harriet's rug. Spent the greater part of the evening at Mr. Powers'. Home at 9 1/4. Feel miserably.

Wednesday, June 11.

Rose at 7. Went to practice at 7 1/2. Home at 12. Afternoon. Working for Susy. Oh! I feel so miserably! I wish I could write down what occurred this afternoon but I cannot—that is I cannot do it justice. I wish night were here. I could sleep and for a while forget my troubles. The resolution I adopted on the 27th of May, I find very difficult to keep. I often meet Snyder at the door, and as he lives very near us, it is not to be avoided except by rudeness and I will not be guilty of that to please anyone, particularly toward him. It is not very likely that I will go in if I chance to be out when I see him coming, and it is very provoking to have my own mother call such accidental meetings "arrangements" etc. etc. To be taunted and snapped at for my innocent chats with the best friend I have, is not very soothing. I may see him twice or three times a day and sometimes not for several days, and of course when I do see him it is all "understood" "a previous arrangement," of course I cannot imagine anything more provoking. I try hard to do what is right but the harder I try the worse I am. Time does not seem to be doing the work I expected him to do— Raining. Evening. Ellie Aughinbaugh was here. I went down street with her. Very disagreeable. Home at 9.

Thursday, June 12.

Rose at 6. Mother and I washed. Finished at 11. Sewing. Clear and pleasant. Warm. Have a dull head-ache. Afternoon. Went down to see Ellie A. with my work. While I was away Jen G. was here with her work. Home at 5. Evening. Mr. and Mrs. Speights and I went to prayer meeting. Mr. Sumwalt led. Did not enjoy it very much. Went down to Jen's and we took a long walk. Home at 10. Very pleasant. Clear and moonlight.

Friday, June 13.

Rose at 7. Ironing. Working at Susie's dress. Clear. Very warm. Afternoon. Working at Susie's dress. Evening. Mrs. Gilbert was here.

Saturday, June 14.

Rose at 6. Busy all morning. Afternoon. Sewing awhile. Went out to practice. Home at 8. Beckie Belch was with me. Jen G. came up and we walked until 9. Home at 9 1/2. Feel very tired. Had quite a hail-storm this afternoon.

Sunday, June 15.

Rose at 6. To S.S. at 9. To prayer-meeting at 10 1/2. Snyder led. Did not enjoy it very much. Had no class. Home at 12. Afternoon. To S.S. at 2. Very pleasant. Stopped at the Catholic Church after school. Home at 4 1/2. The reason why I stop at the Catholic Church so often is because I am fond of the music. Harriet S. is the organist. Evening. Very pleasant. Jen G. went with me to church. Mr. Morgan preached. His text was "And when he is come, he will reprove the world of sin, and righteousness, and of judgment." My mind wandered considerably. Cool. Home at 9. Clear.

Monday, June 16.

Morning. Rose late. At home, washing. Afternoon. Wrote a letter for Harriet. She is so busy. Went out to practice. Did not stay long. Felt like walking and so I went across to Mr. M'Millan's. They were very busy picking strawberries. Snyder was there. Spent a pleasant afternoon. Clear & cool. Evening. Very pleasant.

Home at 9. Snyder came with me. We went over to Harriet's and we (Kate, Harriet and I) were working at the rug. Spent a very pleasant evening. Home at 10 1/2. Mr. Baugher was here while I was away. I am real sorry I was not at home. It is very provoking that he should call the very first evening I have spent away in two weeks.

Tuesday, June 17.

Morning. Very cool. Practicing at Harriet's awhile. Ciphering and studying. Afternoon. Jen Gilbert came up and we were studying together. Beckie Belch was here. Mattie Durboraw & Mattie Robison were here. Had a letter from Lizzie D. Cut a coat pattern for the twins. They will be twenty years old tomorrow. Jen and I took a walk. Sade R. and I were walking. Evening. Cool. Mr. Baugher was here. We had a loud and to me very interesting conversation on school affairs. Feel sick. Have felt so all day.

Wednesday, June 18.

Morning. At home. Practicing awhile at Harriet's. Afternoon. Went down to Jen's. We were ciphering nearly all afternoon. Home at 7. Evening. Very pleasant. Went over to Harriet's and worked at the rug. Home at 10 1/2. Ginnie Powers wants me to come over to their house tomorrow to meet there. I shall go to prayer meeting.

Thursday, June 19.

Morning. Ironing. Uncle Robert Sheads was here a long time settling Grandfather Sheads' estate. He is a director, and we were talking a long time about school affairs. Afternoon. Good news! Good news! Father is home: but poor dear pa is not very well. We were all glad to see him. Went out to practice but precious little practicing I did. Home at 5. Harriet was here. Very pleasant. Evening. To prayer meeting at 8. Mr. Berkstresser led. I enjoyed it more than I have for some time. Cool. Home at 9. Heard some good music.

Friday, June 20.

Morning. Went several errands for mother. Got dresses for the children and herself. Went out to practice at 10. Home at 1. Afternoon. Feel badly. Sleeping nearly all afternoon, which I do not often do. I have not for years. Evening. Jen came up and we were studying awhile. Walked down street with Jen when she went home. On my way home, met Mr. Baugher, and he came home with me. He sent me a book to read. "Horace Mann's lectures on Education." Very pleasant.

Saturday, June 21.

Morning. At home working. Afternoon. Jen was here and we were studying nearly all afternoon. Evening. Jen, Vinie (her sister-in-law) and I were walking. Home at 8 1/2. Snyder and I went over to Harriet's and had some music. Mrs. Speights, Ginnie and Lidie Powers were there. Father was there awhile. Home at 10. Spent a tolerably pleasant evening. Got a letter from Mattie Durboraw and one from Fanny Coshun.

Sunday, June 22.

To S.S. at 9. To preaching at 10 1/2. Mr. Granger of Hanover exchanged with Mr. Morgan for today. His text was "Blessed is the man that endureth temptation, for when he is tried he shall receive the crown of life, which the Lord hath promised to them that love him." Oh! His sermon was splendid. I do not know when I have been a more interested listener. He seemed to feel everything he said. Home at 12 1/2. Very warm. To S.S. at 2. Home at 3 1/2. Evening. Father and I took a walk. I wanted to talk to him about my own private affairs and could not do so at home. I asked him if he thought it would be wrong for me to keep Snyder's company. He said all he objected to was keeping late hours. We had a long talk. I told him that I was not contented, that I thought more of Snyder than of any man I know; that instead of him staying away making me think less of him it had a contrary effect, that I could not keep anyone else's company with any satisfaction. In short, I told him the truth. I told him what I thought of keeping his company, which is this—I enjoy his company and he enjoys mine. Snyder's health (I think) will never allow him to marry and I would not marry him if I could. I do not love Snyder well enough to marry him but there is no one I like better. I can support myself and help father also, and as father is getting old and our family is large, I do not think I ought to marry if I could. Father supported me when I was a child and until I could support myself, and I think I would be very ungrateful to leave him now when I can in a measure repay his care for me. Under the circumstances I think there will be nothing wrong in my keeping his company. I will see what Mother says about it though that won't make much difference. Father says he has no objections, if I don't keep such late hours. That is reasonable and just like my own dear dear father. God bless him! Evening. Jen came up. To preaching at 8. Mr. Granger preached. His text was "Now when Daniel knew that the writing was signed, he went into his house; and his windows being open in his chamber toward Jerusalem, he kneeled upon his knees three times a day and prayed, and gave thanks before God, as he did aforetime." Home at 9 1/2.

Monday, June 23.

Morning. Jen and Emma Aughinbaugh came up for me and we went to the Teacher's examination, or rather the examination of all applicants for election or reelection to the schools of our district. Miss M'Curdy (it is said), is to be married soon, and as she and Miss Martin were not present at the examination they are not considered applicants and there will be two vacancies. Jen was examined. I got a good certificate, a Number one in everything which I have studied since I have left school. I have a better one than I received three years ago, and the standard has been raised considerably. The examination lasted until evening about 4 o'clock. It passed off very pleasantly as far as I was concerned. Eight of my acquaintances were examined. Jen was here for dinner and supper and part of the evening. Had quite a rain this afternoon & evening. Harriet Shillen was here. Feel badly that is, mentally. I am glad the examination is over, but that was the least of my trouble.

Tuesday, June 24.

My twentieth birthday. Morning. Rose at 5. Feel miserably. Washing. Cloudy and cool. Got a letter from Cousin Lib Myers. She scolds me for not writing. I never received her last letter. It is a dear letter just like the writer. Got a note from Beckie. Miss Whiteside and I (I suppose) have our situations, Beckie is 3rd Assistant, Sallie Witherow 4th, Jen Gilbert 5th & Lydia Swope is 6th. I am glad for Jen. Afternoon. Went up street to Uncle Robert's, Rose Guinn's, Mr. Gilbert's and to Mr. Fisher's. Home at 5. Evening. pleasant. Was talking to mother about keeping Snyder's company. She says I will rue it if I do and that I will not do it with her consent. When I asked her last week, she said she had nothing to do with it, and then I asked Father and he had no objections if we did not keep late hours. I told mother that, and she said she did not want to hear any more about it—that she was tired of it and that I had to give him up some time and might as well do it now. She has no sympathy for me, at least she does not act like it. Snyder was here this evening but mother thought there was no use to it. I never in my life spent as miserable a birthday, and hope I never will spend another like it. I have no enjoyment (that is, no lasting enjoyment) in anything. I feel perfectly miserable and in the future I can see no encouragement. Lizzie and Mattie D. want me to visit them. I think I will do so when I get my sewing done.

Wednesday, June 25.

Morning at home. Finished mending my new dress which I tore badly on Monday. Afternoon. Beckie and I went out to Cousin Carrie's. I was practicing awhile. We had not a very pleasant time. The cause of some hard words, was the late election of Teachers. Evening. Beckie Belch and Aunt Emily were here. Beckie and I took a long walk. Sade Rupp was here while I was away. Mr. Baugher was here too. I am sorry I was not at home. Home at 10. Stopped at Harriet's awhile.

Thursday, June 26.

Morning. At home. Sewing. Afternoon. At home. Reading and sleeping. Felt so sleepy that I could not stay awake. Evening. Mother, father and I called on Mr. and Mrs. Berkstresser. They are a very pleasant family. Went to prayer meeting at 7 1/2. Home at 8 1/2. Jen was here. We took a long walk & had (of course) a long talk. Home at 10. Jen, and Mr. Danner came home with me.

Friday, June 27.

Morning. At home. Sewing. Afternoon. At home. Reading. Evening. At home. Thinking. Harriet is thirty years old today. Very pleasant. Working at a dress for mother.

Saturday, June 28.

Morning. Sweeping. Afternoon. At Harriet's sewing. Very warm. Father is not at all well. I am afraid he will never be well enough to go back to camp. He is now taking medicine. I do hope he will soon recover. Evening. Pleasant. Jen Gilbert came up and we were walking. Home at 10. Working at Mother's dress.

Sunday, June 29.

To S.S. at 9. To prayer meeting at 10 1/2. Mr. M'Millan led. Enjoyed it tolerable. Had no class. Afternoon. Raining. To S.S. at 2. There were so few present that Mr. Schick thought it best to dismiss. Home at 3. Very warm. Evening. Went over to Mr. Powers's. Ginnie and I were singing some tunes in the "Shawon." To preaching at 7 1/2. Mr. Berkstresser preached. His text was "And now abideth faith, hope, charity, these three, but the greatest of these is charity." Home at 7 1/2. Feel tired and worried.

Monday, June 30.

Rose at 6. Helped mother wash. Working at mother's dress. Got it ready for Susy to finish. Warm. Very pleasant. Cut out dresses for Jennie and Bell. Teaching Jennie and Susy to sew. Afternoon. At home. Working at the children's dresses. Very warm. Father seems better today. He suffers very much from pain in his legs. There is no inflammation. I hope it is not Chronic Rheumatism.

Tuesday, July 1.

At home sewing. Evening. Anne Zeigler and Lidie Powers were here. Jennie and Vinie Gilbert came up for me to walk. Walked awhile. Stopped at Harriet's to sew at her rug. I was there alone (Harriet had gone downstreet with a lady and left me to keep house) when Snyder passed. I asked him to come in for I felt like talking to him. Home at 10. Had a pleasant chat at the door, but I expect a scolding tomorrow.

Wednesday, July 2.

At home all day. Raining. Sewing at the children's dresses. Sewed until 10. Feel very tired and miserable. As I expected, mother scolded me for sitting at the door so late. Jeff told her it was 1 o'clock. It struck 11 just as I went in. It was rather late but then if mother would let me use my own judgement there would be nothing of the kind. I think I am old enough to judge for myself but she does not seem to think so. I am tired of this way of living. It is unpleasant to all concerned.

Thursday, July 3.

At home sewing. Pleasant. Evening. Went to prayer meeting at 7 1/2. Mr. Berkstresser led. Enjoyed it tolerable. Callie Young and I went down to Mr. Gilbert's. Vinie and Jen went walking with us. Home at 10. Very pleasant. Clear and moonlight. All along the streets persons are taking in their steps, for fear of those "Young Americans" whose delight seems to be to remove steps, gates, etc. etc., as far out of the way as they conveniently can. To use a popular, but not very elegant expression, "Let them go it while they are young." Manhood and the stern realities of life will overtake them soon enough.

Friday, July 4.

Glorious Fourth. Morning. Sewing at Jennie's dress. It was so pleasant at the front door that I sat there with my work a long time. Had quite a conversation with Snyder about the war and the state of the country. Finished Jennie's dress. Very warm. Clear. Afternoon. Uncle Plank was here for dinner. He owns the house in which we live. Finished Bell's dress. Evening. Pleasant. Working. Jen and Vinie went to the country today. Home at 9 1/2.

Saturday, July 5.

Morning. At home working. Afternoon. At home sewing. Evening. Mary and Allie and I took a walk. Home at 9. A glorious night. Clear, warm and moonlight. Kate and Harriet S., Mrs. Speights, & Jennie, father, mother, Susy and I were sitting out until after 10, enjoyed the beautiful night. They were all talking "thoughother" and I—well, it isn't anybody's business what I was thinking about, or rather of whom I was thinking.

Sunday, July 6.

Morning. To S.S. at 9. To prayer meeting at 10 1/2. Snyder led. Enjoyed it right well. Had no class. Home at 12. Ada M'Millan came with me. Very, very warm. Afternoon. To S.S. at 2. Home at 3. Awful warm. Sad pity—the poor soldiers! Evening. Pleasant. Wrote to Mattie and Lizzie D. To preaching at 7 1/2. Mr. Berkstresser preached. His text was "Wherefore seeing we also are compassed about with so great a cloud of witnesses, let us lay aside every weight, and the sin which doth so easily beset us, and let us run with patience the race that is set before us." Very pleasant. A glorious night. Home at 9.

Monday, July 7.

Rose at 4 3/4. Sewing. Warm. Went up street. Got my salary for May. Home at 10. All of the family except Jefferson and me went out to Uncle Plank's. Afternoon. Very warm. Reading the news awhile. Fixing on getting ready to go away tomorrow morning. If nothing happens to prevent, I expect to go to Rural Hill tomorrow morning. Evening. Went up street with Harriet S. Home at 8. Snyder was here. We took a long walk, for mother told me not to dare to ask him to come in. Just to think of it! It is ridiculous. If I had felt like going in the house I would have done so anyhow, but I knew I could not have much of a talk with him at home. I feel miserably. I will have to give up his company, but that is all I shall do. Him, I will never give up as long as he lives and does nothing to forfeit my esteem. All the opposition with which I meet only serves to strengthen the friendship. I feel wretchedly, and no prospect of feeling any better about it. I am afraid it will never be any better and poor Snyder! he feels it worse than I do. I am afraid—I will not write my fears now. I wish it were otherwise.

Tuesday, July 8.

Morning. Rose at 5. Started for Rural Hill at 5 1/2 in the stage. Got here about 7. Was very kindly received but still feel very badly. Made a silk apron. Afternoon. Mr. and Mrs. John Coshun with their children came. He is Mrs. Durboraw's brother. Very warm. Went to the "Taverns" to send some word to mother. Was to see Harriet and Ellen Snyder. Ellen is living here with her Uncle and Aunt. Home at 7 1/2. Feel miserably but have spent as pleasant a day as I could expect and a much pleasanter one (I think) than I would have had at home. I know it should not be so.

Wednesday, July 9.

Rose at 5. Ironing and making some edging for Maggie. Afternoon. Went out and tried to pick cherries but I got dizzy and had to come down from the tree. I nearly fell down. I am sorry for I wanted to get some for mother but I will have to give it up. Evening. At home. Cloudy and raining.

Thursday, July 10.

Morning. Rose at 5. Seeding cherries. Raining. Afternoon. Seeding cherries. Reading awhile to Lizzie and Martha. Evening. Cloudy. Wrote a letter to Grace. Feel very badly. I suppose it is not necessary to state the reason—. Lizzie, Mattie and I started for prayer meeting but found the door shut, though it was cloudy and damp we had a pleasant walk home. Ellen Snyder was here today awhile.

Friday, July 11.

Rose at 5. Think it will clear—at least I hope so. Afternoon. At Mr. Joseph Coshun's sewing awhile for Jane. She picked some sour cherries for me. Carried them to the Taverns about two miles. Felt pretty tired when I got there. Wrote a letter to Grace, sent the cherries to mother. Went to the Post Office. Home at 7 1/2. Pleasant.

Saturday, July 12.

Morning. Sweeping. Afternoon. Martha and I went to the office and then to Mr. Young's and Mr. Conover's on business. Saw Mary, Maggie, Amanda and their younger sisters. Was very glad to see them. Saw Mrs. Baker of Gettysburg at her mother-in-law's. Home at 7. Harriet S. came with me home. Ellen S. came partway. Mrs. David Eiker was here. Spent a pleasant evening. We were singing. Wrote a letter to Bell.

Sunday, July 13.

Morning. Rose at 5. To S.S. at 8. Home at 11. Reading. Afternoon. To preaching at 2. Lizzie, Martha and Snyder went with me to the stone church (Lutheran). I was there last summer when I visited Rural Hill. Mr. Henry preached. His text was "Then said these men, we shall not find any occasion against this Daniel, except we find it against him concerning the law of his God." It is a mile walk going and coming. Home at 4 1/2. Mr. George Hartman was here. Very pleasant.

Monday, July 14.

Rose at 5. Morning at home. Afternoon. Wrote a letter to Snyder. There was nothing said about writing when I left as I did not know how long I would stay. Lizzie and I went over to Mr. Joseph Coshun's. I picked some currants. Sarah, Jen, and Lizzie helped me. Took them to the Taverns to send to mother. Mr. Durboraw took my letter to the Office and was too late and now it will have to be over until tomorrow evening. How very provoking. Reading awhile.

Tuesday, July 15.

Morning. Rose at 5. Ironing. Got letters from Harriet S, Susy and Snyder. They were all welcome especially the last-named. It was written the same day that mine was (yesterday) and if mine had gone when it should have gone he would have had it. They would have passed each other on the road. Afternoon. Had quite a thunderstorm. Martha and I were ironing. Very pleasant. Evening. Reading in "Parson Brownlow's Book."

Wednesday, July 16.

Overslept myself. Rose at 5 1/2. Wrote to Jen Gilbert. Very pleasant. Warm. Afternoon. Lizzie and I went to the store, and several other errands. Home at 4. Evening. Commenced fixing a dress for the girls. Sewing. Spent a pleasant evening. Had some pretty noisy fun.

Thursday, July 17.

Morning. Rose at 5. Got a letter from Snyder; a very welcome one. Perhaps if nothing interferes he will be down to see me next Saturday night. I wish he would come, but I will try and not think of it for fear I may be disappointed. Sewing. Afternoon. Wrote to Susy and Harriet Shillen. Maggie Durboraw picked my basket full of cherries and I carried them to the Taverns and sent them to mother. Home at 5 1/2. Very pleasant. Evening. Commenced answering Snyder's letter. I wish I was at prayer meeting tonight.

Friday, July 18.

Morning. Dreamed last night that some one was trying to stab me in the heart with a steak knife or a knife something like it. Was so frightened I awoke. Finished answering Snyder's letter and Mr. D took it to the office. Cloudy & disagreeable.

Saturday, July 19.

Morning. At home, busy. Afternoon. Spent with Ellen S. Evening. Dr. James [unclear text] and Miss Sophia Lynn came this evening. Miss L. is an old friend of Maggie's from Philadelphia. The Dr. is from Adams Co. and has been practicing his profession for some time away from home. He is Maggie's betrothed. He has been a volunteer Surgeon and has come home to recover his health. George Hartman and Dave Eckert were here. Snyder came and I was very glad to see him. George, Dave, Snyder, Martha, Lizzie and I spent a very very pleasant evening, the pleasantest one I have had for some time.

Sunday, July 20.

Morning. Rose early. Miss L. is going to spend some time here. Mrs. D., Lizzie, Mattie, Snyder and I went to S.S. at 8 1/2. Had prayer meeting after it. Snyder led. Afternoon. We all but Maggie and Mattie went to preaching. Mr. Berkstresser preached. His text was "Quench not the spirit." Dr. went home. Had class after preaching. Mr. Berkstresser led. Enjoyed it tolerably. Evening. Dave came for Mattie to go to preaching and wanted me to go along but I declined. Miss L. went. The ride will do her good. For my part I preferred staying at home and spending another evening with Snyder. We had a very pleasant evening together; no need to be afraid of a scolding.

Monday, July 21.

Morning. Rose early. Maggie, Martha, Snyder and I went over to Mr. Coshun's to pull flax. I never did it before. We were in the patch until dinner time. After dinner the rest went out again and I stayed with the babe while Mrs. C. picked my basket full of nice sour cherries. Started for the "Taverns" with them and S. went with me. We got there just in time to see the stage go through though he was too far up to hear me call if I had done so. I had to carry my cherries back again. Snyder went with me to the school house and we sat there and talked a long time before he started home. He went about sun-down. God bless him! All pleasant visits must have an end.

Tuesday, July 22.

Morning. Cloudy & rainy. At home sewing. Afternoon. Sewing. Put my cherries in the basket (I had put them on driers so they would not mould) and carried them to the "Taverns." Fortunately, I was in time for the stage. Lizzie came down about 6 and stayed awhile. Home at 7. Do not feel well. Have been thinking about Snyder all day. It has been a dull day. I was sewing and had ample time to think. These folks seem to think Snyder has the consumption: that is an agonizing thought, & it may be so. I know not. Oh! God help me to bear my trials—they come fast enough now!

Wednesday, July 23.

Morning. Slept a little later than usual. Had a letter from Snyder. A very welcome one, though not at all unexpected. Afternoon. Maggie, Lizzie & Miss Lynn went over to pull flax. Raining. Evening. Answered Snyder's letter, wrote him a long one, two sheets of the largest sized letter paper. I feel badly when I think of him. I know I will not be allowed to be with him any after I go home and one who never experienced such trouble cannot sympathize with me. I wonder how it will all end. I would like to know, and yet I am afraid. Oh! dear!

Thursday, July 24.

At home all day. Afternoon. Mrs. D. and I went out to pick blackberries this afternoon. I picked a basket-full and sent them to mother. Evening. Lizzie, Martha, Ellen Snyder and I went to prayer meeting. Mr. Jon. Young led. I enjoyed it just tolerably. Home at 9 1/2. Very pleasant after the rain. Got a letter from Papa this morning. He told me of the death of Cousin Melchior Sheads. Poor little fellow. I ought rather to pity his father and mother. Bereft of their only child, they are indeed to be pitied. May God sustain them.

Friday, July 25.

Morning. Rose at 6. Ironing. Miss Agnes Reilly is spending the day with us. Preparing to go home. Afternoon. Got ready, bade them all good bye and then Martha and I started to the Taverns to wait for the Stage. I felt very badly when I parted from them. They have all been so kind to me. They wanted me to stay until next week but I could not, although I would like to do so. Evening. In Gettysburgh. Pretty glad to get home. There was a letter here from Ed, written on the 11th of July and mailed on the 14th. It came early in the week. He is not well & says he would have written sooner but they were under marching orders and he knew not how I should direct an answer. They are still in Havre de Grace but they do not expect to be there long. Went down to Aunt Emily's. Poor soul. She seems like one distracted and Beckie is compelled to bear up on Aunt Emily's account. Beckie says everything she sees reminds her of him and it is indeed a sad, sad household when its light and life is gone. May God sustain them in their sad bereavement. Ginnie and Vinie Gilbert were here. Very pleasant. Feel tired.

Sunday, July 27.

Slept later than I have since I left home for the country. Sorry for it. Will try and do better in the future. Home at 7 1/2. To S.S. at 9. Had to meet my class. To prayer meeting at 10. Mr. McMillan led. I enjoyed it more than I have for some time. Oh! that God may help me to live a more consistent life. Afternoon. Very warm. To S.S. at 2. Home at 3 1/2. Jen G. was here. We took a short walk but had a serious talk. I do not feel as though I had done any sin by it. I think if it had been wrong I would have felt condemned by my conscience. Evening. Went to preaching. Mr. Berkstresser preached. Had a conversation with Mr. Snyder after church. Quite an interesting one.

Monday, July 28.

Morning sewing. Warm. Afternoon. Ann Culp sent for me to come and spend the afternoon with her. Met Mrs. Miller, Mrs. Blessing, Mrs. Reilly and Janie Culp there. Went to the store. Spent a tolerably pleasant afternoon. Evening. Ann Slentz was here. I went down street with her. Walking awhile with Lizzie Rupp. I got home about 8 1/2. About 5 minutes after Mr. Baugher had been here. How very provoking! This is the third time he has been here and I was not at home. Very pleasant. Clear and cool.

Tuesday, July 29.

At home. Sewing. Fixing my clothes. Evening. Ginnie Powers and I were walking. Home at 8. Feel very badly.

Wednesday, July 30.

Morning. Washing. Afternoon. Sewing. Evening. Went down street to see Jennie Gilbert and Rose Guinn. Home at 7. Reading, "Page's Theory & practice of teaching" lent me by Mr. Durboraw. Feel miserably. Wrote to the twins and sent them the trimming I got for their dresses. Very pleasant.

Thursday, July 31.

Morning. Ironing. Afternoon. At home sewing. Evening. Went to prayer meeting. Mr. Berkstresser led. Home at 9. Jen Gilbert came up & we took a walk. Home at 10. Father is worse. He was obliged to retire before dark. God bless my dear father, and speedily restore him to health.

Friday, August 1.

To School at 9. Spent a pleasant morning. Home at 12. Went to the Dr. for father. He came up to see him. It is a bilious attack. To school at 2. Home at 4. Went to the store with Beckie, with her for supper. Home at 7.

Saturday, August 2.

At home all day. Evening. Went with some ladies out to our Alms House. Dear me! what a place. Father seems better, thank God. Harriet Shillen & I were walking. Home at 10.

Sunday, August 3.

To S.S. at 9. To preaching at 10 1/2. Mr. Berkstresser preached. His text was "_____" well, I have forgotten it. After preaching we had communion. It was very solemn. I enjoyed it very much. Afternoon. Raining awhile. There was Union S.S. in the Presbyterian Church but I did not go. I was not very well and had no inclination to go. Evening. Went to preaching. Mr. Paxton a local preacher of Chambersburg, formerly of Gettysburg preached. Home at 9. Father is better.

Monday, August 4.

To school at 9. Home at 12. Afternoon. To school at 2. Home at 5. With the exception of the time I spent with Snyder at Mr. Durboraw's, today and Friday have been the pleasantest days I have spent since school broke up. I have had more to occupy my time & consequently, less time to think about my troubles. I was entrusted with an important secret this afternoon. From its nature I feel very much gratified with the confidence which is reposed in me, & shall do everything in my power to deserve that confidence & to keep it. Jennie Gilbert was here. Mr. Berkstresser walked to see father and the rest of us too, I suppose. Had a very pleasant evening, Jen and I were going to study & it was too late after Mr. B. left so we walked awhile.

Tuesday, August 5.

To school at 9. Home at 12. To school at 2. Home at 5. Evening. Harriet S. and I were walking. Home at 9 1/2. We were singing at our door, at the request of some of the neighbors. We were singing several patriotic songs.

Wednesday, August 6.

At school all day. Evening. At home. Father is getting a great deal better and I am thankful for it. He cannot go down street or in the sun.

Thursday, August 7.

At school all day. Evening. Very pleasant. Jen Gilbert was here. To prayer meeting at 7 1/2. Mr. Berkstresser led. Enjoyed it tolerably. Jen and I were walking after prayer meeting. Home at 10. Very pleasant. Moonlight. Had some fun which I enjoyed very much for the time. Mr. John Wills was at Mr. Shillen's door, and I stopped as I came home.

Friday, August 8.

At school all day. Evening. At home working at some crochet-braid. Sade Rupp and I went down street and were walking. Very pleasant. Home at 10. J.W. was at Mr. Shillen's again and we had more fun of the same kind that we had last night. Harriet says we have our recess in the evening, so we have, and we enjoy it too. Father is still getting better.

Saturday, August 9.

Morning. Cleaned up the front part of the house & scrubbed the pavement. Washed a dress and bound one around the skirt. Afternoon. Very warm. Went over to Mr. Shillen's with my work. Made or rather finished a white skirt. Sewed until 7 o'clock. 8 o'clock—I am too tired to have recess this evening so I will retire.

Sunday, August 10.

To S.S. at 9. To prayer meeting at 10 1/2. Mr. M'Millan led. Had no class. Very warm. Afternoon. To S.S. at 2. After today we have no S.S. in the afternoon until the warm weather is over. It was put to vote, and there was no dissenting voice. I did not vote, for I did not know which way to vote. As far as I am concerned I am glad of it, but still I think it is wrong, although I spoke to Mr. Speights about it among the first. Jen was here after S.S. Evening. Very pleasant. To preaching at 7 1/2. Mr. Morgan preached. His text was "But, I am like a green olive tree in the house of God: I trust in the mercy of God forever and ever." Home at 9.

Monday, August 11.

Morning. Rose late. To school at 9. Very warm. To school at 2. Home at 5. Evening. Very pleasant. Harriet and I went over to Mr. Berkstresser's. She wanted to fit a dress on Mrs. B. Had a pleasant chat with Mr. B. We went down street to hear the music in Christ's Church. This is Commencement week. The Blues Band from Baltimore is here. Home at 8. Prof J.F. Bower, of Littlestown called to see Harriet. He is from Germany and an excellent musician. He played some for us. He took Harriet and me a riding in his buggy. I have not enjoyed anything of the kind so much for a long time. It was so pleasant. Clear & moonlight. Had some fine fun this evening but alas! It cannot afford me any real enjoyment. There is a heaviness of heart under all that is not becoming any lighter, rather more heavy. Wrote a note to my best friend; I mean, of course to except our own family, and I sometimes think he is as good a friend as they. He certainly is better in some things.

Tuesday, August 12.

Rose at 6. Jen G. came up & we took a walk before school. To school at 9. Home at 12 1/2. Got an answer to the last letter I wrote to him while in the country. Very warm. To school at 2. Home at 5. Have no school until Friday on account of the Commencement exercises of Penn. College, which are a month earlier this year. Evening. Jen G. and I were walking while. Very pleasant. Home at 9. J. W. was here awhile. The Catholic S.S. have a picnic one week from tomorrow. Harriet & Kate want me to go along, but I cannot. I do not care very much about going.

Wednesday, August 13.

Morning. At home sewing. Maggie and Amanda Conover were here for me to go to the church with them but I was not ready and it was too late to get ready—. They went and came back for dinner. Very warm. Afternoon. Went with the girls up street to see a lady friend of theirs. Home at 2. Evening. Went with the girls to see our school building and then down to hear a Union speech on the [unclear text] by Mr. Gram Lashell (a young man of our town) who is one of Gen. Buell's bodyguards. Came home with Amanda & we spent quite a pleasant evening. Home at 10 1/2.

Thursday, August 14.

Morning. Rose at 5. The girls started home. I am sorry they could not stay for the exercises this morning. At home sewing. Afternoon. Commenced washing. Rather an unsuitable time but I could not help it. Put the clothes in rinse by 5 o'clock. Evening. Went to prayer meeting. Mr. Berkstresser led. Enjoyed it tolerably. Home at 9 1/2. Feel badly. Oh! if I could forget what has recurred within the last year, but that is idle wishing. I must still remember, though the memory of the past often brings tears to my eyes.

Friday, August 15.

Rose at 6. Helped mother put up the clothes. Harriet S. went to Baltimore this morning to see her brother John. He joined the Porter Guard Band last winter. He is very ill with consumption. Miss Gillespie of Gettysburg visited him while she was in Baltimore and when she came home she told Harriet that the Dr. told her that he did not think he would live a month. Poor fellow! I hope it is not so bad as it is represented. To school at 9. Very pleasant but very windy. Evening. Went down to see Beckie. We were walking awhile. Home at 9 1/2——Had quite a chat with S. at the door.

Saturday, August 16.

Morning. Ironing. Afternoon. Sewing. Father had a letter from Lieut. T.C. Norris of Co. F. 87th Penn Vol. He is to go to York to the hospital and there be examined by a physician. If unfit for duty he will be discharged. I wish he could stay at home. Evening. Went several errands for mother. So see Cousin A. P. Home at 8 1/2. Cool and pleasant.

Sunday, August 17.

To S.S. at 9. Thought we would not have prayer meeting so I went with Rose G. and Will to hear Mr. Bucher preach. His text was "He being dead yet speaketh." The sermon was good. We had prayer meeting for all. Home at 12. Afternoon. At home.

Wrote to Cousin Lizzie Myers. Evening. To prayer meeting at 7 1/2. Mr. M'Millan led. Enjoyed it tolerably. There were not very many there. Home at 9 1/4. Very cool.

Monday, August 18.

Father went at 7. I do hope he will get a discharge and come home soon. He certainly is unfit for duty. Went to the store and got some muslin for myself. Very pleasant. To school at 9. Home at 12. Afternoon. To school at 2. Home at 5. Beckie B., Jennie G. and I went down street. Evening. Reading "Tresch on the study of words." Ginnie Powers & I were walking to see Ann Culp. Home at 9 1/2. Met Cousin Carrie for the first time since June 25th. On that afternoon she used what I considered very insulting language to Beckie and me, because we happened to be teachers in the Public School and dared to defend ourselves and the Directors to the best of our ability from slander and malice. She said, "Quiet, sensible girls that could behave themselves were rejected and flirts and upstarts were retained." I have never been out since but three times have been very cooly treated by the three girls. This evening was the last, and it shall be the last. I can get along without them. They have been doing what I consider beneath me, making false impressions. They have repeatedly talked about Mr. Baugher in a way which is very inpalatable to me, considering he has been so kind to me.

Tuesday, August 19.

To school at 9. Very pleasant. Home at 12. Got Hookers Physiology. Am going to study it this fall & winter. Afternoon. To school at 2. Home at 5. Evening. Harriet came home. John is much better but is still very weak. He will be discharged and sent home in a day or two. Harriet got to Baltimore last Friday in time to see the "Porter Guards" leave for Washington. They were all mounted. Sadie Powers and I were walking. Very pleasant. Kate, J.W. & I had some noisy fun at Mrs. Shillen's door. Home at 9 1/2. Wrote a note to Snyder.

Continued from 18th.

I cannot endure having my friends talked about before me when there is no cause for it, but envy & prejudice and my disposition is not one to overlook anything of the kind myself. I can overlook talk about myself sooner than about friends but their "slang" was to me & Beck as much as anyone. Here after I shall keep at a respectful distance for the further I am from such people the better for both. I can forgive and I have no ill feeling for them but I can not forget it & do not wish to.

Wednesday, August 20.

Went to the shoe shop for mother. Very pleasant. Had a little chat with Snyder at the door. A kind of an answer to my note of yesterday. The Catholic Sunday School went out to Spangler's Springs this morning. Harriet wanted me to ask Mr. Baugher if I might go. He would have had no objections but I told them "Duty before pleasure." They will have a pleasant day. To school at 8 1/2. Home at 12. Afternoon. To school at 2. Home at 5. Evening. Carried wash water or rather helped to carry it. Reading in Hooker's Physiology. Harriet and I were walking awhile. Very pleasant. Ginnie P. & I took a long walk. Home at 9 1/2. Mother got a letter from father. He got to York safely and met with a kind reception. He says he knows nothing as yet about his own case, but thinks he will get a discharge and come home. I do not think there can be any doubt of it, as his health, which has not been good for years is materially impaired. They may detain for some duty at the hospital and in that case he would remain of course. We miss him so much. I wish he was at home to stay.

Thursday, August 21.

Morning. Helped mother wash awhile. Went over to Mr. Berkstresser's for my Hymn Book. He sent to New York for it and also for the 2nd Vol. of Dr. Wheden's Commentary on the New Testament. Like my Hymn Book very much. Warm. Very dusty. I do wish we would have rain soon. To school at 8 1/2. Home at 10. Afternoon. John Shillen came home unexpectedly. He is discharged. He looks better than I thought he would after all I had heard. To school at 2. Home at 5. Jen and I were walking. Evening. To prayer meeting at 7 1/2. Mr. M'Millan led. I did not enjoy it very much. Home at 9. Jen was here and we walked until 9 1/2. Very pleasant. Feel badly Mother and I had a very disagreeable conversation this morning, of which Snyder was the subject. She talked in a way which I will not hear from any one without defending myself. She accused me of being engaged and did it in a way which was insulting as well as unbecoming as a mother and a Christian. I know I said more than I should but the idea of her thinking such a thing of me is, to say the least, absurd. If she does not believe me she need not. I have done all I intend to do to convince her to the contrary. Oh! dear, what shall I do. I feel miserable——

Friday, August 22.

Morning. Ironed my own clothes according to orders. Mother is still angry with me. My God, what a life I am leading. I should better be in my grave. She has not spoken a kind word to me since yesterday morning. She will tell father and I care more for that. If I could tell him too, he would think better of it, but I will not do so. I have said so much to both of them as I intend to say, no differences what happens. If I am attacked again and accused of anything of the kind I will "hold my peace" and they may take out of my silence what they see fit to take out of it. I have repeatedly told them that there is nothing of the kind between us and if they don't believe it, they may leave it alone. To school at 8 1/2. Home at 12. Afternoon. To school at 2. Home at 5. Had sick head-ache. Slept until after 4. Feel little better. Evening. Studying in Fowler's large English Grammar from 3 1/2 until 7. Find it very interesting. I am studying it according to Mr. Baugher's advice. Walking awhile. Home at 9 1/2.

Saturday, August 23.

Morning. Helping at the work. Have the head-ache yet. Sewing at a skirt. Afternoon. Sewing at some things for myself. Evening. At home studying, or rather meditating. Very cool. Reading in Hooker's Physiology. I like it very much.

Sunday, August 24.

Morning. To S.S. at 9. To prayer meeting at 10 1/2. Mr. Warren led. Enjoyed it tolerably. Had no Class. It's been very pleasant. Ada & Laura M'Millan, Callie Young and I went to the Cemetery. Had a pleasant walk. Home at 1. Afternoon. Went to the Lutheran S.S. at 1 1/2. Visited their infant S.S. Stopped at the Catholic Church on my road home. For the first time, got tired of the sounds which seem to me so silly. Home at 4. Evening. Reading. Went to preaching. Mr. Berkstresser preached a pretty long sermon. Home at 9. Cool. Had a talk (a short one) to Snyder at the door about returning my letters. I suppose he will, and I also suppose I will return his though I would much rather keep them. I am afraid he should be taken sick suddenly and then my letters would fall into the hands of those who would use them to my injury. There is nothing in them of which I am ashamed, but they concern no one but ourselves, & in the hands of an enemy would be used in a manner which would be more novel than agreeable. I dislike to return his but of course must do it. As far as he is concerned, I would rather he would keep them but for those reasons I think it best to return them.

Monday, August 25.

Morning. To school at 8 3/4. Home at 12. Afternoon. To school at 2. Home at 5. Evening. Went several errands for mother. Sewing awhile. Cut an apron body for Jennie. Kate Shillen & I were walking. Ginnie Powers and I were star-gazing. We studied Astronomy together some years ago with Mr. Conover, who was Principal of the Gettysburg Public School & our teacher. Had a pleasant time.

Tuesday, August 26.

Morning. Pleasant. Went to the store for mother. To school at 8 3/4. Home at 12. Afternoon. To school at 2. Home at 5. Went to the shoe store for mother. Aunt Agnes was here all afternoon. Evening. Sewed at the children's aprons. Went to see Aunt Lizzie Myers. To see Jen G. She was not at home. Home at 9.

Wednesday, August 27.

Morning. Rose at 5. Carried some wash water. Helped mother wash until 7. Sewed at Bell's apron. To school at 9. Made a change in my Arithmetic and Geography Classes. Home at 12. Afternoon. To school at 2. Went out to see Cousin Carrie after school. At noon I heard that some one had been busy enough to carry some news (not exactly news) for they told some lies. I did not ask who did it for I do not want to know who would be so devoid of principle. I concluded to go out to see her & have a talk with her. I did so and am very glad I did. We had a long talk over it. Carrie says she had no idea of us when she said what she did. She said she considered herself too much of a lady to insult anyone in her own house. She said she did not speak any more than to exchange the civilities of the evening when I met her one week ago last Monday evening, for she thought from what she had heard that it was all I cared for. What she heard was untrue. I will finish my music lessons, I think it best. Evening. Home at 7. Jennie Gilbert was up to see me, also Sade Rupp. Sade & I took Jen home & then we walked a good while. Home at 9.

Thursday, August 28.

Rose at 5 1/2. Helped mother iron. Sewed at Jennie's apron. To school at 9. Feel very badly. I am not at all well. Home at 12. Afternoon. To school at 2. Home at 5. Evening. Sewing. To prayer meeting at 7 1/2. Mr M'Millan led. Did not enjoy it very much. Home at 12. Talking to Snyder at the door. We talked longer than I intended to talk and mother called me in, the first time she ever did anything of that kind. She scolded me after I came in. I don't blame her for it if she had only done it in a different way. Oh! dear, what will I do. I sometimes feel tempted to wish I were dead.

Friday, August 29.

Morning. Feel perfectly miserable. Had a conversation with mother which was not calculated to make me feel any better. From her own words she must have been at the window upstairs listening when I was talking to Snyder. She heard me tell him something that she had said to me about him. It was nothing but the truth and as it concerned him I told him. He is the only confidante I have & as I have every reason to believe that he is a sincere friend, & means all he professes, I intend to tell him all my own troubles as far as I can. There are some things which I can tell no one, & among them I count those secrets which have been confided to me by others and they are not a few. I will not pretend to say whether it was right or not for me to tell Snyder that but this I will say, my conscience does not condemn me. I feel better for having unburdened my mind. To school at 9, but was so disturbed in my mind that I could not hear a class the first half hour. I could not keep from crying—all I could do, I could not even control my feelings long enough to be present in the room. Home at 12 1/2.

Afternoon. To school at 2. Home at 5. Evening. At home sewing. Reading awhile. Very pleasant. Feel badly.

Saturday, August 30.

Morning. At home. Helping mother at the housework. Sewing awhile. Afternoon. Went out to practice at 1. Practiced about three hours. Carrie played & sang some new songs for me. Home at 5. Evening. Sewed until I could not see any more. Went down to see Jen. We were walking a long time & talking about our schools. We are going to study next week or rather we are going to commence then. Got Andrews & Stoddarts Latin Grammar & Reader at Mr. Buehler's. Mr. Baugher very kindly offered to hear my recitations in Latin if I would study it & he also urged me to study it. He says it will be of great benefit to me. I want to study a good deal this winter & think I will unless something should occur which is entirely unforeseen now. I will not forget to ask God's blessing on the endeavor as well as on every other which I shall make. Home at 9. Feel very badly.

Sunday, August 31.

Slept late. To S.S. at 9. To preaching at 10 1/2. Mr. Berkstresser preached. His text was "He that hath on earth [unclear text] let him hear what the Spirit saith unto the churches: To him that overcometh will I give to eat of the hidden manna & will give him a white stone, & in the stone a new name written which no man knoweth saving he that receiveth it." The sermon was very good. Had no class. Home at 12. Afternoon. To S.S. at 2. Home at 3. As I was going out the door to go to S.S. Snyder passed & of course I went down street with him. Who wouldn't, it was raining when school was dismissed & as I had no umbrella he was kind enough to get me one. When I came home, while at the supper table mother commenced scolding me again. She told me I must either give him up as a friend or else give her up. Of course I will do neither simply because it is impossible. I put all his letters in an envelope and sent them to him through the office along with a note telling him that henceforth we must meet as strangers & assuring him of my sincere friendship & love. I never since his recovery would confess to myself that I loved him. Now I know I do. Mere friendship would not stand such a test. I told him it was because I loved him that I thought we should meet as strangers. Then mother will think better of both of us. Evening. To preaching at 7 1/2. Mr. Berkstresser preached. Raining. Had a good sermon. Home at 8 1/2.

Monday, September 1.

Morning. Rose at 6 1/2. Helped at the work. Commenced a dress for mother. Pleasant. To school at 9. Home at 12. Afternoon. To school at 2. Home at 5. Jen came with me. We were caught in a heavy rain. Evening. Sewing at mother's dress. Cut it out at noon. Made nearly all of the body this evening. Pleasant. Clear & moonlight.

Tuesday, September 2.

Morning. Sewing at mother's dress. Went to the office. Got my letters that I had written to Snyder, also a note from him. He begged me not to say we should meet as strangers, but it must be so. When I told him of the change in my feelings six months ago he was surprised & he wished me to promise that if ever I felt the same love for him that I once did, I would let him know. I have not tried to overcome my feelings and have come to the conclusion that I think as much of him as ever. He has thought so himself for some time but as I was fearful of being mistaken I was very positive that it was only friendship and he hardly knew what to think of it. Of course, after promising to tell him of it, I did so. He was very glad. He had said that when I told him what he would like to hear he would tell me how much he thought of me. In his note he said he could not tell me how much he thought of me but he would do the best he could. He said I never could think more of him than he did of me, that I was dearer to him than ever. He said perhaps he would write another note to me that he felt like writing then but he could not. He had this remark in the letter, "This I will say, If my circumstances would justify me in selecting a companion, & the lady I love best would accept my offer, we would both be happier in the future than we have been in the past." He adds, "May the blessing of the Lord rest upon you." I hope God's blessing may rest upon him in all its fullness. I feel to a certain extent better since I wrote the note to him & received his answer, but still it is very hard to give him up forever, for I feel that I am doing so. May God help me. To school at 9. Home at 12. Sewing at noon. To school at 2—Home at 5. Went out to practice. Home at 7 1/2. Ginnie Powers & I were walking. It was so pleasant.

Wednesday, September 3.

Morning. Was very much frightened early this morning about 1 1/2 o'clock. Someone tried to get in the house. Some rascals have [been] committing depredations in our neighborhood and we of course cannot expect to escape. We were awakened & struck a light and by that time whoever it was had "skedaddled." Washed awhile. It is just one year since father entered the army. He is now in York at the Hospital & is slowly improving. To school at 9. Home at 12. Afternoon. To school at 2. Home at 5. Evening. Sewing at mother's dress. Very pleasant. Clear and moonlight. Ginnie Powers & I were walking. Had a very pleasant walk. Home at 9.

Thursday, September 4.

Morning. Ironing. To school at 9. Home at 12. Cool & pleasant. Afternoon. To school at 2. Home at 5. Evening. Sewing awhile. Studying my Latin Grammar. To prayer meeting at 7 1/2. Mr. Berkstresser led. Enjoyed it tolerably. Had a Sunday School meeting after prayer meeting. Mr. John Culp is Superintendent, Mr. Will Guinn is assistant. Home at 9. Delightful. Clear & moon-light.

Friday, September 5.

Morning. Slept late. To see Dr. Fahnestock at 8. Got my salary for August. Gave him all of it. I owed him a bill, for some things which I got in vacation when I had not the money to pay him, & he very kindly waited. To school at 9. Very pleasant. Clear. Home at 5. Evening. It is just twenty-five years since father & mother were married. Went out to Cousin Carrie's. Took a music lesson. Had a very pleasant one. Home at 7 1/2. Very pleasant, Moon-light.

Saturday, September 6.

Morning. Sewing at mother's dress. Several hundred sick soldiers are to be brought from Frederick, Md. to Gettysburg and to be taken on to York to-morrow. Report says the rebels are in possession of Frederick, or are very near it. Afternoon. Went out to practice at 12 1/2. Home at 4 1/2. The soldiers have come, and also some of the Loudon Rangers from Loudon County Vir. Quite an exciting time. Warm. Evening. Walking. Our streets are crowded. Wagons & other vehicles to be seen in every direction. The Loudon Rangers number twenty or twenty-five cavalry. Very pleasant. There is a great excitement all around though for a wonder I feel calm & self-possessed. Hope it will last.

Sunday, September 7.

Morning. Had no S.S. [unclear text] body [unclear text] as every man in town had to go and see that the sick soldiers were safely started. To prayer meeting at 10

1/2. Snyder led. Enjoyed it. We had class in the church after prayer meeting. Had a good class. Home at 12. Afternoon. To S.S. at 2. Our new Superintendent was not there. Our new Ass't was. Very warm. Home at 3 1/2. Evening. Sleeping from 4 1/2 until 6 1/2. Ally Powers and I started for church but every church in town is closed so we came home again. Very pleasant. Went over to Mr. Powers' with Ally. Mr. Sharp of the 82nd Ohio infantry was there. Now 40 more sick soldiers were brought from Frederick. Mr. Sharp was one of them. They were to go to York tomorrow. There is great excitement in town. Reports of all kinds are in circulation. As Brother Jeff says "You can hear any kind of news you wish to hear now." I feel very calm as far as that is concerned though not as calm in some other respects.

Monday, September 8.

Morning. Sewing at mother's dress. She wanted to know if I am going to give up Snyder. I told her that I had returned his letters & received mine from him and that I told him that in the future we must meet as strangers. She says that is not enough, that I am trying to deceive them. Just think of it. She says she has written to father about it & he wrote a few lines & said she might do as she pleased about giving them to me. She says she knows things & has heard things which lead her to believe that I am deceiving her. There is an old adage, "Listeners never hear any good of themselves." I suppose she has got my diary & read it for I had it in a drawer which is unlocked. In the future I shall keep it with me. She does not know whether she will give me father's note or not. She may do as she pleases about it. I shall not ask for it. She says I am trying to make them believe that I do not care anything about Snyder. It is nobody's business whether I like him or not & no one is going to know from me. I have resolved to give him up, & we have met as strangers & will continue to do so, but that is all I will do. To school at 9. Warm. Home at 12. Sewing at mother's dress. Afternoon. To school at 2. Home at 5. Evening. Went out to practice at 6. Home at 7 1/2. Very pleasant. Clear, warm & moonlight. Ginnie Powers & I were walking. Home at 9.

Tuesday, September 9.

Morning. Mending a dress. Working at mother's dress awhile. Very pleasant. Clear. To school at 9. Home at 12. Afternoon. Sewing at mother's dress. To school at 2. Home at 5. Evening. Went out to practice at 5 3/4. Did not practice much. Miss Hester Moore who is in the Country for her health is at Uncle Elias's and she is going home to-morrow. Was talking to her a long time. She is a Methodist from Baltimore. As there is much excitement now she thinks she ought to be at home. The Baltimore American stated today that the rebels were in Gettysburg & Hanover Penna. Home at 8 1/2. Cousin Carrie & Mr. Moore came with me. Very pleasant, clear. Annie Powers & I were walking. Mr. Reynolds one of the Wisconsin Cavalry is there. He was there on last Saturday night. He had been in Frederick at the hospital & went to York on Sunday. He leaves for Frederick to-morrow I believe. Home at 10.

Wednesday, September 10.

Morning. Rose at 6. Washing & carrying water. Warm. To school at 9. Home at 12. Afternoon. Sewing at mother's dress. To school at 2. Met Snyder. He gave me the promised answer to my note, four sheets of large letter paper. I am going to return it. It is no good as a sermon. God bless him. I never before knew how much he thinks of me. Home at 5. Evening. Went out to Carrie's. Took a music lesson. Home at 7 1/2. Went over to Harriet's with my work. Sewed at mother's dress. Home at 9 1/2. Very pleasant but cloudy.

Thursday, September 11.

Morning. Jefferson & Mr. C. Danner went to York this morning. Mr. D to see his brother & Jefferson to see father. Ironing. To school at 9. Pleasant. Cloudy. Hope we will have rain. Home at 12. Studying at noon. Afternoon. To school at 2. Home at 5. Evening. Sewing awhile but there is too much excitement now to do much of anything. Every few minutes there comes a new report & every one is in an uproar. To prayer meeting at 7 1/2. Home at 8 1/2. Practiced after school awhile.

Friday, September 12.

At school all day. Evening. Sewing at mother's dress awhile. Could not work very much. Walking awhile.

Saturday, September 13.

At home all day, sewing at mother's dress. It was reported & believed in town that a party of rebels were coming to Gettysburgh and that our town companies were to go out to meet them. It was a false report however. Evening. Feel very tired but not too tired to walk awhile. Jen & I were walking. Home at 7.

Sunday, September 14.

To S.S. at 9. To preaching at 10 1/2. Mr. Morgan preached. Had no class. Home at 12. Three Regiments of cavalry came from Frederick to-day. The 8th & 12th Pennsylvania & the 1st New York. They are to stay here for further orders. They have seen pretty hard service from their appearance. Afternoon. To S.S. at 2. Home at 3. Evening. The appearance of the town reminds me of when the Porter Guards were here. To preaching at 7. Mr. Morgan preached. Home at 8 1/2. Very pleasant.

Monday, September 15.

Morning. Rose at 6. Washing. To school at 9. Dismissed at 10. The soldiers are going to leave this afternoon & as there is so much excitement the school is small. Harriet, Kate, their uncle & I went down to the camp to see them. They are all packing up ready to leave. Home at 12. Afternoon. Have no school. The three Regiments have left after a great excitement. I am sorry they are leaving, for I think we are in some danger though I am not very much alarmed! Evening. At Mr. M'Millan's. Spent a very pleasant evening. Susie came home with me. Jennie Buckingham & her sister Emma were there. Had quite an interesting chat with Snyder. He was there, I saw him in town only a few moments before I went out. If I had known he was there I would not have gone out. I would not under the circumstances allow him to accompany me home although it would have been very pleasant, & oh! how I enjoyed an hour with him, more so because I seldom can talk to him.

Tuesday, September 16.

Morning. Rose at 6. Sewed until 8 1/2. To school at 9. Mr. Baugher & a great many of our town men have gone to see the battle-ground. It is near Frederick and extends a great way I believe. Home at 12. Afternoon. To school at 2. Home at 5. Evening. Went out to practice but did not practice much. There was company there & we had some fine music. Cousin C. has two new scholars from Baltimore. Misses Emma & Kate Callow. They were singing & playing for us. Aunt Salome & Mrs. [unclear text] were there. Home at 8 3/4. Stopped to see Harriet awhile. Cloudy. Hope we will have rain.

Wednesday, September 17.

Morning. Cloudy & rainy occasionally. To school at 8 1/4. Home at 12. Afternoon. To school at 2. Home at 5. Evening. Went out to Cousin Carrie's. Had a music lesson. I love my music lessons so much. It is only pleasant recreation and not a task. Practiced awhile. Home at 7 1/2. Reading awhile.

Thursday, September 18.

At school all day. Evening. Started out to practice but was caught in the rain & had to come back. Practiced at Harriet's awhile. To prayer meeting at 7. Mr. Snyder led. Enjoyed it tolerable. Home at 8. Cloudy & cool but pleasant.

Friday, September 19.

Rose at 6. Helped mother awhile. She is cleaning house. Got the note referred to on the 8th, but got it without asking for it. I have only one thing to say about it. I am utterly astonished at father, but shall say nothing at all about it to any one. Though hard to bear everything alone, yet I know it is best. To school at 9. Home at 12. Afternoon. To school at 2. Home at 5. Evening. Helping mother "fix up." Sade Rupp & I were walking. Met Ada Mc & Jennie G. & walked awhile with them. Home at 9. Pleasant. Could not go out to practice as mother had too much to do, & I had to help her.

Saturday, September 20.

Morning. At home. Helping mother. Afternoon. At home. Helping mother to clean the entry. Finished the dress at last. I could not go out to practice for I was too tired after I was done. Have not worked so hard for a long time. Felt too tired to dress. Ally Powers was here awhile. Finished a pair of drawers. Very pleasant.

Sunday, September 21.

To S.S. at 9. Did not go to prayer meeting. Thought there would not be any & went with Rose Guinn to her home awhile. Will came home & told us there was prayer meeting. Wish I had stayed. Home at 12. Afternoon. To S.S. at 2. Stopped at Aunt Salome's & they would have me stay for supper. How easily we can do wrong! Home at 6. Evening. To prayer meeting at 7. Mr. M'Millan led. Enjoyed it tolerably. Home at 8. Pleasant.

Monday, September 22.

Morning. Rose at 6. Cut three pairs of drawers. To school at 9. Home at 12. Studying my Latin at noon. Afternoon. Went out to Cousin Carrie's at 5 1/2. Took a music lesson and practiced awhile. Home at 7. Ally Powers & I were walking. Ally brought her work over & I helped mother pare peaches. Very pleasant.

Tuesday, September 23.

At school all day. Evening. Did not go out to practice as I had made an engagement to spend the evening with Miss Whiteside. Spent a very pleasant evening. She made a head-dress for me. Home at 9 3/4.

Wednesday, September 24.

Morning. Sewing awhile. To school at 9. Home at 12. Cool & raining. Afternoon. Studying my Latin at noon. To school at 2. Home at 5. Had considerable rain today. Evening. Did not go out to take a music lesson as Mr. Baugher said he would hear me recite my Latin. He came at 8. Had a pleasant evening. After I finished reciting we had a sociable chat. Pleasant and cool.

Thursday, September 25.

3 o'clock! A.M.

Feel all throughother. We were awakened about 1 o'clock by an alarm of fire. Three or four stables etc. were burned to the ground. The sparks flew in every direction. It was a grand and terrible sight. After the excitement I lay down about 1/

2 an hour & was awakened about 2 o'clock by another alarm. A barn out the old railroad was burned to the ground. Did not attempt to lie down again. It is years since we have had a fire. At school all day. Evening. Went out to practice. Home at 7. To prayer meeting at 7 1/2. Mr. Berkstresser led. Home at 8.

Friday, September 26.

At school all day. Evening. Went out & took a music lesson & stayed to spend the evening. Harriet Shillen & Ann Culp came out. Spent a very pleasant evening. Home at 9 1/2. Cool. Do not feel very well.

Saturday, September 27.

Morning. At home helping at the work. Afternoon. Went out to practice. Practiced about three hours. Home at 5. Evening. Sewing awhile. Ally Powers & I were walking. Home at 8. Stopped at Mr. Shillen's awhile. Very pleasant.

Sunday, September 28.

Morning. To S.S. at 9. To preaching at 10 1/2. Mr. Berkstresser preached. His text was "What shall I do to be saved." His sermon was very interesting & instructive. He discoursed on the question & tonight he will take the answer for his text. Had no class. Home at 12. Afternoon. To S.S. at 2. Home at 3. Wrote to Mattie & Lizzie Durboraw.

Monday, September 29.

Morning. Sewing. To school at 9. Home at 12. Afternoon. Did some errands for mother. To school at 2. Home at 5. Evening. Went out to take a music lesson but Cousin Carrie had some business in town and could not give me one. Practiced until 7. Home at 7 1/2. Sewing awhile. Spent part of the evening at Mr. Shillen's. Home at 9 1/2. Very pleasant.

Tuesday, September 30.

Morning. Sewing. To school at 9. Home at 12. Afternoon. Sewing. To school at 2. Home at 5. Evening. Went out to Cousin Carrie's at 5 1/2. Took a music lesson. Practiced awhile. Home at 7 1/2. Very pleasant. Ginnie Powers and I were walking awhile. Home at 8 1/2.

Wednesday, October 1.

Morning. To school at 9. Home at 12. Sewing at noon. Working at a dress for Bell. Fixing it. Afternoon. To school at 2. Home at 5. Evening. Went out to practice. Ann Culp was there & I stayed later than I would otherwise. Home at 8. Jen Gilbert & I were walking. Got a letter from the Twins. Very welcome.

Thursday, October 2.

Answered the girls' letter and got some ribbon for them. Sent it to them by Mr. & Mrs. Coshun this afternoon. At school all day. Did not go out to practice as I had some scholars kept in and as it was prayer meeting evening it was not worthwhile to go. To prayer meeting at 7. Went down to see Jen & we were walking awhile. Home at 9 1/2. Clear & moonlight. Very pleasant.

Friday, October 3.

At school all day. Evening. Went out to practice. Practiced about an hour and a half. Stopped at Jen's with my work. We walked awhile and then went and spent some time at Aunt Salome's. Home at 9 1/2. Harriet was sewing and I went & worked. I kept her company until 10 1/2. Very pleasant.

Saturday, October 4.

Morning. Helping at the work. Sewing awhile. Afternoon. Got my salary for September. Went out to Cousin Carrie's to practice at 1. Practiced about three hours.

Home at 5 1/2. Evening. Working. Jen came up and we walked awhile. Very pleasant. Janie Culp is dead. She died some time this evening. She had consumption. Poor Janie. When we were school girls together she bode as fair as I for long life.

Sunday, October 5.

To S.S. at 9. Did not stay for prayer meeting. Went down to see Aunt Lizzie. Home at 12. Afternoon. Mattie Durboraw and Mr. Eckert came very unexpectedly & I did not get to S.S. I was very glad to see them. It was too late for us to go to S.S. and we went to vespers. Mattie had never been in the Catholic Church before. Ada Mc & Jennie G. came to see Mattie. Dave and Mattie went home about 4 o'clock. Went part-way with Ada & Jennie. Evening. Prof. Muhlenburg preached a very good sermon. Home at 8 1/2. Moonlight. Very pleasant.

Monday, October 6.

Morning. To school at 9. Home at 12. Studying at noon. Afternoon. To school at 2. Home at 5. Evening. Took a music lesson at 6. Practiced awhile. Home at 8. Very pleasant. Sewing.

Tuesday, October 7.

Morning. Sewing. To school at 9. Home at 12. Studying and sewing at noon. Afternoon. To school at 2. Home at 5. Very warm. Evening. Went out to practice at 5. Home at 7. Ann Culp & I took a walk. Home at 7 1/2. Went over to Harriet's with my sewing. Sewing until 10. Very pleasant. Clear, warm & moonlight.

Wednesday, October 8.

Morning. Helped to wash awhile. Sewing. To school at 9. Home at 12. Studying at noon. Afternoon. Went to school at 2. Home at 5. Evening. Went out to take a music lesson at 5 1/2. Practiced awhile. Home at 7 1/2. Sewing awhile. Jen & Vinie Gilbert were up. Vinie has been away. Very pleasant. Moon-light.

Thursday, October 9.

Morning. To school at 9. Home at 12. Studying and sewing at noon. Afternoon. To school at 2. Home at 5. Evening. Did not go out to practice. Went down to Aunt Lizzie's to see Mother, and stayed for supper. Home at 6. To prayer meeting at 7. Went to see Mrs. Armor about taking something to father. They are going to York on Saturday. Home at 8. Very pleasant.

Friday, October 10.

Morning. Cloudy. Rose late. To school at 9. Afternoon. To school at 2. Home at 5. Did not take a music lesson as there was a soiree tonight. Went out at 7. Ann Culp and I came home about 9. Mr. S[nyder] came home with us. Cloudy and raining.

Saturday, October 11.

At home. Paring peaches & ironing. Great excitement. The rebels are in Chambersburg and up in the mountain stealing horses etc., etc. Every one thinks they will soon be here. A regiment of lancers came this evening from Frederick. I think they will remain until further orders. Harriet & I went to see Sally Wills. Home at 9. Feel miserably & the worst of it is, I have no one to go to for advice, perhaps that is better. Oh! dear!

Sunday, October 12.

Morning. To S.S. at 9. To preaching at 10 1/2. Morgan preached. Had no class. Home at 12. Afternoon. To S.S. at 2. Home at 3. Several thousand infantry came to town from Hanover. They came expecting to fight the rebels. Mother and I went down to the cars to see them. Everyone that could be out was out. There was a great excitement. Did not go to church. Helped Aunt Salome ground and make coffee for the soldiers. One of the men took a fancy to a Bible I had & I gave it to him. Home at 9 1/2. What a Sunday this has been!

Monday, October 13.

Morning. To school at 9. Home at 12. Dismissed in a hurry. Several parents came for their children as the report said the rebels were coming to town in force. Afternoon. Two Regiments of infantry went out to meet the rebels and took their artillery out to Mr. Schultz's Hill. No school. Evening. The report concerning the rebels is false, though they were up along the mountain stealing horses etc. Had two soldiers for supper. They were members of the battery from Indiana. Went to Harriet's with my work. Home at 9 1/2.

Tuesday, October 14.

Morning. Had two soldiers for breakfast. One that was here yesterday evening & another. To school at 9. Home at 12. Afternoon. All the soldiers have come back from Cashtown & they are going to start for Baltimore pretty soon. To school at 2. Dismissed at 3. Jen and I went down to see the soldiers leave. There was a great crowd around the railroad. They all got off about 5. Evening. Feel miserably. I will not attempt to describe my feelings. God help me!

Wednesday, October 15.

At school all day. Evening. Went out to take a music lesson. Home at 7. Ann Culp spent the evening here. Spent a pleasant evening sewing.

Thursday, October 16.

At school all day. Evening. Went out to practice. Home at 6 1/2. To prayer meeting at 7. Snyder led. Enjoyed it very much. Raining very heavily. Home at 8 1/2. Mother is sick. Hope she will soon recover.

Friday, October 17.

Rose at 6 1/2. Got breakfast. To school at 9. Home at 12. Afternoon. To school at 2. Home at 5. Evening. Recited my Latin to Mr. B. Pared apples from 9 till 11. Feel very tired. We are going to boil butter tomorrow.

Saturday, October 18.

Rose at 6. Got breakfast & helped mother put the butter on, rather the apples & quinces to make it. Swept & dusted the house. Got dinner. Did not get through with my work until 3. Got my likeness taken at Mr. Speight's for two of my scholars. Jennie & Mary Reeling (sister Jennie). Home at 5. Evening. Spent part of it with Harriet. Dr. Cress & Sally Wills were there. Harriet & I went down street with Sally. Home at 9.

Sunday, October 19.

Rose at 6 1/4. Got breakfast. To S.S. at 9. To prayer meeting at 10. Mr. M'Millan led. Had no class. Home at 12. Afternoon. Very pleasant. To S.S. at 2. Home at 5. Evening. Writing. Ally Powers & I went to church. Mr. Berkstresser preached a pretty long sermon. Home at 8 1/2. Cool.

Monday, October 20.

Morning. Rose at 5 1/2. Got breakfast. Helped to wash until 8. To school at 9. Home at 12. Afternoon. Sewing until school time. Jen was here. To school at 2. Home at 5. Evening. Went out to Cousin Carrie's & took a music lesson. Practiced awhile. Home at 7. Sewing. Nancy White & Sade Rupp were here while I was away.

Tuesday, October 21.

Morning. Rose at 6. Got breakfast. Ironed until 8. Nancy White was here. She expects to be examined pretty soon & she has a school & wishes me to hear her recite in some of the branches in which we are examined. To school at 9. Home at 12. Sewing. Afternoon. To school at 2. Home at 5. Evening. Went out to practice at 5 1/2. Practiced about 1 1/2 hours. Home at 7. Pared apples. We are going to boil butter tomorrow. Studied my Latin awhile. Feel very tired. Raining.

Wednesday, October 22.

Morning. Rose at 6. Got breakfast. Helped mother with the butter. To school at 9. Home at 12. Very windy. Afternoon. Heard N.W. recite from 12 1/2 till 1 1/2. To school at 2. Home at 5. Windy & cold. Evening. Went out & got a music lesson at 5 1/2. Practiced awhile. Home at 7. Ann Culp came with me. Clear but very cold & windy. Reading awhile in Physiology.

Thursday, October 23.

Morning. Rose at 6. Got breakfast. Sewed awhile. To school at 9. Home at 12. Afternoon. Sewing. To school at 2. Home at 5. Evening. Heard N.W. recite from 5 1/2 till 6 1/2. To prayer meeting at 7. Mr. Berkstresser led. Did not enjoy it very much. Home at 8. Went over to Harriet's with my sewing. Sewed until 10. Home at 10 1/4.

Friday, October 24.

Morning. Rose at 6. Got breakfast. Sewing. To school at 9. Home at 12. Afternoon. Sewing at mother's shaker. Jen came up & we went to school at 2. Home at 5. Evening. N.W. went unexpectedly this morning to the country & she will not recite to me any more. Sade Rupp was up. We were walking. Home at 6 1/2. Finished mother's shaker. Went over to Harriet's with my work. Finished two jobs that have been on hand for some time. Sewed until 10. Clear and cold.

Saturday, October 25.

Morning. Rose at 6 1/2. Got breakfast. Did my usual Saturday work & helped mother clean the dining room. She white-washed & I cleaned the wood-work. Worked until 1 o'clock. Got a fashionable dinner & then helped mother finish cleaning until 5. Got supper. Evening. Fixed the room. Ally Powers was here awhile with her work. Cool and disagreeable. Feel very tired and oh! how sad I feel. I would love to spend my evenings as I once did but alas! that privilege is denied me. How I would appreciate a friend like the one which I had then! More than ever since I know what it is to be deprived of a beloved friend's company.

Sunday, October 26.

Morning. Rose at 7. Got breakfast. Did not go out at all. The air is cold and damp and there is every appearance on rain. I feel very much indisposed. I am sorry I could not go out to S.S. for Dora F. will not be there again until Christmas. She is going to the mountain to teach school. Reading the "Seven Thunders." Got dinner. Afternoon. Raining. At home reading. Feel very badly. Have a very disagreeable head-ache. Got supper. Evening. Ally Powers was here awhile. Writing. Feel miserably. Took cold yesterday & am very hoarse. That is not the only cause of my miserable feeling. Alas!

Monday, October 27.

Rose at 6. Got breakfast. At home all day. Sick. This morning the weather was very inclement & I thought I had better stay at home. Afternoon. The sky is clearing but I still feel unwell. Mr. Baugher sent word that I should not come if I felt unwell. I do feel very badly & so I concluded to stay at home until to-morrow. Father came home in the noon train. He is discharged. Poor father! I wish he was well. I hope home & good nursing will restore him but I am afraid he will be a cripple for life. He has lost the use of one of his legs. Evening. Miss Whiteside was here to see me. Had a sociable chat with her. Feel better in body.

Tuesday, October 28.
Morning. Slept later than usual. Did not get breakfast. To school at 9. Home at 12. Afternoon. Jen & I think of going to Petersburgh to-morrow. The Adams County Teachers Institute meets there. To school at 2. Home at 5. Evening. Have concluded not to go to Petersburgh. I have several reasons but have neither time, room, nor the inclination to state them. The downstairs teachers are going. We are going to teach upstairs. Went down to see Jen. She is going. They have holiday until Monday. I feel a little disappointed but feel as though I have taken good advice in concluding to stay at home.

Wednesday, October 29.
Morning. Rose at 6. Helped to wash until school time. To school at 9. Home at 11 1/2. Practiced out at Cousin Carrie's an hour at noon. Home at 1 1/2. Afternoon. To school at 2. Home at 5. Evening. Went out to take a music lesson at 6. Practiced until 7 1/2. Had an interesting conversation with Carrie. Home at 8 1/2. Reading "Among the Pines, or South in Secession Time." Very pleasant. Clear & moonlight.

Thursday, October 30.
Morning. Rose at 6 1/4. Got breakfast. Ironed until school time. To school at 9. Home at 12. Afternoon. Went out to practice at 12 1/2. Practiced an hour. Home at 1 3/4. To school at 2. Home at 5. Evening. Sewing until prayer-meeting time. To prayer-meeting at 6 1/2. Was late. Mr. Berkstresser led. Enjoyed it tolerably. Home at 7 1/2. Sewing until 9. I was very anxious to go to Petersburgh, & had some good reasons for wishing to go, but I had some better reasons for staying at home. I am so glad I did not go. I know I would have regretted it if I had gone. I may state the reason at some future time.

Friday, October 31.
Morning. Rose at 7. Got breakfast. Helped mother until time for school. She is cleaning the kitchen. To school at 9. Home at 12. Afternoon. Went out to practice at 12 1/2. Home at 1 3/4. To school at 2. Home at 5. Evening. Sewing. Miss Whiteside spent the evening. Spent a very pleasant one, the most pleasant one I have spent for a long time. She stayed until 10. Went part of the way with her.

Saturday, November 1.
Morning. Helping at the work. Afternoon. Went out to practice at 1. Practiced about three hours. Cousin Bob is home. He left home at the same time Bro. Jeff did in the same company and has never been home since. Very glad to see him. Home at 5. Evening. Jen was here. She has just returned from Petersburgh. We were walking awhile. Home at 8. Reading "Among the Pines." Find it very interesting. Very pleasant.

Sunday, November 2.
Morning. To S.S. at 9. To prayer meeting at 10 1/2. Mr. M'Millan led. Had no class. Laura & Callie M'Millan insisted on me going out along with them. I had some "conscientious scruples" about going. But it was so pleasant that inasmuch as no one else knew I was going and consequently could not be injured by my example, I concluded to go. To S.S. at 2. Home at 4. Evening. Ally Powers went with me to preaching at 6. Mr. Morgan preached a very good & interesting sermon. So I thought. Home at 8. Very pleasant. Moonlight.

Monday, November 3.

Morning. Rose at 6 1/2. Helped to wash until school time. To school at 9. Home at 12. Afternoon. To see Ellie A. about fixing a bonnett. Stopped for Jen. To school at 2. Home at 5. Evening. Took a music lesson but was delayed an hour. Practiced awhile. Home at 9. Jeff & Ann Culp came with me. Studied my Latin an hour until 10 o'clock. Very pleasant.

Tuesday, November 4.

Morning. Rose at 6 1/2. Ironed awhile. Recited my Latin at 8 1/2. Recited it in school. Home at 12. Sewing awhile. Afternoon. Sewing until school time. To school at 2. Home at 5. Evening. Beckie and I went out to Cousin Carrie's, I to practice, & she to spend the evening. Home at 8. Helped Harriet to sew awhile. Home at 10.

Wednesday, November 5.

To school at 9. Home at 12. Afternoon. To school at 2. Home at 5. Evening. Went out to take a music lesson but did not. There was company there. Home at 9. Pleasant.

Thursday, November 6.

Morning. Rose at 6 to study my Latin which I expected to recite at 8 1/2 but was so sick that I was obliged to lie down at 7, & could not get up until 12. Ally Powers taught for me. She would teach all day but I think I will go this afternoon as I dislike to lose any more time than I can help. To school at 2. Home at 5. Evening. Working awhile. To prayer meeting at 7. Glad I went. I enjoyed it more than I have for some time. Cousin Carrie has a soiree tonight and they wanted me to come, but I preferred going to prayer meeting, and I was well repaid. Mr. Berkstresser led. Home at 8 1/2. Worked awhile.

Friday, November 7.

Morning. Rose at 6 1/2. Worked until 8 3/4. To school at 9. Home at 12. Snowing. Afternoon. To school at 2. Home at 5. Snowing. Evening. Went over to Harriet's with my work. Worked at a dress for myself. Worked awhile at her rug. Home at 10 1/2. Very cold. Like winter.

Saturday, November 8.

Morning. Rose at 6 3/4. Helped at the work. Very cold and disagreeable. Afternoon. Went up street. Got my salary for October. Did some errands. Sewing awhile. Cold, and very disagreeable. The snow makes such a miserable slush. But—"It all goes in a lifetime." Evening. Sewed awhile. Could not go out to practice. The roads are bad I suppose & I did not attempt to go out.

Sunday, November 9.

Morning. Slept late. Rose at 7 1/2. Could not go to S.S. or church all day. It is so very cold and I did not get my dress done & had none to wear. Sunday seems long when I stay at home all day. Afternoon. Cold. At home. Windy. Evening. We had no preaching. The annual meeting of the "Gettysburgh Female Bible Society" or rather an address before it was delivered in the Ger. Ref. Church by Rev. Mr. Essick. Did not like to stay at home all day, so I wore my school dress, and went, though I felt strangely. Susy and I went. Was tolerably well pleased. Home at 8. Very cold.

Monday, November 10.

Morning. Rose at 6 1/2. Got breakfast. Went to the store. To school at 9. Home at 12. Afternoon. Cut a Garabaldi for Susy & fixed some work for her. To school at 1 1/2. Home at 4 1/2. Evening. Went out to Carrie's at 6. Got a music lesson & practiced awhile. My lesson was a nice one, "Fern Leaf Polka." Home at 8 1/2. Studied my Latin. Cold. Feel very tired.

Tuesday, November 11.

Morning. Rose at 6. Studied my Latin until 8. To school at 8 1/2. Home at 12. Went to the store. Afternoon. Working until school time. Pleasant. To school at 1 1/2. Home at 4 1/2. Evening. Went out to practice at 5. Did not practice long. Mr. & Mrs. Lashell came out to see Cousin Carrie on business I suppose, and of course I could not practice while they were there. So I concluded to come home & work, which I did. Home at 6 1/2. Helped Susy at her body & did some writing. Cool but very pleasant.

Wednesday, November 12.

Morning. Rose at 7. Helped to wash. To school at 9. Home at 12. Afternoon. Sewing. To school at 1 1/2. Home at 4 1/2. Cloudy & raining. Sorry I cannot go out to take a music lesson. Evening. Busy. Sewing for myself and showing Susy. Cut a "Garabaldi" for myself. Feel pretty tired. Studied my Latin about an hour. Disagreeable.

Thursday, November 13.

Morning. Rose at 7. Studied awhile. To school at 8 1/2. Recited my Latin. Home at 12. Sewing at noon. Afternoon. To school at 1 1/2. Home at 4 1/2. Evening. Sewed until 5 3/4. To prayer-meeting at 6. Mr. Berkstresser led. Enjoyed it very much. Home at 7 1/2. Sewing at my dress. Studied awhile. Sewed until 10 1/4. Very pleasant. Cool.

Friday, November 14.

Morning. Rose at 5 3/4. Sewed until 8. To the store. To school at 8 1/2. Very pleasant. Clear & cool. Home at 12. Working awhile. Afternoon To the store. To school at 1 1/4. Home at 4 1/2. Evening. Went out to take a music lesson but Cousin Carrie concluded to wait until tomorrow, as the girls were going away to spend the evening & wanted her along. Of course I had no objections. Practiced awhile. Had a long & interesting conversation with Carrie, on the road to town. Home at 6 1/2. Jen Gilbert was here & spent the evening with me. Sewing at my Garabaldi. Spent a very pleasant morning. Took a walk with Jen, when she went home.

Saturday, November 15.

Morning. Rose at 5 1/2. Sewing. Helped at the work, and then sewed until noon. Afternoon. Sewing. Did not go out to Carrie's. I was so anxious to get my work done. Sewed until 4 1/2. Mary Jane Slentz & Ann, M. Rupp were here. Had a long talk with Ann. Evening. Jen & I went to see Annie Kuntz. She is an old school-mate. Her father moved from Gettysburg some years since. We were both scholars of Mr. Conover, & Annie was a pupil of Mr. Baugher, the first session I taught. Went to see Sade Rupp. She is sick. Jen came for me when choir-meeting was over. Home at 9. Got a good pair of calf-skin boots. Writing awhile.

Sunday, November 16.

Morning. Rose at 8. To S.S. at 9. To prayer meeting at 10 1/2. Mr. Culp led. Enjoyed it very much. We had class in Church at Mr. Culp's request. Enjoyed it very much. Home at 12 1/4. Afternoon. To School at 2. Home at 3 1/2. Went down to see Ann Culp a few minutes. I am sorry I went, inasmuch as I think Sunday visiting injurous unless in particular cases. Evening. To preaching at 5 1/4. Mr. Berkstresser preached a very good sermon. On the road home, Brother Morgan & Ginnie Buckingham overtook me and asked me to go along around to the Colored Church, I mean the Colored People's church, for the church is white. Stayed about an hour. We had a hearty laugh coming home, which was wrong on Sunday night, if we had a minister with us. The preacher while describing the damnation of a sinner from the land of Bible and Christian priveleges, described him as going down, down, down, into the "Bottomless Pit" until he came to the Sodomites, and telling them to get out of the way & let him down, farther; then going on down until he came to the Antidiluvians & telling them to get out of the road further & let him down, further, & going down, down, forever down. The idea was original & very good, I thought.

Monday, November 17.

Morning. Rose at 5 1/2. Sewed until time for school. To school at 8. Home at 12. Recited my Latin at Recess. Afternoon. Raining. To school at 1. Home at 4 1/2. Evening. Raining. Did not go out to Carrie's. Sewing at my dress, & showing Susie at hers. About 9 1/2 o'clock as the rest were about retiring (I intended to study) there was an alarm of fire, which I thought to be a stable or barn on Railroad street. Harriet and I went downstreet & found it to be a new hay stable belonging to Mr. Weible. The night was wet, or the fire would have been more destructive. When it was about half burned down there was an alarm in the eastern part of the same street & presently the fire burst from an old stone bank barn belonging to Mssrs. Codori & Doersom. There was great excitement. It is certainly the work of an incendiary. Susy & I went down to see Aunt Lizzie Myers. She has erysipelas very badly in her head and face. She is no better. Sat up awhile to study after I came home & did not—fell asleep. Did not awake until 12 o'clock. What an evening this has been.

Tuesday, November 18.

Morning. Rose at 7. To school at 8 1/2. Recited my Latin. Cloudy. Home at 12. Afternoon. To school at 1. Recited my Latin. Home at 4 1/2. Evening. Raining. Working at my dress & showing Susy. We worked until after 10 o'clock. Feel pretty tired. The Railroad hours have been changed. They leave at 7 3/4 in the morning. The hours for the return of the morning train and the departure of the afternoon train are irregular, I think, & at night they do not come in until between 9 and 10. Tonight they were after 10 sometime. Very disagreeable.

Wednesday, November 19.

Morning. Raining. Rose at 7. To school at 8. Very disagreeable. Home at 12. Afternoon. To school at 1. Home at 4 1/2. Evening. At home sewing. Very disagreeable. Sewing at my dress & helping Susy.

Thursday, November 20.

Morning. To school at 8. Studying my Latin. Home at 12. Raining. Afternoon. To school at 1 1/2. Home at 4 1/2. Evening. Working until 5 1/2. To prayer meeting at 6. Mr. McMillan commenced leading and Mr. Berkstresser closed. Home at 7 1/2. Very disagreeable. Sewing awhile & studying my Latin.

Friday, November 21.

Morning. Rose at 6 1/2. To school at 8. Studying my Latin lesson. Home at 12. Sewing. Afternoon. Sewing. To school at 1 1/4. Home at 4 1/2. Evening. At home. Sewing until 8 1/2. Took my work & went over to Mr. Shillen's. Harriet is very busy. We sewed until 11 1/2. Did considerably more than I expected to do. Home at 11 1/2. Good hours for ladies of our standing in the community. Ahem! Spent a very pleasant evening.

Saturday, November 22.

Morning. Helping awhile at the work. Sewed from 9 1/2 until 12. Clear & cold. Pleasant. Afternoon. Sewed from 1 until 4. Went up street on an errand.

Home at 5. Snowing. Evening. Sewing. Finished my dress and Garibaldi & Susy finished hers. Very pleasant but cold. Clear. Feel very tired. Writing awhile.

Sunday, November 23.

To S.S. at 9. To preaching at 10 1/2. Mr. Morgan preached, he said unexpectedly to him. His sermon was good. Did not stay to see if we would have class, for I felt so sick I was glad to get home. Afternoon. To S.S. at 2. Home at 3 1/4. Evening. Jen Gilbert was here until church time. She went to their church & I went down for Ann Culp to go to church. We went too soon & had a good long "set" before Mr. Finney came. He is the Presbyterian minister & Mr. Berkstresser exchanged for this evening. Mr. Finney's subject was "Faith" and his sermon was elegant. Just the kind I needed. Home at 7 1/2. Ann & Jefferson came with me.

Monday, November 24.

Morning. Rose at 6 1/2. Washed until school time. Went to the store. To school at 9. Home at 12 1/2. Uncle & Aunt Plank were here. They came about 10 o'clock. They look very well for their age. Uncle is over eighty years old, and Aunt is a few years younger. I wanted to stay until they went, but the bell rang and I had to go. To school at 2. Stayed after school to write. Home at 5 1/2. Evening. Went down to the store. To see Aunt Polly Myers a few minutes. She is knitting some for me. Home at 6 1/2. Sewing. Feel badly. Am not well and have a bad cold. Spent a quiet pleasant evening. Writing awhile.

Tuesday, November 25.

Morning. Ironed awhile. To school at 8 1/2. Home at 12 1/2. Afternoon. To school at 1 1/2. Home at 4 1/2. Evening. Harriet, Kate S. and I went down street awhile. Home at 6. Worked on Harriet's rug. Home at 9 1/2. Feel very tired and sleepy. No wonder when I wrote until after 10 last night. It struck 11 before I was ready to retire. Pleasant but cold.

Wednesday, November 26.

Rose at 7. Ironed awhile. To the store. To school at 8 1/2. Home at 12. Afternoon. To school at 1 1/2. Home at 4 1/2. Evening. At home sewing. Should have gone out to Carrie's but felt too badly. I am not very well. Commenced a dress for Jennie.

Thursday, November 27.

No school. Thanksgiving day. To preaching at 10 o'clock. Mr. Berkstresser preached an excellent sermon. Home at 12. Afternoon. Sewing for Harriet. Evening. To prayer meeting at 6. Mr. Berkstresser led. Enjoyed it tolerably. Home at 7 1/2. Pleasant. Did not spend a very pleasant day. Missed one with whom is associated every Thanksgiving day for four years. Now, alas! how changed.

Friday, November 28.

At school all day. Evening. Went to see Miss Whiteside with my work. Spent a very pleasant evening. Worked at Jennie's dress. Miss W. and [unclear text] came with me & we all stopped to see Harriet awhile. After the girls went home, I sewed until 11 1/2 with her. Feel pretty tired.

Saturday, November 29.

Morning. Snowing. Finished Jennie's dress. Afternoon. Received a letter from Mr. Casey. He is at home in Holland, Erie County, New York. He is discharged from service & was pretty sick for some time after he got home, but he is getting better & thinks he will entirely recover if he takes proper care of himself. It is more than four months since I received his last letter, which remains unanswered, and he writes with the same friendship which he did then. Ann Culp & I went down to help Aunt Lizzie Myers to sew. Stayed until evening. Beckie Belch wanted me to come there for tea but I could not. Evening. Home at 8. Writing awhile. Feel very tired.

Sunday, November 30.

Morning. To S.S. at 9. To prayer meeting at 10. Had no class. Home at 11 1/2. Afternoon. To S.S. at 2. Home at 3 1/2. Went to see Jen a few moments. She was here at noon. Evening. To preaching at 6. Mr. Morgan preached a pretty long sermon. I could not pay very much attention to it. It was very warm. I was so sleepy & my thoughts were to some extent preoccupied. Oscar & Ada M'Millan came home with me. Cloudy and disagreeable.

Monday, December 1.

Morning. To school at 9. Home at 12. Afternoon. To school at 1 1/2. Home at 4 1/2. Evening. At home sewing. Very disagreeable. Cloudy.

Tuesday, December 2.

Morning. To school at 9. Home at 12. Afternoon. To school at 1 1/2. Home at 4 1/2. Evening. Went over to Harriet's awhile. Reading aloud to her. The evening being so very pleasant I thought I would go down street. Went to see Jen but she was not at home. To see Rose Guinn. Home at 8 3/4. Harriet & I went down street with Miss Gillespie who was spending the evening with her. Home at 9 3/4. This is a glorious night, Clear, cold & moon-light. How I could enjoy it under other circumstances, and as it is, I enjoy these nights very much.

Wednesday, December 3.

Morning. To School at 9. Home at 12. Afternoon. To school at 1 1/2. Home at 4 1/2. Jen and I went to get our salaries for November. We had a long talk with Dr. Fahnestock. He is treasurer of the school board. He is Lieutenant Colonel of the regiment of "Drafted men" now in camp at "Camp Gettysburg." I am sorry he is to leave. We lose a good director. Went to the store. Bought several things & spent more than I intended to spend. Bought two Hymn-books for prizes for my S.S. class. Home at 7.

Thursday, December 4.

Morning. To school at 9. Home at 12. Working at noon awhile. Afternoon. To school at 1 1/2. Home at 4 1/2. Evening. Had a long interesting and very welcome letter from Martha Durboraw with a very pressing invitation to come and spend the holidays with them. I cannot accept it though I expect to visit them a short time after New Year. To prayer meeting at 6. Mr. McMillan led. Enjoyed it very much. Home at 7 1/2. Worked at Harriet's hearth-rug until 10 1/2 and finished it, all that I am to do at it. Harriet & I had a very sociable and interesting chat after we finished work. Home at 11.

This is a glorious night. Clear and moon-light. I would love to take a moon-light stroll with a gentleman (not a thousand miles away) who I know would enjoy it fully as much as I. Why must we be separated? I think it unjust and cruel and more than that, I think it is sinful in those who have been the cause of our separation. I hope God will forgive them and help me to do so, for I find it very hard to forgive them and cherish for them the feelings which I did before.

Friday, December 5.

At school all day. Evening. Snowing. Went over to Harriet's with my sewing. Cut the body and sleaves of Susy's dress and worked at the body. Sewed until 11. Feel miserably and it is no wonder!

Saturday, December 6.

Morning. Sewing at Susy's dress. Trimmed hats for Jennie and Bell and fixed a dress for Bell. Afternoon. Sewing for Susy. Evening. Sewing awhile. Helped Harriet awhile. Writing.

Sunday, December 7.

Morning. Dreadfully cold. To S.S. at 9. To preaching at 10 1/2. Mr. Morgan preached. Had no class. Afternoon. To S.S. at 2. Home at 3 1/2. Evening. Writing. To preaching at 6. Mr. Berkstresser preached but I was so much worried that I could not fix my mind on the sermon.

Monday, December 8.

Morning. To school at 9. Home at 12. Afternoon. To the store. To school at 1. Home at 4 1/2. Evening. To the store. Got myself a dress and vail. Home at 5 1/2. Sewing at my dress. Cut the body and sleeves. Sewed with Harriet until 10 1/2. Very pleasant after 10. Clear & moonlight.

Tuesday, December 9.

Morning. Washed awhile before school. To school at 9. Home at 12. Working at my dress at noon. Afternoon. To school at 1 1/2. Home at 4 1/2. Evening. At home sewing.

Wednesday, December 10.

Morning. To school at 9. Home at 12. Afternoon. To school at 1 1/2. Home at 4 1/2. Evening. Aunt Polly sent for me to come up and show her at her dress. Stayed until 8 with my work. Home at 8 1/4. Writing until 10.

Thursday, December 11.

Morning. To school at 9. Home at 12. Afternoon. To school at 1 1/2. Home at 4 1/2. Evening. To prayer meeting at 6. Mr. Berkstresser led. Did not receive much benefit. From the nature of some the exercises I could not. Home at 7 1/2. Mr. Morgan came home with me. Sewed at my dress until 10 1/2. Would have sewed longer but my lamp "gave out" and I was obliged to retire. Pleasant overhead. Damp and muddy.

Friday, December 12.

Morning. To school at 9. Home at 12. Afternoon. To school at 1 1/2. Home at 4 1/2. Evening. Sade Rupp came up and we went down to Mr. Gilbert's to spend the evening. Spent a very pleasant evening. Home at 9 1/2. Jen and Vinie came home with me. Sewing at the sleeves of my dress. Went out to Carrie's after school. Home at 5 1/2.

Saturday, December 13.

Morning. Helping at the work. Finished Susy's dress. Working at mine. Afternoon. Sewing at my dress. Made the skirt. Evening. At home sewing. Jeff and Ann Culp were here a while. Sewed until 11 1/2.

Sunday, December 14.

Morning. To S.S. at 9. To prayer meeting at 10 1/2. Mr. M'Millan led. Had no class. Home at 11 1/2. Afternoon. To S.S. at 2. Jen was there & we took a walk to the Cemetery. Had a delightful walk. Home at 4 1/2. Evening. To preaching at 6 1/4. Mr. Berkstresser preached. His sermon was pretty long but very good. Home at 7 1/2. Ada, Sally & Oscar McMillan came home with me.

Monday, December 15.

Morning. Rose at 6 1/2. Sewing at my dress. To school at 9. Home at 10 1/2. Afternoon. To school at 1 1/2. Home at 4 1/2. Evening. Pleasant. Went down to see Jen awhile with my work. Stopped at Harriet's on the road home & sewed until 10 3/4. Finished my sleeves. Home at 11. Very pleasant. Warm & windy. Feel miserably. I wish had a friend to whom I could unburden my mind. I should say I wish it was my privelege to do so, for I know I have such a friend. I know no other whom I would trust in that way. God bless him!

Tuesday, December 16.

Morning. Rose at 7 1/4. Overslept myself. Sewing at my dress. To school at 9. Home at 11 1/2. Sewing at noon. Afternoon. To school at 1 1/2. Cold & windy. Very disagreeable. Home at 4 1/2. Evening. Sewing at home until 9 1/2. Took my work over to Harriet's and sewed with her until 11. She has so much to do, and it is pleasanter for both, when we sew together. Home at 11.

Wednesday, December 17.

Morning. Rose late. Washing awhile. To school at 9. Home at 12. Afternoon. To school at 1 1/2. Home at 4 1/2. Went to the store to buy Christmas presents for the family & for two of my S.S. scholars. Home at 5 1/2. Met Rose G. and accepted an invitation to spend the evening with her. Took my sewing along. Home at 9. To Mr. Shillen's. Sewed until 11. Home at 11. Very cold and windy.

Thursday, December 18.

Morning. Very pleasant. Clear & cold. To school at 9. Home at 12. Afternoon. To school at 1 1/2. Very pleasant. Miss Swope's, Miss Witherow's, Miss Gilbert's and Miss Belch's schools closed today. Home at 4. Evening. To prayer meeting at 6 1/2. Enjoyed it tolerably. Home at 8. Sewed until 10.

Friday, December 19.

Morning. To school at 9. Home at 11 1/2. Mr. Little's school closed this morning with an examination. Afternoon. To school at 1 1/2. Had a public examination. There were not many present but we had a very creditable examination. Our school closed until January 19th. Home at 5. Evening. Went out to Cousin Carrie's Christmas Soiree. Was very much pleased. Stayed after it was over until 10 o'clock. Sewed with Harriet until 11.

Saturday, December 20.

Morning. Our Quarterly meeting commenced. Our Presiding Elder cannot be here but Mr. Mourne, a son of one our former ministers, and his colleague, Mr. Carrol are here. Mr. Carrol preached at 11. His sermon was splendid. Home at 12 1/2. Saw Mrs. Durboraw. She will not be in town any time. Afternoon. At home sewing awhile. To the store. Got Christmas presents. For Father & Jefferson, handkerchiefs, for mother a purse and a pair of gloves, for Susy handkerchiefs; for Jenny and Bell, blue veils; and for Grace a pair of gloves. Evening. To preaching at 6 1/2. Mr. Mourne preached an excellent sermon. "Work out your salvation with fear and trembling." Home at 8. Writing.

Sunday, December 21.

Morning. To lovefeast at 9. Had a very solemn meeting. Did not enjoy it much. I felt too much cast-down. To preaching at 10 1/2. Mr. Mourne preached another and better sermon. His subject was the witness of the spirit. Oh! how I did appreciate it. After preaching the Sacrament of the Lord's supper was administered. I enjoyed it very much. I felt so much encouraged, though I did not feel as happy as I could wish. Nevertheless I can take courage & press onward. May God aid me. Home at 1. Afternoon. At home all afternoon. Evening. To preaching at 6 1/2. Had a splendid sermon by Mr. Carrol. Home at 8. Feel badly. Have been sick all day.

Monday, December 22.

Morning. At home. Feel very badly. Sewing at some handkerchiefs. Afternoon. To Mr. F. Got my salary for Dec. Jefferson and I bought several presents, candy, nuts etc. for the children. We are going to have a Christmas tree. Went down to see Jen start off. She has gone to Frederick, Md., to visit her mother's relations. Went out to practice. Practiced about 2 hours. To see Miss Whiteside. She is going home tomorrow. Her home is at York Springs. Home at 5. Evening. To preaching at 6 1/2. Mr. Morgan preached a very good sermon. Home at 8 1/2. Writing.

Tuesday, December 23.

Morning. At home sewing. Afternoon. Went out to practice at 1 1/2. Home at 4 1/2. Evening. To preaching at 6 1/2. Mr. Berkstresser preached. Home at 8 1/2.

Wednesday, December 24.

Morning. At home sewing. Afternoon. Practiced at Harriet's & went down to the fair awhile. Home at 5. Evening. To preaching at 6 1/2. Mr. Morgan preached a very good sermon. Home at 8 1/2. Helped to fix a Christmas tree for the children. Wrote awhile. It is just six months since Mr. Snyder has been in our house. I sincerely hope it will not be six months before he comes again. It will not be if I can help it. Writing awhile.

Thursday, December 25.

"Christmas Day."

Morning. Rose at 5. Susy & I got breakfast and made some arrangements about presents. Sewing awhile. Afternoon. Had company to dinner. The house has been more like some public show. The children are continually (big children too) running in to see the tree. Evening. To preaching at 6 1/2. Mr. Berkstresser preached. Home at 8 1/2. Met Mr. Snyder when I was going to preaching, & took a longer road than I would, if I had been alone. Had a pleasant walk, and a still pleasanter conversation, only it was too short—both the walk and the talk.

Friday, December 26.

Morning. Intended practicing at Harriet's so I could go to the fair and help her at their table, but just as I had cleverly commenced Mr. Morgan came to our house and I had to go home. He stayed to dinner and there was an end to my practicing for to-day. Afternoon. Went down to the fair & stayed until 4 1/2. Wrote a letter to Mattie & Lizzie Durboraw. Julie Gilbert is in town and is going home to-morrow. She lives in their neighborhood. Wrote a letter for Harriet. Her mother is very ill. Evening. To preaching at 6 1/2. Mr. Berkstresser preached. Home at 8 1/2.

Saturday, December 27.

Morning. At home fixing my bonnett. Afternoon. Went out to practice at 2. Home at 5. Feel very badly. Evening. Went down to the fair for Harriet. Did not spend a very pleasant evening though it has been as pleasant as I generally spend now. Home at 10 1/2.

Sunday, December 28.

Morning. To S.S. at 9. To prayer meeting at 10 1/2. Had no class. Afternoon. To S.S. at 2. Gave my scholars their Christmas presents. Home at 3 1/2. Jeff, Ann C. and I took a walk to the Cemetery. I enjoyed it tolerably well. I would have enjoyed it more if Snyder had been there with me. Home at 5. Evening. To preaching at 6 1/2. Mr. Morgan preached and closed the meeting. Home at 8. Feel perfectly miserable. Oh! God help me to bear my trials patiently and Oh! help me to cherish a forgiving spirit toward those who have been the cause of trouble.

Monday, December 29.

Morning. Washing. Finished at 1. Afternoon. Went out to practice at 2. Home at 5 1/2. Evening. At home awhile. Went up street on some business. Mrs. Shillen is very ill and they have just received news of Tom's death. He was mortally wounded at the late battle of Fredericksburgh and since died. I wrote several letters at Harriet's request, for the purpose of finding out the particulars about his death. Clear & moonlight but the beauty of night affords me very little pleasure. It only recalls to my mind the happiness which once was mine and which might be mine now had it not been for my thoughtlessness. How true that "Remembrance of past pleasure augments present pain."

Tuesday, December 30.

Morning. Ironing until 12. Afternoon. Went out to practice. Home at 4 1/2. Went to see Dora Flemming. Evening. Mrs. Shillen is no better. Working awhile.

Wednesday, December 31.

Morning. Helping Harriet to sew. She has some work which must be done & poor girl she does not feel much like working. Afternoon. Rainy. Went out to practice. Learned "Maryland my Maryland" though not quite perfectly. Home at 5. Evening. At home reading. This is a glorious night. Clear calm and moonlight. Ann & Jefferson were here until 9 O'clock. Father, Susy and I are going to watch-meeting. A year ago to-night I was not reading before meeting & I would not have been this evening if I had had the same company.

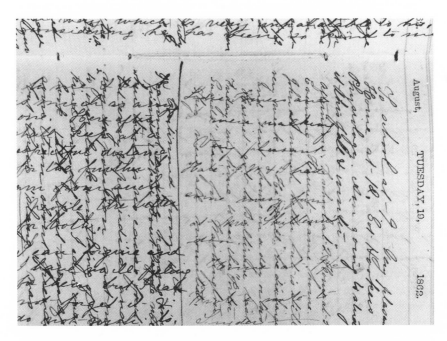

Page from Sallie Myers diary, 1862.

2

AND THE BATTLE CAME RAGING:
"I AM NOT AFRAID OF THEM"

Early in 1863 the Myers family experienced some happier times. Without the 1863 diary, there is no record of daily events to document Sallie's life in detail, and the typescripts for January through May are sketchy at best. But happiness in the Myers family can be surmised because of several circumstances that are known. Sallie's father was home from the war and mending nicely. Her brother Jefferson had also been discharged from the army on a medical certificate[1] and was also back at home, working in Gettysburg as a printer. His romance with Sallie's friend, Ann Culp, had deepened and they were married in May.

Other circumstances in the town of Gettysburg were less than pleasant. As 1863 unfolded, Sallie Myers and the inhabitants of Gettysburg found themselves in an unusual position. Daily activities continued as always, but underlying a "life goes on" philosophy adopted by the townspeople simmered the very real threat of invasion by the Confederate Army. The realization had hit the local populace that the Civil War was intensifying and would not end any time soon. Additionally, it was no secret that an all-out invasion of the North by General Robert E. Lee's army was more than a possibility. Major General J.E.B. Stuart had threatened the western portion of Adams County in October 1862, and the illusion of safety that was the Mason-Dixon Line had been shattered. Lee's men were riding the crest of victory after victory, and morale was high among his troops. Bolstered with confidence in his seemingly unbeatable army, the likelihood existed that General Lee soon would lead his men into the unscarred region of the North and seek victory there.

Gettysburg's geographic location as a border town with close proximity to Washington, D.C. and the South, spelled tension for its population. "Raids and rumors of raids" flew from the lips of farmers and businessmen, fathers and mothers, as they went about the business of living. As early as January of that year, Sallie's diary contains an allusion to the invasion rumors with the simple statement, "Report the Rebels are coming."[2] As weeks passed by, the tension grew worse as the number of rumors increased. Sallie recalled years later, "Whenever we saw a farmer come into town on horseback, or in a wagon, leading a couple of horses we knew he had heard that a raid was imminent. It seemed to be the great worry of the farmers that their horses would be taken."[3]

Another source of tension in the border town of Gettysburg was the existence of political division and disagreement concerning the war in general. Public sentiment was primarily Union, but given the political atmosphere of Gettysburg, a sufficient number of anti-war Democrats, or Copperheads, inhabited the town to fan the flames of dissent. Robert Goodloe Harper's *The Sentinel* described Republican meetings as "patriotic," and accused the Democrats of holding "Copperhead Meetings" attended by traitors to the Union.[4] Sallie described these Copperheads as being "not very open in upholding the Southern cause, but just seemed to think the South was right, and we often squabbled on that subject."[5]

Springtime in Gettysburg, along with warm sun and freshly plowed gardens, brought increased rumor activity which affected the lives of the townspeople on an increasingly large scale. By early June, the first serious reports that the Rebels were coming surfaced, and local reaction reached fever pitch. Sallie's description of Gettysburg during the month of June told a tale of people distracted with worry and fear:

> Naturally, the people of the town became terribly excited and business was at a standstill. Bankers sent their money away. Merchants sent their goods to Philadelphia and other places for safety. Day after day the people did little but stand along the streets in groups and talk. Whenever someone heard a new report all flocked to him. The suspense was dreadful. Of course there was no social life in the town at the time, though the young folks would meet and sing patriotic songs.[6]

Likewise in her diary entry for June 15, Sallie wrote, "The town is all in an uproar. Merchants are packing their goods & sending them off and every one shares in the confusion caused by the news 'The rebels are coming.'" She later described the nervous state of the citizenry, and the accompanying feelings of dread, caused by the terrible waiting and wondering what would happen next:

> The dangers of our situation kept us in constant turmoil, and not much work was done. We were like Micawber "waiting for something to turn up" or like those people the Bible tells of who "spent their time in nothing else, but either to tell, or to hear some new thing." Oh, those were awful times![7]

Local merchants, bankers and businessmen were not the only ones in Gettysburg with much to lose. Far worse than the possibility of lost inventory was the possibility of lost freedom faced by the black population of the town. These people fearfully believed that if, indeed, invasion rumors turned into reality, they ran the risk of capture and a life of slavery in the South. Sallie's compassion ran high for the plight of Gettysburg's black people, and her June 17 entry reflected this when she wrote, "... I pity the poor darkies. They seem perfectly bewildered." Sallie later described their fears, and reaction to the threatening rumors by affectations of disability:

We have a population of between 300 & 400 colored people.[8] Their fear of the rebels was caused by the belief that they would be captured and sold as slaves if the Rebels came north into the States. I know not how much cause they had for their fears, but it was a terrible reality to them. All who could got away and those who were obliged to stay at home were at the shortest notice suddenly transformed into limping, halting, and apparently worthless specimens of humanity.[9]

The final week of June brought the fear and commotion in Gettysburg to a peak. Sallie recorded the report that the "rebels have taken possession of Millerstown, about 8 miles from here, or rather Fairfield, which is its proper name...."[10] Church services were suspended and even the Methodist preacher, The Rev. David Eisenberg,[11] had "skedaddled." She described Gettysburg as a town empty of "darkies of both sexes" as well as empty of some "white folks of the male sex." Observing these peculiar circumstances, she wrote, "I am glad I am neither a man nor a darky, though girls are not so much better off. Oh dear, I wish the excitement was over."[12] Although Sallie could not have known it on June 21, the excitement was far from over. The excitement, in fact, had scarcely begun.

On June 26, several elements of Lee's Army of Northern Virginia made their first appearance in Gettysburg. The 35th Virginia Battalion (White's Cavalry), followed by General John B. Gordon's brigade of Georgians, rode into town from the Chambersburg Pike after a brief engagement at Seven Stars. With the whereabouts of the Union Army unknown, Gettysburg civilians stood witness to the fact that their greatest fear, the invasion of their homes and their village, had become a reality. Uncertain about just what to expect from the Rebels, the townspeople tried to avoid them. Sallie would later remember,

> On the last Friday in June the raiders really came, and they occupied the town for a day and a night and had their headquarters in the court-house. We had a vague idea that the Rebels were a dreadful set of men, and we didn't know what horrid things they might do. So we mostly kept in our houses out of their way. They demanded a great sum of money of the townspeople. We couldn't give it to them, and we were nearly scared to death.[13]

Although "nearly scared to death," Sallie faced the presence of the Rebels with bravery and just a bit of anger. In her diary entry for June 26, she expressed both outrage over the Rebels' occupation of Gettysburg, as well as a curious interest in their activities:

> In Rebeldom. About 4 O'clock the long looked for Rebels made their appearance, and such a mean looking lot of men I never saw in my life.... It was very provoking to see them riding around doing just as they pleased. Several hundred Cavalry came first, then followed several thousand Infantry with their old red flag flying and they were yelling like fiends. I am not afraid of them and did not believe they were

coming as I stood on the corner until two of them rode by furiously brandishing their sabres and pointing pistols. At last we have seen the rebels.[14]

Later that same evening, Sallie wrote further in her diary and described an interesting conversation which took place between some Rebels, her father, and herself at the door of her home on West High Street:

How exasperating the thought that tonight we are under the control of "armed traitors." Two of them were at our door about two hours talking to father about the war and their southern rights, etc. Father and I told them we were for the Union unconditionally. They were very reasonable and our conversation was interesting.

Regardless how reasonable the Rebels appeared to Sallie and her father that evening, they disrupted everyday routine and inflicted considerable damage east of town before leaving the next morning for York, Pennsylvania. Sallie's entry for June 27 details some of the destruction:

We were awakened by the Rebs' Band playing a rebel march in our Court House where they were quartered for the night, only a part of them were there. They went out in a hurry about 11 o'clock last night for our own men are near and of course they heard of them. The rebels have gone on towards Oxford & Hanover after burning 15 or 20 cars and the bridge over the creek. The cars cannot run into town now. The news conflicts, some say there are more Rebs coming and some say the Union troops are near. I suppose both tales are true and we may look for strenuous times. Hooker & Lee with their armies are in Maryland and Pennsylvania.

With no certain knowledge that the Union troops were by this time advancing north, and conflicting reports concerning the positions of both General Joseph Hooker's and General Lee's armies circulating everywhere, the townspeople could do nothing but wait, and wonder what the immediate future would hold. They did not wait long, however, for on June 28 came the arrival of advance pickets of Hooker's army, an event received with a combination of relief and fear. Sallie wrote the next evening, "Rebels are reported near. Their camp fires can be seen in the Mountains. Our men in great numbers are advancing from Frederick and we may expect a battle both near and soon. God help us! for surely our cause is one of justice and humanity."[15]

The next day, June 30, saw a division of Union cavalry under the command of General John Buford enter the town around noon. Enthusiastic, and motivated by energetic patriotism, groups of local girls stood on the street-corners and greeted the men with food, drink, and patriotic music as they rode by. Song after song they sang, among them "The Battle Cry of Freedom," "When This Cruel War is Over," and "Tramp, Tramp, Tramp," each received by Buford's cavalry with waves and cheers. A lively touch was added when the girls also sang "John

Brown's Body" and "We'll Hang Jeff Davis." Many young ladies of Gettysburg participated in thus greeting the soldiers. Among them were: Eliza Martin, Eliza Ziegler, Theresa Warner, Maria Warner, Jennie Myers, Elizabeth S. "Sallie" Myers, Susie M. Myers, Carrie Young, Alice Powers, Dora Flemming, Vinnie Wierick, Anna Garlach, Amanda Reinecker, Sallie McClellan, Mary Culp, and Sophia Culp.[16]

The revelry and enthusiasm of June 30 turned overnight to quiet desperation and anxiety with the early morning sun of Wednesday, July 1. Tense, expectant with fear, the people of Gettysburg waited as the storm gathered force west of town. Acting on the advice of soldiers, many people had packed some belongings and left the town. Others, like the Myers family, did not, for they had "packed up their clothes and got as far as the door, then they decided not to go and went in again."[17]

As the morning progressed, the air began to shake with the intense roar of artillery, and men, women, and children "sat on their doorsteps, their hearts beating with anxiety, looking at one another mutely."[18] Gettysburg soon turned into a scene of intense activity, as the citizens were spurred into action:

> Troops were constantly arriving hurrying to the battlefield, and we brought out some buckets of water and several tin cups. There were five of us girls in our family, and we handed the water to the soldiers as they double-quicked through the town. They drank without ever stopping and threw the cups back to us. Besides giving them water, we handed them cake, bread and butter, and anything at all we could find in the house that was good to eat.[19]

Soon the sights and sounds of men running toward the battlefield took a dramatic turn, as the conflict produced its inevitable casualties. Gettysburg stood witness to the horrible results of that morning's intense fighting west of Seminary Ridge. With each passing hour, the war's result, the wounded soldiers with their bandages and blood, became more visible. Sallie described her horror at the first sight of blood which met her eye that morning:

> At 10 O'clock that morning I saw the first blood. A horse was led past our house covered with blood. The sight sickened me. Then three men came up the street. The middle one could barely walk. His head had been hastily bandaged and blood was visible. I grew faint with horror. I had never been able to stand the sight of blood. But I was destined to become accustomed to it.[20]

By late afternoon, a mighty force descended upon the streets and alleys of Gettysburg as the retreating Union Army filled the town with wounded men. The slow, bloody collapse of the Union line of defense along Seminary Ridge brought the possibility that the Confederate Army might turn its wrath on the town itself. Word quickly spread through the local population with the order, "Women and children to the cellars—the rebels will shell the town."[21] Their home located in the direct line of retreat, Sallie Myers and her family heeded the order, huddled in their cellar, and remained there from four to six in the afternoon while battle noises raged above ground, and the Union army's desperate last attempt to hold Seminary Ridge was crushed:

> Those two hours I can never forget. Our cellar was a very good one and furnished a refuge for many besides our own family. The noise above our heads, the rattling of musketry, the screeching of shells and the unearthly yells, added to the cries and terror of the children, were enough to shake the stoutest heart. I am sure that never were more fervent prayers borne heavenward.[22]

By early evening, the Rebels had full possession of the town, and Gettysburg settled into the temporary, oppressive quiet which comes when artillery and musketry end their deadly exchange. Retreating soldiers had overrun the town on their way south to Cemetery Hill, trampling through yards and flower beds, in through back doors and out front doors in their retreat to safety. Sallie Myers' home was no exception. Strewn in her backyard was the debris of hasty retreat; several muskets and pistols, a cartridge box and other personal items were found, abandoned by Union soldiers in their haste. Sallie described the rush of soldiers into town:

> The Union troops retreated through the town in a regular stampede. Some of them came up an alley behind our house and in at the rear door and out at the front. Afterward we found in our back yard a number of guns loaded and capped that they'd thrown away. They could easily have pillaged the house, but the only thing we missed was a little linen apron I'd been ironing. I think perhaps a soldier took it for a handkerchief.[23]

Sallie's sister Sue would later recall that the situation was "awful; the men ran in every direction, in their desire to escape being taken prisoners. They did not wait to find the doors, but rushed through their houses, jumping through windows in order to get away."[24]

Looking out her cellar window to observe the commotion, Sallie saw a group of captured Union soldiers, prisoners of war who now waited, tired and exhausted, for their eventual trip to a Southern prison. Sallie later recalled their conversation:

> As we were looking out of one of the cellar windows we saw some of our men who'd been taken prisoners, and they were standing so near that we spoke to them. They said they expected to be sent off South and wished we would write to their home people. Then, one after the other, they gave us their names, and the addresses of the persons to whom we were to write.[25]

Prisoners of war were not the only sights that caught Sallie's eye. Coming up from the cellar, she observed that the town was "full of Rebels...and we could see a Union soldier lying out in the street with his head cut off."[26] Sallie's brother Jefferson confronted one Rebel in front of their house, who was threatening to shoot a Union soldier for refusing to give up his sword. Jefferson "walked up to the rebel, turned the pistol towards him and said: 'If you must shoot, shoot a rebel, not a Union man.'"[27]

All available churches, schools, and other public buildings were quickly filled beyond capacity with wounded soldiers. Converted from places of worship, education, and community service, they became places of pain, suffering and death. Private homes were also pressed into service. Townspeople went to work cooking meals, boiling linens, and providing additional aid as Gettysburg turned its full attention to the care of the wounded. In Sallie's section of town alone, along both East and West High Streets, six public buildings and most of the private homes were used. Included in that number were the St. Francis Xavier Roman Catholic Church, the United Presbyterian Church, and the home of Peter Myers and his family.

The Catholic church, only six doors east of the Peter Myers residence, was filled to bursting with the casualties of war. Dr. James Fulton, assistant surgeon of the 143rd Pennsylvania Infantry, worked without rest through the long night to provide relief for the suffering. He asked permission to use the Myers' kitchen and cookstove for the unending task of cooking for the soldiers. Instantly, the Myers house was transformed into a hospital auxilliary service as the family cooked, boiled linens and bandages, and otherwise tried to meet the demands of

United Presbyterian Church, West High Street, Gettysburg, Pa., c. 1888.
(ACHS)

St. Francis Xavier Catholic Church, West High Street, Gettysburg, Pa., as it appeared in 1863, where Sallie Myers "sat down on the steps and cried." (ACHS)

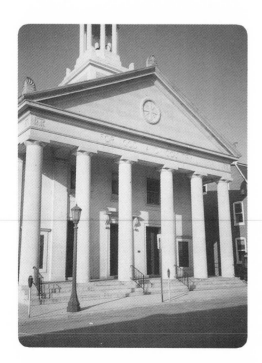

St. Francis Xavier Catholic Church as it appears today.

151

row upon row of wounded soldiers who awaited food, water, and medical attention.

Understaffed and overburdened with the monumental task of tending so many with so few, on Thursday morning, July 2, Dr. Fulton walked into the Myers home and said to the daughters, "Girls, you must come up to the churches and help us. Our boys are suffering terribly from want of attention."[28] Sallie's initial reaction to Dr. Fulton's request was uncertainty, for as she later wrote:

> It didn't seem as if I could do such work, but I went. The doctor led
> the way to the Catholic church, which, like all the other public buildings,
> had been turned into a hospital. Some of the wounded lay in the pews,
> and some lay on the floor with knapsacks under their heads, and there
> were very few persons to do anything for the poor fellows. Everywhere
> was blood, and on all sides we heard groans and cries and prayers.[29]

Thus, Sallie Myers found herself drawn into nursing the wounded. This young woman who only the day before had turned her head away in horror at the sight of a bleeding horse and a soldier's bandaged head, had now turned herself in the direction of St. Francis Xavier Church. The sights and sounds inside the church were terrible at first. Sallie's first encounter there was with a critically wounded man who, after she climbed the steps and walked through the door, was lying just inside the vestibule:

> I went into the Roman Catholic Church. The men were scattered all
> over it, some lying in the pews and some on the bare floor. The suffer-
> ing and groans of the wounded and dying were terrible to see and hear.
> I knelt by the first one inside the door and said, "What can I do for
> you?" He looked up at me with mournful, fearless eyes, and said,
> "Nothing; I am going to die." To be met thus by the first one I addressed
> was more than my overwrought nerves could bear, and I went hastily
> out, sat down on the church step and cried. In a little while, by a great
> effort, I controlled myself, re-entered the hospital, and spoke again to
> the dying man. He was wounded in the lungs and spine and there was
> not the slightest hope. He was Sgt. Alexander Stewart (Company D) of
> the 149th Pa. Vols.[30]

As she talked to Alexander Stewart, he asked her to read to him the 14th chapter of John, which he and his wife Lizzie, his brother Henry, and his parents had read together at the family altar before the brothers departed for the war. Opening her Bible, Sallie read, "... Peace I leave with you; my peace I give to you. Not as the world gives do I give it to you. Do not let your hearts be troubled or afraid. ..." Alexander then described Lizzie, his mother Jane and his father John, at home on the family farm in New Brighton, Pennsylvania. He also spoke of his younger brother, Henry, telling her how they had enlisted together after Henry's graduation that past August, comrades and brothers even in war. But Alexander was in Gettysburg without Henry, for in January, Henry had been injured, discharged, and was back home recuperating.[31] Sallie listened to the dying man, then wrote down the address of his family and promised to write to them of his love. The nature of his wounds meant that medically, there was nothing further that could be done for Alexander Stewart in the hospital. At his request, he was moved at noon to Sallie's house. She cared for him there, and soon a dozen other wounded soldiers would find their way to the Myers home.[32]

Through the long hours of July 2, Sallie worked with little rest, tending to wounds and requests for water, comforting the men in their pain and misery. Back and forth between the Catholic church hospital and home she traveled, for instructions and supplies, carrying food and linens in her arms. She later wrote in her diary of Alexander's deteriorating condition, and noted, "He seems better and worse by times. Watched by him all day and all night except two hours during which I rested. Our men were taken prisoners and we had three of them in the cellar. What awful noises, heavy shell flying over the town from 4 to 9 o'clock."[33]

That evening, as the battle intensified south of Gettysburg, the order came once again that civilians were to go to their cellars, for the shelling and rifle fire had accelerated to tremendous proportions. With all doors and windows closed, the heat was oppressive, the air unbearably thick, and Alexander Stewart urged Sallie to go to the safety of the cellar. But Sallie would not leave Alexander, who lay in the front room of the first floor and could not be moved below. For her loyalty and devotion to a dying soldier, Sallie almost lost her own life:

> That night we were again ordered to the cellar. He [Stewart] insisted on my going to the cellar—said nothing could save his life and I must not risk mine—but I could not leave him to suffer in the stifling atmosphere, for we were obliged to close all doors and windows. While fanning him, being in an uncomfortable position, I changed it and a moment later a ball struck the floor where I had been sitting, scattering over us the plaster which it had displaced.[34]

July 3, the final day of the battle, Sallie wrote that she was "at the Hospital occasionally through the day and watched by Mr. Stewart. He seems better but the poor fellow will not get well...I have been very busy all day." As she went back and forth between the hospitals and home, she offered what comfort she could to Alexander and the other soldiers under her care, and she would later write in her diary, "Mr. Stewart cannot bear to have me away from him."[35]

The conditions in the churches were horrendous. Along with the stench of unwashed bodies and infected wounds was the sight of blood everywhere, on walls and floors, covering pews, doorways and even the altars themselves. Amputated limbs quickly accumulated in piles, hastily carried or even thrown out doors and windows, part of a grisly, grotesque assembly line of heart-rending proportions.

The Fourth of July, Independence Day, had a special meaning that summer for Sallie and all of Gettysburg. Robert E. Lee's army had abandoned the town, and was encamped along Seminary Ridge. By the following day, July 5, Lee's army was in full retreat, through Fairfield to Maryland and south toward the Potomac River. No longer threatened by the invaders, the home ground had been contested and the Union was victorious. Sallie wrote, "The rebels have left and we are again in possession of the town. I never spent a happier Fourth. It seemed so bright when the surly rebels had gone."[36]

Sergeant Alexander Stewart died on July 6, and the soldier who first drew Sallie's attention in the Catholic Church was temporarily laid to rest nearby, until a few days later when John Stewart came to Gettysburg, took Alexander's body home, and interred it in the Presbyterian churchyard in Clinton, Allegheny County, Pennsylvania.[37] Emotionally attached to Alexander, Sallie poignantly wrote of his final hours in her home:

> He has been sinking gradually all morning. About 9 o'clock he had a hard spell of coughing and until 10 he suffered dreadfully. I held him in my arms until nearly 11 when his head sank on the pillow and he died with only a slight struggle. I have never been so much interested in a stranger. I was with him almost constantly, wrote to his wife and friends. They will come for the body.[38]

Thus, the aftermath of war does not disappear with the retreat of the defeated. Long after the final guns are fired and the last soldier falls on the field of battle, the dying and destruction continue. Gettysburg found itself facing the monumental task of clearing debris, restoring the fields and farms left in ruins, and trying to meet the demands of caring for the wounded and burying the dead, both Union and Confederate, left behind by the thousands. The rains that fell after the battle filled hastily dug graves with water, and bodies previously laid to rest required that boards be laid over them to keep them in place. The hot July sun beat down on bodies lying yet unburied, quickly turning dead flesh and bone to bloated rot and stench. Farmers, for weeks trying to restore destroyed fields, plowed up live shells and battle debris, hands, arms, legs and feet, and various other pieces of what were once whole men.

For Sallie Myers, too, the battle did not end. Throughout the months of July and August she worked, walking with tired feet to the church hospitals and later to Camp Letterman, the field hospital located one mile from Gettysburg on the York Pike where many of "her boys" were moved. She nursed fourteen soldiers in her home, and as their families came to Gettysburg to see about their loved ones, Sallie and her family provided them with food and a place to rest. She later described, "Our house looks like a tavern, all but the liquor, and we have plenty of that, of different kinds, but not for sale."[39] Routine activities such as worship services were suspended indefinitely, until the churches were cleared of the wounded.

For many weeks after the battle, Sallie lived the life of a soldier. She slept in her clothes on the upstairs hallway floor of her home, the only available space not occupied by a wounded soldier:

> All our rooms were kept full, and I slept on the floor in the hall upstairs with a roll of carpet for my pillow. That was the only bed I had, and for weeks I didn't have my clothing off at night. Our ordinary household routine was very much broken up. We came in and ate when

we wanted anything, and it was a long time before we all sat down together.[40]

Sallie did not want the rest of the soldiers in her home and in the Catholic Church to be moved, but she had heard of the plans to do so. A tent hospital had been erected on the George Wolf farm east of town on July 20, in an effort to remove the wounded from scattered locations around Gettysburg into one place.[41] She wrote on July 23, "They are talking about moving all to a general hospital about a mile and a half from here. I am afraid they will take our boys but I hope not." By the next day, the operation was completed and all wounded who were fit for travel had been moved. Sallie continued to nurse "her boys," but some in a much different setting. On July 24, she noted in her diary:

> They have moved all from the churches and private houses to a General Hospital near where the Porter Guards were encamped two years ago. Some of them have been taken to Harrisburg, and among them one of ours. Private Decker disliked to go very much. His foot is painful. Andrew Crooks has been taken to the General Hospital....Went to the hospital. Andrew is doing very well. Home at nine, folded the clothes—feel very tired.

Sallie traveled back and forth between the United States General Hospital (Camp Letterman) and home, with passes issued to her by the surgeons in charge. These passes authorized her entry into the field hospitals, as well as access to any

United States General Hospital (Camp Letterman). (ACHS)

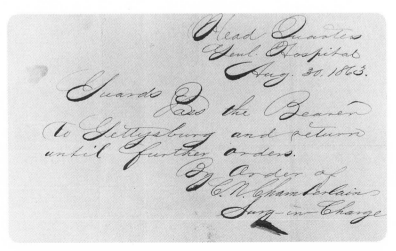

(top of photo) U.S. Sanitary Commission authorization for supplies as needed, granted to Sallie Myers, dated July 13, 1863. (bottom of photo) Pass granting access to the General Hospital (Camp Letterman), the tent hospital located on the York Pike, dated August 10, 1863. (ACHS).

Pass dated August 30, 1863, granting Sallie Myers access to and from Camp Letterman. (Scott Hann collection) and all supplies necessary while caring for the wounded. She would later describe her passes as being "among my most precious possessions."[42]

On July 25, Sallie was also needed at home to take care of her mother and sister, Susie, who were both sick. Cooking and ironing through the morning, she busily finished her chores, and after supper headed for Camp Letterman. She had not walked far when it began to rain. Her trip turned out to be quite adventurous, for she later wrote:

> I was fortunate enough to get into a buggy which was passing and I knew the man. He took me out and promised to come for me again, but he did not. It rained very hard and I could not go back so I went to the ladies tent & looked at soldiers fashions. The beds were all occupied and I got a gum blanket and laid it on the ground and on it I put two government blankets. Then I lay down and covered two over me and slept very soundly. The rain coming on the tent was very entertaining.[43]

Trips to Camp Letterman continued through the remainder of the summer, as Sallie volunteered her services alongside the ranks of enlisted nurses. Some of these women, like Cornelia Hancock, would become lifelong friends. Camp Letterman officially closed on November 20, 1863, four months from the day it opened.[44] Sallie's nursing experience ended with the striking of the tents at Camp Letterman, but the impact of the experience would last her entire lifetime. An innocent bystander caught in the destruction of war, a "thoughtless, lighthearted girl" who "never could stand the sight of blood," Sallie somehow found the courage necessary to face the blood, the suffering and agony, and the screeching of shells as she answered the call from Dr. Fulton and first walked up those steps into the Catholic church. Years after her experience, she recalled:

> The sight of blood never again affected me and I was among the wounded and dying men day and night. While the battle lasted and the town was in possession of the rebels, I went back and forth between my home and the hospitals without fear. The soldiers called me brave, but I am afraid the truth was that I did not know enough to be afraid and if I had known enough, I had no time to think of the risk I ran, for my heart and my hands were full.[45]

Fate, or destiny, whichever word is preferred to describe the course of events that serve to affect a life, and sometimes alter its direction completely, often occurs from sheer circumstance, without personal intention, prior knowledge of cause and effect, or possible outcome. As Sallie Myers cradled Alexander Stewart in her arms and offered what comfort she could as he breathed his last, the future connection between them could hardly have been foreseen. As she helped to lay his body to rest, and then wrote to his family back home, Sallie could not have known that because Alexander's life had ended, her own would have a new beginning.

On July 29, 1863, Sallie received a letter from Sergeant Alexander Stewart's brother, Henry F. Stewart. This letter marked the beginning of a correspondence and courtship that would last over the next three years, and result in their marriage on October 17, 1867. Her diary entry for July 29 noted, "Received a letter from Henry Stewart, a brother of Sergeant Stewart. It was a splendid letter coming from a grateful heart."

The remainder of the typescripted entries for the year 1863 are filled with notations regarding Sallie and Henry's romantic correspondence. The only exceptions to this type of entry occur in November, when Sallie commented on President Lincoln's arrival in Gettysburg with his entourage to dedicate the Soldiers' National Cemetery. She wrote on November 18, "President Lincoln and a number of others, members of his cabinet, came this evening on a special train," and the next day she noted, "The long looked for 19th is here at last. Went up the street and saw the procession going out to the cemetery and then came home to work. Saw the President and a great many distinguished men but had little time to look at them."

Thus ends Sallie's eventful year, but many changes in her life would occur as a result of her participation in that battle. The letters exchanged with the many soldiers she cared for, and the kindness she showed to their families, would result in friendships that lasted her entire life. She would later move to western Pennsylvania as a minister's wife, and within a year's time, bury her young husband, then give birth to their son, alone and far from loved ones and home.

DIARY 1863

The Salome Myers Stewart diary for the year 1863, once housed with the Stewart family collection at the Adams County Historical Society in Gettysburg, Pennsylvania, mysteriously disappeared from the Society during the late 1960s. To date, this historically significant diary has not been recovered, and its where-abouts are unknown. The following few entries contained in the typescripts for the months of January through May 1863, are reproduced here:

Friday, January 2.
Report the Rebels are coming. Had our Christmas tree lighted.

Monday, February 2.
To see Uncle Lewis Myers. He is home on a furlough but is going back to the York Hospital tomorrow. Was taking music lessons from Cousin Carrie Sheads.

Thursday, April 2.
Gave father $15.00 for rent & paid Mr. Schick all I owed him. Hurrah.

Friday, May 29.
The lower floor of our school is divided into four school rooms. The upper floor has one school room with two recitation rooms. The upper floor is to be divided into four school rooms with glass partitions like the lower floor.

——— *June and July, 1863* ———

Most of the entries for the months of June and July are taken from the typescripts conducted by Dr. Henry Stewart. Some additions to his work are included, for in 1897 Sallie wrote a personal memoir she titled, "Recollections of the Battle of Gettysburg, Written for my son, Harry." In this memoir she quoted directly from her diary entries, and some of her quotations are much more exten-sive than Henry's typescripts conducted many years later when the diary pages were more faded and harder to read.

The challenge was to put both Sallie's quotations and Henry's typescripts together in the most precise way possible. At times Henry's quotes differed slightly from Sallie's; when this occurred I chose to use Sallie's own words from the memoir in an attempt to achieve the most accurate representation of the diary.

Sallie interspersed her diary quotations with reflective remarks throughout the 1897 memoir. Several of these reflections have been included. They have been identified in an effort to separate them from the actual diary writings, for the sake of clarity.

From the 1897 memoir:
It has long been my desire & intention to write an account of my experiences during the eventful summer of 1863, for your benefit, so that you might know something of what was done and endured by your Grandfather Myers' family during and after the battle.

At that time our family consisted of my father, 47 years old, my mother Margaret (Sheads) 45 years old, my brother Jefferson, 23 years old (he had been married in May of that year), myself, 21 years old, my sister Susie (15 years), Jennie (12 years), Belle (10 years), and Grace (6 years).

Our house was on West High St., the sixth house West of the Catholic Church, at this time (Dec. 1897), occupied by Mr. Stover. It is a frame two story house.

My father had been a member of the 87th P.V., and my brother of the 1st Penna. Reserve, but both had been discharged for disability. My Father was Justice of the Peace. I was teaching in the Public Schools as 2nd Assistant. My sisters were still in school & my brother was a printer.

From Henry A. Stewart's typescripts:

Monday, June 15.

The town is all in an uproar. Merchants are packing their goods & sending them off and every one shares in the confusion caused by the news 'The rebels are coming.'"

Tuesday, June 16.

Last night the "darkies" made such a racket up and down by our house that we could not sleep.

Wednesday, June 17.

The Rebels are still coming. Another report that the Rebels were coming set the town in a perfect uproar. The excitement was intense for a while but it died down when it was found that the report was false. I am getting very tired of all this fuss consequent upon border life though the numerous reports do not alarm me. On the contrary I am sometimes quite amused by seeing the extremes to which people will go. I pity the poor darkies. They seem perfectly bewildered.

From the 1897 memoir:

Gettysburg is only about 7 miles from Mason & Dixon's Line, and we have a population of between 300 & 400 colored people. Their fear of the rebels was caused by the belief that they would be captured and sold as slaves if the Rebels came north into the States. I know not how much cause they had for their fears, but it was a terrible reality to them. All who could got away and those who were obliged to stay at home were at the shortest notice suddenly transformed into limping, halting, and apparently worthless specimens of humanity.

Thursday, June 18.

The rebels are coming. That again is the latest.

Friday, June 19.

The excitement is intense. Some of our boys from the 87th P.V. who were in the battle of Winchester, Va., last Sunday, came home today. Among them were Uncle William Culp & Cousin David Myers, of my other two Uncles and cousins they know nothing. The boys retreated. Their ammunition gave out and they "made for home!" Poor fellows! They have been on the road since Monday evening. Dear me! What times! All week I have been pretty busy and steady, but today I could no longer control myself & I was out nearly all day.

Saturday, June 20.

The excitement is still intense. Some Cavalry from Philadelphia who armed & equipped themselves, came tonight. They are entirely and altogether volunteers.

Sunday, June 21.

Afternoon. The excitement grows worse than ever. I think it is about as bad as it can be. For the first time for more than 2 years I have been alarmed and excited.

The Rebels have taken possession of Millerstown, about 8 miles from here, or rather Fairfield, which is its proper name. Evening. Had no preaching. Rev. Eisenberg has "skeedaddled." The town is pretty clear of darkies. They have nearly all left. I pity the poor creatures. Darkies of both sexes are skeedaddling and some white folks of the male sex. I am glad I am neither a man nor a darky, though girls are not so much better off. Oh dear, I wish the excitement was over.

Monday, June 22.

Went to the stores but there is very little to be bought. They look quite desolate.

Tuesday, June 23.

About three o'clock another excitement was gotten up. The rebels were coming certainly. Nearly everybody looked for them but they disappointed us again.

Thursday, June 25.

There is a great deal of excitement, the "Rebs" are near "they say."

Friday, June 26.

In Rebeldom. About 4 o'clock the long looked for Rebels made their appearance, and such a mean looking lot of men I never saw in my life. They flew around after any stray horses and it was very provoking to see them riding around doing just as they pleased. Several hundred Cavalry came first, then followed several thousand Infantry with their old red flag flying and they were yelling like fiends. I am not afraid of them and did not believe they were coming as I stood on the corner until two of them rode by furiously brandishing their sabres and pointing pistols. At last we have seen the rebels. Evening. How exasperating the thought that tonight we are under the control of "armed traitors." Two of them were at our door about two hours talking to father about the war and their southern rights etc. We talked to them as we would to any one else. Father and I told them we were for the Union unconditionally. They were very reasonable and our conversation was interesting.

Saturday, June 27.

We were awakened by a rebel band playing a rebel march in our Court House where they were quartered for the night. Only a part of them were there. The greater part of them left last night about 11. They went out in a hurry for our own men are near and of course they heard of them. Afternoon. The rebels have gone on towards New Oxford and Hanover after burning 15 or 20 cars and the bridge over the creek. The cars cannot run into town now. Evening. The news conflicts. Some say there are more Rebs coming and some say the Union troops are near. I suppose both tales are true and we may look for strenuous times. Hooker and Lee with their armies are in Maryland and Pennsylvania.

Sunday, June 28.

Morning. The advance pickets of Hooker's army (I think) came in town this morning about 10 1/2 and now we are expecting a large part of Hooker's cavalry. Hope they will come. Afternoon. Several thousand cavalry came to town today. They are a Division of Hooker's army. They stopped at the East end of town and sent out scouts in every direction. We feel safe now as the Artillery & Infantry are not very far off. We did not have Sunday School this afternoon—too much excitement. We were too glad to see our noble looking Union troops. Quite a contrast to the dirty mean looking rebels who call themselves Southern Chivalry.

Monday, June 29.

Washed today but could not put up the clothes, it is raining. The rebels are near and our men have gone to meet the rest of our men. God be with them. Afternoon.

Reports of all kinds abroad. Made an apron for myself. Evening. Rebels are reported near. Their camp fires can be seen in the Mountains. Our men in great numbers are advancing from Frederick and we may expect a battle both near and soon. God help us! for surely our cause is one of justice and humanity.

Tuesday, June 30.

Several thousand cavalry came into town, they commenced coming about noon. They were very enthusiastic. We sang for them and they cheered.

From the 1897 memoir:

...the surrounding country. It was never equaled even when the rebels came. We felt utterly defenseless. Naturally we girls thought all the chivalry of the town took its departure in the morning and our imagination pictured the most outlandish things which would be done. Children and women went about wringing their hands, alternately bemoaning our impending fate & praying for deliverance. Many of the remaining men and darkies left. Jefferson had gone to Harrisburg, and father hunted up an old gun, loaded it and left it in the house and then went out to hear what could be heard. Mother said, "There is this gun ready loaded for the rebels to shoot us." In the midst of our terror we laughed, for not one of us knew how to handle a gun. In an hour or two we were assured that the report was false, and the town quieted down.

From Henry A. Stewart's typescripts:

Wednesday, July 1.

Feel dreadfully, about 10 1/2 o'clock. The shells make me feel pretty badly. Afternoon. Our infantry which was behind came up and the fighting was awful. About three o'clock our men were driven back and the rebels took possession of the town. All afternoon I stood in a driving rain giving water to our infantry as they went into battle tired, hungry and thirsty.

Thursday, July 2.

Morning. Went to the hospital. Saw a poor man by the name of Stewart of Barington, Pa., who was shot through the lungs and will die. Brought him down to our house at noon. He seems better and worse by times. Watched by him all day and all night except two hours during which I rested. Our men were taken prisoners and we had three of them in the cellar. What awful noises, heavy shells flying over the town from 1 to 9 o'clock. While I was fanning Mr. Stewart a minnie ball came through two walls and struck the floor where I had been sitting but a few minutes before. Had I stayed a few minutes longer I would have been struck through the neck. One of my young companions was killed by a ball.

Friday, July 3.

At the hospital occasionally through the day and watched by Mr. Stewart. He seems better but the poor fellow will not get well. He reminds me of Mr. Casey very much. I have been very busy all day. I feel Mr. Stewart bear to have me away from him. Lieut. Col. H[uidekoper], Major Chamberlain & Capt. Leslie are staying with us. Lieut. Col. has lost his right arm. Major is wounded in the shoulder & Capt. Leslie in the face. They are doing very well. I wish Stewart was doing as well. The rebels have possession of the town.

Saturday, July 4.

Brought from the Hospital Mr. Andrew Crooks, a friend of Mr. Stewart who was wounded while helping Mr. S off the field. He has his right leg amputated. He is in the same company & from the same neighborhood as Mr. Stewart. The rebels have left and we are again in possession of the town. I never spent a happier Fourth.

It seemed so bright when the surly rebels had gone. Evening. Brought Andrew Wintamute of Wyoming to our house. He is wounded in the arm and stomach. Mr. Stewart is worse. Capt. Leslie left. Our house is used as a sort of a kitchen to cook for the wounded in the Hospital. The Catholic and United Presbyterian churches are used as hospitals. Kept pretty busy. Get little rest at night.

Sunday, July 5.

Of course we had no services today. Busy with our own affairs & at the Hospital. Mr. Stewart's brother in law came to see him. His name is Barton. We thought Mr. Stewart dying in the afternoon but he rallied and seemed better. Evening. Feel very tired.

Monday, July 6.

Mr. Stewart's brother in law left. He has been sinking gradually all morning. About 9 o'clock he had a hard spell of coughing and until 10 he suffered dreadfully. I held him in my arms until nearly 11 when his head sank on the pillow and he died with only a slight struggle. I have never been so much interested in a stranger. I was with him almost constantly, wrote to his wife & friends. They will come for the body. Lieut. Col. H & Maj. Chamberlain left this morning. I felt sorry to see them go.

Tuesday, July 7.

Morning. At 11 we buried poor Mr. Stewart. His funeral was very affecting. Mr. Bushman officiated. Afternoon. Busy. Cleaning up. Evening. Capt. James Ashworth from (?) Penna. Vols, and Lieut. Ruth came. Captain is pretty badly wounded, and Lieut. Ruth very weak.

Wednesday, July 8.

Busy all day. Lieut. Ruth left but the Capt is still with us. He cannot be moved. Very busy all day going to the Hospital and back. Get very tired as I do not get enough time to sleep. Captain Blair, who had his right arm amputated came to stay with us for some time. His servant Cato came along. Frank Decker, a friend of Andrew Wintamute, came also from the hospital.

Thursday, July 9.

Our patients are all doing very well. Captain Ashworth's brother came to help take care of him. Feel pretty tired and sleepy. Our house looks like a tavern, all but the liquor, and we have plenty of that, of different kinds, though not for sale.

Friday, July 10.

Busy all day. Our men are doing finely. Capt. Blair's brother is here. Wilson Race is doing finely at the hospital. I wanted to have him brought down but the Dr. objected and he concluded to stay until Thursday when he will be able to walk down. Will Sheriff of Pittsburgh, wounded in both legs is better. The Dr. would not let me bring him down.

Saturday, July 11.

We have four men here from New York who came to render any assistance in their power. Our men are doing well. Capt. Ashworth's mother is here with us, taking care of her son. He is still very low. Will Sheriff's father & mother came to take him home. They are staying with us and I seldom liked strangers as well. Will gave me his photograph some time ago.

Sunday, July 12.

Mr. Stewart's father came to get the body of his son. He is a poor weak old man. He is very much distressed about his son. Mr. Baldwin came with him. His son was killed and buried by the rebels. The weather was not fit for Wilson Race to come to our house, and I suppose he will have to stay in the hospital. Poor Mr. Stewart, how I pity him and Mr. Baldwin.

Monday, July 13.

Morning. Brought Amos Sweet from the Catholic Church. He has lost his right leg. He may recover. Wilson Race's father came to see him, but I am afraid it will make him worse. He is shot through the right lung, and his recovery is doubtful, though men live through it. His father is a very pleasant man. It affects him very much, so much that he cannot speak of it without crying. Evening. Wilson is worse. His father cannot stay with him. His business requires him to return home today. Oh, what trying times.

Tuesday, July 14.

Mr. and Mrs. Sheriff left with Will. Felt very sorry to have them go but it could not be helped. I am so glad he is getting home for his own sake. Our two New York men left also. Mr. Race left. Poor man. I pity him. I am afraid he will never see his son alive. Corp. George Bates of Philadelphia, shot in the leg and arm is doing well. The ball is still in. Evening. Our boys are doing very well. Capt. Ashworth seems to be improved.

Wednesday, July 15.

Mr. Sweet died at noon. Busy all day. Andrew Wintamute, his brother and friend left today. Sorry to see them go though I am glad he can go home.

Thursday, July 16.

Captain Blair, his brother, wife, son, and darky left this morning. Also Mr. Stewart, with the remains of his son and Mr. Baldwin who found his son unfit to be moved and will leave him until winter. Evening. Dr. Wilson of Ohio left today. Mrs. Thiele of Phila. came to our home today, hunting Capt. Ashworth to find out about her husband who was shot and is dead. Poor woman. She is almost distracted. Dr. Loughman, in whose hospital he died was very kind. Wilson Race is worse. Had Mr. Berkstresser talk & pray with him. I wrote Mrs. Sweet & Judge Richard.

Friday, July 17.

Busy ironing, going to the hospital and doing errands. Afternoon. Did several errands and wrote some letters. Our boys are doing finely. Capt. Henry A. Eaton & O.S. Eugene L. Eaton came to our house to stay overnight. Their hospital was four miles out of town, broken up and they were not able to go further. They belong to Co. A, 16th Reg't Vermont Vols. Went to see Wilson Race. He is better and his symptoms are decidedly more favorable.

Saturday, July 18.

Our men are doing well except Capt. Ashworth, who is very ill. Afternoon. Busy. Went to the store, & so forth. Evening. Mr. Jas. Goodrich of Co. K, 14th Vermont came this evening. He is not wounded, but is sick.

Sunday, July 19.

All our men are doing well except Capt. Ashworth is not so well. He is very ill. Busy all day. Evening. Mr. Henry Frazer, of Co. C, 14th Vermont came to stay with us for a day or two. Wilson Race is very low. He will hardly live long. Very pleasant. Mrs. Thiele went to Philadelphia this afternoon. Poor woman. How I pity her, left with three small children.

Monday, July 20.

Capt. Eaton's father came from Illinois to see his two sons. Our boys are doing well. Capt. Ashworth is better but I suppose it will not amount to much. Our family physician is attending him. Wilson Race is better. I had him moved out where he will get fresh air. It seemed to do him good.

Tuesday, July 21.

Morning. Warm. Feel sick. Have a headache. Capt. & Orderly Serg't Eaton, Mr. Goodrich, and Mr. Frazer left this morning for New York. Evening. Writing several letters. Wrote to Mrs. Race. He is much better. Had a letter from Will Sheriff with photographs of his mother and sisters, Annie and Becky. Our boys are doing very well.

Wednesday, July 22.

Busy all day. Our boys are doing well. Wilson Race seems to be improving and things look encouraging. Evening. Went to the store. Jennie Gilbert and Mr. Boyer of Massachusetts were here a while. Evening. Very pleasant, clear and moonlight. Mrs. Sweet came today to see her husband, not knowing he was dead. She had not received any of our letters. One written by a gentleman in the hospital which was encouraging was all she had received.

Thursday, July 23.

Mrs. Sweet left this morning. She is almost heartbroken. Very busy all day. Afternoon. Wrote to Mr. Sheriff. Sent him two letters that came after he left. Evening. Wilson Race is very much worse. I am afraid we will have to give him up after all. Poor Wilson and his poor father & mother. Feel badly. They are talking about moving all to a general hospital about a mile and a half from here. I am afraid they will take our boys but I hope not.

Friday, July 24.

Morning. Rose early and went to see Wilson Race. He failed rapidly and died about 8 o'clock. He died peacefully and happily. He was not afraid. His last words were "Tell mother I died loving Jesus and trusting him for salvation." Washing. Afternoon. They have moved all from the churches and private houses to a General Hospital near where the Porter Guards were encamped two years ago. Some of them have been taken to Harrisburg, and among them one of ours. Private Decker disliked to go very much. His foot is painful. Andrew Crooks has been taken to the General Hospital. Went down to see Frank before the cars started, but was too late. Went to the hospital. Andrew is doing very well, and is pleasantly situated. George Bates is gone to Harrisburg. Evening. Received a very loving letter from Cousin Lizzie Myers, of Centreville, Wayne Co., Ind. Have not heard from her for some time. Home at nine, folded the clothes—feel very tired.

Saturday, July 25.

Rose at 4 1/2. Got breakfast and ironed until 8. Sadie Rupp helped me. Mother and Susie both sick. Mother is overdone. Afternoon. Busy. Went to the store and bought portfolio & ink stand for Andrew Crooks and took them out to him after supper. It began to rain but I was fortunate enough to get into a buggy which was passing and I knew the man. He took me out and promised to come for me again, but he did not. It rained very hard and I could not go back so I went to the ladies tent & looked at soldiers fashions. The beds were all occupied and I got a gum blanket and laid it on the ground and on it I put two government blankets. Then I lay down and covered two over me and slept very soundly. The rain coming on the tent was very entertaining. I see I am writing in advance of the time but the facts are here never the less. I was sorry to be away from home.

Sunday, July 26.

Rose at 5, feeling very well after my first experience in camp life. Home at 6. Mother is better. Also Susie. Got breakfast and did the work. Afternoon. Busy. Mrs. Krause could not get off and stayed until tomorrow morning. Mother and Susie both improved. Evening. Mr. Spencer took me out to the hospital in a buggy about 8 o'clock. Had a very pleasant ride. Met nearly all the boys I know in the hospitals and out street. It was moonlight and cool enough to be pleasant.

Monday, July 27.

Evening. Wm. Rupp, Sadie Rupp, Mr. Wallace & Mr. Casey went to the hospital. Pa came for me in a hurry. Mr. Race had come for Wilson's body. Poor Mr. Race. I gave him all the consolation I could. He mourns very much for his son's early death. I took a last look at him and put some flowers on the coffin. Wrote to Mrs. Race. Wrote till 11, but was too sleepy to finish. It is just 2 weeks since Mr. Race was here before. How different the circumstances. God help them to bear their bereavement.

Tuesday, July 28.

Finished Mrs. Race's letter and wrote to Wilson's brother from whom I received one last night. Wrote to Nellie Myers of New York, who made a house wife which fell into my hands under rather peculiar circumstances, and in it was a request from the maker to acknowledge the receipt of it by a letter. Evening. Mr. Wm. Decker came for his brother Frank and found him gone to Harrisburg. Dr. Willing of Carlisle, originally one of our Volunteer surgeons, spent the evening here. He has been sick and tomorrow morning will start for his regiment according to orders.

Wednesday, July 29.

Joe Lewis, a hospital steward who has been boarding with us, with Dr. Gates and Mr. Spencer left for their regiments. Perhaps Dr. Williams went, though if he can stay he will. Felt sorry to part with them, especially Joe, who seems like a brother to us. Wrote to Mrs. Rankin, Mr. Stewart's pastor's wife, from whom I received a letter some time age. Received a letter from Mrs. Thiele, of Philadelphia. Evening. Joe came back on the afternoon train. There was something wrong with their transportation papers. He brought with him a friend of the same name but no relation. Received a letter from Henry Stewart, a brother of Serg't Stewart who died with us on the 6th of this month. It was a splendid letter coming from a grateful heart.

Thursday, July 30.

Received a letter from Serg't J. B. Wilson, a wounded soldier who lay in the Catholic Church. He was moved to Harrisburg some time ago.

At this point, the 1897 memoir written by Sallie ends, and none of the additional pages have been located. Therefore, the remainder of 1863 entries depends solely on Dr. Henry A. Stewart's typescripts.

Sunday, August 23.

The Provost Marshall has been changed & I went to get my recommendation renewed by Dr. Loughman of the 20th N.Y., and get my pass renewed.

Monday, August 24.

Brother Jeff and a good many of my friends are drafted. I am sorry but I don't think they will keep him, or rather take him.

Saturday, September 19.

Commenced an answer to Harrie Stewart's letter.

Monday, October 10.

Letter from Harrie Stewart and news of a package on the way from Lizzie.

Tuesday, October 11.

Received my express package today. It was a large case containing a heavy gold ring inscribed as a "token of her regard and appreciation of my devoted kindness to her beloved husband"

Monday, October 19.
> School began. I am teacher of #4.

Wednesday, October 21.
> Wrote a note to Harrie Stewart, a sort of a business note.

Saturday, November 7.
> Received a letter from Harry Stewart.

Tuesday, November 11.
> Received a letter from Mrs. Stewart with the pictures of Mr. and Mrs. Stewart, Son. Mr. Stewart's is very good, but I never saw Mrs. S.

Monday, November 16.
> Hon. Edward Everett, General Couch and several distinguished personages are in town. They came in a special train, also some soldiers.

Tuesday, November 17.
> School dismissed today—in anticipation of the approaching 19th on which day our National Cemetery will be dedicated.

Wednesday, November 18.
> President Lincoln and a number of others, members of his cabinet came this evening on a special train.

Thursday, November 19.
> The long looked for 19th is here at last. Went up street and saw the procession going out to the Cemetery and then came home to work. Saw the President and a great many distinguished men but had little time to look at them.

Friday, November 20.
> The town is all excitement—persons from abroad are as anxious to get away as they were to get here. Details an accidental shell explosion.

Friday, November 27.
> Had a letter from Harry Stewart, a long and interesting one—he writes splendid letters. In answer to a question which I asked him Harry S. told me he graduated from Jefferson College on the 5th day of August.

Thursday, December 3.
> Note from Harry Stewart enclosing his photograph. I like his appearance.

Friday, December 4.
> Wrote to Harry Stewart a note in reference to my photograph which he wants, and partly in answer to his note.

Friday, December 11.
> Commenced an answer to Mr. Stewart's letter of the 23rd.

Sunday, December 13.
> Finished Harry Stewart's letter and mailed it.

Wednesday, December 16.
> Wrote a note to Harry Stewart & sent him my photograph.

Thursday, December 24.
> Note from Harrie Stewart.

3

THE SOLDIERS:
"I SHALL NOT SOON FORGET THE FAMILY OF
MYERS"

While engaged in the serious business of nursing the battle wounded, Sallie Myers earned the highest respect and admiration from the soldiers whose suffering she eased during those hot summer weeks. Many of the soldiers she tended became her friends. Some of those friendships would last a lifetime, bonded together for years by the kind of camaraderie known only to those who have journeyed together to the brink of Hell and back, faced death head to head and, dependent on each other for survival, lived to tell the tale. Friendships formed from such beginnings evolve into a kind of symbiotic relationship, each party a participant in the ongoing story of the other, never again to exist as truly separate entities, always and forever tied to the past and each other.

And so it was with Sallie and her soldiers, her "boys,"[1] as she liked to call them. For the remainder of her life, she would be spoken of by these men with reverence, described in memoirs and speeches as an angel incarnate who stayed by their side and eased their pain. They called her brave; they called her kind, loving and merciful. Many of them, like Lieutenant Colonel Henry S. Huidekoper, who, along with the 150th Pennsylvania Volunteers, faced the rebel onslaught on McPherson's Ridge, took a minnie ball in the right arm and lost it under the surgeon's knife, and was awarded the Medal of Honor in 1905 for "most distinguished gallantry in action at Gettysburg," called her a hero.[2]

Sallie Myers tended a great many soldiers during the days of the battle and the many weeks which followed. Just how many cannot be estimated, for her nursing experience at Camp Letterman alone placed her in contact with hundreds of wounded men. Within her diary, however, is contained a record of some of these soldiers; descriptions of their name, rank and regiment is combined with their stories of pain, suffering, and sometimes death. As many of their stories as possible have been collected and presented on the following pages:

Lieutenant Colonel Henry S. Huidekoper
150th Pennsylvania Infantry

On July 2, after his arm had been amputated, Lieutenant Colonel Huidekoper
lay in the Catholic church. Asked by two
young girls if he was badly wounded or
needed anything, he replied that he was
hungry. The girls "went away, but returned in ten minutes from their homes
near by and gave me a glass of home-
made wine and one cracker, which Miss
Myers had to carry hidden under her shawl
lest she might encounter some hungry
rebel." The girls came back for him later,
and he was moved to the Myers house,
where he "was fed and given a bed until
about the ninth of July."[3]

Years after the battle, then General
H.S. Huidekoper gave the oration at the
Reunion of the Survivors of the 150th
Regiment, Pennsylvania Volunteers, on

Lt. Col. Henry Huidekoper.
(ACHS)

August 13, 1894. His speech included the following comments about Sallie
Myers and her family:

> John Burns has been termed the hero of Gettysburg; but that title
> should go to one of the many women who, through the shot and shell of
> the second and third days of July, or in the pain and misery of the next
> few days, forgot all danger and all personal comfort to drop tears over
> dying men as they gave their last messages for dear ones at home, or
> cheerfully ministered to the wants of the helpless wounded in their own
> homes and in the hospitals. I say this knowingly and feelingly, for
> while I was a prisoner one of these good women took me to her own
> house, where she and her sister were caring for others, to whom, by
> chance, Major [Thomas] Chamberlin was added to make the house full,
> and between my surprise at having him—whom I had seen killed two
> days before—dumped onto my bed, as though, having been tentmates
> for a year, we should not be separated longer, and my admiration and
> reverence for the family, I shall not soon forget the little house a few
> doors from the brick church, nor the family of Myers.

General Henry S. Huidekoper never did forget Sallie, for in her diary many
years later, she recorded visits from him whenever he came to Gettysburg.

Major Thomas Chamberlin
150th Pennsylvania Infantry

Major Thomas Chamberlin of the 150th Pennsylvania Volunteers also found
his way to Sallie Myers' house, where he was reunited with his comrade, Lieu-

tenant Colonel Henry S. Huidekoper, who had seen him shot and believed him to be dead.

An 1858 graduate of the University of Lewisburg (renamed Bucknell University in 1886)[4] Chamberlin entered the war as a Captain in the Fifth Pennsylvania Reserves. Severely wounded in the Peninsula Campaign of 1862, Chamberlin was later commissioned Major of the 150th Pennsylvania Volunteers on September 4, 1862, and served under regimental commander Colonel Langhorne Wister.[5] As part of the famous "Bucktail Brigade," Chamberlin took part in the furious fight at McPherson's Barn on July 1, and there received the wound that would affect him the rest of his life and cause his early discharge from service on March 16, 1864.[6]

Col. Thomas Chamberlin.
(Scott Hann collection)

Chamberlin was shot through the back and right shoulder; Sallie Myers tended his wounds until July 6, when he and Lieutenant Colonel Huidekoper left her home. Sallie wrote in her diary that day, "I felt sorry to see them go."[7]

Captain Brice X. Blair
Company I, 149th Pennsylvania Infantry

Captain Brice X. Blair of Company I, 149th Pennsylvania Volunteers, received a severe wound in the left arm during the fighting of July 1. Taken prisoner at the Seminary, he was "without surgical attention for several days."[8] His wound became infected and his arm required amputation at the shoulder joint in order to save his life.

One T. A. Appleby, in an article in the *Huntingdon Daily News*, published February 4, 1929, remembered this about Blair:

> Captain Blair was 40 years old, while his boys, as he called them, were an average of 21 years. He felt deeply for their welfare. During the fiercest of the fighting, in the field directly east of the McPherson buildings, a bullet struck his left arm near the shoulder and shattered the bone to pieces, almost cutting the arm off. It bled profusely, but he stayed with his men and directed them in the battle until the loss of blood was threatening his collapse, when he called Levi Graham to help him off the field. He took him to the cemetery, but our troops were being pressed back almost as fast as the wounded Captain could walk. When they reached the west side of the Seminary building, the bullets were knocking holes in the wooden steps so rapidly that they went around the big brick building and went up the stairs. Capt. Blair was

helped by Graham to an upper story bedroom, and as the "Rebs" were soon swarming all over the place, he (Graham) bloodied one of his arms and put it in a sling so that they might think him wounded and so leave him with the Captain. This deception worked all right for some time, but he was soon detected and sent off to the prisoner's camp. Capt. Blair received no medical attention until July 5th, when his wound seemed so hopeless that the Chief Surgeon would not take the time to cut his arm off. Finally, a junior surgeon undertook the job. It took many months before Capt. Blair recovered.[9]

Captain Blair stayed in the Myers home until July 16. Sallie noted in a later memoir that Captain Blair was left-handed. Note the glove above the sabre on his left, probably used to hide a wooden arm and hand.

Capt. Brice X. Blair, 149th Pennsylvania Volunteers. (Scott Hann collection)

Sgt. Levi G. Graham, 149th Pennsylvania Volunteers, who helped Capt. Blair off the field. (Ronn Palm collection, USAMHI)

Private C. Frank Decker
Co. K, 142nd Pennsylvania Infantry

Private C. Frank Decker, Company K, 142nd Pennsylvania Volunteers, came to the Myers house from the hospital on July 8.[10] Wounded in the foot, he joined his friend Andrew Wintamute, who had been at the Myers house since July 4. On July 24, he was shipped by train to a Harrisburg, Pennsylvania, general hospital instead of to Camp Letterman when the reorganization of the wounded took place. Sallie wrote, "Private Decker disliked to go very much. His foot is painful."[11]

In a later memoir, Sallie would recall that after recovery, Private Decker "joined his regiment, served out his time, and a few years later was drowned in the Susquehanna River in sight of his home."[12]

Pvt. C. Frank Decker.
(Scott Hann collection)

Private Andrew R. Wintamute
Company K, 143rd Pennsylvania Infantry

Private Andrew R. Wintamute, Company K, 143rd Pennsylvania Volunteers, was brought to Sallie Myers' home on the evening of July 4. Wounded in the arm and stomach, he nonetheless recovered and went home on July 15 for a long recuperation. Sallie wrote that, "Mr. Wintamute, another of our boys, recovered, rejoined his regiment, and in the first engagement was instantly killed."[13] The "first engagement" referred to by Sallie was the Wilderness, where Private Wintamute was killed on May 5, 1864.[14]

Captain Henry Eaton and Sergeant Eugene Eaton
Company A, 16th Regiment Vermont Infantry

Captain Henry Eaton and his brother, Orderly Sergeant Eugene Eaton, of Company A, 16th Vermont Volunteers, arrived at the Myers home on the evening of July 17. Sallie wrote, "Their hospital was four miles out of town, broken up and they were not able to go further."[15] On July 3, Orderly Sergeant Eaton was struck in the neck by a shell which passed into his left shoulder. Sallie later recalled that:

> Sgt. Eaton was suffering very much. His back had been very badly injured by a piece of shell, and he could neither stoop nor turn his head. The doctors and nurses were all busy. Capt. Eaton said he knew how the wound should be dressed, but as he was not able to do it, he would take the responsibility and superintend the job if I would do the work. I went to work and we succeeded in relieving him.[16]

Pvt. Andrew R. Wintamute,
149th Pennsylvania Volunteers.
(Scott Hann collection)

Capt. Henry Eaton,
16th Vermont Volunteers.
(Scott Hann collection)

Dr. James M. Fulton
143rd Pennsylvania Infantry

Dr. James Fulton, assistant surgeon of the 143rd Pennsylvania Infantry, was the surgeon in charge of both the St. Francis Xavier Catholic Church and the United Presbyterian and Associated Reform Church hospitals on High Street in Gettysburg.[17] Overworked and understaffed like every other surgeon in the battlefield hospitals, it was Dr. Fulton who first approached the Myers family and asked permission to use their kitchen. By the next morning, he made his request of Sallie and her sisters to assist the soldiers who were "suffering from want of attention."[18]

Dr. Fulton fell in love during his stay in Gettysburg. One of Sallie's girlhood friends and fellow teachers, Miss Alice (Allie) Powers, drew his attention as she assisted with the wounded in the Catholic church and at her home, on the corner of Washington and High Streets,

Dr. James Fulton, 143rd Pennsylvania Volunteers. (Scott Hann collection)

only several doors down from the Myers family residence. Allie Powers refused Dr. Fulton's repeated proposals of marriage. She had earlier betrothed herself to a young seminarian whose family objected to him marrying a poor schoolteacher. He, faced with being disinherited, chose money over love, and Allie vowed to never marry.[19]

Dr. Fulton eventually married another, and had two daughters. He tragically ended his days a complete invalid, for in early 1892, his daughters Susan and Helen filed a petition on behalf of his wife, Matilda, for management of his lands and goods. His pension claim papers describe him in 1892 as age 78, blind and utterly helpless, suffering from dementia.[20]

Private Andrew Crooks
Company D, 149th Pennsylvania Infantry

Private Andrew Crooks, Company D, 149th Pennsylvania, was severely wounded in the right ankle while trying to carry Sergeant Alexander M. Stewart from the field.[21] Stewart, wounded in the lungs and spine, could not walk. When Company D could no longer hold against Perrin's Brigade, and collapsed the line, Alexander was left on the field of battle, where he had fallen. Private Crooks helped to carry him across town and to the Catholic church, where he lay until Sallie Myers had him moved to her home.

Private Crooks' wound was severe enough to require amputation of the leg at the upper third portion; the surgery was performed in the Catholic church by regimental surgeon William F. Humphrey. Sallie remembered Andrew Crooks' amputation many years later:

I, who a short time before was ready to faint at the sight of blood, stood near to be of use if needed while the surgeons amputated his leg. We became acquainted without the formality of an introduction, and it was the beginning of a friendship which has stood the wear and tear of forty years.[22]

Many references to Andrew Crooks can be found in Sallie's diaries, some as late as 1906. Descriptions of visits, attendance at functions in Philadelphia with Andrew as escort, and letters and conversations shared between them, give testimony that their friendship was indeed one which "stood the wear and tear of forty years."

Captain James Ashworth
Company I, 121st Pennsylvania Infantry

On July 7, Captain James Ashworth of Company I, 121st Pennsylvania Volunteers, was moved to Sallie Myers' home. Shot in the right knee joint and elsewhere, she described him as having "seven severe and painful flesh wounds," and called him "pretty badly wounded."[23]

Ashworth's mother arrived in Gettysburg on July 11, and like many other relatives of the wounded in the Myers home, she stayed at Sallie's house where she could care for her son. His recovery was slow and painful, and Sallie wrote on the 18th, "Our men are doing well except Capt. Ashworth, who is very ill," and on the 20th she described him as "better but I suppose it will not amount to much."

Ashworth stayed at the Myers home for six weeks. He did recover, however, and served until the end of the war. His wound left him permanently lame, and he could walk only with great difficulty for the rest of his life.

Corporal George Bates
Company F, 150th Pennsylvania Infantry

Corporal George Bates, Company F, 150th Pennsylvania Volunteers, received wounds in the left shoulder and the right thigh during the fighting west of town on July 1. Cared for by Sallie and her family, Bates was removed by train to the hospital in Harrisburg on July 24. The minnie ball in his right thigh was never removed, and his right leg remained lame.[24]

Private William J. Sheriff
Company F, 150th Pennsylvania Infantry

Private William J. Sheriff, Company I, 142nd Pennsylvania, was shot in the leg during the fighting west of the Seminary. He stayed at the Myers home until July 13, when his parents came to Gettysburg and took him back home to Oil City, Pennsylvania. He and Sallie Myers became lifelong friends and when he died, he remembered her in his last will and testament.[25]

Other soldiers mentioned in Sallie Myers' diary of 1863 stayed for brief periods of time and moved on, either home to finish the task of recuperation, or to a field hospital, whether in Harrisburg or nearby Camp Letterman. Some she cared for in her home; others at the Catholic church, Presbyterian church, or

Camp Letterman. Names like Captain Leslie, Lieutenant Ruth, Mr. James Goodrich, Mr. Henry Frazier, Joe Lewis, Dr. Gates and Mr. Spencer are included in her diary, names with stories attached that still need to be uncovered.

Of the dozen or so men Sallie cared for in her father's house, only two died: Sergeant Alexander M. Stewart (149th Pennsylvania), and Private Amos P. Sweet (150th Pennsylvania).[26] Corporal Wilson D. Race (149th Pennsylvania), who Sallie wanted moved to her home, was nonetheless ordered to remain in the Catholic church by the surgeon, who felt he was unable to be moved. Sallie visited Corporal Race several times daily, caring for him at the church until his death on July 24. She also welcomed his father when he came to Gettysburg to visit his wounded son. In her diary for 1863, as well as in some later articles, Sallie described these men, their suffering, and their subsequent deaths.[27]

In none of her writings, however, does she describe the final moments of these men with more poignancy than in a memoir she later wrote, titled "Reminiscences of Gettysburg Hospitals." Earmarked "For Mr. Young," identified by her son Henry as a Methodist minister in Gettysburg during the 1870s[28], the handwritten pages are undated, the letter unsigned, the compassion of a witness to horrendous suffering unmistakable:

For Mr. Young
Reminiscences of "Gettysburg" Hospitals

Alexander Stewart was wounded on the 1st day—A ball passing through the lungs & near the spine produced complete paralysis of the lower limbs. At no time did he or his physicians entertain any hope of his recovery; yet, during those terrible days, amid the suffocating smoke & heat, & the deafening roar of battle, he conversed composedly in reference to his temporal affairs; inquired frequently concerning the progress, and probable result of the contest, & received the news of the Rebels' retreat with a fervent "Thank God."

When asked if he felt resigned to what was evidently God's will concerning him, he replied with a smile, "Oh! yes: I feel as though it will be gain to die. My long desire is to depart & be with Christ, which is far better." He lingered until the 6th & then without a struggle passed from earth. When a young man, the idol of aged parents, a devoted wife & a younger brother; with everything to make life desirable, dies thus, sustained by the religion of Christ, comment is unnecessary. His father arrived a few days after his death & took his remains home where loving hands laid him gently to rest in "the old church yard."

Amos Sweet was wounded on the 2nd day by a minnie ball which rendered necessary the amputation of a limb. He seemed to be doing well, had written for his wife & was daily expecting her. About the 9th he began to sink & on the 12th when in distress caused by intense pain, the bandage became loose & a hemorrhage from the limb was the result. Everything was done that could be done but in vain. He sank until midnight when he died with these words upon his lips—"Tell—my wife—I'm—going—home." That midnight death-bed scene I shall never forget. Myself & Alexander Stewart's father (who had arrived in the meantime) stood by his bed, the old man with tears in his eyes, exclaimed "Oh! had it but been God's will that I could have stood by my son's death-bed." His wife came after his burial, expecting to see him living, & was met with the sad news of his death.

Alas for the broken hearts, the desolate homes, & the blighted lives of such as she!

Wilson Race was wounded on the 2nd through the lungs but the wound was of such a nature that his physician entertained hopes of his recovery. I wrote for his father & he came a short time after, intending to take him home as soon as he was able to travel. His father was so much excited at the thought of meeting his son under such circumstances that he did not give me sufficient time to inform him of his arrival, but rushed to him & the two wept in each other's arms. He never recovered from the shock but commenced to decline. His father's business would not allow him to remain more than a few days & he started for home leaving directions with me in reference to Wilson. (At the same time another son was engaged at Vicksburg). Wilson was very calm & spoke but little. In a conversation with me the evening before his death he remarked "I have always been governed by religious principles." He died on the 24th & the body was embalmed & sent home.

In the following article, Sallie wrote about an Alabama soldier, one Private Hardy Graves, Company C, 6th Alabama, part of O'Neill's Brigade. Wounded in the action of the first day, Hardy Graves drew her attention, first in the Catholic church and later, at Camp Letterman:[29]

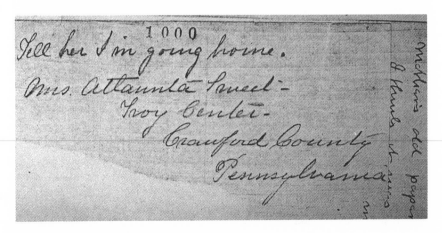

Message written to Mrs. Atlannta Sweet, widow of Amos Sweet, as Sallie cared for him during his last hours. Original on file in Adams County Historical Society, Gettysburg, Pa.

As I entered the Church the first men I saw lying on the floor to the right of the entrance, were three Southern soldiers. To the best of my knowledge they were the only ones there who were not Union soldiers. I did what I could for them, and had some conversation with them. One of them particularly attracted my attention. He was, or seemed to be, a large man, though he was lying down and I could not very well tell. His complexion was dark, and he had the blackest eyes and hair that I have ever seen. That was fifty years ago, but I can see him as distinctly as then, lying there helpless and the appealing look in his great black eyes. Those three were there but a short while and I never knew where they had been taken, or how they were wounded, but later, as you will read further on, I saw one of them again.

Among the wounded southern soldiers was Major Goldsborough. I think he was a Marylander. He had some acquaintances in and around Gettysburg. He was in Camp Letterman, a tent hospital about a mile and a half east of Gettysburg, and was in use about the 1st of August. He sent word to a lady in C[ashtown], whom he had known before the war, to come to see him. We found him in a tent with four other wounded southern soldiers. One of them was Captain Bailey. The names of the others I have forgotten. At that time there was a great fad for writing your name with some sentiment attached, in books prepared for the purpose. We wrote our names—Harriet C. Shillen and Sallie E. Myers. The sentiment I wrote was "The Union Forever"—and one of the gentlemen wrote in mine "The Union is lost to us forever, but let us be friends". I wonder what he has been thinking all these years, if still living. A few years ago I heard of the death of Major Goldsborough. I know nothing of the others.

In the course of the conversation one of the gentlemen said—"In the next tent are several of our boys lying ready for burial. Perhaps you would care to go in." We went into the "dead tent," and there lay the man who had attracted my attention in the Catholic church, but the great black eyes were forever closed. On his breast was pinned his name—Hardy Graves and below it was his wife's name, Julia Graves, Brundidge, Pike Co., Alabama. I cut off a lock of his hair and some time after I wrote to her and sent her the lock of hair, and told her what I knew of her husband. She replied and asked if I could find his grave—a long time after I found his grave. He had been buried with many others in a plot of ground near Camp Letterman. I gathered some wild flowers and enclosed them to her, telling her how her husband's grave was situated and that it was marked. Later the bodies of the Union soldiers were removed to the National Cemetery and the southern soldiers were taken to Richmond. I never knew whether Mr. Graves' body was removed with the other soldiers or taken to Alabama.

Although Sallie does not recount the rest of the Hardy Graves story in this article, there is, indeed, more to tell. Apparently Julia Graves, the grieving widow to whom Sallie was so kind, could not believe her husband was really dead. Mistaking Sallie's kindness for a deeper, more romantic attachment to her husband, Julia obtained the services of an attorney from home to write the Gettysburg Postmaster an inquiry about Sallie. The following letter is reprinted from the original still in the Salome Myers Stewart files at the Adams County Historical Society. Spelling and punctuation are not edited:

Brundidge, Alabama
December 10th/,68

Mr. Post Master,

Dear Sir   do you wonder, why a stranger thus addresses you, if you do a few words will l explain & perchance the word at the head of this page by awakening sad memories of the past will convey to your mind an idea of the subject of this letter, it is simply to make a few inquiries about a native of this vicinity who left his home & joined the Confederate army in 1862 & at the battle of Gettysburg he received a Gun shot wound in the arm & when the Rebs retreated from that part he was left in the hands of the Federal Troops & has not been heard of directly Since & the supposition is that he has abandoned his wife here & has married in your Town.

I will give you all of the details concerning of him so far as I know in Sept 1866 there was a one Miss Sallie Myres wrote his wife a letter stating to her that her Husband was dead. She lived in Gettysburg & said that She visited the Hospital & saw a man there paid some attention to him & in a few days after she visited there again & found one Mr. Hardy Graves lying on his cooling Board waiting for Burial for that was his name. She said that she saw his address on his blanket H Graves Co. C 6th Alabama Regt and the supposition is that he had remained in Gettysburg & he and this Miss Sallie E. Myres is married & his wife requested me to write this letter to you this Lady also said in her letter that she visited the Grave yard about 2 miles from Town & there she saw his Grave with his name Co & Regt on his head Board, and the question is why did she put her self to so much trouble concerning this one Mr. Graves, it looks rather suspicious that there is something green about the affair it is true it does not look as bright as Gold, this woman wrote in her last letter to Mrs. Graves that she had just returned from a trip to the western part of your state & had that day wedded her self to one Mr. Stuart a Presbyterian Minister and his wife seems to think that Mr. Graves was the Mr. Stuart that she married on that day & had Changed his name.

She requested me to write to you & request of you if it is not too much to visit the Grave yard & hunt for his grave. She said in her letter that he was buried at the Grave yard was about 2 miles from Gettysburg on the York Pike & it would be no difficulty to find it as his name was plain to be seen. She supposed that no [one] would ever go in search of it, the reason she gave such a strict direction of it. Mrs. Graves requested me to write to you to answer this & write if you know this woman & if she has married the Mr. Stuart a presbyterian Preacher or not & if you knew him before they were married, if you did not give a description of him in your letter, if this supposition of hers is not true & you ever chance to meet this Mrs. Stuart do not vulge to her this for it would insult her after her kindness to her. If you knew this woman at that time she wants to know it & what sort of a woman she is if are acquainted with her husband & know him not to be this Mr. Graves it will settle the Question & if you are not originally acquainted with him give a description of him & where he came from.

You will please answer this as soon as you get it. Please visit the graveyard & hunt for his grave. Direct your letter to W. F. Williams

Brundidge
Pike, Co
Alabama
and I will get it answer imediately & bil me
W. F. Williams

In Sallie's 1913 article referring to Hardy Graves, she described her actions as more or less a heartfelt gesture of sympathy for his widow. The gesture was based, no doubt, on the fact that Graves made quite an impression on her, both in the hospital and later, in the "dead tent" at Camp Letterman. That she could "still see him as distinctly as then" in 1913, reveals the impact he must have made on her, but hardly convicts her of adultery and Mr. Graves of bigamy. Correspondence with families of soldiers killed in battle was commonplace, and Sallie did this for many of the soldiers she encountered that summer.

The original letter from the Pike County attorney is preserved in her records at the Adams County Historical Society. No records exist regarding the Postmaster's reply, if indeed he wrote one, or of Sallie's reaction to the inquiry. By 1913 Sallie likely knew of Mr. Williams' letter and in all probability had it in her possession. Interesting is the fact that instead of destroying the letter, the Postmaster chose to give it to Sallie.

The Confederate soldiers identified and buried at Camp Letterman were moved to Richmond, Virginia, between 1871 and 1873. Thus, by 1868, when the inquiry was written, Hardy Graves had not made it home to Alabama, Julia was cheated of properly mourning her big, dark-eyed soldier, and Sallie's kindness had become the object of jealousy.

Located in Hollywood Cemetery, Richmond, Virginia, are many sections of Confederate soldiers, mostly unmarked and without headstones, designated only by plot markers. Stepping off the distance to Section I, lot 30, the visitor today can stand at the gravesite of Hardy Graves, Company C, 6th Alabama Regiment.[30] One hundred and twenty-two years after removal from Camp Letterman, Hardy Graves still has not made it home to Alabama.

In the later years of her life, Sallie Myers would look back on her nursing experience that fateful summer and fall with a combination of respect for those

Letter from Pike County, Alabama, on behalf of Julia Graves, widow of Hardy
Graves, Co. C. 6th Alabama Regiment. Original letter on file in Adams County
Historical Society.

his name &c & Regt on his head Board, and the
question is why did she put her self to so much
trouble concerning this one Mrs Graves
it looks rather suspicious that there is something
green about the affair it is true it does not
look as bright as Gold,
this woman wrote in her last letter to
Mrs Graves that she had just returned from
a trip to the western part of your state &
had that day wedded her self to one
Mr Stewart a Presbyterian Minister
and his wife seem to think that Mr Graves
was the Mr Stewart that she married on that
day & had changed his name
she requested me to write to you & request of
you if it is not too much to visit the
Grave yard & hunt for his grave She said
in her letter that he was buried at the
Grave yard was about 2 miles from
Gettysburg on the York Pike & it would
be no difficulty to find it as his name
was plain to be seen She supposed that no
would ever go in search of its the reason she
gave such a strict direction of it Mrs Graves
requested me to write to you to answer this & write if
you know this woman & if She has married the
Mr Stewart a presbyterian Preacher or not & if
you knew him before they were married & if
you did not give a description of him in
your letter, if this supposition of hers is
not true & you ever chance to meet this
Mrs Stewart do not divulge to her this for
it would insult her after her kindness
to her. If you know this woman at that time

Last page of the letter from Pike County, Alabama, on behalf of the widow of Hardy Graves, Co. C. 6th Alabama Regiment. (Adams County Historical Society)

soldiers under her care, gratitude for the opportunities and friendships that developed, and pride in a job well done. Sallie's own words, written in 1903 for the *San Francisco Sunday Call*, describe it best:

> This work enlisted all my sympathies, and I received many kind and appreciative letters from those who could not come. Besides caring for the wounded, we did all we could for the comfort of friends who came to look after their loved ones. Many pleasant and enduring friendships were the result of this part of my work. It is a great pleasure to remember that during that long, trying summer, I was treated with the greatest courtesy and kindness by the soldiers. Not one, in either army, ever addressing me except in the most respectful manner. They were men. They bore their suffering in the hospitals with the same matchless courage and fortitude with which they met the dangers and endured the hardships of army life. Their patience was marvelous. I never heard a murmur. Truly, we shall not look upon their like again.... I have always regretted that I did not enlist as a nurse. My heart was in the work, but I

could not see my way clear to leave home at that time. In conclusion, I wish to say that while I would not care to live over that summer again, yet I would not willingly erase that chapter from my life's experience; and I shall always be thankful that I was permitted to minister to the wants and soothe the last hours of some of the brave men who lay suffering and dying for the dear old flag.

Sallie Myers, c. 1863. (ACHS).

4

TWO BROTHERS:
ALEXANDER AND HENRY STEWART

As Sergeant Alexander Stewart lay mortally wounded inside the St. Francis
Xavier Catholic Church, he told Sallie Myers about his family back home in
Allegheny County, Pennsylvania. Sallie listened with patience and a young girl's
compassion for a dying soldier far from his loved ones, and she promised to write
to his family, to send them his dying message of love. That Alexander Stewart
and his younger brother Henry were to become forever intertwined with her and
her future was not even a thought. Yet the destiny that brings people together,
whether in friendship, love and marriage, or even across a deadly battlefield, was
at work by the time Sallie encountered Alexander in the Catholic church and
"went out on the church steps and cried."[1]

The Stewart family of Allegheny County, Pennsylvania, traced its beginnings to Lancaster County and Adams County, Pennsylvania. Part of the Scots-
Irish immigration to America in the early 1700s, the Stewart family grew and
scattered throughout Pennsylvania. Alexander's and Henry's ancestors eventually settled into a portion of the Marsh Creek settlement circa 1735-36, dissenting
Presbyterians who sought their livelihood as farmers east of the South Mountain
range.[2]

William Stewart, grandfather of Alexander and Henry, was born in Adams
County in 1775. He moved west to Allegheny County in 1800, taking with him
his wife Jane and his two children, Margaret, aged 2, and baby John, born that
August.[3] There the family stayed, farming the land and raising their five children.

William and Jane's son, John White Stewart, married Jane McFarland, and
together on the family farm they raised two sons, Alexander McFarland Stewart,
born May 4, 1834, and Henry Ferguson Stewart, born eight years later, on October
15, 1842.[4] The two boys grew into adulthood in Allegheny County, worked hard
on the farm, went to school, and were raised in the strict Presbyterian tradition of
their early ancestors.

John White Stewart, 1800-1870.
(ACHS)

Jane McFarland Stewart, 1808-1875.
(ACHS)

That Alexander M. Stewart would meet his death within a few miles of his ancestral settlement might be termed coincidence. It also might be regarded as destiny, for his death in Gettysburg set into motion a series of events that brought the Stewart family full circle, back to the region of Penn's Woods where his forebears first sought refuge.

The saga of Alexander McFarland Stewart and Henry Ferguson Stewart is tragic, notable for its representation of the Civil War's impact on families. At the outbreak of the war, Alexander was 27 years old, operated the family farm with his father in Allegheny County, and was married to a young woman named Elizabeth Barton.[5] Alexander and Lizzie had no children. Henry, slated for the Presbyterian ministry, was 19 years old and enrolled in the Washington and Jefferson College Preparatory Department. He would graduate in August 1862, and begin his studies in the seminary upon graduation to fulfill his family obligation and his calling.[6]

The country was at war, however, and with Henry's graduation in August 1862, Alexander decided to enlist. John Stewart was determined that if one son went, so must the other.[7] And so it was that the two brothers set off for the business of war together. Mustered in at Pittsburgh, Pennsylvania, on August 23, 1862, as newly enlisted members of Company D, 149th Pennsylvania Infantry, Alexander achieved the rank of sergeant, and Henry the rank of corporal.[8] Part of Colonel Roy Stone's newly formed "Bucktail Brigade," authorized by Governor Andrew Curtin in July 1862, they followed the legendary reputation of the first regiment so nicknamed, the 13th Pennsylvania Reserves (Kane's Rifles). The following account describes their formation:

Henry F. Stewart, 1862, in full regimental dress.
Note the "bucktail" on his kepi. (ACHS)

Alexander M. Stewart, c. 1862.
(ACHS)

Mrs. Alexander Stewart,
(nee Elizabeth Barton) c. 1862. (ACHS)

[T]he 143rd, 149th, and 150th P.V., all made up the Bucktail Brigade, formed on the idea that a brigade should be raised like the original Bucktails, the 1st Penna. Rifles of the Reserve, which had performed so well during the first year of the war. So, in July of 1862, Major Stone was authorized by the secretary of war to proceed to Pennsylvania, for the purpose of raising a Bucktail Brigade. Soon the 149th and 150th Regt's were formed, and were quickly ordered to Washington when the rebels invaded Maryland. Mid-February, 1863, the brigade was actually formed, to include the 149th, 150th and 143rd, under now-Colonel Stone, and became the 2nd Brigade of the 3rd Division of the First Corps.[9]

Each soldier proudly wore the bucktail on his kepi, symbolic of proficiency with a rifle achieved during long experience hunting deer. These Pennsylvania mountain men represented the state's finest fighters.

Brotherly camaraderie was not to last long, however, for on January 28, 1863, Henry received an injury which landed him in the hospital tent, and under a surgeon's knife. Encamped with his company at the corner of 15th and I Streets in Washington, D.C., Henry tackled the chore of splitting wood for his camp "mess" and severely axed his foot. The surgeon amputated his big toe and a portion of the metatarsal bone.[10] Hospitalized for two weeks, Henry received his discharge on February 13, 1863, just three days after the regiment had received orders to join Hooker's army at Falmouth, Virginia.[11] Alexander and Henry would have to part company, with the older brother marching south into active service, and the younger heading back home to Pennsylvania. When able, Henry departed for home as an invalid, unable to walk, with erysipalas [a type of infection] set in the wound. Alexander would have to finish the war without his beloved brother.

Letters sent to Henry from Alexander posted addresses like Belle Plain, dated February 28 and April 3, 1863; Camp Near Falmouth, Virginia, dated May 9, 1863; and Headquarters, Provost Guard, dated June 10, 1863.[12] They trace the path of the 149th Pennsylvania Volunteers from its Washington, D.C., camp in the fall and winter of 1862-63, to its departure south for active service. The letters also describe the regiment's move toward Chancellorsville, and the days preceding the march north to Gettysburg. Alexander's letters are heartfelt, descriptive narratives to the little brother who is sorely missed. Sometimes chatty, sometimes marvelously earnest, the letters to Henry tell tales of camp life, illness, screaming battle experiences, and moral and political beliefs.

These four original letters still exist among the Stewart family files at the Adams County Historical Society. Typed as written, all spelling and punctuation are unchanged. Any editing is for clarification only.

Bell Plain
Feb. 28th/63

Dear Brother

I will now answer your letter which I received three days ago. We get our mail about 6 o'clock in the evening. The morning after I got your letter had to start out on "picket" and just returned a few minutes since.

I was glad to hear that you were likly to have no more trouble with the eresypelas in your foot as I think it a bad thing to have. I want you to tell me all the particulars about your foot, and when you will be able to go home but you must not move until you are sure you are able can you sit up and let your foot hang down yet? tell me all about it.

I have not much additional news from last to write you, we had a more plesent time on picket this then last, out twice.

Well, Henry! Col. Dwight can't handle the men like Stone. I do not think he will ever make a military man, he has tactics of his own differing widely from either Hardee or Casey—your place has been filled by D— Phillips.—Bell was badly disappointed. Easton is to be detailed as acting Lieutenant, but the order has not yet been issued. There has been an order issued that all promotions will be made by the commanding officer, the companies not being consulted. The adjutant goes on the staff, the vacancy was offered to Slagle but he would not accept it, he has one of the best positions in the army—division judge-advocate, it is worth $200 per month. I believe I told you Dalgliesh was on the Col. staff as acting aid, but the trouble is these are all temporary appointments, and leave no vacancies. Henry, I stand it well so far, am now better than when I left Washington, for which I desire to be thankful to God, who has been so merciful to me thus far. It is awful to be sick here, no accommodations for sick at all, several of the company have measles, but, the men stand it much better than you would expect, because we have endured nothing but hardship so far. I am well fixed now. The Capt has taken Easton and I in with him. I had heard of Isaac's death. It made quite an impression upon me.

Truly, "in Life we are in death." I think really you have also cause to be thankful, you met with quite an accident, and suffered much but you have been saved much toil and suffering you would have had to endure had it been otherwise, you have enlisted, and served your country faithfully until you were hurt and now you have another and more important work to perform, and now Brother let your every energy be applied in the great work God in his providence is calling you to perform and Henry, I must tell you, for I cannot help it. I have a presentiment that I will never come out of this contest, why it is I cannot tell, but by the grace of God enobling I hope to be prepared for what seems to me will be the result. This Henry is strictly confidented. Will you not make me particularly the subject of your prayers, but I must close may God's blessing rest and abide with you at all times and in what ever circumstances you may be placed is the prayer of your Brother

A. M. Stewart

P.S. Capt. Slagle, Easton, Jones, & Momyer send their kind regards to you

Write to me frequently
A. M. Stewart

I wish you could send me a paper occasionally. I had to write this on my knee and in a hurry and I think it will bother you to read it.

❦   ❦   ❦

Camp Near Belle Plain
April 3rd/ 63

Dear Brother,

I will now attempt an answer to your letter, received a few days ago. As you are doubtless interested in the affairs of "(D) Co. 149th P.V."

We are still incamped as usual. I see no more signs of moving now then when we first received marching orders.

To day, have had a grand review of our division by Gen. Hooker. It was rather a splendid affair. There was quite a display of Shoulder staff and starred gentry on hand, it would have been very plesent but for the wind and dust, which made it quite disagreeable. There is so much sand in the dust here that makes it very hard on the eyes. We started for review this morning at 9 o'clock and returned by 1 P.M.

Gen. Hooker is a fine looking man, his hair is quite gray but he seems to have all the spirit and energy of youth. It is the prevailing opinion here now that should we remain another week, our Corps will be stationed here for some time to come. There is one Corps to be left behind and it is reported that ours will be the one. This morning Rick Minser and Momyer received there discharge papers and started for Pittsburgh at 8 o'clock. Cooper was very much disappointed that he did not get his discharge also. I am informed that he will be, in a few days. Means is of no account to the Co. but the surgeons will not discharge him. We have not had to drill so hard for a few days as for some time after we came here. Dwight does not make so good a Col. as Stone nor never will. But such men as Stone as military men are scarce in my opinion. Should we be permitted to remain here, I think will make an application for leave of absence for a few days.

I was sorry to hear that you had trouble with your foot. I had hoped by the time you got home, you would have no further trouble. Dr. Robb was down on a flying visit to our camp this week, he came one evening and returned the next morning, he said he thought when you left it would have to break and run as it healed up too fast, he says had he been twenty four hours later in seeing it you would have had trouble with it. George Templeton is mending slowly he is very weak. Marks is able to be out of the Hospital, your old messmates are all well. Will looks better than ever I saw him look before he is now in the pioneer corps, he perhaps did not care about you knowing this as the men that were not well drilled were assigned to this service. he has not to leave the company, there are two from each company, you need not say anything about it to any of their folks.

You know Will never had much taste for drilling.

I do not know as I've much more to write. I am in excellent Health and getting along fine. The Capt. and I are quite intimate more so than ever before, he of late makes me quite a confident. He treats me so kindly I cannot help but like him. He says I will get the first furlough out of the company, some things I look on differently then I did some time ago, Henry you understand me. I must close, My kind regards for your welfare, I remain as ever your Brother

A. M. Stewart

Most likely, Alexander's longed-for furlough never happened. April 28 saw the Second Brigade moving from camp near Belle Plain to the Rappahannock River. By May 2, the 149th was moving into Chancellorsville, where it took its position at the right of the Union line on the Ely's Ford Road, setting up a defense position and scouting the Confederate action.[13] Although not heavily engaged, the 149th nonetheless "was of great service" in the battle that produced the death of Lee's right arm, Lieutenant General Thomas J. "Stonewall" Jackson, mortally wounded by a nervous regiment of his own men.[14]

On May 6, after Chancellorsville, the 149th crossed back over the Rappahannock where it awaited its next call to battle.[15] From the encampment across the Rappahannock, Alexander wrote home to Henry of the terrible battle which had just occurred at Chancellorsville. His description of the events of May 1-4 as "grand, sublime, terriffick, awful" attempts to tell brother Henry of the horror that was Chancellorsville:

Camp Near Falmouth, Va.
May 9th, 63.

Dear Brother

It has been longer than I intended it should be since you have heard from me, but under the circumstances I could not well help it. But now Brother the noise and din of battle has again passed away and we are now enjoying a quiet day in camp. Since I last left home I have endured many hardships and privations, and witnessed many sickening heart-rending scenes. Many of which would like to narrate, but I am afraid my ideas are so much mixed up that I cannot get them into anything like a readible shape.

But I will try to give you a short account of our doings since leaving camp at "Belle Plain." After we left our old camp, our Corps (the First) was moved to a ford some four miles below Falmouth. I was not able to get the name of the ford. We remained there some three days, supporting a battery that was trying to destroy a Reble battery on the opposite side of the river, shell was thrown around and over us but fortunately no one of our Regiment was injured. Although quite a number narrowly escaped being killed. A number of the enemys shell failed to burst which was well for us. A shell struck within three feet of Jos. Pettit and did not hurt him from the fact that it did not explode. since commencing this letter I have found out the name of the place at which we were below Falmouth. It is called Pollock's Mills. We then had orders to march to United States Ford, some ten miles above Fredericksburg. The march was a hard one, to reach it we had to travel near twenty five miles, a good part of the way after night. We reached our position on the right of the line about twelve o'c at night, that was Saturday. The battle had been raging furiously all day, and our men had been forcing the enemy slowly back all day untill late in the evening, when the Eleventh Corps ingloriously broke and ran, thus losing all we had gained, and driving back our forces three miles. We arrived on the field and formed line of battle as soon as possible, but the enemy did not see fit to further follow up the advantage gained, so we laid on our arms all night. The next morning at daylight the battle again commenced and raged furiously untill noon. The position of our Brigade in the line was fortunately posted along the edge of a thick piece of woods through which the Reb's were unable to pass. We were completely protected, we were out of the range of there musketry, but there shells flew fearfully over our heads and close at that, but we lost ownly two or three men. No casualties in our company. I would like to give you an idea of a battle field, but I cannot do it. It was grand, sublime, terriffick, awful. Those that were in both engagements say that for severity it far exceeded Antetam, it shook the earth for miles arround. I tell you the noise of shell is the most unearthly noise I ever heard in my life, I prefer never to hear any more of them for my part, it is said that our Corps performed a very important part in covering the opperations of the left of the army. Our loss is heavy, but nothing compared to the rebels, this time they had to fight us in the open field and suffered terribly, we have also lost a great number, some of them two acquaintences of yours. McEwen, an acquaintance & class mate perhaps, had his head taken off by a cannonball. Also a young man by the name of Prine, a student of Jefferson, McNary of Cannonsburgh told me to inform you of this he is acquainted with you. I also met a Lieut by the name of Coleman who is acquainted with you he told me to tell you he had come through it all and was safe, but this is not all. Calvin Eaton and Elijah Lewis was both killed. I can learn no particulars of the former but the latter (poor fellow) was shot through the head with a minie ball and killed instantly. They belonged to Segdwick's Corps. and fought opposite Fredericksburgh and suffered severly.

Well Henry we are all back again on this side of the river. Why it is I cannot tell as yet it is all shrouded in mystery, we could have held our position on the right against all the force they could have brought against us. I suppose the withdrawal of the army will be a great thing for the "copperheads" to make capital of. The army has not lost confidence in Gen. Hooker, he was always up to the front with the men. I seen him myself ride along the very front of the line—Our Brigade is now encamped within a mile of the river 4 miles below Falmouth in a beautiful place, we came here yesterday noon and Capt Glenn Snodgrass and Easton and I have been busy building our house, it is quite tosty and Ceeder shrubery planted all a round it we will live very nice so long as we stay here, we are all in good health. It is surprising how I stand exposure. And now Henry I wish you all at home to unite with me in gratitude and prayer to God for his mercies in preserving my life through danger seen and unseen. On tomorrow I hope to write to Lizzie and will give her some further particulars. She will think me a long time writing but I have written three times to her since leaving home and received but two, I received one yesterday evening from you, was glad to hear that your foot was improving I also received one from you today, written a few days after I left, in it you told me about the chickens, but I must close this scrible and go to bed. I believe I could sleep now eighteen hours out of twenty four, there was for 8 days I did not more than average two hours a night. You have my thanks for a bundle of papers received yesterday evening. The Boys are all well, Easton tells me he received a letter from you lately. My kind regards to Father, Mother, Lizzie, and Taylor and all my friends.

A. M. Stewart

The following letter shows that Alexander Stewart was an exception to the general notion that soldiers from the North did not particularly care about the freedom of the black man, nor did they generally regard them as capable of offering much use to the Union Army. He eloquently argues his conviction that the black man must join ranks with the army and fight, to secure the right to live free from oppression. He describes his desire for "putting down this rebellion, I don't care how it is done." Alexander also argues that, contrary to rumor, General Hooker was perfectly sober at Chancellorsville, for he saw him several times with his own eyes:

H'dQrts, Provost Guard
3rd Division 1st C,
June 10, 1863

Brother Henry,

I have just this moment received a letter from you and so will just answer it.

You asked my opinion in regard to an argument or rather the points involved in a certain discussed by you and others. Well! The mere Tecnichality upon which you seem to Hinge your argument I have nothing to say. The relation between the master and slave you say still exists the same as before the Rebellion. Not so with a good many of them at least—a number of them ain't there any more. But as to the "moral right," now the master has no moral right to hold a slave at all. In short no right save what municipal or state authority gives him and that is ownly founded on might, not justice nor right and is of no binding effect save the slaveholders ability to hold the Negro. Now the government is no longer bound to assert its authority in assisting the rebelious slaveholder in the possession of his slave property—Now under these circumstances you will not pretend to deny the Negro's right to freedom, and that [unclear text] by whatever means God has placed in his hands. I should not be surprised if the people of the south would be visited with the horrors of St. Domingo, if so they have no one to blame but themselves, they alone are responsible—The Negro will yet in my opinion play an important part in the History of this war, I believe he will fight and I say let him fight. I am for putting down this rebellion and I don't care how it is done so it is done, if necessary I will take a commission and drive sambo up to the work they are as much interested as any other class, but I must stop. My health is improving, I am now about as well as ever. Mr. Barton has written to you. Dalgleish is still on Stone's staff, we are now having a very plesant time. I do not think we will now move for some time. Gen. Hooker has made a bold reconnoisance for the purpose of ascertaining the exact positions and numbers of Lee's army in front, it was successful. I have been asked was Gen. Hooker drunk during the battles of the first of May. I answer emphatically No—and I do know—for on Sabbath I seen him three different times through the day, on Monday I seen him different times and he was as sober as any man.

I believe it would be morally right to hang some of the copperheads in your neighborhood a while at least, but I close

My love to all   Your affectionate Brother
A. M. Stewart

Whether this is the last letter Alexander wrote to Henry is difficult to determine, but it is the last one that still exists. June 24 found Hooker moving north out of Virginia, and by June 30, Reynolds' 1st Corps was in Pennsylvania, encamped within four miles of the spot where General Buford was to make his cavalry stand on July 1, and hold his position until Reynolds could arrive with reinforcements. Part of Reynolds' 1st Corps, the 149th Pennsylvania arrived on the western outskirts of Gettysburg to join the savage fight.[16] It was on this day that Sergeant Alexander Stewart received the wound that fulfilled his "presentiment" of impending death.[17]

Alexander's "presentiment" confided to brother Henry in his letter home on February 28 became a terrible reality in the late afternoon hours of that first day's fighting at Gettysburg. Serving as General Abner Doubleday's headquarters guard and detached from the rest of the regiment, Company D saw little of the bloody action that morning near McPherson's barn located on the Chambersburg Pike.

Monument to the 149th Pa. Inf. located on Rt. 30 West, Gettysburg, Pa.
Note McPherson's barn in right background.

As one Company D soldier recalled, "Up to this time our Company had not fired a gun, but our time was coming."[18] As the fighting continued throughout the afternoon, the Confederates slowly gained ground. Pender's Division pushed the Union line to the crest of Seminary Ridge and beyond. The Confederate Army closed in on the last ragged lines of the Union defense, and General Doubleday ordered Company D to plug a hole in the line left of the Seminary. Doubleday later described his decision:

> As the enemy were closing in upon us and crashes of musketry came from my right and left, I had little hope of saving my guns, but I threw my headquarters guard, under Captain Glenn of the One Hundred and Forty-Ninth Pennsylvania, into the Seminary and kept the right of Scales's brigade back twenty minutes longer, while their left was held by Baxter's brigade of Robinson's division, enabling the few remaining troops, ambulances, and artillery to retreat in comparative safety.

Positioned south of the Seminary at the Hagerstown Road, with only portions of Buford's already exhausted cavalry to their left, Company D found themselves cut off from the the right of the Union line, which had already collapsed and was in scattered retreat through the town.[19] In a valiant attempt to hold the line, with the Seminary grounds to their right in possession of the Rebels, Company D

Marker showing approximate spot where Alexander M. Stewart fell mortally wounded, July 1, 1863, at approximately 4:00 p.m.

Post-war view of Hagerstown Road, looking west from Seminary Ridge. Approximate area where Alexander Stewart fell mortally wounded. (ACHS)

1863 view of southern portion of Gettysburg from Seminary Ridge. The spire of St. Francis Xavier Church where Alexander was carried from the field is visible in background, center. (William A. Frassanito collection)

faced off against Perrin's assault, and attempted to stop the Confederates at the Hagerstown Road. For an eternal twenty minutes, Company D "opened fire and kept it up, but the rebels moved slowly and steadily forward, and it soon became evident that we could not hold the position."[20]

Alexander M. Stewart was shot through the lungs and spine and left on the field as Company D made its way toward the town.[21] Killed outright in the standoff against Perrin was Joseph H. Baldwin, and shot through the ankle was Private Andrew Crooks, wounded while trying to carry Alexander off the field. Baldwin and Crooks were also left on the field in the haste of retreat.[22] Cut off from the Seminary hospital by the presence of the Confederates, Private Crooks carried Alexander to the Catholic church on High Street.[23] It was there, in the vestibule of St. Francis Xavier Church, as Sallie "knelt by the first man inside the door,"[24] that the destiny of the Stewart brothers and Sallie Myers became forever intertwined.

When Alexander's father came to Gettysburg for his son's body, he and Sallie began a friendship which extended to the rest of his family back in Allegheny County. Alexander's widow, Lizzie Barton Stewart, wrote to thank Sallie for her kindness in caring for Alexander through his final days, and on July 29, Sallie received the first of what was to be many letters from Alexander's brother Henry. Their correspondence continued through 1863, and the following summer of 1864, the Stewart family, Henry F. Stewart included, traveled to Gettysburg to meet Miss Sallie Myers, who had so compassionately tended their loved one in his final hours. And it was during that visit that Sallie and Henry fell in love.[25]

5

WIFE, WIDOW, MOTHER:
"THE HAPPINESS IS ALMOST TOO GREAT."

The aftermath of a battle takes many forms. Long after the last visible remnants of destruction are cleaned from the streets and fields where troops once wreaked havoc in a deadly encounter of misery and death, the battle impact remains. Just as no soldier emerges truly unscathed from the horror of war, neither do the innocents caught by chance in the nightmare of battle. Its effect is felt forever in the hearts and minds of those civilians who experienced the terror of gathering huddled in cellars while shells scream overhead, and men in retreat run through their homes and gardens. Life after such trauma can never go on as usual, for there cannot exist again a real sense of peace and security, a certainty that life will be unaffected by indescribable horror.

And so it was for Great-great grandmother Sallie. The year 1864 meant a return to normal life for her and others scarred by the previous summer and fall. Yet this return to normal was in appearance only, for 1864 was filled with changes wrought by the events of the past six months. For Sallie Myers and the other residents of Gettysburg, the war would never again seem far away. Reports of battles that year would be received with a greater understanding of their ferocity, and casualty lists would always serve as grim reminders of the broken and battered men, recipients of canister and case shot, bullet and bayonet wounds, who once filled the town of Gettysburg.

Sallie's family continued to feel the effects of the war. She recorded many tragic events in her diary which resulted from the terrible conflict that continued to ravage the nation and tear at the heart of America. During 1864 several of Sallie's relatives were killed in action or died as a result of the war. Sallie's Uncle Isaac Sheads received a bullet wound in the head in early June. Her cousin Robert Sheads was killed just two weeks later at the Battle of Monocacy.[1] November brought the news of the deaths of two cousins, Elias Sheads, age twenty-two, and Jacob Sheads, age eighteen. Sallie wrote on November 20, "They were buried with the honors of war." On December 15, Sallie recorded the news that another cousin, David Myers, who had been taken prisoner of war, had possibly died of starvation at Andersonville Prison in Georgia, with: "To Aunt Lizzie—It is feared that Cousin Dave is dead, a prisoner starved to death—God grant that it is false. Poor Aunt! She is almost heartbroken. She seems to have nothing but trouble."[2]

The magnitude of the Civil War's impact on Sallie's family was great indeed. To what degree they were affected can be shown by Sallie's later description, part of an interview she granted in 1913. The four cousins she described in this article were the four brothers of Cousin Carrie Sheads:[3]

> I had five uncles and eight first cousins in the Union armies—all from this town. When they enlisted they thought they would get back in two or three months. One of my cousins starved to death in Andersonville Prison. Another was shot in the throat and never spoke a loud word afterward, but made himself understood chiefly by motions. A brother of his had both feet shot off and died in an ambulance that picked him up on the battlefield. Another brother was killed at Cold Harbor. Their father wouldn't let the youngest son go into the army, and the boy ran off and died in camp of measles.[4]

The casualties of war did not come only from the battlefields. Evidence of this occurred in early 1864, when Sallie recorded in her diary, "Kate Shillen is much worse. They think she is dying," and on January 4 are the words, "Kate Shillen is dead. She died about midnight. Poor Kate! It seems but a short time since she was among us, well. She has declined since the battle, after which she worked harder than she should have done." Another friend from Sallie's girlhood died that year as well, Martha "Mattie" Durboraw, with whom Sallie spent part of her summers at Rural Hill. Hearing the news on February 20, Sallie sadly wrote, "Dead! can it be. I cannot realize that one I loved and with whom I spent so many happy hours is no more." Yet another, Julie Culp, was affected physically by her battle experiences. On August 27, Sallie described Julie's affliction: "Julie Culp had a spasm of some kind in church. Poor Julie, I pity her. She has been subject to spasms ever since the battle of G— ... They seem like catalepsy & the Dr. says they are caused by trouble."

Julie Culp certainly had her share of "trouble." Julie and her sister Ann, who had married Sallie's brother Jefferson in May 1863, had mourned their brother, Wesley Culp, the previous summer. He was killed at Gettysburg, not far from his former home, fighting for the Confederacy.

The year 1864 was also spent corresponding with new friends made the previous summer because the soldiers Sallie nursed during the battle contacted her often. Some of these friendships ended tragically, as in the case of Andrew Wintamute, who, after being tended by Sallie, undertook a long convalescence in the hospital at York, Pennsylvania. He finally rejoined his regiment in mid-March, and on June 1, 1864, Sallie saw his name on a list of killed in action. Her worst fears after hearing reports of the terrible fighting of that May were realized.[5] Her diary entry for May 10 reflected her anxiety:

I feel very anxious to know if any of my friends have been killed or wounded. I hope not but I am afraid to hear. Oh! this cruel war! I think the most of my friends were engaged in the fight and it is but natural & reasonable to suppose that some of them have suffered. God bless our noble Army! Amen and Amen!

The following day, unable to ease her fear and anxiety about her friends fighting in the fiercely contested battles of the Wilderness and Spotsylvania Courthouse, Sallie's thoughts echoed those felt by families everywhere, North and South, as news of the conflicts spread:

So far no one I know has been killed or wounded. I should say in the lists I have seen. I am afraid to see the lists & yet I am anxious. In such a terrible struggle, some of my friends will certainly fall. Some persons say the fighting is worse than that of any battle on record—Oh, how I wish the struggle would end. I hope it will soon terminate in an honorable peace. God grant it.[6]

Sallie also corresponded with a soldier named Ben Jones. In their letters to one another, they sometimes addressed each other as "Cousin."[7] A member of the 149th Pennsylvania Volunteers, Sallie's friendship with him apparently began as a result of the battle, when she met and nursed many soldiers from the "Bucktail Brigade." There is a hint that perhaps Sallie felt an affection for Ben that was temporarily more than friendship, for Sallie wrote on April 25th that she received a letter from Ben Jones, with "an answer to the proposal I wrote to Ben on the 6th." She continued with,

He cannot "in justice to himself & others" correspond with an ultimate view to matrimony but will be all too happy to have my name as a 'bright addition' to his list of correspondents, & is proud to acknowledge as his friend one of the "heroines of Gettysburg." Hoping to hear again soon, he closes. Alas! Benjamin.

No further references of this type occur regarding Ben Jones. The friendship between them continued, however, throughout 1864 and to the end of the war. Some of their written exchanges survive in Sallie's files, among them one particularly poignant letter that Ben wrote to Sallie from City Point, Virginia. On the following pages, Ben eloquently describes the irony of finding passion-flower blossoms growing over battlefield breastworks. He also enclosed a number of general's autographs which he collected for Sallie, among them Sedgwick and Warren, which exist today among Sallie's papers at the Adams County Historical Society.

Head-Quarters, Army of the Potomac
City Point, Va. August 7th, 1864

Dear cousin Sallie.

Having nothing to do is in itself an affliction but to have no ideas is absolutely deplorable. Here I have been for the past fifteen minutes scratching my head and the result is ... three lines in commencement of an apology; now I dislike apologys especially when used in connection with such a duck of a letter as your last one was. If I could write such letters, I should never think of offering an excuse even for the worst, it is said that the nearer we attain to perfection the more diffidence we have in our own powers. That is your case exactly. I was going to scold you for your tardiness in not answering my letter sooner but the old saying has just occurred to my mind, "Don't scold a woman, lest she should scold better than thee." Sallie if the question be not impertinent I would with due deference inquire: how many corres. [some lines of text are missing] opinion [unclear text]. Oh! for that "spot of earth supremely blessed a dearer sweeter spot than all the rest" called "Home" where everything comes at your bidding and where the green eyed monster is not always floating before your eyes in the shape of "G_____" [appears in text like this; meaning is unclear]. Now Sallie write often and tell your lady friends to do likewise for a letter is to me like an oasis to the burning desert of Gobi, excuse the simile.

I enclose you a Passion Flower; they grow in good profusion over the fortifications, gracefully draping the very uninviting Breastworks. This faded specimen can give you but a faint idea of the brilliancy of the flower which so forcibly reminds us of Him whose blood was shed for the redemption of sinners. The contrast is indeed startling and it strikes one painfully to see this graceful vine wreathing its tendrils around works reared for the destruction of beings whom God hath made. Well I must close. Remember me with love to your good Mother and Father, Susie, Mrs. Eyster, Miss Reynolds, Harriet, and all enquiring and write soon. I suppose you will recognize the autographs of some of our Generals among them is that of the lamented Sedgewick.

> That every happiness may attend you
> is the sincere wish of
> Ben C. Jones

Ben Jones served in the army throughout the Civil War. Nothing further is known of his life until 1884, when he re-enlisted in the U.S. Marine Corps as a nurse, serving until November 10, 1891, when he was discharged as "unfit for service."[8] Struggling with alcoholism, Ben spent the last two years of his life in the National Soldiers' Home, Elizabeth City, Virginia, separated from his wife Jennie. He died there in 1898.[9]

Sallie also corresponded with a soldier named Granville Gilbert, who fell deeply in love with her and proposed marriage in January 1864. Referring back to her relationship with Thomas Snyder, she wrote, "I told him in my letter that having almost overcome one uncomfortable early love, I was disposed to guard well the citadel of my affections."[10] Gilbert continued to press his suit, completely undiscouraged, and even showed up on Sallie's doorstep unannounced on March 12:

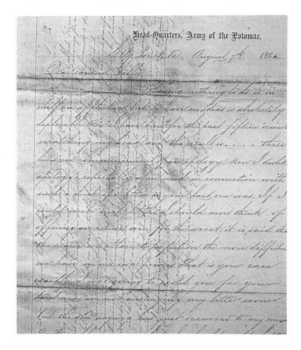

Ben Jones' letter from City Point, Virginia, 1864. The page contains an imprint of a passion flower along with several generals' autographs collected for Sallie Myers. Original in Adams County Historical Society.

I was surprised by a visit from a soldier friend, Mr. Granville Gilbert. I knew he contemplated visiting me but thought he would tell me when he was coming...I find Mr. Gilbert very intelligent and excellent company but my heart does not respond to his ardent love...I am sorry father is not at home.[11]

Gilbert again asked Sallie to marry him, or to at least pledge herself to him until his term of service was over, using the age-old argument that love would grow in time. Sallie's entry for March 13 describes her response to him. "He said he could not blame me but would be only too happy to have the hand if the heart did not go with it. I differ from him in regard to such things & will never marry anyone I do not love." In July of that year, Sallie received word that Granville Gilbert was killed in action on June 2. His last words to a comrade were, "Tell my mother I died like a soldier."[12]

By then, however, Sallie knew exactly where her affection was directed. The long correspondence with Alexander Stewart's brother Henry resulted in a long-awaited visit from him on June 8. Pleased to meet the Stewart family, Sallie noted that Henry was much different in person than he had appeared in his photograph: "Thought he was very large & he is not. The face of his photo is not at all good."[13] Just two days later, on June 10, she wrote in her diary that "I am loved by one whom I have learned to love within a year, & yet I could not acknowledge it to myself. It seems as though the happiness is almost too great."

Sallie and Henry, (sometimes called "Harry") spent their days visiting friends, gathering strawberries, and attending church services. They also found some time for long walks together, out to the college, the Seminary, and the spot where Alexander fell. Sallie described a picnic at the Round Top on June 10, "Ate our dinner on the top of that dear old hill. Enjoyed the walk. Have not been there for many fine years. The walk home I will never, never forget."

The Stewart family left Gettysburg on June 15.[14] Sallie and Henry parted with promises to write, and plans for another visit the next summer. On June 30, Sallie received a letter from Henry which she carefully copied onto the pages of her diary:

Miss Sallie,

I will not call you by any more tender name until I have your consent. I am now free to tell you all—when I met you face to face & talked with you & my heart yearned towards you I knew that I loved you & acknowledged it for I could not help it. I do love you & will you accept it & love me and marry me?—do you think you can accept my heart, & trust me? If you can, it will be the strongest proof I can ask of your love. —I reaffirm my devoted love for you. It is very late & I could only write on the same subject were I to lengthen this letter to three sheets, but it is useless to multiply declarations for one from an honest heart as I now know mine to be, is as good as an hundred. And therefore I will close & sign myself as I truly am,

Your sincere lover, Harry

And Sallie replied:

> Mr. Harry F. Stewart,
> I love you devotedly & truly & I love you only. I can & will trust you & I will say in the language of Ruth to Naomi, whither thou goest, etc. And now, "May the Lord bless thee & keep thee, etc., etc.—So prays one who is and hopes to be through life & after death,
> Thine only.

The romance continued, and Sallie and Harry made their plans to marry when he finished his studies at the United Presbyterian Seminary in Allegheny, Pennsylvania. Their love is evident throughout the remainder of the 1864 diary. Sallie recorded her happiness every time she received his letters, and her sadness when one did not arrive as expected, as on November 26: "Thought I would certainly get a letter but was woefully disappointed."

July 1864 turned out to be an eventful month for other reasons as well. Exactly one year from the battle that held Gettysburg in its grip, Sallie recorded the serene contrast between the past and present with,

> One year ago tonight, just in this same room but under far different circumstances. Now all is calm & peaceful, then I would scarcely hear my own voice for the deafening roar of artillery & the quick sharp volleys of musketry. When I think of the narrow escape I made, I cannot sufficiently thank my heavenly Father for his goodness unto me....[15]

The serenity Sallie felt on July 2 would soon be shattered as the threat of invasion once more hit Gettysburg. That first week of July brought to town the news of Confederate troops near Frederick, Maryland, only thirty miles to the south. With Washington, D.C., as the objective, it was obvious that the Rebel advance would be contested nearby. As reports of the Battle of Monocacy streamed into Pennsylvania, the citizens of Gettysburg realized all too well what that could mean. Sallie's entry on July 9 explained her worries: "There is considerable excitement. I am a poor soldier. The news when unfavorable fills me with dread—I have been more alarmed in the last week than I was all last summer." On the 10th, Sallie wrote, "Report says there is fighting near Frederick & the rebels are within miles of Baltimore. I do hope they will not come here. I dread them coming more than ever." And on July 11, Sallie described Gettysburg as existing in a threatening death-grip:

> Yesterday noon our Engine with all the cars left, it was feared that the rebels would cut off our communication with Baltimore & Washington, & it was deemed advisable to "skeedaddle." The Postmaster left. Evening. No trains all day and consequently no news, no papers, no letter, in short nothing except vague rumors to break the oppressive quiet which reigns supreme. Everything is painfully still ... I hope this state of affairs will not long continue. It is worse than excitement.

Trains and other communication in and out of Gettysburg came to a stand-still until the afternoon of July 14, when the first mail train in five days arrived in town. Postmaster Buehler returned to Gettysburg that evening, when privately carried news reports brought assurance that the Rebels had been repulsed without having reached Washington, D.C., and were making their way back into Virginia.[16]

Relief at the Rebel repulse was to be short-lived, for in August 1864, Get-tysburg again had reason to worry. On July 30 Chambersburg, Pennsylvania, only twenty-five miles west of Gettysburg, had been evacuated and burned by two cavalry brigades, sent by General Jubal Early and led by Brigadier General John McCausland. Sallie's concern was recorded on August 5 with, "Wrote to Harry. He is very uneasy about us, having heard of the burning of Chambersburg, & the probability of G & Hanover."

The threat of another invasion diminished after that, and the remainder of 1864 went by in a flurry of activity for Sallie. She spent her days teaching, taking long walks with friends like Ada McMillan, Allie Powers, Rose Guinn, Beckie Belch, and Jennie Gilbert, corresponding with soldiers, and, of course, writing to Harry. That October, Gettysburg would celebrate the return of the 87th Pennsyl-vania Infantry.[17] And in November much of Gettysburg would celebrate the re-election of Abraham Lincoln to the presidency.[18] Pleased that Lincoln was re-elected, Sallie wrote in her diary this exclamation, "LINCOLN & JOHNSON!!"[19] Yet the irony of the celebration surrounding this event, while so much death and destruction still continued, did not escape her, for on the 19th she reflected:

> The town is lively. A grand Demonstration in honor of Lincoln's re-election will be made. An illumination & torchlight procession.... Evening. Was up street awhile but did not enjoy anything except some singing with accompaniment. It seems out of place to have such a jubilee now. True, we have much for which to rejoice but I feel sad.

Sallie's diary for 1865 contains few entries, for reasons she explains on February 27, when she wrote, "My diary has been sadly neglected this year. Mother's illness has been partly the cause. The best reason I will not state— Suffice it to say it is a good one." No diaries exist anymore for 1866 or 1867. Other family records show, however, that on October 17, 1867, Sallie E. Myers married Henry F. Stewart in Gettysburg,[20] and together they traveled to western Pennsylvania, where Henry was to assume his first pastorate in the United Pres-byterian Church at Jamestown. Henry's wartime injury was not yet healed, and Sallie, still in her role as nurse, planned to restore him to good health.

The following letter to her friend Ada McMillan back home in Gettysburg was written just ten days after Sallie married Henry. Written with all the enthusi-asm of a new bride, this letter describes her wedding, the trip to New Brighton where she would greet his family as their daughter, and her hopes for a happy future.

Marriage Certificate of Henry F. Stewart and Sallie Myers, October 17, 1867. (ACHS)

Photographs taken of Henry F. Stewart and Sallie Myers Stewart, around the time of their marriage, 1867. (ACHS)

New Brighton, Penna.
Monday, October 27, 1867.

My dear Ada,

Am I not a model of punctuality? But though I am all ready to write, I must confess I hardly know how or where to begin. Suppose I commence just where I left you.—

We had a very quiet pleasant wedding & everything passed off without the least embarrassment on the part of any; at least as far as my observation extended.

Mr. Bouse did splendidly. Mr. S. was very much pleased with him. He was very cordial. I met with an accident before leaving G. I tore the back width of my dress a little more than half-way up. It was torn nearly three inches two ways. You can imagine how it vexed me, but I did not [know] what the future had in store for me.

We had a very pleasant ride to Harrisburg. Reached it in due time & concluded to wait until the 4:10 fast line. Just as we were going into the hotel Mr. S. tramped on my dress & it tore nearly all the way across the width in the place where it had been torn in G. Wasn't I in a pretty fix? Nothing to mend it with & no hope, or very little, of matching it. I put on my walking dress (didn't I look birdish?) & Mr. S. & I walked out to try to match it. We searched in vain. What to do I did not know. We left H. at 4:10. Met John Odell on the train. He talks fully as much as ever & just the same way. At Altoona Sallie B. & a very nice man called to see us. Sallie looked sweet. They stayed as long as they could. She had just returned home a day or two before. Eunice has improved somewhat. I wish I could have seen her. The ride from A. to Pittsburg was exceedingly disagreeable. The night was cold & there was no comfort in the car. I was unromantic enough to fall asleep & miss the mountain scenery. We reached Pittsburg at 2 on Friday morning.

After breakfast we started out to find alpacca & fortunately in the second store we called at, I found a piece exactly like the dress. I was so glad for the dress could be fixed to look as well as new. At 10 Rev. Witherspoon called for us & took us over to Allegheny up "Henderson Hill" & we spent several hours very pleasantly. About 3 we descended & crossed over to Allegheny city to meet the 3:20 Acc. train for New Brighton.

About half-way between Pittsburg and Brighton Uncle Alexander & Aunt Sarah McFarland got on the train & accompanied us to New Brighton. Father S. met us at the depot & his cordial grasp of the hands & his hearty "welcome" did much to reassure me. At the door Mother S. met me with a kiss but was too full to speak.

A few of Mr. Stewart's friends were here for tea & the time passed very pleasantly. They left on Saturday morning. In the afternoon we had company. We are now entirely alone with father & mother S. It is quiet & pleasant. I am sure I shall love my new home & my new friends very much. I am as happy as I can be until Mr. Stewart's health is restored. His general health is better & I think there is hope for him. I mean to take good care of him. I wish I could talk with you this afternoon. I feel like telling you how happy I am, what kind friends I have met & last but not least what a dear good husband I have, but I am afraid it would look foolish on paper.

Yesterday I went to church with him & it seemed so odd. I thought of the dear ones worshipping in the church at home, but I did not wish myself there as I had always done before when away from home.

Well I suppose I must stop. I hardly have the time to write much more now. On Friday we leave here to visit some of Mr. Stewart's friends. We will be gone two weeks I suppose. I have my dress to fix & am never sure of being uninterrupted by callers. Write soon Ada dear. Tell me all the news, all your "trials & triumphs," all your hopes & fears, & rest assured you will have my sympathy as you ever had.

Love to your family. Remember me to Will when you write to him. I am anxious to hear of your plans. Mr. S. is not here but if he were, I know he would want to be remembered to you, so I take the liberty of doing so. I shall look for a letter at the appointed time. Direct to Mrs. Sallie M. Stewart

> Box 139, New Brighton
> Beaver Co.
> Penna.[21]

In January 1868 the young couple, having left the Stewart family home in New Brighton, started for Jamestown to begin their life in the ministry. They set up housekeeping in a modest house where their dreams for a long life together could begin. Pleased to be in their own home for the first time, on March 28 Sallie recorded that they "had our first dinner in our own house."

But a long and happy life together was denied them. All of Sallie's efforts to restore her beloved Henry to good health were not enough. Unable to fully recover from the injuries received in the winter of 1863, Henry's health declined despite Sallie's careful attentions. By August 2, Henry had deteriorated badly, so disabled that he could no longer fulfill his duties as pastor. Henry's short tenure as the pastor of the Jamestown Presbyterian Church was described with, "though of short duration, [it] left its peculiar fragrance. Rev. Henry F. Stewart lived only one year and four months after his ordination, but he lived long in the hearts of those who knew him."[22] On August 27, Sallie wrote, "Mr. S. suddenly very ill." Finally, on September 18, Sallie sadly entered these words into her diary, "Have no hope."

On October 17, Sallie's diary contains the following words:

"One year ago today I left home a happy bride. This morning the cold snow is falling thick & fast upon my precious husband's grave." Less than one year after her wedding to Henry F. Stewart, with all its hopes and dreams for a bright future, Sallie was left a widow.

United Presbyterian Church, Jamestown, Pa., where Henry was pastor in 1868, until his death. (ACHS)

House where Sallie's son, Henry A. Stewart, was born. Jamestown, Mercer County, Pennsylvania. (ACHS)

Not all of Sallie's hopes and dreams ended when she laid Henry to rest. One part of her beloved Henry was with her still, and would be with her for the rest of her life. Just ten days after Henry died, Sallie gave birth to their son. She named him Henry Alexander, for his father, now lying beneath the snows in Jamestown, and his uncle, who had died in her arms five years before in Gettysburg. On October 27 she wrote simply, "Our babe, a fine large boy was born about noon."

Henry Alexander Stewart was christened on February 14, 1869, by Rev. Alexander McFarland, in the Jamestown Presbyterian Church.[23] During the span of eleven months, Sallie Myers had become a wife, a widow, and a mother. Her beloved husband never got to see his son, and his son would never have the chance to see his father. Yet Sallie was determined to raise young Henry with her memories of his father, whose short time on earth had brought her so much happiness.

Sallie with son, Henry Alexander Stewart, at approximately six months old. (ACHS)

Henry Alexander Stewart, age approximately one year. (ACHS)

Diary 1864-68

From the diary of Salome Myers Stewart. Quite a few of these pages have text too faded to read. Inscribed on the front inside page is the following:

"Let love and truth indite
Whatever here I write."

Friday, January 1.

Morning. Clear and pleasant. Rose at 5. Feel badly continually. Afternoon. At home sewing. Clear & cold and windy. Evening. Wrote to Mr. Gilbert in answer to a letter received last night and to which he wished an immediate answer. I could not give him the answer he wished for in his note. He said, "after our short acquaintance I have a regard for you which I never felt for any one else." etc. I of course do not feel as he does, & consequently could not reply in the same way. I feel sorry for him if he is sincere & I have no reason to doubt his sincerety. I hardly knew how to write a reply without saying something to inflict a wound, however I did the best I could. I never was more surprised in my life, than when I read his letter. Reading awhile. Went to see Miss Whiteside & Mrs. Martin. Very cold and windy.

Saturday, January 2.

Very cold. To preaching at 10 1/2. Mr. M'Murray our Presiding Elder preached an excellent sermon. Text "Nevertheless I have somewhat against thee, because thou hast left thy first home, Remember, therefore, from whence thou hast fallen, & repent & do thee quickly, & will remove thy candlestick out of his place, except thou repent." The sermon was peculiarly appropriate. Mother and I went to the store. Home at 1 1/4. Afternoon. At home. Evening. Went to see Jennie Gilbert & Miss Bell Stewart. Miss S. went to church with me. Mr. Eisenberg preached. Text—"For I am the Lord, I change not." Home at 8. Kate Shillen is much worse.

Sunday, January 3.

To preaching at 10 1/2. Mr. McMurray preached an excellent sermon. After the sermon the Sacrament of the Lord's Supper was administered. It was very solemn. Home at 1 1/2. To Love-feast at 2 1/2. Spoke but did not enjoy it very much. Evening. To preaching at 6 1/2. Mr. McMurray preached a good sermon. Home at 8. Kate Shillen is much worse. They think she is dying.

Monday, January 4.

Kate Shillen is dead. She died about midnight. Poor Kate! It seems but a short time since she was among us, well. She has declined since the battle, after which she worked harder than she should have done. I pity Harriet very much. She will miss Kate. At school all day. Snowing. Susy and I went to preaching. Mr. Berkstresser preached. Home at 8 1/2.

Tuesday, January 5.

At school all day. Feel miserably. —I do think that there was never a person as peculiarly situated as I am. I sometimes wish I had never been born or that I had died when a child. I know such thoughts are sinful but when I think of my situation &

realize it as I do now, I cannot help writing such things. I know not what [unclear text]

Wednesday, January 6.

At school all day. Evening. To preaching at 6 1/2. Mr. Berkstresser preached. Did not enjoy the meeting at all. Home at 8. Today mother is 46 years old & yesterday father was 48. How time flies!

Thursday, January 7.

At school all day. Snowing. Evening. To prayer meeting at 6 1/2. Mr. Kitzmiller led. Did not enjoy it at all. Home at 8. Received a letter from Andrew Crooks & one from Beckie & Sherrif, with fine Photograph of Fannie Culp, Aunt Salome's little daughter who died some time ago, & whose pictures Beckie was painting.

Friday, January 8.

At school all day. Pleasant. Evening. At home. Did not go to church, as mother is unwell. Received a very interesting letter from Harry Stewart. This afternoon I received a letter from a stranger, a soldier who wishes to carry on a correspondence with me for fun, mutual improvement & to while away the dull hours of camp life. He says my address was given him by a messmate. He is in the 62nd P.V. but I cannot imagine who gave him my address. I do not know whether I will answer or not. The letter is right well written and composed. Cold but pleasant. Clear & starlight.

Saturday, January 9.

At home all day. Mother is sick, but is better today. Sewing. Evening. Wrote to Mr. Hall & did some other writing. Very cold but clear and pleasant.

Sunday, January 10.

To S.S. at 9. To preaching at 10. Mr. Berkstresser preached. Had no class. Home at 12 1/2. To S.S. at 2. Home at 3. Evening. To preaching at 6. Mr. Berkstresser preached an interesting sermon. Very cold— Home at 8. Reading awhile.

Monday, January 11.

At school all day. Mother is better. Evening. Ann and I went to preaching. Mr. Eisenberg preached from the parable of the prodigal son. Had a good meeting. Home at 8. Clear & very pleasant. Wrote to Mr. Bergen & to Mr. J. M. Watson.

Tuesday, January 12.

At school all day. Evening. To preaching at 6 1/2. Mr. Berkstresser preached a very good sermon. Three penitents were at the altar, and one professed to find pardon. Oh, for a greater manifestation of the power of God. Home at 8. Sewing awhile. Cold. Reading.

Wednesday, January 13.

At school all day. Evening. Cousin Mary, Sister Susie and I went to preaching. Mr. Kitzmiller preached an excellent sermon. Did not enjoy the meeting very much. Home at 7. Received a letter from Mr. Gilbert. He is now in Rochester, N.Y. recruiting. I told him in my letter that having almost overcome one uncomfortable early love, I was disposed to guard well the citadel of my affections. He says he is glad that no one else possesses my affections & he will live in hope that he will possess the love of my heart at which time he will be the happiest person in the world. He gave me the address of the Methodist minister in his native place and wishes me to "please write to him." Perhaps I will. He would like to spend an evening with me and thinks it would be worth what it would cost.

Thursday, January 14.

At school all day. Evening. Went to preaching. Mr. Eisenberg preached an interesting sermon, but as I was suffering from sick-head-ache, I could not enjoy it or appreciate as [unclear text] under other and [unclear text] circumstances. Home at 9. Reading & sewing awhile.

Friday, January 15.

At school all day. Evening. To preaching at 6 1/2. Feel badly. Mr. Berkstresser preached but I did not enjoy the sermon very much. Home at 9. Writing awhile. Very pleasant.

Saturday, January 16.

Morning. Sick. Have a dreadful head-ache. Could not work. Afternoon. Feel better. Working. Received a very interesting letter from Ben Jones. Evening. Received the "United Presbyterian" of last Sept. containing the "Lines" I wrote on Mr. Stewart's death, also the catalogue of the U.P. Seminary in Allegheny City which Harry Stewart is attending. Very pleasant. Clear and moonlight. Writing awhile. Father came home. Very glad to see him.

Sunday, January 17.

Morning. Have head-ache. Could not go to S.S. or prayer meeting. Afternoon. To S.S. at 2. Ann went with me. Home at 3 1/2. Pleasant. Ann & Jeff came home with us. Evening. To preaching at 6. Home at 8. Reading awhile.

Monday, January 18.

At school all day. Raining. Evening. Did not go to church. Mother thought we had better stay at home. Received the Penn School Journal. Sewing. Received a letter from Mr. Hall and wrote to him. Busy all evening and feel pretty tired.

Tuesday, January 19.

At school all day. Evening. At home. Sewing at Jennie's dress. Very cold. Reading and writing awhile—Father is going back to Littlestown tomorrow morning. I do wish he had employment at home.

Wednesday, January 20.

At school all day. Evening. At home. Sewing. Reading awhile in the "School Journal." Find it very interesting indeed. Finished answering Andrew's letter. Heard some good singing by some young men of our town. Very cold and disagreeable. Quite a sudden change——Cloudy.

Thursday, January 21.

At school all day. I like my school very much and find it growing pleasanter every day. Received a letter form Sergt. Thos. G. La Clear of the 94th N.Y. Evening. Susie and I went to prayer meeting. Mr. Kitzmiller led. Enjoyed it tolerably. Sewing, reading and writing awhile. Cloudy. Heard something this evening which made me feel miserably. I hope however, that it is not as serious as I feared it. Truly there seems to be nothing but trouble in store for me, but I suppose I deserve it all. May God help me to bear it.

Friday, January 22.

At school all day. Received a very interesting letter from Mr. Beyer. Evening. At home. busy. Sewing at Jennie's dress. Lou and Harriet and [unclear text] were here. Writing awhile. Feel badly. It seems as though my efforts to be a Christian are fruitless. I feel weary in the way though I do not think I am weary of the way. Oh Lord, bless me and give me more of the mind that was in thee!

Saturday, January 23.

At home all day. Finished Jennie's dress and did some sewing for myself. In the early part of the evening I was alone and had a pleasant time meditating, and taking perspective as well as retrospective views. Later in the evening I went up street and made some calls but came home early. Annie was here. Very pleasant. Clear, warm and moonlight. Received a letter from Mr. J.M. Watson in answer to the one I wrote under a fictitious name. He sent me 1 two cent stamps & two [unclear text] ones though he does not understand why I told him to "address" with stamp & wishes me to explain, says he is not posted & if I mean him to send a stamp to pay the reply I shall tell him & he will act accordingly. He calls this an age of cheap postage and though he has no stamp now, but will get some in a day or two & will send me a dozen or two when he writes again.

Sunday, January 24.

To S. school at 9. To prayer meeting at 10 1/2. To class after prayer meeting. Our new leader is C.M. Kitzmiller, an old resident of G[ettysburg] and a local preacher. He has been living in York for some time. Enjoyed it tolerably. Home at 12 1/2. To S.S. at 2. Home at 3 1/2. Evening. Reading. Very pleasant. To preaching at 6. Mr. Eisenberg preached.

Monday, January 25.

At school all day. Evening. Annie Rupp, Sister Susie and I spent the evening with Aunt Pollie Myers with our work. Spent a very pleasant evening. Clear and moon-light and of course very pleasant.

Tuesday, January 26.

At school all day. Received a letter from Mr. Hall, a very interesting one, also one from Laurie Coshun of Johnstown containing her photograph. Annie & Sade Rupp, Cousin Annie Myers, Sister Sue & I spent the evening with Jennie Gilbert. Did not spend a very pleasant one. Wish I had stayed at home. Very pleasant.

Wednesday, January 27.

At school all day. Evening. Writing awhile. Rose Guinn & Sister Annie spent the evening here. Will Guinn and Bro. Jeff came up for them and we were singing from our "Golden Chain." Spent a pleasant evening.

Thursday, January 28.

At school all day. Evening. To prayer meeting at 6 1/2. Mr. Berkstresser led. Did not enjoy it very much. Home at 8. Very pleasant.

Friday, January 29.

At school all day. Evening. At home. Sewing at Bell's dress. Feel very tired. Reading & writing awhile.

Saturday, January 30.

Morning. Raining. Busy. Finished Bell's dress. Afternoon. Raining. Cut & fit Susie's dress. Working for myself. Evening. Disagreeable. Annie Rupp was here. Father came home. So glad to see him. Wrote to Mr. Gilbert.

Sunday, January 31.

To S.S. at 9. To preaching at 10 1/2. Mr. Isenberg preached. To class. Home at 12. To S.S. at 2. Home at 3 1/2. Evening. To preaching at 6. Mr. Eisenberg preached. Home at 7 1/2.

Monday, February 1.

At school all day. Evening. Wrote to Mr. Watson. Wrote from "Raccoon Valley" as the scene of my labors. I am keeping a copy of my letters.

Tuesday, February 2.

At school all day. Evening. Sade & Annie Rupp were here. Wrote to Mr. Beyer & to Ben Jones. Commenced to answer Mr. Stewart's letter. Sade Rupp & I were walking. Received a letter from Mr. Hall. A very interesting one.

Wednesday, February 3.

At school all day. Did not go home at noon. Stayed at school & finished answering Mr. Stewart's letter. Cloudy and disagreeable. Evening. At home.

Thursday, February 4.

At school all day. Evening. To see Mrs. Speights. To prayer meeting at 6 1/2. Mr. Snyder led. Did not enjoy it very much. Home at 8. Received a letter from Andrew Crooks. He is still in the Hospital in Pittsburgh. To see Harriet a few minutes.

Friday, February 5.

At school all day. Evening. At home. Feel badly. Oh! my father in heaven, if one so unworthy may call thee father, look kindly on me & enable me to bear meekly the trials which I have to endure. Give me more grace & increase my faith.

Saturday, February 6.

At home all day. Made a dress for Grace. Feel tired and sad. It seems that there is nothing but trouble for me. How sadly I miss one in whom I was accustomed to confide & who was ever ready with kind words of advice & sympathy.

Sunday, February 7.

To S.S. at 9. To prayer meeting at 10 1/2. Mr. Kitzmiller led. Did not enjoy it very much. To class. Home at 12. To S.S. at 2. Susie & I went to see Laura Berkstresser. She has had rheumatism but is now suffering from an affliction of the heart. She looks badly. To preaching at 6. Mr. Berkstresser preached a splendid sermon. I have not very lately been so much interested in a sermon. His text was "Let not your heart be troubled." The sermon was excellent. Home at 8. He could not have selected a text more appropriate to me. Sade Rupp is twenty-three today.

Monday, February 8.

At school all day. Received a letter from Mr. Wm. Barton and one from Mr. J.R. Hall. Evening. Answered Mr. Hall's letter. Feel badly. Went down street on an errand. Home at 7. Do not feel like working. Read awhile—Cold.

Tuesday, February 9.

At school all day. Dismissed at 2:20. Room cold & full of gas. Rec'd a letter from Mr. Watson. he addressed me as "Cousin Rosa—if I would allow him to use the term." The letter is very interesting & well written. He will take the dozen or two stamps all back and take my advice to send but one at a time. He thinks our correspondence will be rather interesting. He signs himself, "Yours until Lee makes his annual [unclear text]." "National cousin," "John." Evening. At home sewing. Feel badly.

Wednesday, February 10.

At school all day. Evening. At home. Sewing and reading.

Thursday, February 11.

At school all day. Received a good letter from Maggie Carpenter & also one from Mr. Beyer. Answered Sergt. La Clear's letter. To prayer meeting at 6 1/2. Mr. Berkstresser led. home at 8 1/2. Stopped at Aunt Pollie's. Ellie Carpenter is twenty one years old today. She is one yr. older than Maggie.

Friday, February 12.

At school all day. Evening. Received a letter from Mrs. Stewart. Her father, (Mr. Barton) is ill. He has had a paralytic stroke and Lizzie says she thinks he cannot live very long: her mother-in-law is very old and on the 7th they sent to the city for Harry. She was a little better when Lizzie wrote. Poor Lizzie! Received a "Waverly" from Mr. J.M. Watson. Pleasant.

Saturday, February 13.

Morning. Washing. Mother is not able to do it, and we cannot afford to get it done, so I have concluded to do it on Saturday. Afternoon. At home. Feel pretty tired. Evening. Father came home and was called upon to hold an inquest over the body of a man who was found dead on the steps of the Eagle Hotel & though not dead when first seen, he died before a physician could be brought. He was drunk— what an awful death & what a curse is "liquor selling."

Sunday, February 14.

At home all day. Did not go out. Am not very well and it is so cold and windy. Answered or rather finished answering Andrew Crook's letter, for I commenced it on Friday night. Evening. Very cold. Feel badly. Mr. Casey came yesterday. He is one of the old "Porter Guards" & has re-enlisted, is here on furlough. From here he goes to Elmira to stay until spring. He looks very well. He is here visiting his lady-love.

Monday, February 15.

At school all day. Received a very interesting letter from Ben with Gen. Doubleday's photo—also a letter from Mr. Hall. Evening. Received a letter from Andrew Wintamute, a wounded man who lay in our house awhile. He belongs to the 143rd P.V. and is now in York Hosp. also a very interesting letter from Mrs. Race, with her own and Mr. Race's pictures Annie Race sent hers to Susie. They are real nice pictures. Finished Andrew Crook's letter & wrote to Mr. Watson. Answered an advertisement in the Waverly by one who calls himself Fred Ryman, [unclear text] of the 2nd Brig., 2nd Div 6 Corps. Answered under an assumed name, of course. Sade Rupp & Mr. Casey were here, also Annie & Mollie with two gentlemen. Cold and snowing. Disagreeable.

Tuesday, February 16.

At school until 2. The room was so cold that I was obliged to dismiss. The thermometer down to 46 and three large panes of glass are broken and nearly out. Home at 2 1/2. Sewing at mother's dress. Evening. At home—Very cold & windy. Disagreeable.

Wednesday, February 17.

At school all day. Very cold & windy. At home. Sewing at mother's dress. Evening. Clear and moonlight but dreadful cold. Twenty four refugees from Page and Rockingham counties, Va. came to town last Sunday. They profess to be Union men who have escaped from being conscripted by the Rebel Army. They may be spies for all we know. I could not trust them.

Thursday, February 18.

[unclear text] this morning. Poor fellow, how he hated to go. To school at 9. Dismissed at 20 minutes past 10. The thermometer was down to 44. Home at 10 1/2. Sewing at mother's dress. Cold. To school at 1 1/2. Home at 4 1/2. Ellie Carpenter was up at school. Evening. To prayer meeting at 6. Mr. Berkstresser led. Home at 9. Clear & moonlight but very cold. Wrote to Ella May of St. Louis, Mo. She advertised in the Waverly for a correspondent "with a view to matrimony." Her name is assumed of course. I write as a gentleman—E.D. Hastings. Mr. Little copies the letters for me. I hope she will answer. If she does I expect to enjoy it—Sent "Cousin John" a stamp.

Friday, February 19.

At school all day. Wrote to John Franklin, 1st Mass., & to Lieut. Will Claryton, 36th Ind.—advertisements in the Waverly & wrote "just for the fun of the thing" & I keep a copy of all I write & write nothing which I would not show. I may be wrong but I think not. Martha Durboraw is very ill with Typhoid Fever. I did not know she was ill until noon. Went to see Mrs. Cress (her sister) and she says she is very low. Asked the Doctor about her and he thinks she will die. Poor Martha. I hope she will get well. Bell is eleven to-day.

Saturday, February 20.

At home all day. Busy sewing. Very pleasant. Have a bad cold, no wonder. Evening. Martha Durboraw is dead. Dead! can it be. I cannot realize that one I loved and with whom I spent so many happy hours is no more. I would love to attend her funeral but as I am not well, and she died with Typhoid Fever, mother thinks I had better not go. Jennie Gilbert was here. She had a letter from Fred K_____ [as appears in text; name unknown]. He says he is not married. The stories that were told of him were told to inquire. He says he loved me & would have made any sacrifice for me, that the hours he spent with me were so pleasant, etc. He says I took the word of an entire stranger and gave him no opportunity to explain, That my inconstancy has shaken his faith in the [unclear text] & I was false to a promise that he considered sacred in the sight of God and man—and he thought of putting himself out of his misery, & ended by enlisting for five years and is sorry now he did. All of which sounds very nice but must be received with every [unclear text] of allowances. For I did not give him the chance to explain.

Sunday, February 21.

At home all day. Wrote to Lizzie Hartman to express my sympathy etc., though it was a feeble effort. Poor dear Martha. I can hardly think she has gone, and how sadly will she be missed by her twin sister Lizzie. May God enable her to bear this heavy trial. Jennie Gilbert came up after S.S. and stayed all evening. Mother went to church. Jen and I had quite a chat over old times and ardors. She is 21 today. How time does fly. Oh Lord help me to improve it as I should. Help me to live a more consistent Christian life. Feel badly. Poor Martha! Can it be that she is gone, never more to return.

Monday, February 22.

Washington's birthday. At home all day. Washing. It was really enough to bring the old gentleman out of his grave but I could not help it. Very disagreeable. Received a note and some specimens of penmanship from Mr. Byer. He is a splendid penman. Evening. Mrs. Berkstresser was here. Had a very interesting letter from Harry Stewart. His mother is better and he is again in the city pursuing his studies.

Tuesday, February 23.

At school all day. Evening. Ann and I went over to Mr. Rupp's with our work. Spent a very pleasant evening. A lot of young men disguised as "Sisters" came in and contributed to our amusement. Sade's brother, Jen's brother and their chums. Aunt Lizzie was here spending the evening. Grace is seven today. Very pleasant all day. Clear, warm and very much like spring. Feel in pretty good spirits. The weather is so delightful it seems to "drive every dull care." Susie received a very pretty "Photograph Album" from "somebody" today.

Sunday, February 28.

At home all day, did not feel well, and had another good reason for staying at home. Answered Mr. Gilbert's letter. Mother is not at all well.

Monday, February 29.

At school all day. Susy is sixteen today and we gave her a "surprise party." It seemed to be enjoyed by all, but I take no pleasure whatever in such things, though, I do not by any means condemn those who do. Writing and preparing my class book & Register for the coming month. Wrote until 12.

Tuesday, March 1.

At school all day. Evening. Cousin Mary Myers was here for supper. Spent the evening with Ann and her sister. Home at 8 1/2. Worked at my school report until after 11. Feel very tired. Snowing and very cold.

Wednesday, March 2.

At school all day. Evening. Received a letter from Andrew Crooks. He is getting better slowly, of late he is improving some. Went over to Mr. Rupp's awhile with my work. Home at 8. Working at my school report. Clear and very pleasant. Feel very badly. Will I never never learn to control my temper. It seems as though the more I try the worse it gets. Oh! Lord. help me by thy grace to subdue it and to be more consistent.

Thursday, March 3.

At school all day. Evening. To prayer meeting at 6 1/2. Home at 8. Reading & sewing.

Friday, March 4.

At school all day. Evening. Received a note from Ben with his picture, also one of his old mess mates standing with him, now Capt. Templeton of the U.S. Colored Troops so Ben says but they are so much alike that I think they are brothers. Writing.

Saturday, March 5.

At home. Washing. Afternoon. Busy. Evening. Went to the store & to see Mrs. Berkstresser. Home at 7. Writing. Wrote to Andrew Wintamute and commenced to answer Harry Stewart's letter. Wrote several hours. (during several hours)

Sunday, March 6.

To S.S. at 9. To prayer meeting at 10 1/2. Mr. McMillan led. Enjoyed it. Had no class. To S.S. at 2. Home at 3. Evening. Our ministers have gone to Conference and I went to hear the priest preach. Wish I had stayed at home. Wrote awhile & read.

Monday, March 7.

At school. finished and sent Miss Stewart's & Wintamute's letters. Received a letter from Mr. Beyer & one from Sergt. Isaac La Clear with a handsome engraving of Camp Parole, Annapolis, Maryland. Evening. Went over to Harriet's with my work. Working at a head-dress for myself. Home at 9 1/2. O-h d-e-ar!

Tuesday, March 8.

At school all day. Received a splendid letter from Mr. Watson. He believes, or professes to believe that I am what I profess to be and says "on the honor of a soldier" he is "scribing under true colors" and his "motives are honest." He does not want me to practice a piece of strategy and send me one of my friends. Mr. Hogan is at Mr. Powers'. He was one of the wounded at Mr. Powers' and is in Mr. Gilbert's company. He knows him well and says he is a good boy and as brave a soldier as he ever saw. He knows him very well and knew him before they enlisted. He lives less than five miles from East Rush, the native place of Mr. Gilbert. Was glad to hear him speak well of Mr. G.

Wednesday, March 9.

At school all day. Evening. Received a pattern from Mr. Beyer but no letter with it. Sewing at my dress (an old one) and writing awhile. Very pleasant. New Moon.

Thursday, March 10.

At school all day. Evening. At home. Wrote to Beckie Sherriff. Sent her sister Susy's photograph and a shell ring. Very disagreeable. Raining. Feel miserably.

Friday, March 11.

At school all day. Received a letter from Dr. Little, Ass't Serg. 143rd P.V. who was with us & at the Cath. C. Hospital during and after the battle. He sent four photos & one of Mrs. Eyster, one for Harriet, one for Mrs. Powers and one for myself. Evening. Very disagreeable, raining. Wrote to Mr. Watson.

Saturday, March 12.

Busy all morning. Very pleasant. Afternoon. Received a letter from Ben Jones, & just as I was reading it I was surprised by a visit from a soldier friend, Mr. Granville Gilbert. I knew he contemplated visiting me but thought he would tell me when he was coming. Did not know him at first, but when he inquired for Peter Myers, I knew him. He is very pleasant & entertaining & improves upon acquaintance. He has been since Thursday night on the road & has borrowed furlough. The Provost told him that orders from Washington forbade him giving any passes, but he said he didn't care where he went as he was soldier enough to take care of himself. Evening. Spent a pleasant evening. Cousin Mary Myers is sixteen today & she had a party. Mr. Gilbert & I went down a few moments though neither of us cared to stay. I find Mr. Gilbert very intelligent and excellent company but my heart does not respond to his ardent love. However, he is nowise discouraged. I am sorry father is not at home. Mr. Gilbert will be 24 on the 24th of May. I will be 22 on the 24th of June. His term of service expires on the 14th of next October.

Sunday, March 13.

To S.S. at 9. To preaching at 10 1/2. Mr. Berkstresser preached. Had no class. Home at 12. Afternoon. Mr. Gilbert and I went to Dr. Carpenter's. They were all at home, and fortunately Mr. G. met in the Drs. one of his soldier friends whom he has known all his life. The surprise was as agreeable as it was unexpected. Had a pleasant ride there and home. Got home at 7, too late to go to preaching. Was very sorry. Had a very pleasant evening and on acquaintance I find that Mr. Gilbert is very much of a gentleman & has excellent principles, besides being very anxious to become a Christian though his religious opinions puzzle me not a little. He wishes me to accept if I can in justice to myself & him accept his attentions as a lover until his term of service expires. I told him I would but I feared at the end of that time I would not feel any differently toward him than I do now & feared he would think it unkind of me. He said he could not blame me but would be only too happy to have the hand if the heart did not go with it. I differ from him in regard to such things & will never marry anyone I do not love. Those friends or acquaintances whom we met speak very highly of him. He is skeptical & eccentric but of good family & highly connected.

Monday, March 14.

Mr. Gilbert left this morning. He would have liked to stay but we all thought it prudent for him to go, although we could have spent a week in visiting and getting better acquainted with each other. At school all day. Clear & pleasant. Mr. Durboraw is dead. He died at one o'clock. His son Newton got home at 10 in time to see him die. Had a note from Maggie Cress.

Tuesday, March 15.

At school all day. Evening. Received a note from Mr. Stewart in answer to a request I made in my letter. Answered it & then tore it up. Do not know when I will reply. Cold and windy. Clear and moonlight. Feel badly. I wish I had never at the request of the family written to know whether Mr. Gilbert had been killed. He was at our house on July 1 & gave the children books in which was his address. The children & mother thought so much of him that I yielded to their request & to my own curiosity & wrote to the "Commanding Officer" to inquire of him. I did it with the best of intentions, little thinking it would lead to this. Mr. G. says it made it more embarrassing to him, than if he had commenced the acquaintance & he said that nothing was further from his thought then that it was anything but mere curiosity which prompted my writing. I [unclear text].

Wednesday, March 16.

At school all day. Evening. Wrote to Mrs. Stewart. Received a letter from Beckie Sherriff. Susy had one from Andrew Crooks with a Photograph for her & one for mother. Was agreeably surprised by a visit from Rev. J.S. Rankin & Rev. J.P. Caldwell of the U.P. Church who have been with the Army of the Potomac for six weeks. The former is, or was, Mr. Stewart's pastor. I was very glad to see them & especially Mr. Rankin. Had a very interesting visit. They are on their way home & will be in town over tomorrow. The cordial shake of the hand and the thanks again rewarded me for what I did for Mr. Stewart. I like Mr. Rankin very much. His wife wrote to me soon after Mr. Stewart's death with warm expressions of regard. Mr. Rankin thinks I ought to visit a place where I have so many friends.

Thursday, March 17.

At school all day. Evening. Had company for tea and all evening. Did not go to prayer meeting. Bro. Jeff, Sis. Annie, Rev. J.S. Rankin of the U.P. Rev. W.B. [unclear text], Rev. J.P. Caldwell of the O.S. Presbyterian Church took tea with us, and spent the evening with us. Spent a very pleasant evening. I like Mr. Rankin very much indeed. He spoke very highly of the Stewart family & thinks if Harry is spared he will make an excellent preacher. I wish we had had a better opportunity to get acquainted with Mr. Rankin. They leave in the early train tomorrow. Mrs. Berkstresser & Annie were here. They also leave tomorrow. I am so sorry they are going. Sade Rupp and Julie Culp were here. Feel badly. The pleasure of meeting & being with friends is marred by the thought of bidding them adieu, perhaps forever.

Friday, March 18.

Went down to the Cars to see Mrs. Berkstresser. I love her dearly and feel afraid that her place will not soon be filled. At school all day——Evening. Went down to see Ann & spent the evening with very pleasantly. Home at 10.

Saturday, March 19.

Morning. Went to the Gallery and had a picture taken, an Ambrotype for Mr. Gilbert. I think it very good. He wishes it and it costs me nothing. I would like to have his but I do not wish to encourage him any more than I can help. I do not think I will ask him for it. He sent me his photo last fall. Afternoon. Received a letter from Mr. Barton. He has been at home on a twelve day furlough. Enjoyed his visit very much. Evening. Rose Guinn & Sister Annie were here a long time. After they left wrote to Mister Waterman of Decatur N.Y., who was here some weeks with a wounded friend. I heard from him last Dec. Wrote to Mr. H. Stewart in answer to that note & began a letter to Andrew Crooks.

Sunday, March 20.

To S.S. at 9. To preaching at 10 1/2. Our new preacher in charge preached a very good sermon. He will finish it tonight. Had no class. Home at 11 1/2. To S.S. at 2. Home at 3 1/2. Evening. Father, mother, Susie & Jennie went to church. Bell, Grace & I stayed at home. Sewing & reading. Finished Andrew's letter & wrote to Mr. Hall & Dr. Fulton. Clear & moonlight. Very pleasant.

Monday, March 21.

At school. Miss Emma Wolf & Mrs. Fink (the latter I met at our County Convention in Fairfield last Dec.) both teachers visited our school this morning. [unclear text] & Maggie Carpenter were to see me. Maggie's school is over. Pleasant. Afternoon. At school. Evening. Bell received a letter from Mr. Gilbert. He got home safely. He sent for a copy of Mr. Detterline's map & description of the Battle of Gettysburgh. Sent it to him and also sent my picture to him. Received a letter from Lieut. Will Clayton, also Lieut. Frank Nash, of 36th Ind. Inftry. He advertised in the Waverly for correspondents. I answered on the 19th using the name of Justina D. Sellingham. The letter is tolerably well written. Do not know whether I will answer or not. At Harriet's with my work.

Tuesday, March 22.

At school all day. Had two teeth plugged at noon & was half an hour behind time by the operation. Evening. Went to the store for mother & for myself. Home at 7. Sewing busily all evening. Cloudy & very cold. Went over to Harriet's & did some cutting out.

Wednesday, March 23.

At school all day. Evening. Susie and I went out calling. Called to see the Misses Fink, & Miss Mary went with us to see Miss. Emma Wolf. I like them both very much. Home at 10. Clear & moonlight. Pleasant but very cold. Feel badly.

Thursday, March 24.

At school all day. Evening. At prayer meeting. Received a letter from the House of Representatives from a Mr. Wesley Benjamin who says he was wounded at the battle of G— & that I attended to him. He wishes to know if I still live in G. as he expects to visit the town in a short time & wishes to thank me in person. He addresses me "My very revered friend—Miss Myers." I do not remember any one of the name. As he sent a stamp & wished an answer I answered immediately & also wrote to Beckie Sherriff & Fannie Coshun. Feel very badly and I hardly know why. Received a letter from Mr. Watson and a picture which he says is his own. I do not know whether it is or not.

Friday, March 25.

No school but went and worked at our curriculum. Snowing. Received a letter from Mr. Beyer. Last month I wrote to Mr. Beyer & sent him the address of the M.E. Minister of Mr. Gilbert's native place. he wrote to him to inquire concerning Mr. G—'s personal character & family connections. To-day I received the letter which the minister wrote in reply to his inquiry. The letter confirmed what Mr. Hogan & the Zimmerman's have said. But it is to a great extent immaterial to me, for I do not & cannot love him. It troubles me not a little more because I think he is honest & that his motives & intentions are honorable. I wish I had never had a beau. Since I had the first one I have had nothing but trouble.

Saturday, March 26.

Very busy all day. Evening. Wrote to Mr. Beyer, Ben Jones and Sergt. Isaac G. La Clear. Feel tired. The weather is very disagreeable. Received a paper from Mr. Watson addressed to Sallie Myers. I do not know why he sent it to me. I have received two addressed to Rosa Howard, but I don't know why he sent the last one to me unless he wanted to find out whether I am scribing under a "nom de plume" or not. He disclaims anything of the kind, as far as he is concerned.

Sunday, March 27.

To S.S. at 9. To preaching at 10 1/2. Our pastor preached a splendid sermon. Enjoyed it very much. Home at 12. To S.S. at 2. Beckie Belch went with me. Home at 3 1/2. Pleasant. Evening. Feel miserably. Am not well. Did not go to church. Stayed at home with Grace while the rest went to church. Annie Rupp came over and we had a very pleasant chat together about matters & things in general. I like Annie very much.

Monday, March 28.

At school all day. Received a letter from Mr. Hall and one from Andrew Wintamute. They are both with their Regiments. Evening. Received a letter from Andrew Crooks. Poor brother! The hand of affliction has been heavily laid upon him. He has lost his dearest earthly friend. His heart is almost breaking & as I confided in him as a brother he has honored me by his confidence. He wishes me to pray for him & I shall certainly do so. Sadie had measles and while she was fast recovering, she took diptheria and only lived four days. He told her sister to tell me I was not forgotten. She did not see Andrew. They did not send for him as she was not considered dangerous and the [unclear text] were very. Poor Andrew. May God bless him.

Tuesday, March 29.

Rose at 5 1/2. Washing until 8. At school as usual. Pleasant. Miss Zimmerman & Miss Carpenter were at school this afternoon. I took them into all the rooms. Miss Z—is a professional teacher from Brown Co. N.Y. Evening. At home. Very busy. Feel badly.

Wednesday, March 30.

At school all day. Evening. Sewing. Very disagreeable. Feel disappointed. Did not get a letter and was confidently expecting one. So much for expectations. If I never meet with a worse disappointment, though, I shall consider myself fortunate.

Thursday, March 31.

At school as usual. Had not more than 1/3 of my scholars. Disagreable. Dismissed early. Evening. To prayer meeting. Mr. Souser led. Home at 9. Received two letters, one from Mr. H. Stewart & one from Mr. Gilbert. Mr. G. starts for his Regt on the 1st of April. His letter is just like himself, earnest and honest. I am sorry this affair has occurred. He says, "What a privilege to have for a friend one whom we love." He begins, "Much loved friend" & at the end he says "My feelings justify my in subscribing, Your devoted lover."

He seems confident that the day is not far distant when I will treat him with much more favor than at present. For my picture "an acknowledgement of friendship and confidence" he will not attempt to thank me "in words" but will by God's help live so that I will not be ashamed to have it seen with him. Poor Mr. Gilbert. I pity him.

Friday, April 1.

Morning. At home. Baking & ironing. Had several invitations to "help to move" but not caring about it I declined. Afternoon. Helped Ann to clean her garrett. The house in which she moved was horribly dirty. Julie and I stayed until late. Answered Mr. Watson's letter. Very disagreeable. Feel disappointed. Was expecting to go home with Ellie Carpenter today until Sunday evening, but when she came I could not go. I could not see my way clear to spend so much time in visiting. It is very likely that Mr. Harry, & Mrs. Lizzie Stewart will visit us in June. Mr. S. says "if nothing providential occurs to prevent." I hope nothing will occur for I would like very much to see them.

Saturday, April 2.

Helping Ann all morning. Afternoon. Home at 3. Very busy—Sewing. Evening. Received a "return letter" which I wrote on last November. Was glad to get it. Received a letter from Mr. Stephen Moore of Co. I. 150th P.V. He was a nurse at the Catholic Church Hospital. He writes to have a note delivered to a lady whose name he had almost forgotten. Received a note from Ben with his pictures. His own is a picture of evening, very pretty. His own is splendid. I am so glad he sent it for the other one I have is not good. Father came home. Was very glad to see him.

Sunday, April 3.

To S.S. at 9. To prayer meeting. Mr. Snyder led. Had no class. Home at 11 1/2. Afternoon. To S.S. at 2. Home at 3 1/2. Evening. Wrote a note to Ben Jones in answer to the one received with the pictures. Did not go to church. Was afraid my nose would bleed again as it bled twice today. Grace, Bell & I kept house. Writing & reading.

Monday, April 4.

Rose at 5 1/2. Washing until 8. At school all day. Evening. Went to the store. Raining. Very disagreeable. Went to the store. Our Junior preacher Mr. Lantz was here. I like him very well so far. He is very sociable & also very intelligent. Sewing all evening. Feel pretty tired.

Tuesday, April 5.

At school all day. Evening. Went up to stay with Annie. She was alone & was afraid. Sewing. Fixing an old dress. Received a very interesting letter from Beckie Sherriff with a photo which she sent to me to send to Mr. Watson in exchange for the one he sent me. It is a beautiful young lady, though the card is a good deal soiled. It is a vignette. I do not know whether I will send it or not.

Wednesday, April 6.

At school all day. Evening. Annie Rupp was here a long time. Sewing at my dress. Finished it & made out my school report for the present month. Pleasant. Clear.

Thursday, April 7.

At school all day. Received a letter from Mr. Barton. Evening. To prayer meeting at 7. Mr. Lantz led. Enjoyed it. Home at 8 1/2. Pleasant. Went down to the depot to see Maggie Carpenter. She started for Monroe County, NY with her step-aunt & uncle to stay six months or a year. Mrs. Hattie Zimmerman, another step-aunt, came last November to spend the winter here as her health was very poor, and their own climate was too severe for her. She was expecting to go home with them, but on the beginning of the week she became much worse & on Sunday afternoon about 2 o'clock she died. She died calmly though at first the thought of dying without seeing her mother was very trying. She was the youngest in the set. Poor Hattie! She was a sweet girl, though death to her is gain. What a sad going home for her brother & sister & her poor father & mother.

Friday, April 8.

At school all day. Evening. At home. Sewing. Working at my circular. Want to finish it this week. Am braiding it.

Saturday, April 9.

At home all day. Finished my circular. Evening. Cut out a collar & a pair of cuffs for myself. Raining. Very disagreeable.

Sunday, April 10.

To S.S. at 9. To preaching at 10 1/2. Mr. Consor preached a splendid sermon. His subject was the ladder which Jacob saw in his vision when fleeing from Esau. Had no class. Home at 11 1/2. Mr. Drum is here. He looks well. To S.S. at 2. Maria Ziegler went with me. Had a pleasant session. Home at 3 1/2. Evening. Mrs. Speights & Jennie were here. To preaching at 7 1/2. Mr. Consor finished the discourse which he commenced this morning. It was good. I like him so far, very much—Home at 8 1/2. Feel miserably. Oh, Lord, look in great mercy upon me. Lead me in paths of peace if not joy.

Monday, April 11.

At school all day. Received a very interesting letter from Mr. Watson. He thinks Rosa F. Howard a beautiful name & asks to be excused, but he cannot help thinking every time he sees it that it is assumed— Evening. Jennie Speights & Cousin Mary Myers & Al are going to Baltimore tomorrow morning. I am sorry they are leaving for I like Mrs. S. so much. Jennie gave me her photograph. Ann & I went down street to Mr. Gilbert's, Mr. Rupp's & Mr. Powers'.

Tuesday, April 12.

Went to the depot at 6 o'clock to see Mrs. S. and her family leave. Went at 8 to see Maggie Benner go to Philadelphia. Evening. Mr. Benjamin of Co. I. 142 P.V. now discharged, came in the afternoon train. I was very much surprised as I was not expecting him until the House adjourned. He spent the evening here. He has lost the use of his right arm, & will probably never be able to use it. He seems very young to be a member of the house. He is discharged from service. I like him very much, very pleasant. He was in the same company with Will Sherriff & knows him well. He gave me a very handsome photograph album which will hold fifty pictures. I was surprised. Had a letter from Andrew Crooks. He is doing well. Is attending Iron City College. Our ministers were here to see us but I was not at home, was at school.

Thursday, April 14.

At school all day. Evening. To prayer meeting at 7 1/2. Had a very interesting meeting. I enjoyed it very much. Mr. Drum led. I like Mr. Drum very much. Mr. Consor and Mr. Lantz were also there. Home at 8 1/2. Writing awhile.

Friday, April 15.

At school all day. Mother and I went "shopping." How I dreaded it, & how thankful I am that it is over. Answered Mr. Watson's letter. Sent him my photograph.

Saturday, April 16.

At home all day. Working at my silk dress. Evening. Wrote to Mr. Gilbert and to Miss Mollie Winfield, Centerville, Wayne County, Indiana. She advertised in the Compiler for correspondents and I answered getting Bro. Jefferson to copy the letter. I signed myself "Rufus P. Barton." Hope she will reply.

Sunday, April 17.

To S.S. at 9. To prayer meeting at 10 1/2. Had no class. To S.S. at 2. Home at 3 1/2. Evening. Went down to see Aunt Agnes Sheads & Rose Guinn on an errand.

To preaching at 7 1/2. Mr. Drum preached an elegant sermon. I was very glad to hear him once more.

Monday, April 18.

At school all day. Evening. At home. Busy.

Tuesday, April 19.

At school all day. Evening. Julie Culp had company & I went up awhile, but did not enjoy it & came home. Feel miserably. Have had head-ache all day.

Wednesday, April 20.

At school all day. Feel miserably. Am not well. Evening. Received the School Report for 1863 from Mr. Burgwin. Commenced an answer to Mr. Stewart's letter of March 24th. I ought to have answered sooner but could not find time. Have a terrible head-ache. Can not imagine the cause of it.

Thursday, April 21.

At school all day. Evening. Finished answering Mr. Stewart's letter, and wrote to Ms. Hall & Mr. Burgwin. To prayer-meeting at 7 1/2. Mr. Snyder led. Had a very interesting meeting. Had a pleasant walk. Home at 9.

Friday, April 22.

At school all day. Evening. At home. Busy.

Saturday, April 23.

To preaching at 10 1/2. Mr. Lantz preached a very good sermon. Home at 12. Went to the store, and did several errands. Working at my silk dress. Evening. Received a Waverly from Mr. Watson. To preaching at 7 3/4.

Sunday, April 24.

To preaching at 10. Mr. McMurray preached an excellent sermon. After the sermon commenced, had a very interesting meeting. Home at 12 1/2. Afternoon. To Love-feast at 3. Enjoyed it tolerably. Home at 4 3/4. Evening. Mr. McMurray preached an excellent, though rather a long sermon. Home at 8 1/2.

Monday, April 25.

At school all day. Received a letter from Mr. Watson and one from Ben Jones, also an answer to the proposal I wrote to Ben on the 6th. He cannot "in justice to himself & others" correspond with an ultimate view to matrimony but will be all too happy to have my name as a "bright addition" to his list of correspondents, & is proud to acknowledge as his friend one of the "heroines of Gettysburg." Hoping to hear again soon, he closes Alas! Benjamin. He has been home on a short furlough & enjoyed it very much.

Tuesday, April 26.

At school all day. Evening. Working at my dress all evening. Feel pretty tired.

Wednesday, April 27.

At school all day. Evening. Received a very welcome letter from Mrs. Stewart. If it suits us, she, her sister Mary & her brother-in-law will visit us in June. I am so glad they are coming. I anticipate a very pleasant visit. If only nothing happens to prevent it. Wrote another proposal to Ben Jones. Working.

Thursday, April 28.

At school all day. Received a letter from Mr. Beyer & one from Mr. Hall. Mr. Consor & Mr. Lantz both know Mr. Beyer & spoke very highly of him. Evening. Received a letter from Sadie White's sister Jennie, giving me the particulars of

Sadie's death. I think I will like Jennie very much. She writes a very nice letter, & wishes me to answer at my earliest convenience. To prayer meeting at 7 1/2. Mr. Lantz led. Home at 8 3/4. Sewing at my dress until 10. After Sadie White had said farewell to those who were about her & sent messages to two who were absent she whispered to Jennie, "Tell Sallie she was not forgotten." Poor Andrew, how I pity him. From all accounts, Sadie was a sweet girl. Her death was happy & triumphant.

Friday, April 29.

At school all day. Evening. Busy. Working at my dress. Wrote to Mr. Watson, to Mrs. Stewart, to Mr. Wintamute, to Mr. Crooks & to Miss Beckie Sherriff. Have so many letters to answer that I hardly know where to commence.

Saturday, April 30.

Morning. Busy. Afternoon. Finished my dress. Received a letter from Mr. Gilbert. Evening. Wrote to Mr. Gilbert and Mr. Barton. Feel badly. I always do when I read Mr. Gilbert's letters. His letter deserved an immediate answer. If I would consult my feelings I would not correspond with him but he does not ask me to stop writing to him & he says it really does him good to hear from me. Poor fellow! I feel so sorry for him.

Sunday, May 1.

To S.S. at 9. To prayer-meeting at 10 1/2. Mr. McMillan led. Did not enjoy it very much. To class. Did not enjoy it. Our old leader, Mr. John Culp led. To S.S. at 2. Home at 2 1/2. Evening. To preaching at 7 1/2. Mr. Consor preached an excellent sermon. Text—"What shall it profit a man if he gain the whole world & lose his own soul?" Rachel Lashell went with me.

Monday, May 2.

Morning. Washing until 8 1/2, at school all day. Received a package of songs from Ben Jones addressed to "Rosa Howard" alias Nellie Sinclair, alias Sallie Myers, with the compliments of the "charming Bucktail." Ha! ha! ha! What fine fun!! though I am not "Nellie Sinclair." Received a note from Mr. Burgwin. He will be here on Friday or Saturday if it suits me. One of the girls proposed to Ben under the name of Nellie Sinclair & Ben accepted, only he thought she knew him & was only sending under a "nom de plume." She does not know him and he blames both of them on me. How we enjoyed it.

Tuesday, May 3.

At school all day. Evening. Wrote a note to Mr. Burgwin telling him it will be convenient for me, to have him come on Friday or Saturday. Sewing for myself. Feel miserably! Oh for a friend in whom I could confide, but alas even that privilege is denied me. I have friends enough, but none whom I care to trust in this respect.

Wednesday, May 4.

At school all day. Evening. Working awhile. Feel badly. Feel as though I have nothing to live for. Oh God! drive away these clouds and may I be enabled to rejoice in the glorious sunlight of the presence of God in my heart. Oh Lord grant my prayer.

Thursday, May 5.

At school all day. Feel most dreadfully. Evening. Busy. Filie Culp, Julia Culp, Mollie Kendlehart & I were walking before prayer meeting. To prayer meeting at 8. Mr. Lantz led. Did not enjoy it. Received a letter from Henrietta S. Houck of Centerville Ind. in answer to the one I wrote to Mollie Winfield a few weeks ago. It is grand (?). Commences Mr. Rufus G. Barton, "affectionate friend." Don't know whether to answer or not. At present do not feel like it.

Friday, May 6.

At school all day. Received a letter from S.S. Hubert of the 149th P.V. in answer to the last proposal I wrote to Ben. Ben requested him to answer & he says, It may be Ben himself; writing under an assumed name. I will not answer over the name I signed when I wrote to Ben, but as the letter is well-composed & beautifully written I think I will correspond under another assumed name. He wishes me to do it & I may. I want to exchange photos. Evening. Received a letter from Mr. Burgwin. He cannot come. He received a letter from home stating that his brother was very sick & requesting him to come home immediately. He will stay at home until August when he will return to the Capital & will then visit us, if agreeable.

Saturday, May 7.

At home all day. Afternoon. Mrs. Pepple is here from Illinois. She is an old friend & also a second cousin. Evening. Ginnie Gilbert was here. We were over at the Shillens awhile & up at Bro. Jeff's. Spent a pleasant evening.

Sunday, May 8.

To S.S. at 9. To preaching at 10 1/2. Mr. Consor preached a very good sermon. To class. Mr. Consor led. Enjoyed it. To S.S. at 2. Home at 3 1/4. Evening. To preaching. Rachel Lashell went with me. Mr. Consor finished his discourse. Home at 9. Feel badly.

Monday, May 9.

At school all day. Evening. Julie Culp, Mollie Kendlehart and I called to see Miss Lizzie Consor, our minister's niece. Walking awhile. Working at my dress, at Harriet's until 10 1/2. pleasant; Moon-light & star-light. Feel sad.

Tuesday, May 10.

At school all day. Evening. Working at my dress. Feel miserably. The news from the army is encouraging, if true, but I fear that our men are being drawn into danger. I feel very anxious to know if any of my friends have been killed or wounded. I hope not but I am afraid to hear. Oh! this cruel war! I think the most of my friends were engaged in the fight and it is but natural & reasonable to suppose that some of them have suffered. God bless our noble Army! Amen and amen!

Wednesday, May 11.

At school all day. Evening. Sewing at my dress. So far no one I know has been killed or wounded. I should say in the lists I have seen. I am afraid to see the lists & yet I am anxious. In such a terrible struggle, some of my friends will certainly fall. Some persons say the fighting is worse than that of any battle on record—Oh, how I wish the struggle would end. I hope it will soon terminate in an honorable peace. God grant it.

Thursday, May 12.

At school all day. Received a letter from Maggie Carpenter. She is well, enjoying herself & is attending school. Did not go to prayer-meeting. It was raining very heavily, & we (Susy, & I) concluded to stay at home. Sewing at my dress. Have as yet not seen the names of any I know among the killed & wounded. The news is good. Thank God. Oh that the cause of right would triumph speedily over rebellion & tyranny. May God in mercy grant it.

Friday, May 13.

At school all day. Susy received a letter from Mr. Hall. He was wounded on the 5th and is now in Washington. He was wounded in the left hand & will lose one of his fingers. He made a narrow escape. The man beside him was killed. Evening.

Received a very interesting letter from Andrew. He is getting along very well. Expects to go home in a week or ten days. Poor dear brother! Sewing until 11 1/2. Felt in the humor. Could have sewed until morning. The news is excellent.

Saturday, May 14.

At home all day. Very busy. Evening. Feel very much disappointed, was expecting a letter & did not get it. Father came home. Busy sewing until 11 1/2.

Sunday, May 15.

To S.S. at 9. Raining very heavily. Had a very short session. Had no prayer-meeting. Went with Julia Weygandt & Maggie Bailley to the Presbyterian church. Home at 11 1/2. Afternoon. Did not go out. Writing. Wrote to Jennie White & Mr. Beyer. Evening. Feel tired & not very well. The weather is very unpleasant. There was an appointment for Quaker meeting in our church by one of the Orthodox society of Friends, but it turned out to be a genuine "Quaker Meeting" for the creek was so high the speaker could not come & after waiting awhile, the congregation one after another with illy suppressed laughter retired—I was too indignant to laugh—Hope they will get our church again. Did not go to preaching. It was raining heavily, but I am sorry I did not go. Mr. Lantz preached.

Monday, May 16.

At school all day. Evening. Lizzie Consor was here. Received a real good letter from Mr. Stewart. He is without exception my best correspondent, and I have some elegant ones. It is still their design to visit us in June if nothing occurs to prevent, though if Mr. Barton should be wounded or killed I suppose Lizzie & Mary will not feel like going any place, & if he needs care Mr. Stewart will go to him if possible. Sewing until 11 at a wrapper & dress. Feel very tired but I must work for I have so much to do & expecting company.

Tuesday, May 17.

At school all day. Evening. Sewing at my wrapper. Worked until 11. This is a glorious night. Clear & moon-light. Oh! I love the sweet silver moon—perhaps I am a lunatic. The twilight is pleasant & how I enjoy the "Calm grey nightfall When the light falls, From the [unclear text], And the splendor, Pale & tender, Of the full moon gleams on high—God Bless our brave soldiers, Amen and amen!

Wednesday, May 18.

At school all day. Received a letter from Mr. Gosten of the 94th N.Y. He was in G__ after the battle for several months. They are at Annapolis, at Camp Parole, He is from Canada— Evening. Commenced an answer to Mr. Stewart's letter. Went to see Miss Catherine Reynolds awhile. Very pleasant—Moon-light.

Thursday, May 19.

At school all day. Received a letter from Beckie Sherrif with the news of a box containing an album with photographs of Will & his lady-love—was quite anxious to see it. Finished & mailed Mr. Stewart's letter. To prayer-meeting at 8. Home at 9. Feel very tired.

Friday, May 20.

At school— Received an interesting letter from Mr. Barton. He was slightly wounded under the great toe by a minnie ball when our men fell back. He had not received my last letter. He is doing very well. Afternoon. Mr. Little's, Miss Whiteside's, Miss Belch's & my own school went out to the woods to rusticate. Enjoyed it tolerably. Feel very tired. Home at 5. Called to see Maggie Cress & Rose Guinn. Answered Mr. Barton's letter & sewed until 11— Feel badly. Oh! Lord look in great mercy on thy erring child. Help me to be a better, a more consistent Christian.

Saturday, May 21.

Morning. Went to the store & to see the President & Secretary of the Board of School Directors on business. Had a satisfactory interview. Home at 10 1/2. Afternoon. Up street on business. Very tired. Home at 3. Sewing. Evening. Sewing. Rose Guinn & Jennie Gilbert were here. Sewing until 11 1/2. Feel very tired. Received a very interesting letter from Mr. Watson written last Saturday. He was unhurt though his old school mate & most intimate friend was shot through the heart by a rebel sharp-shooter. He says he will answer my letter as soon as they get settled again. Feel dreadfully.

Sunday, May 22.

To S.S. at 9. To preaching at 12. Mr. Lantz' sermon was excellent. To class. Mr. Lantz led. Did not go to S.S. Wrote to Mr. Watson though he did not request me to write & did not consider his letter in answer to my last. He sent me some Virginia flowers from the "battle-field of the Wilderness." They are highly prized. Evening. Ada Mc was here. To preaching at 7 3/4. Mr. Lantz preached a splendid sermon on "Prayer." It suited my case exactly. Ada Mc left and I took a walk after church. She was waiting for her father who had gone to the country to hold a prayer-meeting. Had a very pleasant chat. She has been away from home a year with her sister, Mrs. Drum and Mr. E. Ministers. The moon is bright. Perhaps it shines on wounded & dying. God bless the soldiers of every description & under all circumstances—

Monday, May 23.

At school all day. Jennie had a letter from Mr. Gilbert. He is well. —Was glad to hear of his safety— Evening. Busy. The regular class met tonight at our house. Did not go in as it is not the one to which I belong but was in the parlor listening. Enjoyed it almost as much as though I had been in. The moon is bright. Oh, how I enjoy a moon-light night. I love to pray in the light of the moon. It is so holy, so calm & soothing. I feel very grateful to God for his many mercies. I feel within me a new source of happiness & I fear the joy is too great. I feel calm & peaceful, & so thankful to my kind heavenly father. Oh may my gratitude be lasting.

Tuesday, May 24.

At school all day. Evening. At sister Annie's with my work. Raining very heavily. Feel well, better indeed than I have felt for a long, long, time. I fear it will not last, but oh my father in heaven, look in mercy upon me & help me under all circumstances to be a consistent Christian. If there is one thing I desire above another, it is that I may be an humble follower of the Lamb. Oh God! for the sake of thy son, my saviour & intercessor, help me to love thee & serve thee devotedly.

Wednesday, May 25.

At school all day. Evening. Feel very tired. The album for which I have been looking came this evening. It is from Mrs. Sherrif " 'a very inadequate recognition' of my [unclear text] 'to our wounded soldiers during the battle of Gettysburg July 1st, 2nd & 3rd, 1863.' " It is beautiful and has my name on the back. It contains pictures of Will & his lady-love. She is very sweet looking but Will's are not as good as the one he gave me in July, also a letter from Will.

Thursday, May 26.

At school all day. Evening. Mr. & Mrs. Pepple came from Emmittsburgh— They are going home to-morrow morning, or rather start for home. Did not go to prayer-meeting as it was raining & I thought there would not be any. Spent a pleasant evening—Singing. Mr. Pepple is Lutheran & was a lay delegate to the Synod at York. They live in Adams Co. Illinois.

Friday, May 27.

Mr. & Mrs. Pepple went away. Felt sorry to see them go. I like Mrs. P very much. To school at 9. Had an examination, Four of the Directors were there. School closed until August 1st. Afternoon. Very busy—Sewing. Could not get time to attend any of the examinations.

Saturday, May 28.

Very busy all day. Evening. Feel so tired that I can hardly walk. This is a good beginning for vacation—however, I am as able to work as any one of the family and I am thankful for it. What a blessing is good health.

Sunday, May 29.

Did not go to S.S. To prayer-meeting at 10 1/2. Did not enjoy it. Had no class. Afternoon. To S.S. Evening. Went to Mr. Blessing's funeral. He died yesterday of consumption. His wife is sister Annie's first cousin. It is the first time I have been to the cemetery since early in December. Evening. To preaching. Mr. Lantz preached a very good sermon. Feel badly.

Monday, May 30.

Morning. Washing & scouring. Afternoon. Sewing. Did some errands. Evening. Received a splendid letter from Mr. Stewart. They will "Providence permitting" leave Pittsburg at 8 1/2 on the evening of the 6th of June—I am so very anxious to see them. "Brother Harry" is a good correspondent.

Tuesday, May 31.

Morning. Ironing. Afternoon. Very busy—Sewing. Evening. Sewing. Wrote a note in answer to Mr. Stewart's letter. It was not necessary but I wanted to see his photos & I wrote to request him to bring them along.

Wednesday, June 1.

Very busy all day. I saw Andrew Wintamute's name in the list of killed. He was wounded & lay at our house more than a week last July. Poor Andrew! I feel sorry for him. He was in the 143rd P.V. Finished a wrapper & began a calico dress for myself.

Thursday, June 2.

Busy as usual. Evening. To prayer-meeting. Mr. Snyder led. Did not enjoy it. Wrote to Ben Jones. Have been owing him a letter for more than five weeks. Went to see Miss Whiteside. She is going away tomorrow & doesn't know when she will return. She has resigned her situation as 1st Assistant in our school.

Friday, June 3.

Busy—Finished my calico dress, & hemmed & marked two sheets. —Went to the store & to see Jennie Gilbert. She is going to Washington tomorrow morning.

Saturday, June 4.

Busy— "Cleaning up" Afternoon. sewing. Ironing. Did some shopping & errands for mother. Evening. Annie Slentz, & Allie Powers were here. Pleasant. Feel badly.

Sunday, June 5.

Did not go to S.S. Felt too badly. To preaching at 10 1/2. Mr. Taylor, once our Junior preacher preached—To class. Home at 12 1/2. To S.S. at 2. Beckie Belch &

I went to vespers—Home at 4. Evening. Wrote to Maggie Carpenter and Beckie Sherriff.

Monday, June 6.

Morning. Washing. Finished at 10 1/2. Father is home very unexpectedly. Afternoon. Went up street to the store. Received a letter from Mr. Gilbert. Poor Mr. Gilbert. I wish he had never seen or become acquainted with me. Evening. Received a very good letter from Mrs. Race—and a note from Mr. Stewart. He says "Circumstances compel us to delay—one day. We will therefore not leave Pittsburgh until Tuesday evening." Wrote a note to Andrew Crooks with Annie E. Rupp who is writing to her brother Henry in Pittsburgh.

Tuesday, June 7.

Morning. Ironing until 12. Afternoon. Sewing. Received a letter from Mr. Hall and also a paper. He is in Baltimore. Evening. Very pleasant. Very busy.

Wednesday, June 8.

Morning. Busy. Went to the cars to meet Mr. and Mrs. S__ & Miss B__. Met them though it was almost more than I expected. I have been anticipating this visit for so long, since last fall & I was afraid something would occur to prevent them from coming. Like them all very much. Miss Mary Barton is (so far) one of the "nicest" ladies I ever met. She has been a teacher of common schools for a great many years. She is very entertaining & improves very much from acquaintance. Mrs. Stewart is very sad. She talks very little, but I know I will love her. Poor dear Lizzie! Mr. Stewart is very different from what I expected after seeing his photo— Thought he was very large & he is not. The face of his photo is not at all good. Afternoon. At home. Evening. Went out to view the spot where Mr. Stewart fell. Had a very pleasant walk. Stopped to see Cousin Carrie on our way home & had some music. Home at 9—Became considerably better acquainted with Mr. S. after the rest retired.

Thursday, June 9.

Morning—at home. Afternoon. Had a pleasant walk around Culp's Hill & through the "Soldiers Cemetery" & "Evergreen Cemetery." I was walking most of the time with Mr. S— & found him very entertaining, very pleasant, & very sensible. Home at 5. Evening. At Ada McMillan's. To prayer-meeting at 8. Mr. Lantz led. Did not enjoy it very much. Home at 9. Had company. Had a very interesting conversation with Mr. S. Find him very much a gentleman, & like him much better than I expected and indeed I like them all much better than I thought I would.

Friday, June 10.

Morning. Harry & I went out to see Ada McMillan about some strawberries & afterwards started out to "Round Top." Mr. Stewart & I were together & had a delightful walk & a more delightful conversation. Ate our dinner on the top of that dear old hill. Enjoyed the walk. Have not been there for many fine years. The walk home I will never, never forget. Saw some scenes which were beautifully grand— some that were lovely & some that were very sad, sad indeed, but then conversation on road home was more interesting that all we saw, & yet I fear it is the forerunner of trouble. I cannot write it now, for a want of space. Suffice it to say that I am loved by one whom I have learned to love within a year, & yet I could not acknowledge it to myself. It seems as though the happiness is almost too great.

Saturday, June 11.

Morning. At home. Harry has gone out to see an old friend of his father's. Dear Harry & yet I have no right to call him that. I would not if anyone, himself not excepted, I would not have thought six months ago that I could love again & would not believe it myself until I was told that I was beloved, & that too by one who is in every way worthy of my love & highest respect. Yet there is a circumstance, which I cannot name which makes me feel as though— Well, I cannot be more explicit at present. Afternoon. Spent at Bro. Jeff's not as pleasantly as I would at home but we had to go. Feel badly. Evening. Harry & I called on Mr. Woodburn of the U.P. Church, & an old college friend of Harrie's. Had a pleasant call, at Harriet's awhile. Home at 9. Had a pleasant chat.

Sunday, June 12.

Morning. Did not go to S.S. Had no preaching & we went to the U.P. Church. Harry & Lizzie are members of that church. [unclear text] is the O.S. Presbyterian Church. I like them all very much— Home at 12 1/2. Afternoon. Mary, Susie, Harrie, & I went to S.S. Home at 3. Evening. Went to preaching. Mr. Lantz preached an excellent sermon. Home at 9. Had another delightful chat & yet my conscience condemns me. How hard it is to do right. ! Lord guide me by the spirit in the path of duty. Show me the path of duty & give me grace to walk therein. Never did I need grace more than at this time.

Monday, June 13.

Morning. At home. Working on the frames and little mementoes to send to our friends in Western Penn. Allie Powers was helping. —Spent a pleasant morning. Afternoon. Visited the college, & Seminary Hall. Uncle Isaac Sheads is dead. He was shot in the head and only lived one day. Poor Dear Uncle Isaac! Evening. Mr. & Mrs. Bushman were here. Also Ginnie Gilbert. Harry and I went home with her & had a delightful walk. Clear & moonlight. Spent an hour or two with Harry. Dear Harry! I am so happy! I fear it will not last. Never will I forget dear old Round Top, & the walk there & back. Oh God may I not forget thee, he gives of every good & perfect gift.

Tuesday, June 14.

Morning. Busy. Afternoon. Harry, Mary & I went to see our school building & the Jail, & then we all spent the afternoon & took tea with Aunt Emily Sheads. After tea, visited the gas works. Home at 8. Mr. Woodburn was here. This is the last evening I will spend with those I have learned to love under peculiar circumstances. Spent perhaps the last evening with Harry—oh! so pleasantly. I feel so sorry to part with them & especially with one who is dearer than life. Oh! may I be worthy of the love of that noble heart. God bless him abundantly with every needed blessing & fit him for the sacred office—I tremble for fear my joy is too good. Oh! God! look in mercy upon me.

Wednesday, June 15.

Morning. Our friends left at 11:30. It seemed more like parting with the friends of a lifetime than with persons whose existance one year ago was unknown to me. I cannot describe my feelings as the cars moved away bearing within them those I love & especially one dearer than life to me. I hope God will forgive me if I have erred in loving too well one whom I have now no right to love. But I must write no more now on that subject at present. I cannot hear from him under two weeks is the nearest calculation. Oh, how long it will seem. Had I asked or rather had I willed it he would write as soon as he gets home but dearly as I love him & anxious as I am to hear from him, I told him not to write until [unclear text]. I will hear from Mary & Lizzie but that will not be from Harry. God bless him! Amen and amen. Afternoon. Feel miserably. Evening. Ada McMillan was here for me to go up street but I did not feel like going. At home.

Thursday, June 16.

Morning. Washing until 2. Had a large wash. Afternoon. At home— Feel better than I did yesterday—After the first burst of sorrow—I began to think & I feel how highly I have been blessed notwithstanding my unworthiness. Evening. Did some errands—To prayer-meeting. Mr. Lantz led. Enjoyed it. Home at 9 1/2. Folded & sprinkled the clothes.

Friday, June 17.

Morning. Ironing. Afternoon. Busy. Evening. Feel strangely. My feelings are not to be described. In every respect but one I am happy. Oh! so happy, & yet I tremble for fear my cup of joy will be dashed to pieces & I left again one of those most miserable of human beings. That needs some qualification. I can never be one of the most miserable for my religion forbids it,—but I may have to drink the cup of sorrow to its dregs. God forbid & yet help me to make thy will mine. Help me to bow with submission to the holy will. Wrote to Andrew Crooks.

Saturday, June 18.

At home. Very busy. Afternoon. Busy. Evening. Mother and I went down street to get some further information in reference to Uncle Isaac Sheads' death. It is only too true! Poor Uncle Isaac—After a life of unhappiness, yea, misery, to think he ended his life on the battle-field. I almost forgot that Harry's father sent me & Grace a dress. One that he chose himself. I like it very much & mean to keep it until I visit them, which it should & with the permission of providence will be next summer. However, I mean not to build my hopes too high for the past has taught me the folly of building air-castles.

Sunday, June 19.

Rose at 6. To S.S. at 8 1/2. Spent a pleasant morning. To preaching at 10. Mr. Lantz preached an excellent sermon. His subject was the prodigal son & more particularly the character of the elder brother as representing a certain class of Christians. To class. Enjoyed it. Mr. Humelbaugh led. Home at 12. Ada Mc came with me for dinner. To S.S. at 2. Home at 3 1/2. Ada wanted me to go along with her today until time for evening service but I did not think it would be right though I would have enjoyed it. Spent a delightful hour reading in the Bible, & praying. Have not spent so holy a Sabbath evening for so many years. Was alone. Evening. To preaching at 7 1/2. Mr. Lantz preached an excellent sermon. The subject was Heaven, & he spent considerable time in proving that it was not merely a state, but a place. It was good —very good. Ada stayed with me until her father returned from the country. We walked awhile, for which I am sorry & our conversation was not of the proper kind. Oh Lord, forgive me. Help me to be more [unclear text].

Monday, June 20.

Rose at 5. Washing. Finished at 9. Pleasant. Busy. Afternoon. Feel badly. Evening. Rachel Lashell was here & we took a walk awhile. I am so anxious to hear from Allegheny County & yet I will not hear from Harry, though it will be a pleasure to hear of him. God bless him & all of them.

Tuesday, June 21.

Morning. Very busy. Am not well. Afternoon. Received a letter from Mr. Barton. He is still in Washington City & is detailed. He would have liked to have made us a visit while his sister was here but it was impossible. We would have [been] pleased to see him. Evening. Received a very interesting letter from Mr. Watson. I feared he had been killed but on the 10th he was well & in excellent spirits. My letter was received on the night of the 10th & read by camp-fire at the dead hour of midnight—7 miles from Richmond. He confesses to "thrill of emotion" passing through his "weary frame" when Rosa's letter was received & cannot account for it unless it is the romance connected with it. After thanking me for my wishes & hopes for his safety & return to home & loved ones he says "It is certainly more than I could have asked of a stranger. Somebody's prayers have been heard for I am still unharmed." Feel miserably. Ginnie Gilbert was here—Heard that cousin Bob Sheads is killed—Oh! I hope it is not true.

Wednesday, June 22.

Morning. Ironing & baking. Afternoon. Working. Answered Mr. Watson's letter. Feel badly. Two weeks ago we met those dear friends, one week ago we parted with them. Such is life. We meet, know love, & then part, perhaps forever. God grant it may not be so in this case—& yet it may be. Received a very interesting & very welcome letter from Harrie, dear Harry. He addresses me as "Miss Sallie." Part of the letter was written in Harrisburg on the night of the 13th, the day they left. They were unfortunate. Lizzie became very sick & they were detained at Hanover 1 1/2 hours, at the Junction 2 1/2 hours & in Harrisburgh 3 1/2 hours—but they got home safely. He says, "You gave me tacit permission to write provided I did not ask you to answer. I do not ask it, for I fully appreciate your feelings & position & while it is anything but pleasant for me to forego the extreme pleasure of hearing from you, & knowing what I do, I admire the moral courage you display in forbearing to write to me." "You can only imagine from your own feelings how sorry we all were to leave you." "After we started I was sitting with my back toward my destination & shutting my eyes. I imagined that I was nearing G__ instead of leaving it. It was but for a moment, when the unpleasant reality that we were actually leaving forced upon me. That was a hard parting for me & I know it was for more than me." Oh! that quivering lip while it pained me & increased my sadness, filled my heart with joy, for well I knew for whom it quivered." —God bless him—& me.

Thursday, June 23.

Morning. Started out to spend the day with Ada McMillan. On the way out I could not help thinking of the walk I took out the same way nearly two weeks ago with one who is now so far away. Within those two weeks what a change has "come over the spirits of my heart." I shall know before another week rolls around what my lot will be, whether the future will be bright or dark, whether life will be happy, or a dreary waste, whether my life will be shared by one I loved devotedly, or whether I must sail over the ocean of life alone! alone!—May God in mercy forbid & yet what have I done to deserve such unspeakable happiness. Afternoon. Lizzie Consor came out & we spent a pleasant afternoon. Enjoyed the whole day as well as I can enjoy anything with my present feelings. Came home early. Ada did not come in as the sky had every appearance of rain. To prayer-meeting at 8. Mr. Consor led. Enjoyed it tolerably. Home at 9 1/2. Reading awhile in Young.

Friday, June 24.

My birthday! 22 years old! Can it be? How the years fly! Oh! God. whatever may be in store for thy erring child, make her a true Christian—& fit temple for the indwelling of thy holy spirit—Hear & answer for the sake of thy son, my blessed Saviour. What changes have occurred since my last birthday. On the whole I feel better than I did then. I feel that I am making some progress in the divine life & though not by any means what I ought to be, yet I thank God that I am what I am. I am learning to be happy & though now surrounded by peculiar & in some degree painful circumstances, yet I am comparatively happy. Whatever may be my future lot, I feel that I am on my way to a better land, & "the rougher the way the shorter my stay." I feel that I can bow to the will of my heavenly father. Oh God, continue to bless me. Evening. Aunt Emmie, her sister Jane were here. I like them very much.

Saturday, June 25.

Morning. Very busy. Baking & doing the usual "Saturday work." Very warm. Afternoon. Wrote to Mr. Barton. Oh! God. I thank thee for the comfort I feel in leaning on thy strong arm, & for the confidence I feel in thy infinite wisdom & kindness. Help me always to trust in thee, I know dark days will come, but oh! help me to trust thee in sorrow as in joy. Evening. At home—Working at a crotchet tidy. Father came home. Very glad to see him.

Sunday, June 26.

Rose at 4. Prepared breakfast. To S.S. at 8 1/2. Had a pleasant session. To prayer-meeting at 10. Mr. Humelbaugh led. Did not enjoy it very much. It was entirely too long. Had no class. Home at 12. Afternoon. In S.S. awhile & reading in the Bible. Prepared test. Evening. Spent another pleasant hour alone, reading & praying. Oh God, help me always to honor thy day. I thank thee for giving us this sweet day of rest. T o preaching—Mr. Woodburn preached instead of Mr. Consor. I was very sorry for I do not like him— His text was "The carnal mind is enmity against God etc., etc." It was a long & tedious sermon & besides he stood up & prayed & did not read the hymn which we sang—. Rachel Lashell was with me to S.S., prayer-meeting, and preaching. Mr. Young came home with us, one of the returning Penn. Res's.

Monday, June 27.

Rose at 4 1/4. Washing. Finished at 10. Father went away. Very warm. Feel tired. Afternoon. Received a very good letter from Rufus P. Northrop of the 90th P.V. He received my address from one of the 94th New York with the privilege of writing if he chose. He was taken prisoner on the 1st of July, paroled & sent to Harrisburgh. Was home awhile, rejoined the army, was slightly wounded at the battle of the Wilderness, has recovered & is detailed by the Surgeon at the Campbell Hospital in Washington. He says, "I trust you will not consider me rude for presuming so much as to write you without any invitation. This is the first time I have ever had time to write anyone except intimate friends or relatives. So you will see I am not in the habit of "writing to girls" as the boys say. Trust me, I wish to receive a line from you ere long, I will close. Very sincerely, Rufus P. Northrop." He thinks it would be "decidedly interesting as well as novel to hear from me, residing in that portion of the state made memorable, etc." The letter is well-written & well-composed. Do not know whether I will reply or not—Warm. Sewing awhile. Evening. Received two interesting & welcome letters, one from Mary Barton & one from Andrew Crooks. Mary writes a very good letter, Andrew & Harry took her with them one week ago. Andrew's leg is well. He is back at the hospital [unclear text].

Tuesday, June 28.

Morning. Went out with mother. Pleasant. Afternoon. At Sister Annie's with my work. Evening. A short time before school I received a note of which the following is a copy—"May 18th. '64. Miss Myers, I have been wanting to get up to the school for some days but have been prevented. I have engagements for tomorrow also. Under the circumstances I thought best to advise you by note that complaints have been made that certain exercises made obligatory in your school are more or less neglected, that spelling has been entirely omitted for a week at a time, that writing is frequently omitted and neglected, scholars being allowed to prepare their own copies without supervision. Also that large portions of your time in the schoolroom are occupied by reading books & papers, writing, etc. I regret the necessity of bringing these complaints to your notice but justice to yourself requires that you should be advised of them as they are officially made to the board. They merit your prompt attention as if well founded they might seriously prejudice your claims for a re-election unless satisfactorily explained. In a day or two I may get up to the school to see you personally. Respectfully, I.A. Buehler, Secretary of the Board." This evening I received another note from Mr. Buehler which I will also copy. "June 28, '64. Miss Myers, I have the pleasure of announcing that you have been re-elected teacher of School No. 4—for current year, Salary $20.00 per month. Respectfully yours, I. A. Buehler." Comment is unnecessary. At home all evening.

Wednesday, June 29.

Morning at home. Afternoon. At sister Annie's. Evening. At home. Feel badly. Am disappointed. Thought I would certainly get a letter from Harry and I did not. I must try & wait patiently until tomorrow evening. I will certainly get one then. I hope the news will be favorable. Oh! Lord, prepare me for any dispensation of the providences. Help me to bow in submission to thy holy will.

Thursday, June 30.

Morning. Went out to Ada's for some cherries. She came with me to attend a funeral. Afternoon, at home. Evening. Rachel Lashell went with us to prayer-meeting. Home at 9 1/2. Wrote to Harry but I am anticipating. Received a real good letter from Beckie Sheriff and one from Chattanooga from a soldier who was taken prisoner in front of our house on the 2nd of July '63, and to whose father I wrote at his request, also a copy of Brother Harry's first sermon. Last but by no means least a letter from, not Brother Harry, but dear Harry, dearer far than a brother. He says "Miss Sallie, I will not call you by any more tender name until I have your consent. I am now free to tell you all—when I met you face to face & talked with you & my heart yearned towards you I knew that I loved you & acknowledged it for I could not help it. I do love you & will you accept it & love me and marry me?—do you think you can accept my heart, & trust me? If you can, it will be the strongest proof I can ask of your love. —I reaffirm my devoted love for you." He wished an immediate answer & accordingly I wrote in answer to his declaration of love & offer of marriage. "Mr. Harry F. Stewart—I love you devotedly & truly & I love you only. I can & will trust you & I will say in the language of Ruth to Naomi, whither thou goest, etc. And now "May the Lord bless thee & keep thee, etc., etc." So prays one who is and hopes to be through life & after death, Thine only." He closed his letter thus, "It is very late & I could only write on the same subject were I to lengthen this letter to three sheets, but it is useless to multiply declarations for one from an honest heart as I now know mine to be, is as good as an hundred. And therefore I will close & sign myself as I truly am, Your sincere lover—Harry." May God bless him & help me to be worthy of the love of his noble heart. Amen!!

Friday, July 1.

At home all day. Afternoon. Mrs. McFadden, Aunt Emmie's sister, & Cousin Mary Gosnell were here for tea. Spent a pleasant afternoon. Received a letter from Will Barton. Evening. Received a very interesting letter from Mr. Watson. There are allusions in it which made me laugh heartily. Want of space forbids mentioning them. Went over to the parsonage according to appointment to meet the committee appointed by the church to raise funds to repair the parsonage. Home at 10. Ada came with me to study all night. Ada, Miss Susan Warren & myself compose a sub-committee. We can meet as often as we please but the committee proper meets once a month only. I think I will like it. It seems as though we are being of some use when we are active. We have as yet no plans matured. Pleasant.

Saturday, July 2.

Morning. After Ada left about 5 1/2, I took a good sleep. We talked until long after midnight & of course I felt sleepy. Afternoon. At home. Received a letter from Mr. Isaac LeClear. Wrote to Miss Mary Barton, Mr. Andrew Crooks & Mr. J. S. Beyer. One year ago tonight, just in this same room but under far different circumstances. Now all is calm & peaceful, then I would scarcely hear my own voice for the deafening roar of artillery & the quick sharp volleys of musketry. When I think of the narrow escape I made, I cannot sufficiently thank my heavenly Father for his goodness unto me, one of his most unfaithful & unworthy creatures. Oh! that he would be with me still & preserve me not only from personal danger but from the power of sin for Jesus' sake.

Sunday, July 3.

To S.S. at 8 1/2. To preaching at 10. Mr. Consor preached an excellent sermon. His subject was the first resurrection and the satisfaction of those who will participate in it. His remarks were instructive & suited me very much. To class. Enjoyed it. Home at 12 1/2. To S.S. at 2. Marisa Zeigler went with me. Home at 3. Warm. After preparing tea & doing the evening work, I spent an hour, perhaps longer, in reading, prayer & meditation. How I do enjoy it. I find it difficult sometimes to keep my thoughts fixed on proper subjects but yet by trusting in God, the hour is not only pleasant but profitable. —To preaching at 7 1/2. Mr. Consor's remarks were upon the state of the country, the war, etc. —and his text "preach liberty." I like his address very much though I know there were some who did not like them. After preaching Rachel Lashell & I were walking & talking a long time. As we were talking only upon religious subjects & wished to talk without interruption we thought it no harm to walk. Had a very interesting conversation. "The rebels are coming." So says reports, I will believe it when I see them.

Monday, July 4.

Morning. Preserving cherries & baking pies. Rather inappropriate for the 4th but I wasn't going to let the cherries spoil. All the rest attended the celebration held in "Culp's Woods." One of us must stay at home & I care very little for such gatherings. I was elected, to let the rest go. Spent a very pleasant morning—alone nearly all the time but not lonesome, far from it. Ellie, Lizzie & Will Carpenter were here. They wanted me to go home with them but I did not care about going away. Jennie Gilbert was here— Writing awhile. Evening. Very pleasant. Quiet. Very different from one year ago!

Tuesday, July 5.

Morning at home. Have head-ache. Afternoon. Writing. Lizzie Consor was here. Evening. At home. Feel better than I did this morning. Report says the the rebels are coming—Do not credit it & will not until I see them. One year ago poor Mr. Stewart was living, though suffering. What an eventful year has this last one been for me—& for many others. Wonder where I will be and what my condition & circumstances ere another year rolls into eternity. Oh, God help me to live for thee, to thy honor & glory.

Wednesday, July 6.

Morning. Washing. One year ago I stood by the dying bed of Mr. Stewart & for the first time witnessed the arrival of the dread messenger death. My feelings can be imagined but never by me described. May I be as ready as he, when the summons comes. I have no doubt he is now enjoying all the ineffable glory of a home in heaven. Oh, God, prepare me for a home in heaven, & help me to do my duty here in all things. Evening. Dreadful excitement! Strangers are leaving town in crowds &

merchants are sending off their goods which have been packed since Monday. Wrote to Harry & sent also a sheet which I wrote on Monday while all the rest were away. I didn't know when I would have a chance to send a letter again & so I improved the present. A train left at 9 & as I was too late for the mail, sent it by a lady who will mail it in Baltimore City.

Thursday, July 7.

At home all day. Evening. Received a very good letter from Jennie White—& also one from Harry— His letters, always highly prized, are more doubly dear—it is so much like him. Ada Mc, Laura Mc, Kate Wills, Susy & I went to prayer-meeting. Mr. Consor led—Enjoyed it— Home at 8 3/4. Wrote to Harry, in compliance with his request for a good long letter. There is some excitement in town though not near so much as last night. I hope there will be no more & yet we have as good a right to suffer as any others—& should be willing to bear our part of the distress occasioned by this "cruel war." Oh, God guard us from danger, In thee alone can we put our trust —Forsake us not.

Friday, July 8.

Morning. Was very much surprised by a call from a cousin of mother's, Mr. John Troxell. He has not been here for twelve years. He is in the "Three years service" & is home with his Regt. on a veteran's furlough. He is Captain of A Co. 46th, Department of the Gulf. I like him. cousin Mollie came with him & they were here about two hours. I like him very much—He is so entertaining—he was in the siege of Vicksburgh & all the engagements in that Department. Afternoon. Went out to hunt up books in my S.S. class. Was very successful. Called to see Cousin Gertie Height of Clearfield Co. who is visiting Aunt Polly Slentz (her grandmother). She is not more than 18—I like her very much. Her father is a Lutheran minister. Home at 5. Wrote to Mr. Barton.

Saturday, July 9.

Morning. At home. Very busy. Afternoon. Received a letter from Louis Rottleman, a soldier of the 94th N.Y.—Cousin John Troxell, Cousin Mollie Gosnell & her sister Jennie spent the afternoon & part of the evening here. Spent a pleasant evening. I like Cousin John very much. Evening. Received the Pittsburgh Post from Mr. Watson. His Reg't has returned home. Ada McMillan was here. After they left I wrote to Harry—though I will not send it until I hear from him. I have so much to write to him. How I would love to talk to him instead of write to him. However, as that is impossible I will do the best I can. There is considerable excitement. I am a poor soldier. The news when unfavorable fills me with dread—I have been more alarmed in the last week than I was all last summer.

Sunday, July 10.

To S.S. at 9. To prayer-meeting at 10 1/2. Mr. Consor led. Enjoyed it. To class. Mr. Warren led. Enjoyed it very much. Afternoon. At home. Had no S.S. Report says there is fighting near Frederick & the rebels are within miles of Baltimore. I do hope they will not come here. I dread them coming more than ever. Evening. Spent an hour reading & praying & felt calm, notwithstanding there was considerable excitement. To preaching at 7 1/2. The congregation was small—Mr. Consor preached an excellent sermon—though it was rather long. Home at 9. Reading awhile. It is reported that a body of cavalry & a Provost Marshall are coming to Gettysburgh.

Monday, July 11.

At home all day. Yesterday noon our Engine with all the cars left, it was feared that the rebels would cut off our communication with Baltimore & Washington, & it was deemed advisable to "skeedaddle." The Postmaster left. Evening. No trains all day and consequently no news, no papers, no letter, in short nothing except vague rumors to bread the oppressive quiet which reigns supreme. Everything is painfully still. Writing to Harry—though I have no idea when I will hear from him & will not send it until I do hear. I hope this state of affairs will not long continue. It is worse than excitement. Yesterday was the 10th—One month since my memorable walk to "Round Top." How time flies!!!!

Tuesday, July 12.

At home all day. It is rumored that the rebels are advancing against Washington in force & that they have captured the 8 o'clock train from Philadelphia to Baltimore —That at the Riley House our men drove the rebels back & again our men were driven back by the rebels. I do wish we could hear something reliable. No papers, and no news (reliable) of any kind.—It seems so lonesome without the noise of the locomotive.

Wednesday, July 13.

Washing. Finished at 11. A train came from Bridgeport. Carrying a part of the "Christian Commission" & a car-load of provisions etc., for the wounded. They will go in wagons or carriages from here to the scene of the late battle near Frederick. They brought us news but I was so glad to hear the engine once more. The train I believe immediately returned—How I wish I could go with the Commission to the relief of our brave suffering men. No news yet except reports which are not reliable. Evening. Papers came by private conveyance, but the news is unfavorable. So many conflicting reports & dispatches that it is believed by all that there is fighting at or near Washington.

Thursday, July 14.

Morning. Ironing from 9 till 11. Report says that the Rebels have been repulsed & are trying to get back into Virginia. The news is more favorable. I do hope it is reliable—No trains yet, & no mail of course— Our Postmaster is away & no one else can open the mail though I believe there was one from Chambersburg which was sent back. So Mr. [unclear text] says though I do not credit it. Afternoon. At last the welcome sound is heard. A train came bringing papers & a mail—what mail I do not know, but our P.M. not being at home it is unopened. Evening. Mr. Buehler, our P.M. came home—The mail was very large but as it was not the regular western mail I did not get a letter— Feel a little badly but I know I will soon get one—& I am very anxious to hear, not only from Harry but from the rest of my Allegheny Co. friends. To prayer-meeting— Mr. Consor led. Home at 9.

Friday, July 15.

Morning. Went up street—Home at 9. Have a dreadful head-ache. It is my own fault. For several evenings we have had such magnificent nights that I have been sitting up later than usual & then sleeping in the morning. —I know it is wrong & mean to stop it. —Head-ache is always my penance for indulging in this injurous habit. Evening. Feel badly—Feel very much disappointed in not getting a letter. I fear mine was miscarried. Very pleasant. Moon-light—Received a letter from Ben Jones—He is a clerk at Meade's Hdqtrs, also one from Maggie Carpenter. She is enjoying herself finely.

Saturday, July 16.

Very busy all day—Evening. Cousins Ann Slentz & Gertie Height were here. Very pleasant. Evening. Received a good long & of course a very interesting letter from Harry. He has been very busy—as they are harvesting—Received one from

Andrew Crooks—He is well & attending Iron City College—Also received a letter from a Mr. Chamberlin of Co. B—8th N.Y. Cavalry with the intelligence of Mr. Gilbert's death. He was shot dead on the 2nd of June. His last & only words after being shot were "Tell my mother I died like a soldier." I felt very sorry to hear of his sad fate, but respected him highly.

Sunday, July 17.

To S.S. To preaching. Mr. Lantz's text was "Ye are the salt of the earth." It was elegant. To class. Home at 12. Afternoon. At home—Reading & sleeping. Evening. To preaching at 7 1/2. Mr. Lantz preached from "Ye are the light of the world." It was very good but I would not follow him as intelligibly this morning. My thoughts wandered & I lost "The thread of the discourse." Cousin Gertie Height went with me & Mr. [unclear text] came home with us. Spent a pleasant hour in meditation, reading & prayer.—I try to keep the Sabbath Holy. It is hard sometimes.

Monday, July 18.

Washing. Finished at 10.—Got dinner. This is my week in the kitchen. Afternoon. Went up street on business. Home at 4. Evening. Writing until dark—Anna Zeigler was here—Cousin Bob Myers was here. Was rather agreeably disappointed in having a pleasant interview instead of an unpleasant one as I feared. Very pleasant.

Tuesday, July 19.

Morning. Ironing and baking. Afternoon. Writing. Evening. Writing until 7. Very pleasant—Clear & moonlight. Finished & mailed a letter to Harry—This full moon brings to my mind thoughts of what occurred during the last reign of "the lovely queen of night."

Wednesday, July 20.

Morning. At home. Cousin Mollie Gosnell was here—Afternoon. Wrote to Mr. Chamberlin. He wished me to acknowledge the receipt of his letter & we want to know more of the particulars of Mr. Gilbert's death—Very warm—Evening. Pleasant. Moonlight.

Thursday, July 21.

Cousin Gertie Height spent the day with us. Spent a very pleasant day. Evening. To prayer-meeting at 8. Mr. Consor led. Home at 9. Did not enjoy prayer meeting very much.

Friday, July 22.

Morning. At home. Sewing. Afternoon. Allie Powers was here—Ada McMillan was here for tea. Evening. Ada and I went out shopping & then went walking. Feel pretty tired. Allie Powers & I were walking.

Saturday, July 23.

Busy all morning. Ada was here. Afternoon. Ellie Carpenter was here. Evening. Did not dress & of course got company—Mr. Hillpot & Cousin Gertie Height were here. They wanted me to go with them up to Mr. Zeigler's but I wouldn't & they stayed here. Writing. Feel very tired & didn't mean to stay up as late but couldn't help it. How glad I am that to-morrow is the blessed holy Sabbath— May I keep it holy. Pleasant but cool.

Sunday, July 24.

To S.S. To prayer-meeting. To class. Feel badly. Did not enjoy the services this morning. Afternoon. At home. Reading & sleeping—Feel badly—Mr. Consor preached a continuation of his sermon on the intractability of those who "make war with the Lamb." This evening he spoke of the inactivity of that class of persons— His sermon was good. Home at 8 1/2. Jefferson & Annie were here.

Monday, July 25.

Morning. Went up street on business. Was caught in the rain. Stayed at Uncle John Slentz' for dinner. Cousin Gertie is not well. Afternoon. Received a very interesting letter from Mr. Barton. He is still in Washington City. Evening. Susy and I went home with Cousin Mollie Myers & we all went over to Uncle John Slentz' & got a "boon" by the operation—A theol. student & his name is "Harry"—Ahem— Home at 10.

Tuesday, July 26.

Morning. At home. Afternoon. Went up street. Was at Jennie Gilbert's for tea. Home at 7. Ada was here. We were walking awhile. She, Laura & Mr. Snyder are going up to "Chambersburg" to-morrow for huckle-berries & they wanted me to go along. I would love dearly to go, for I know I would enjoy the ride in the country but mother disapproves & of course I will not go— Walking awhile.

Wednesday, July 27.

Morning. Washing— Finished at 12. Feel badly. Afternoon. At home writing. Evening. At home—Received two good letters from Harry. —I suppose they are about done harvesting— He has not much fancy for a farmer's life & is glad they are nearly done.

Thursday, July 28.

At home. Writing all afternoon. Evening. Received the "United Presbyterian" of July 20th from Harry—It has some very good reading in it. Lizzie Consor was here—To prayer-meeting at 8—Mr. McMillan led. Home at 9—Reading.

Friday, July 29.

At home. There is considerable excitement caused by the uncomfortable proximity of the rebels. Answered & mailed Harry's letter. Oh! God help me to be more like the meek and lowly Saviour—Help me to be in reality & not in profession a follower of the Lamb. Amen.

Saturday, July 30.

At home all day. Afternoon. Received a letter from Mrs. Howard, Mr. Gilbert's only sister telling me of her brother's death. The letter contains not a single regret, not one word of sorrow for the loss of her brother. I know he was kind to her. She would like to have an answer but it is a matter of doubt whether I will answer. Evening. Very exciting news. At one time I thought the rebel army was really in town.

Sunday, July 31.

Rose early. To S.S. at 8 1/2. Very few present. To preaching at 10. Mr. Consor spoke of the "apostary of those who make war with the Lamb." His remarks were good. Had a sort of a General class. Afternoon. At home. Evening. To preaching. Mr. Consor told us how an "inefficient" & an indifferent ministry "makes war with the Lamb." He was pretty severe on the ministry. Home at 9.

Monday, August 1.

My week in the kitchen. Washing, cooking etc. Evening. At home. Writing. Spent a pleasant evening all by myself though there was a good deal of company in the house, not the kind however that I enjoy.

Tuesday, August 2.

Morning, baking, cooking. At home all day. Evening. At home writing & reading. Spent my time very pleasantly.

Wednesday, August 3.

Cooking !!!! Afternoon. Received a letter from Mr. Beyer & one from Mr. Chamberlin in reference to Mr. Gilbert. The letter is very satisfactory. Mr. C was in Rochester last Spring & Mr. G. showed him one of my letters telling him that he contemplated visiting me & would never feel satisfied until he did visit me & that after his visit he (Mr. C.) was satisfied that Mr. G. knew that I considered him as a friend only. He also said that previous to his visit here Mr. G. was a strong Universalist but after it he was more inclined to Orthodox views of God & his government & he (Mr. C) thought the change had been brought about through my influence. I am glad I have done some good, & Mr. G always said my acquaintance was a blessing. He had no letter when he was shot. Mr. C. has my picture & will forward it as soon as he gets into camp.

Thursday, August 4.

Morning. To preaching at the U.P. Church. Mr. Woodburn preached a very good sermon. I liked it very much but his delivery was not good. Afternoon. At home. Evening. Received a splendid & unexpected but none the less welcome letter from Harry. Went out to Ada's to stay all night & occupied myself along the road reading that precious letter. It was mailed in Canonsburg where he is attending the annual commencement of Jefferson College, his alma mater, though I suppose he is at home now. Met Mr. Snyder but he did not stay. He & Mr. Mc came to town to attend religious services in the College Church. We did not go, as we thought it would be too much crowded to be comfortable. Spent a very pleasant evening with Ada & Laura.

Friday, August 5.

Spent a pleasant day with the exception of a talk with Mr. Snyder who came out this afternoon. I may have been severe in my remarks but however that may be I was just to myself & feel a good deal better since it than I did before. I have been wanting an opportunity to speak to him, yet wished it to appear accidental—& it was purely so. He evidently did not relish some things I said & I was pretty plain, but the circumstances required it, also justice to those dearest to me. I may as well say, one dearest to me. How [unclear text] is life! & how happy I am! Oh God! may I not forget thee in my happiness. Wrote to Harry. He is very uneasy about us, having heard of the burning of Chambersburgh, & the probability of G & Hanover.

Saturday, August 6.

At home. Did my usual work. Afternoon. Received a letter from Mr. Beyer containing $3.00 to purchase some pens for himself. Evening. Writing late. Was going to stay with sister Annie to-night. Bro. Jefferson is away.

Sunday, August 7.

To S.S. at 8 1/2. To prayer-meeting at 10 1/2. Mr. Snyder led. Did not enjoy it. Had a general class meeting in the church. Mr. Snyder led also. Did not enjoy it. To S.S. at 2. Have a new class & a very nice one. Gracie & 3 little girls her size. Evening. Was sick. Had a dreadful head-ache & did not spend a pleasant evening. I missed my "sacred hour." To preaching—Mr. Consor preached from the last clause of the verse from which he had preached four times before. His sermon was good. Rachel Lashell went with me. Feel something better, but did not spend as pleasant a Sabbath as I would have wished.

Monday, August 8.

Rose at 4 1/2. Washed until 8. To school. Did not spend a pleasant day owing to several things I cannot write. Evening. Wrote to Harry—Mailed the letter. Home at 8. Feel very tired & sleepy.

Tuesday, August 9.

Rose at 6. Ironed until school time. To school. Spent a pleasanter day than yesterday. The Directors transferred 23 pupils from my school & 25 into it. I think I will like my school very much. Received a good letter from Ben with a "passion flower" from the fortifications at City Point & the autographs of eight generals.

Wednesday, August 10.

Rose at 4:45. At school all day. I like my school very much, better indeed than I thought I would. Received from Mr. Chamberlin the picture of me, which Mr. Gilbert had. I was very glad to get it & am exceedingly grateful to Mr. C. for his kindness in sending it. Few gentlemen under the circumstances would have done as he has done. Evening. Writing. Sade Rupp, Allie Powers, Jennie Gilbert, [unclear text] were here. Have laughed more this evening than I have for a long time. Aunt Pollie & Aunt Lizzie Myers were here, & cousins Annie & Mollie.

Thursday, August 11.

No school. Rose at 4:45. Got breakfast & did my usual work. Sewing all morning. Very warm. Afternoon. At home. Extremely hot. Evening. Wrote to Mr. Barton. Susie & I went to prayer-meeting. Mr. Consor led. Did not enjoy it very much. Feel disappointed. Thought I would surely get a letter & I did not.

Friday, August 12.

At school all day. Spent a very pleasant day. Evening. Writing awhile & received an elegant letter from Harry. He is at home again. Harriet & I started to go down to see Maggie Cress & she met company & had to go back. Julie Weygandt, Lizzie & Virgie Consor were here. Kate Menchey & I were walking. Feel very tired & sleepy. Have been getting up earlier than usual of late & of course feel sleepy in the evening. Very pleasant.

Saturday, August 13.

At home all day. Very busy. Evening. Received another very welcome letter from Harry. It was not altogether unexpected. He writes splendid letters & of course existing circumstances make them better. I am afraid this happiness is too great to last. Harriet & I were going again to see Maggie Cress, & just as I was done "dressing" Cousins Annie Slentz & Gertie Height came. Gertie is going home on Monday or Tuesday. I am real sorry. Sue & I went down street with them to see the "gas-works" & Harriet & I then went to see Maggie. Sue & I called to see [unclear text], a cousin of Annie's from York. She was here when we were children. Spent a pleasant evening. Home at 9 1/2. Wrote in Gertie's album & did some other writing. A splendid night—moonlight—Oh, how I enjoy it!

Sunday, August 14.

To S.S. at 8. Rachel Lashell went with me. Had a pleasant time. To preaching at 10 1/2. Mr. Lantz preached [unclear text] was very good but rather long. To class. Rachel went with me. My dear old [unclear text] Mr. John Culp was there [unclear text]. I joined the church more than six years ago. Afternoon at home. Slept very little last night, not five hours & I fell asleep while reading the Bible. The "spirit was willing but the flesh was weak." Evening. [unclear text]

Monday, August 15.

At school all day. Spent a pleasant day. Cousin Gertie Height came up to school & after dismissal we ran around a little. Evening. At home. Writing awhile. Feel very tired. Was over at Harriet's. Mr. [unclear text] of Petersburgh, a professional teacher was there. Harriet is going to Shickshinny, Luzerne Co. to visit the friends of a soldier who died in their house. She will be gone a few weeks.

Tuesday, August 16.

Morning. Washing until 8. At noon went down to see Cousin Gertie to give her good bye & found she had deferred going until to-morrow. At school as usual. Evening. Received a letter from Andrew Crooks—He is still in Pittsburgh Genl Hospital, & attending Iron City College—Very tired. Writing awhile. Pleasant.

Wednesday, August 17.

At school. Cousin Mollie Gosnell was up at school this morning. Evening. Cousin Mollie Gosnell, her sister Emma, now Mrs. Coon, were here, also Beckie Belch. Cousin Emmie was here a long time ago when we were children but she is so changed, & so care-worn. She is a year or two my senior.

Thursday, August 18.

At school as usual. Evening. Writing—Went to prayer-meeting. Mr. Warren led. Did not enjoy it very much. Home at 8 1/2. Mr. Bales was here when I got home—He is pretty intelligent, agreeable & entertaining when he chooses to be. Feel very tired. Pleasant. Received a letter from Harriet.

Friday, August 19.

At school all day. Feel tired but spent a pleasant day. Evening. Went up to Sister Annie's. Writing until after 10. It was imperative. Feel very tired.

Saturday, August 20.

Sue & I started out to Mr. Herbert's. 1 1/2 miles to "see about" her getting a fall school near there. It was engaged. Came home & started out to Mr. Abraham Plank's 2 1/2 miles on a similar errand. It was also engaged. Came back to town & started to Mr. Samuel Coleman's 2 miles, & found it was not positively engaged. She may get it. Home at 2. After walking 12 miles since breakfast it is to be presumed I am tired. Writing all afternoon. Evening. Feel tired & sad. Received a very good letter from Harry. Mr. Barton is dead. He has been ill for some time & now he is dead. Poor Lizzie! I feel sorry for her & for all of the family, but Lizzie seems to have more trouble than the rest. He was resigned & fully prepared for the solemn change.

Sunday, August 21.

At home all day. Did not feel well enough to go out. The day seems so long. Evening. Went over to see Rachel Lashell. She is going to Dayton, O, to teach school to-morrow morning. I intended going over last evening but really could not. To preaching—Mr. Consor preached a good sermon but I not being well, could not appreciate it.

Monday, August 22.

At school as usual. Evening. Wrote to Harriet Shillen & did some other writing. Wrote at Annie's until after 10— Brother J— has gone to Hanover to work. He will come home every Saturday night & I am to stay with Annie & Julia while he is away. I would prefer staying at home.

Tuesday, August 23.

At school all day. Evening. Wrote to Mr. Chamberlin & then did some "other" writing. Wrote until after 10 at Annie's. Feel badly. Am not well & feel depressed mentally: why I cannot say, or write. Ada McMillan was here. We were walking awhile.

Wednesday, August 24.

At school all day. Evening. Received a dear letter from Harry. Finished that "other" writing & sent it on its mission. Mr. Bales was here & I wish he had not been. I wanted to be alone & if his conversation had been sensible it would not have been so bad but I was positively disgusted at the frivolity of a man of his years. Wrote to Harry though not in answer to the letter received this evening.

Thursday, August 25.

At school all day. Evening. Wrote to Maggie Carpenter. Went to prayer-meeting. Mr. Consor led. Did not enjoy it very much. Felt too badly both mentally & physically. I could not sing with any degree of satisfaction, being hoarse, & of course did not enjoy that part of the prayer-meeting, which to me is the most pleasant generally. There were other & unfavorable circumstances which are unnecessary to state. Wrote a note to Harry.

Friday, August 26.

At school all day. Evening. Wrote to Jennie White. Went to prayer-meeting at 8. Mr. Consor led. Did not enjoy it. Am not at all well & besides I feel much depressed in spirit. I hope it will not long continue. There will at least be an end of suspense before another week, but whether satisfactory or not I know not.

Saturday, August 27.

At home all day. Evening. Annie Rupp was here. Ada came & stayed until time for General class. Did not enjoy it very much. Went from a sense of duty & not from inclination. Julie Culp had a spasm of some kind in church. Poor Julie, I pity her. She has been subject to spasms ever since the battle of G— though she has not had any for some time. They seem like catalepsy & the Dr. says they are caused by trouble.

Sunday, August 28.

To S.S. at 8 1/2. To preaching at 10. Mr. Corson preached an excellent & very appropriate sermon from Acts [unclear text]. He confined himself to a short & very interesting account of the life & death of "this man." After the sermon the sacrament of the Lord's Supper was administered. I never felt so deeply its import & never was so much benefitted. May I never forget it but profit by it. To class after church, did not enjoy it. Had no S.S. Evening. Brother & sister were here for tea. Bro. likes working in Hanover very much. To preaching at 7. Mr. C. preached from the latter part of the verse from which he preached this morning. The sermon was good but very long, the house was full, & my head ached—After it, a short prayer-meeting, which did not help my feelings any.

Monday, August 29.

At school all day. Morning. Took a pleasant walk. Evening. Writing until dark. Went up to Annie's. Feel bad. Very cool & not at all pleasant. Julie Culp is well again, at least she seems so.

Tuesday, August 30.

At school all day. Do not yet feel very well but feel better. Cool & pleasant. Evening. Received a letter from Mr. Beyer, the 3rd since I wrote. He, some time since, sent me $3.00 for pens, & not receiving them or hearing from me, he came to the conclusion that the money was lost. For some time I could not get them, & when I did get them I was afraid to send them owing to the excitement. Sent the pens &

answered his letters this evening though I really had not time. I wanted to write to Harry or write a little in the letter but was several times interrupted & finally Jen Gilbert came & I gave it up. Cool but pleasant.

Wednesday, August 31.

At school all day. Evening. At home all evening writing & making out my monthly report. Wrote at home until 9 & at Annie's until after 10. Received a darling letter from Harry—dear Harry! Though not an answer to my last, yet is none the less welcome. Oh! I am afraid this happiness is too great. Oh, Lord help me never to forget thee, the giver of every good & perfect gift. Help me to love & serve [unclear text] supremely.

Thursday, September 1.

Writing until school-time. Six years ago I commenced my career as a teacher. How checkered has been my life! & now blest with so great a boon, how happy I am. At school all day. Very busy. Evening. To prayer-meeting. Mr. Lantz led. Had a S.S. meeting & re-elected all our officers. Oh! God, help me to love thee supremely, help me not to forget thee in my great happiness, but let every feeling & thought be subordinate to thy honor. Oh, look in mercy upon the erring child & keep her in the path of duty.

Friday, September 2.

At school all day. Evening. Mailed a letter to Harry. Was a little disappointed in not hearing from him in answer to what I wrote on Aug. 24th. However, as he lives a good way from the office it cannot be helped. Received a very good letter from Cousin Lizzie Myers of Centerville, Ind. Uncle John talks of coming East this fall. I hope he will & I do wish he would bring Lizzie along, though I suppose he will not.

Saturday, September 3.

At home all day. Very busy. Evening. Writing to Harry. Did not get a letter. Cannot imagine why. I really do not know how to wait until Monday evening for I will certainly get one then.

Sunday, September 4.

To S.S. at 8 1/2. Went to the Ger. Ref. Church to hear Mr. Deitrick & heard Mr. Reilley. To S.S. Home at 3. Evening. To preaching. Mr. Lantz preached. Do not feel very well.

Monday, September 5.

At school as usual. Afternoon. Received a letter from Sergt. Jefferson Reisinger, a soldier who was wounded at Gettysburgh & lay some time in the Catholic Church. He is at [unclear text] General Hospital, & as it is a dreary life he would like to correspond with me. If I had time I would but it is impossible. I have too much to do. Evening. Went down to Aunt Lizzie's. She has more trouble. It really seems as though she has nothing else. Very cool & raining heavily. Received a good letter from Harry—& one came for pa from him, a rather significant answer to what I sent him on the 24th.

Tuesday, September 6.

At school as usual. Evening. Received a very welcome letter from Cousin Gertie Height. She is home at last after being away all summer & having had a "splendid time." She writes a good letter. I like her very much. Went down to Uncle John Culp's partly to tell them I had heard from Gertie & partly to get my correspondence with Mr. Watson which has been there ever since I gave it to Gertie to read. Went to see Aunt Lizzie. She is better. Aunt Agnes was there & as she had heard of

Mr. W, she would like to read the correspondence if I had no objections. I had not & she took it home with her.

Wednesday, September 7.

At school all day. Afternoon. Received a letter from Mr. Barton. He is at Camp Distribution. He speaks of his father in terms of love, respect & praise. Finished & mailed a letter to Harry. The weather is cool & very disagreeable. A good deal of rain.

Thursday, September 8.

At school all day. Received a letter from Mr. Beyer. He received the pens I sent him & wishes some holders to suit them. Evening. Went to prayer-meeting. Mr. Lantz led. Did not enjoy it very much. Have been reading "Dred: a tale of the Great Dismal Swamp, by Harriet Beecher Stowe."

Friday, September 9.

At school all day. Commenced a letter to Andrew. Evening. Received a letter from Jennie White, very unexpected, with her photo. I like her appearance very much. Her letter is very good. She is a teacher. Finished Andrew's letter & wrote a few lines to Mr. Beyer, sending him some pen-holders to suit those pens. Went down street & heard "the immortal J. N." Poor man, he seems indeed to be a wanderer. I would like to know more about him. If insane, there is a "method in his madness." Home at 9. Very cool. Do not feel at all well.

Saturday, September 10.

Attended a "Teacher's Examination" & as a natural consequence got nothing else done. Feel ill. I hurt my head the other day & have had the head-ache ever since. Evening. Writing awhile. Bell, Gracie & I took a walk. Went down to Aunt Salome's awhile. Home at 8 1/2. Pa came home this evening.

Sunday, September 11.

Did not go to S.S. Caught cold last night by leaving my window open to which I am not accustomed at Annie's. My neck is stiff, my throat is sore, & I am so hoarse I speak with difficulty. Went to preaching. I like the ministers so much that I dislike to stay away from preaching when I can possibly go. Afternoon. At home. Writing awhile. Evening. To preaching though I felt so badly that I had better been at home. Oscar McMillan came home with Sue & me. He has a furlough, but returns to his Reg't tomorrow morning. Feel badly. Clear & cool. Pleasant.

Monday, September 12.

At school as usual. Wrote to Mr. Hall. Received a letter from Cousin John Troxell. His Reg't is at Lexington, Kentucky. Evening. Paring (or helping to pare) peaches for butter. Annie, Julie, Cousin Mollie, Sade Rupp were here. I did not spend a pleasant evening. Finished reading "Dred"—I do not like the end of it. Through the 1st, & part of 2nd Vols. I was deeply interested & then the heroine died of cholera, & my interest declined. However, as an illustration of love in the midst of slavery, I suppose it is correct. Julie & I took Sade home. Very pleasant. Moon-light.

Tuesday, September 13.

At school all day. Evening. Hattie & I took a little walk. Lizzie Consor was here all evening. Went part of the way with her & we took a walk. Very pleasant. Clear & moon-light. Feel a little disappointed. Thought I would get a letter. My cold is a little better. Mr. Little has been elected in place of Mr. who has gone into the army so Capt. Bob McClean has Mr. L's situation. The salaries of the female teachers have been raised $2.00 per month.

Wednesday, September 14.

At school all day. Evening. Lizzie Consor was here & we went down to the store & to several other places. Went to see Aunt Salome on business. Home at 8. Writing awhile.

Thursday, September 15.

At school all day. Evening. Wrote to Ben Jones. Went to prayer-meeting. This evening it met at the parsonage. Did not enjoy it very much. After prayer-meeting Julie Weygandt, Lizzie Consor & I took a walk. The evening was very pleasant. Clear & moon-light. There was no mail this evening. I feel as though I ought to have had a letter from Harry but I must patiently (?) wait until to-morrow. After we came home Nettie & Barbara were singing. This is a glorious night, too pleasant to be in the house, but we can't stay out all night.

Friday, September 16.

At school all day. Afternoon. About 2 1/2 Sue came up to school with a letter in a well-known & dear hand. I was expecting it. Went home at recess to read it. It is just like the writer, good & unexpressibly dear to me. Evening. Alone. Writing in my "diary" until dark, & then lit the lamp & wrote until 8 1/2. Walking awhile. This is another beautiful night.

Saturday, September 17.

Morning. Sewing until 8. Went to see our Treasurer in reference to promoting three of my scholars. To see Beckie Belch, Jennie Gilbert & Annie Rupp. Stopped at Harriet's awhile. Sewing. Went up street & stayed a good deal longer than I intended. Evening. Received "The [unclear text]" a paper issued in Aug. '59 previous to The Annual Commencement of Jefferson College, Wash. Co. where Harry graduated, also the Testimony of the U.P. Church." Read the former hastily & then spent some time in carefully reading the latter. Writing awhile. Very pleasant. Moonlight again.

Sunday, September 18.

To S.S. at 9. Rose Guinn & I went to hear Mr. Deitrick preach. This time I did hear him. To S.S. at 2. Home at 3 1/2. Evening. Reading. With the "Confession of faith," "Theological [unclear text]," "Testimony of the U.P. Church" & last but not least the Bible. I spent a long time in careful & I trust not unprofitable study. Mr. Consor preached. Julie Culp & I went to church together. His text was "Alleluia, the Lord God omnipotent reigneth." I liked the sermon pretty well. Home at 8.

Monday, September 19.

At school all day. Evening. Wrote to Harry. I mailed the letter. Went down to Uncle John Slentz's & to Aunt Lizzie Myers's. Home at 8. Writing a long time, part for myself & part for others. Susy, Julie & I took Cousin Mollie Myers home. Had a long (of course) & not a very pleasant walk. Wrote to Cousin Gertie Height.

Tuesday, September 20.

Morning. Wrote to Mr. Barton. At school as usual. Pleasant. Evening. At sister Annie's. While busily writing we were very much surprised by a visit from Mr. Will Lee of Phila. & his sister Amanda, who are stopping with Aunt Lizzie Myers. Will belonged to the 72nd Penn. Vols. He is now discharged & has come with his sister to visit the Battlefield in general & Cousin Mollie in particular. I like his sister's appearance very much.

Wednesday, September 21.

Morning. Went to the store for mother & made a morning call at Aunt Lizzie's & accepted an invitation to dine with them. Went down after school & spent a very pleasant hour. Evening. While writing to Harry, I was astonished for I was not looking for him. Was very glad to see him. He walks on crutches & looks a little thinner than when he was here before [unclear text] Spent a very pleasant evening.

Thursday, September 22.

At school all day. Evening. Jennie Gilbert, Sade Kendlehart were here. Andrew & I went down to Aunt Lizzie Myers'. Stayed longer than I intended & started home about 7. There was a republican meeting in town to-night. I would not go & Andrew did not care about going. Came home and found my brother home. I was so glad. Received a good letter from Maggie Carpenter. She intends staying in New York until spring. Andrew & I had a very interesting chat. He is on his way to Phila. to get an artificial limb. Aunt Lizzie & their visitors went to Round Top today. I would have gone along but could not or would not leave my school.

Friday, September 23.

At school all day. Evening. Susy, Andrew & I went out to the National Cemetery & also visited Evergreen Cemetery. Had a very pleasant walk. Came home about dark. Intended going to Harriet's this evening but then Mollie sent me word that they were coming up & we could not go. They came after we had been home 1/2 an hour. We spent a very pleasant evening. Amanda is a splendid girl. She is about 25, intelligent, agreeable, sociable and entertaining. We have by mutual consent dropped "Miss" & call each other by our names. They were here until after 10. Very pleasant.

Saturday, September 24.

At home all day. Susy went with Allie Powers to Heidlersburg. Busy all day. Mollie, Will, & Amanda took tea & spent the evening with me. Spent a delightful evening. I love Amanda, & like Will pretty well. Received a splendid letter from Harry dear. How welcome it was I will not attempt to say nor is it necessary for me to do so. After the company left (It was after 10 & I had not yet read my letter) I ran upstairs & enjoyed it all alone. Andrew & I talked a long time about affairs in general. I like Andrew very much.

Sunday, September 25.

Rose early. I stay at home while Andrew is here. He went with me to S.S. Mr. Consor did not preach & as I did not care to hear the one who did preach, Andrew, Maggie Bailley & I went to hear Mr. Woodburn. Andrew (though not a member) attends the U.P. church when at home. After his leg was amputated, on July 2nd, 1863 he was removed to the U.P. church where he lay until he was removed to our house. Afternoon. At S.S. Evening. Pa, Ma & Andrew took tea with Jefferson. I stayed at home & wrote to Harry. I have not written since Wednesday. I could not get 10 minutes to myself without Andrew & I went to church. Mr. C. preached. Home at 8 1/2.

Monday, September 26.

Andrew left in the 8 o'clock train. I felt sorry to see him go, & he disliked to go, but thought it best not to stay any longer. He may have to stay in Phila. several months. At school all day. Do not feel very well. Writing awhile. Sade Rupp & I were walking awhile. Cool & pleasant.

Tuesday, September 27.

At school all day. Evening. Sue & I pared apples until dark & then went down to Aunt Lizzie's. The girls & Nell were out. Stayed awhile & then came home. Wrote to Cousin Lizzie Myers & mailed the letter.

Wednesday, September 28.

At school all day. Mr. Consor was in my room this morning a short time & Bell, Amanda & Mollie were up this afternoon. I like Amanda so much. We are boiling apple-butter today. Evening. Just as I was dressing Susy brought me two letters from Harry, mailed at Pittsburgh. They were unexpected but so welcome. I enjoyed reading them very much. Harry's father has purchased a house in New Brighton, Beaver County, Penn. They will move on the 1st of April next. Susy & I went down to Aunt Lizzie's & I went over to Slentz's awhile. Will & Amanda are going home to-morrow morning if it does not rain. Spent a pleasant evening. Will came up with us. Cousin Will! Ahem!! Andrew's friends in Alle. Co. are very much alarmed about him. They know he was in the train which was burnt (or a part of it was) & they have not heard of him since & they know that a soldier with one leg was burnt. I guess it was not Andrew. I suppose they know before this that he is safe.

Thursday, September 29.

At school all day. Morning. A dispatch came from T.A. Crooks in Harrisburg to pa, dated 10 A.M. this morning inquiring whether Andrew had been here within a week. I went down from school & telegraphed that he left G— on the 26th for Phila. Evening. Was a little surprised by having Mr. Thomas Crooks call to see us. He stayed in Harrisburg until 1 1/2, & there not receiving a reply from G— he started & came to see. His friends are very uneasy. Thomas left home at 2 on Monday morning, telegraphed from Pitts. to Gett., received no answer, telegraphed to Phila. & found out that Andrew had not yet returned there, came to Harris., telegraphed to G— & receiving no answer came to see. He is younger than Andrew—Did not go to prayer-meeting. Spent rather a pleasant evening.

Friday, September 30.

At school all day. Morning. Walked out around the Seminary with Mr. Crooks, showed him as near as I could the place where Andrew had been wounded. Had a pleasant walk. Home at 8 3/4. Susy went with him out to Cemetery Hill, National Cemetery & Culp's Woods. He left on the 11:30 train. Had to leave then in order to reach home this week. Night. Working at my school reports. Worked until around 11.

Saturday, October 1.

Morning. Worked at my reports until 9. Did some homework, served some, washed, dressed, etc. dinner, then wrote to Harry until 3. Went up street. Received a letter from Ben Jones, Bell received a paper from Andrew. I suppose he got to Phila. safely. I thought I would hear from him but did not. Evening. Feel tired. Writing. Finished a letter to Harry.

Sunday, October 2.

To S.S. at 9. To prayer-meeting at 10 1/2. Home at 11 1/2. To S.S. at 1. Home at 3 1/2. Evening. Wrote to Harry in answer to a part of two letters in reference to the distinctive doctrines of the U.P. Church. I do not approve of Sunday letter-writing generally but think there is no harm in writing as I did to him almost entirely excluding everything which did not relate to religion. Gave him some of my experiences in trying to be a christian. It is such a blessed privilege to have a dear friend in whom one can confide without reserve. He is one of that kind. May God bless him abundantly & may I be worthy of him.

Monday, October 3.

At school all day. Evening. At home. Wrote to Jennie White but it was too late to mail the letter. Had a busy day in school. Sent one of my scholars to a lower school & three to a higher. received 3 new ones & now have 39.

Tuesday, October 4.

At school all day. Received a letter from Andrew. He is at Broad & Cherry Hospital. He was not well for a day or two after he left here, but is getting better. Doesn't know how long he will stay there. Mailed Jennie White's letter. Allie Powers & I were walking awhile.

Wednesday, October 5.

At school all day. Evening. Received a splendid & rather unexpected letter from Harry. Working at my Register. Was at Harriet's awhile. Raining.

Thursday, October 6.

At school all day. Evening. Answered Harrie's letter. Susy is going to mail it, either at Heidlersburg or York Sul. Springs. Received a very unexpected letter from Amanda Lee: rather a note accompanying "Gail Carrolton's" last book—"Stumbling Blocks." Went to Prayer-meeting. Did not enjoy it very much. Home at 8. Writing & reading.

Friday, October 7.

At school all day. Evening. Wrote a note to Amanda Lee acknowledging the receipt of the book she sent me. Annie & I went down to Rose Guinn's for tea & spent the evening there. Spent a very pleasant evening. Wrote after I came home. Susy & Allie Powers went to Petersburg this morning to see about a school which has no teacher & which we think Susy can get.

Saturday, October 8.

Busy all day. Susy was successful & goes five weeks from today to teach for four months at "Flohr's School-house" 3 miles the other side of Petersburgh. Evening. At home. Writing awhile.

Sunday, October 9.

To S.S. at 9. To preaching at 10 1/2. Had no class. To S.S. at 2. Home at 3 1/2. Evening. Reading "Stumbling Blocks." Like it very much. Allie Powers went with me to church. Mr. Lantz preached two excellent sermons to-day. I liked his morning sermon the better. I was more interested in it.

Monday, October 10.

Evening. Received a letter, or a note, from Mr. Beyer requesting me to send him the amount due him, in stamps. Had no school all day. This morning there was no fire & this afternoon there were too few scholars. I had only 12. There is a Democratic meeting to-day in town. Working at my circular & doing other sewing.

Tuesday, October 11.

At school all day. Evening. Wrote to Mr. Beyer & sent the stamps. Also answered Andrew's letter. Allie Powers, Sue & I went up street. Stopped at Annie's on the way home. This has been a quiet election day, as far as I have heard & seen.

Wednesday, October 12.

At school all day. Just one year ago, Mr. Hall, Will Lee & Fred left. I wish I had never seen Fred. Evening. Feel disappointed. Was looking for a letter & did not get one. Did not feel like working. Pleasant but cool. Clear & moonlight.

Thursday, October 13.

At school all day. Did not get along very well. Evening. Went down to Aunt Emily's but did not go up in Beckie's room. She has Typhoid Fever. Received a welcome & expected letter from Harry, a good long one too. Each letter is if possible more anxiously looked-for & more welcome than the one preceding. How I would love to see him & spend an evening with him. I would know how to appreciate such a privilege. Wrote at sister Annie's until 10 1/2. Mr. Lantz led prayer-meeting. Did not enjoy it very much. Went to the store with Ada & Laura McM.

Friday, October 14.

At school all day. Evening. Wrote to Harry & mailed the letter. Mr. Wallace of the 10th N.Y. Cavalry (now discharged) & Annie Rupp were married last night at Annie's home. Long life & happiness to them.

Saturday, October 15.

Morning. At home busy. Helping to clean house. Afternoon. Working at my circular. Finished it & like it much better. Evening. Writing. Mrs. Lashell is dead. She died of erysipelas & leaves twin daughters not two weeks old.

Sunday, October 16.

To S.S. at 9. Went with Rose Guinn & Susy to the St. James Lutheran Church. Wish I had gone to the O.S. Presbyterian church where I intended going in the 1st place. To S.S. at 2. Julie Culp & I went to Mrs. Lashell's funeral but the house was crowded & it was so windy that we did not go to the Cemetery. Jennie G. was here. Evening. Reading the "Testimony" & the U.P. which Harry sent me. Evening. Went to the Presbyterian church & was well repaid for going. Mr. Carnahan preached. Text "I would not live always." The sermon was splendid. He is an elegant preacher— Home at 8 1/2. Moon-light.

Monday, October 17.

At school all day. Evening. At home. Sewing for Susie until 8 1/2. Received an unexpected letter from Harry mailed in Pittsburg. Writing awhile. Feel tired.

Tuesday, October 18.

At school all day. Evening. Synod meets at the O.S.P. Church to-night. I would like to go but really cannot spare the time. Sewing for Susy until 8 1/2. Feel tired. Sewing steadily is hard work, for me.

Wednesday, October 19.

At school all day. The 87th P.V. Inftr. are home. Heard some good music. There was a meeting in the C.H. & a speech in honor of their return which I would like to have heard but could not go. The bride & groom are at Annie's for tea, & I declined an invitation to take tea with them because I would not leave my school & for other good reasons. Sewing for Susy until 9. Writing awhile.

Thursday, October 20.

At school all day. Evening. Writing awhile. To prayer-meeting at 7. Home at 8 1/2. Received a very welcome & interesting letter from Andrew. He called to see Mrs. Lee on Monday.

Friday, October 21.

At school all day. Evening. Sewing for Susie. Received an unexpected letter from Harry, also the Nov. No. of Godey, & the sermon he (Harry) preached on Tuesday before Presbytery at [unclear text] Church. Feel tired. Finished & mailed a letter to Harry.

Saturday, October 22.

Morning. Out. Was at Mrs. Martins, Aunt Emily's, Aunt Salome's, Aunt Lizzie's, Uncle John Slentz's, Jennie Gilbert's, Sister Annie's & at Harriet's— Afternoon. At home busy. Received a letter from Mr. Beyer. Evening. At home. Writing.

Sunday, October 23.

To S.S. at 9. To preaching at 10 1/2. To class after preaching. Reading at noon. To S.S. at 2. Evening—Reading in the U.P. Testimony & "Stumbling Blocks." To preaching at 6 1/2. Mr. Eisenberg preached upon the 2nd coming of Christ. Julie Culp was confirmed to-night.

Monday, October 24.

At school all day. Received a letter from Mr. Barton. Writing at school until dark. Evening. Do not feel well. My head aches, why, I cannot imagine.

Tuesday, October 25.

At school all day. Capt (now Col.) Ashworth, who lay in our house 6 weeks last summer visited us to-day. We were very much surprised to see him for we never thought he would walk, he was so severely wounded. With the exception of being lame, he has entirely recovered. He is very intelligent & has travelled extensively, and was in England all summer. Evening. Col Ashworth was here. He leaves town to-morrow morning. Reading awhile. Feel badly. Am not well.

Wednesday, October 26.

At school all day. Evening. Called to see Mrs. Wallace but she was not at home. Thought I would certainly get a letter to-night from Harry & did not. Feel badly. Have had the head-ache all week. I wish Saturday was here.

Thursday, October 27.

At school all day. Evening. Annie Slentz was here & we went to prayer-meeting. Mr. Warren led. Home at 8. Allie Powers was here with her work. Raining & very disagreeable. Do not feel at all well.

Friday, October 28.

At school all day. Evening. Received two letters, a good & dear letter from someone who is also good & dear. Finished & mailed one to him. How I wish I could talk to him instead of writing. Received one from John M. Watson. He writes to Sallie to inquire of the doings and whereabouts of one Miss "Rosa" who on looking over his books, he finds is marked "deserter." If she be dead then break it to him lightly. If Rosa, how that name haunts him, be married then let him know the worst at once & the name of the happy man so if perchance they ever meet, he can have sweet revenge [unclear text] Villian! to mar my bright anticipations. He says, "being posted on the rules & customs of your place I enclose a stamp & my address,
Miserable"
Eldersridge, Indiana Co. Pa.

Do not yet know how I will reply. Had he not sent a stamp, I would not reply at all.

Saturday, October 29.

Morning. At home, busy. Writing awhile. Afternoon. Ironing. Evening. Vice-Pres. Hamlin is to speak in the Court-House to-night but I was not going. I know the house will be crowded & besides I care but little about either seeing or hearing him. Went down to Aunt Agnes Sheads'. Home at 9. Writing awhile. Reading.

Sunday, October 30.

To S.S. at 9. To preaching at 10 1/2. Mr. Carrshan preached an excellent sermon from the text "lovest thou me?" Home at 12. To S.S. at 2. Home at 3 1/2.

Evening. Reading & writing. To preaching at 6 1/2. Annie went with me. Mr. Lantz' sermon was good. His subject was "temptation." Home at 8. Do not feel well.

Monday, October 31.

At school all day. Evening. Working at my monthly reports & getting my class books ready for Nov. Busy until 10 1/2. Do not feel at all well. Was at Jennie Gilbert's awhile. Met Mr. & Mrs. Johns, Miss Johns, Mrs. Eisenberg & Mollie Kendlehart. Cold & windy.

Tuesday, November 1.

At school all day. Busy every spare moment fixing my class books for Nov. & making out reports.

Wednesday, November 2.

At school all day. Evening. Feel tired. Reading awhile in Stumbling Blocks. Like it very much. It is very pleasant & not unprofitable reading.

Thursday, November 3.

At school all day. Raining & very disagreeable. Evening. Susie & I went to prayer-meeting, but did not enjoy it much. Mr. McMillan led. Home at 8 1/2.

Friday, November 4.

At school all day. Evening. At home. Cold & windy. Feel disappointed. Received a letter from Andrew. Intended answering his letter received two weeks ago but will now wait until next week. He has gone home to vote. He sent me his picture. It is good.

Saturday, November 5.

Sewing for Susie all day. Clear & pleasant. Evening. At home reading & writing.

Sunday, November 6.

To S.S. at 9. To preaching at 10 1/2. Mr. Lantz preached an excellent sermon. His subject was "Charity." Mr. Culp led our class. Home at 12. To S.S. at 2. Evening, reading. Allie Powers & Kate Menchey went with me to preaching. Mr. L's text was "what is man?" I liked the sermon very much.

Monday, November 7.

At school all day. Evening. Wrote to Andrew. Received a letter from Mr. Hall & one, a good long one, from Harry. The letter should have been here on Saturday night. Mollie, Jane, & Helen Myers were here. Cut out a flannel sacque for Susie — Feel tired.

Tuesday, November 8.

At school all day. Evening. Received a real good letter from Cousin Gertie Height. She has not been very well. She commenced teaching yesterday. Susie had one from her sister Alice. She is also teaching.

Wednesday, November 9.

At school all day. Evening. At home. Feel tired

LINCOLN

&

JOHNSON!!

Thursday, November 10.

At school all day. Evening. Sue & I went to prayer-meeting. Mr. Lantz led. This is a beautiful night.

Friday, November 11.

At school all day. Feel tired. I am anxious for the end of the session. I have worked hard & am beginning to feel the effects of it, besides I have so much sewing to do. Received a good letter from Harry, mailed in Pittsburgh. He is in the city now, & will soon commence his studies. Susie is going to-morrow to teach at Flohr's school-house, about 4 miles the other side of Petersburgh. Willie Sheads is going to drive for us: I am going along & will return in the evening.

Saturday, November 12.

Sue & I started at 8 & reached our destination at 12, after a ride of 18 miles, neither pleasant nor unpleasant. [unclear text] They seem to be a nice family—Have three very interesting children. After dinner, about 2, Willie & I started home. Did not have a pleasant ride, got home about 5. Very cold. Received a letter from Mrs. Rankin. She writes an interesting letter. She thinks a great deal of Harry & teased me about him—She comes pretty near the truth.

Sunday, November 13.

To S.S. at 9. To preaching at 10 1/2. Rose Guinn & I went to hear Mr. Cannahan. His text was "It is finished." To S.S. at 2. Evening. At home. cold. There is a sermon to be preached to-night in the O.S.P. Church before the Female Bible Society of Gettysburg. All the other churches are closed. I preferred staying at home. Reading & writing (not letters). Very cold & windy.

Monday, November 14.

At school all day. Evening. Received two letters, one from T. A. Crooks, Andrew's brother, & one from Harry, mailed in Pittsburgh, though it was written at home. Wrote to Mr. Watson & sent back the letter I received from him on Oct. 28th inquiring about "Rosa."

Tuesday, November 15.

At school all day. Evening. Mother received a letter from Susie though it was written on Sabbath & contains no news of her school. I wrote to her & mailed her a letter from Washington which came this evening.

Wednesday, November 16.

At school all day. Evening. Annie & I went out to Uncle Elias Sheads's. How I pity them. Cousins Carrie & Lou came from Washington last Saturday & Uncle has gone for the remains of his two sons who one died from wounds in an amputation & one died in a Camp Hosp. Cousin Lou is sick & probably has the consumption. She looks bad. Home at 7 1/2. Clear & moon-light.

Thursday, November 17.

At school all day. Evening. Did not go to prayer-meeting. Had no bonnet & would not wear my hat. Received a letter from Julie Culp. Uncle Elias Sheads came home this morning with the remains of his two sons, Elias & Jacob. Poor boys.

Friday, November 18.

Morning. Received a letter from Mr. A. Armor, Galion Ohio inquiring of Mr. Stewart's brother. Should have received it last night. As he enclosed a stamp & envelope I answered—At school all day. Evening. At home. Was disappointed in not getting my bonnett colored & now I cannot get it until Thursday & must stay at home.

Saturday, November 19.

Morning. Ironing. Busy. Afternoon. The town is lively. A grand Demonstration in honor of Lincoln's re-election will be made. An illumination & torchlight procession. Several of pa's Littlestown friends were here. Evening. Was up street awhile but did not enjoy anything except some singing with accompaniment. It seems out of place to have such a jubilee now. True, we have much for which to rejoice but I feel sad. Received a good letter from Rachel Lashell & a splendid one (of course) from Harry. Both were welcome, especially the latter. Answered Harrie's but will not mail it until Monday.

Sunday, November 20.

Morning. At home. Raining. Annie & I started out to Uncle Elias Sheads's about 11—through the rain. It was sad & when we went into the parlor Lizzie was at the head of one of the coffins & Annie at the foot of the other—their heads bowed down—After awhile the other members of the family came in & oh, how my heart ached for them. The funeral was at 2. Mr. Baugher officiated. They were buried with the honors of war. Elias was 22 & Jacob 18 & Poor boys— Annie & I came home about 7. —Raining & very disagreeable. Feel tired.

Monday, November 21.

At school all day. Evening. At home. Do not feel well. Jefferson went to Hanover this morning with his furniture & Annie & ma go down in the early train to-morrow. We shall miss them. Mailed a letter to Harry. Cloudy & raining.

Tuesday, November 22.

Pa & I went to the cars with Annie & ma. At school all day. It seems odd without ma & we shall miss Annie too. Evening. At home. My room was cold to-day & I am far from being well. Have a bad cold.

Wednesday, November 23.

At school all day. Clear, pleasant & my room comfortable. Evening. Amanda Conover is here. She came from her school 2 1/2 mi. from town. Spent a pleasant evening. Wrote & mailed letters to Mr. Barton & Mr. Beyer. Received a letter from Susie very unexpectedly. Working at a pair of pulse warmers for [unclear text]. Ma came home in the evening train.

Thursday, November 24.

Thanksgiving Day. At home all day. No bonnett. I was so sorry I could not go out to church & the day was so pleasant & I felt like going out with Amanda. Worked at the pulse warmers but could not finish them. Had not wool enough & had to go to the store which took some time. Amanda went about 3. Jennie Gilbert was here awhile. This has been a lovely day. Could not go to prayer-meeting.

Friday, November 25.

At school all day. Finished & mailed the pulse-warmers also a Star with a notice of Uncle's boys funeral. Evening. Did several errands & got nearly all the things to my bonnet though I will not get it until next week. In the beginning of the week I was not well, was busy & the weather was so bad that I did not get out to get the trimmings & so cannot get it for Sabbath. Reading & writing awhile.

Saturday, November 26.

Morning. Did several errands up street. Did my part of the work at home. Afternoon. Sewing at Harriet's. Evening. Did some errands. Thought I would certainly get a letter but was woefully disappointed. Am going to stay at Mr. Lashell's to-night. Cannot go out to-morrow. I wish I could. The day will seem long. Writing awhile & reading.

Sunday, November 27.

Did not undress last night at all. The babies were troublesome. Lay down about 3 & slept until 7. Came home about 8. Did not of course feel very good. Slept from 11 1/2 until 3. Evening. Wrote to Susie, [unclear text] McElroy & Kate Menchey came to go to church with me but I could not go. I hope this will be the last Sabbath that I will spend in this way. It was a mis-spent day— Very pleasant. Clear & not very cold.

Monday, November 28.

At school all day. Evening. Received two very welcome letters, one from Annie & one from Harry. Did not answer Harry's but mailed my weekly missive to him—Was very glad to hear. The letter should have been here on Saturday.

Tuesday, November 29.

At school all day. Evening. Wrote to Annie. Feel tired. This has been a delightful day. Warm, clear & pleasant.

Wednesday, November 30.

At school all day. Do not feel well. Rose Guinn was here this evening & we were "running around" awhile. Working at my monthly reports. Feel real tired. Writing awhile to [unclear text].

Thursday, December 1.

At school all day. Afternoon. Received a letter from Susie. Evening. Went to prayer-meeting. Mr. McMillan led. Ada & I went down street. Met Mr. Bales. Home at 9 1/2.

Friday, December 2.

At school all day. Afternoon. Received a letter from Andrew Crooks. Evening. Received a good letter from Harry —His health is improving & he says he is getting along very well. I am very glad he is. Answered his two last letters but cannot mail them to-night.

Saturday, December 3.

At home all day. Busy. Received a letter from Mr. A. Armor of Galion O. I did not wish an answer to my last brief reply. Wrote to Harry. Am going to stay at Mr. Lashell's to-night. Do not feel very well.

Sunday, December 4.

At S.S. & church as usual. Do not feel at all well & did not enjoy the services of the day. I am very anxious to have the session close. I am so tired. I have worked hard.

Monday, December 5.

At school as usual. Evening. At home. Feel too tired to do anything.

Tuesday, December 6.

At school as usual. Evening. Our S.S. Teachers met at Mr. Schick's to consult each other about an exhibition. Spent a very pleasant evening. We meet again to-morrow night.

Wednesday, December 7.

At school all day. Evening. Went to Mr. Schick's according to appointment. Did not spend an unusually pleasant evening. I hardly have the time to spare. Received a letter from Sister Annie. They are well.

Thursday, December 8.

At school all day. Evening. Received an unexpected but none the less welcome letter from Harry. Went to prayer-meeting. Did not enjoy it very much. Wrote to Susie.

Friday, December 9.

At school as usual. Evening. Wrote to Harry & to Andrew. Went down to Will Guinn's to meet with the teachers. Spent a very pleasant evening. Had a good deal of fun. Home at 9 1/2. Snowing.

Saturday, December 10.

At home all day. Busy. Evening. Pa came home. Writing and reading.

Sunday, December 11.

At S.S. Went to hear Mr. Carrahan. To S.S. at 2. Evening. Feel badly. Am not very well & feel as though it is an impossibility for me to do anything except what must be done. Wrote to Susie. Heard Mr. Consor preach.

Monday, December 12.

At school as usual. Received a real good letter from Harry. Was not looking for one. Writing awhile.

Tuesday, December 13.

At school all day. Evening. Answered Harrie's letter. Feel unwell. Am very hoarse—Could hardly get through in school. To-morrow I am free. No one could be more rejoiced than I. My examination is to-morrow morning.

Wednesday, December 14.

Evening. Free for a month! My examination was pronounced by the Sec. of the Board, "an improvement over last year" as though he knew. I was more gratified by the [unclear text] remarks of some of the ladies there by all he could say. Commenced a dress for Jennie. Worked all afternoon & evening. Feel tired.

Thursday, December 15.

Morning. Finished Jennie's dress. Afternoon. Busy. Evening. Went up street. Received a letter from Sue & one from Andrew's sister Margaret—Wrote to Susie. To prayer-meeting. Mr. Lantz led. To Aunt Lizzie—It is feared that Cousin Dave is dead, a prisoner starved to death—God grant that it is false. Poor Aunt! She is almost heartbroken. She seems to have nothing but trouble.

Friday, December 16.

Writing nearly all day. Copied a sermon of Harrie's. Sent him my copy, at his request. I kept his copy. Also wrote a letter to him. Did several errands. Home at 7. Writing awhile. Very disagreeable. Have a miserable cold. There was no mail, of course, when I look for a letter.

Saturday, December 17.

Morning. At home. Evening. Received a good letter from Harry.

Saturday, December 24.

Evening. Susie came home. Went several places with her.

Sunday, December 25.

Could not go out to-day for two very good reasons. Evening. Went to church. Mr. Lantz preached. Very cold.

Monday, December 26.

Writing nearly all day. Evening. Ada came in & we took a walk. Had a long & interesting chat.

Tuesday, December 31.

Morning, busy. Evening. Received a letter from Mr. Mc A. Armor which I will send back by return mail—for reasons not necessary to state. Went over to Mr. Consor's to practice singing with the children.

—— 1865 ————————————

Wednesday, January 1.

To Sunday School at 9. To preaching at 10 1/2. Mr. Lantz preached a good sermon. To class. Home at 12 1/2. To S.S. at 2. Home at 4 1/2. Evening. Susie and I went down to Aunt Lizzie's. To preaching at 6. Mr. Lantz preached. Ada & Mr. Bales came home with me. Laura is going to stay here to-night. She and Sue go in the morning in the stage to their schools. Clear and moonlight. Very cold.

Thursday, January 2.

Rose at 6. Sue and Laura went at 5 1/2. Washed. Finished at 10. Writing—Mr. Wallace was here. Evening. Clear and cold but pleasant.

Wednesday, January 8.

At home all day. Evening. At home. Wrote to Rachel Lashell. Disagreeable —Raining. Feel disappointed—thought I would get a letter & did not.

Sunday, January 19.

Emma Zeigler is teaching for me today. I cannot & will not let mother to be taken care of by anyone else. Though better, she is still very weak.

Monday, January 20.

Mother is better today but she is still very weak. No one is allowed to go into her room except those who wait on her. Wrote a letter to Harry. Cold but pleasant. Clear.

Tuesday, February 18.

Mother has not been so well during the past week but she is better now. I think she is out of danger. She has been very ill indeed and for some time shows fears. We were much alarmed that she would not recover. Thank God! she is still spared to us. May she be for many many years.

Thursday, February 20.

Received a letter from Harry & one in answer to a letter I wrote in August 1863 & which only reached its destination last week.

Sunday, February 23.

Received a good letter from Harry. I should have had it last night but we did not hear the train & were too late to get in the P.O.

Wednesday, February 26.

Mother sat up to-day for the first time for 6 months and some days. How glad I was! At home all day.

Thursday, February 27.

My diary has been sadly neglected this year. Mother's illness has been partly the cause. The best reason I will not state —Suffice it to say it is a good one. Of course. Mother still improving. Received and read Enoch Arden, Tennyson's last poem.

Friday, February 28.

At school all day. Mother is still improving rapidly, though she looks very pale & weak. I am so glad she is convalescent. I hope nothing will occur to retard her speedy recovery. Looked for a letter and——didn't get it. Provoking! Feel very much indisposed.

Saturday, March 1.

Mother still better but P seems not well. Have a bad cold, & cough, & have had a head-ache for about 2 weeks. A request was made to the Dr. He says I have been confined too much—recommended a mild physic & if I do not feel better, come to him again. Also exercise in the fresh air.

—— *1866* ————————————————

Dr. Henry Stewart's typescripts state that the diary for this year was missing, so a typescript could not be completed.

—— *1867* ————————————————

In his typescripts, Dr. Henry Stewart made the following comment, "The diary of 1867—I had it but it has mysteriously disappeared, like some of the others." Therefore, no typescript could be completed for this year.

—— *1868* ————————————————

From Dr. Henry Stewart typescripts.

January & February.

Notes their daily life in New Brighton and on the 28th they left for Jamestown.

Saturday, March 28.

Had our first dinner in our own house.

Tuesday, May 26.

Mr. S. is a little better but has not regained what he lost within a month.

Sunday, August 9.

Mr. Snodgrass preached for Mr. S. He has been in unusually poor health during the last month. (Aug. 2 last recorded preaching)

Thursday, August 27.

Mr. S. suddenly very ill.

Thursday, September 3.

We moved today into our new house. Mr. S. was not able to walk over but was carried over. However we were thankful that he was able to come, even if in a chair.

Thursday, September 17.

Mr. S. seems quite poorly today, while hoping for the best, we fear the worst.

Friday, September 18.

Have no hope.

Saturday, September 19.

Sinking very fast, almost unable to speak.

Saturday, October 17.

One year ago today I left home a happy bride. This morning the cold snow is falling thick & fast upon my precious husband's grave.—

Thursday, October 27.

Our babe, a fine large boy was born about noon.

Sallie, sitting beside Henry's grave in Jamestown, Pennsylvania. (ACHS)

6

THE LATER YEARS
"I HAD MY BLACK BREAD FIRST"

The fourteen years of Sallie Myers' life following the birth of young Henry are more difficult to document. No diaries have yet emerged for the years 1869 through 1882, and in Henry's typescripts those years are omitted except for a few entries from 1875. However, Sallie Myers Stewart's story is examined through personal records on file at the Adams County Historical Society. Other records are available from the National Archives. Also extant is one particularly revealing letter by Dr. Henry A. Stewart, written to his sons Henry, Horace, and Donald in 1931. This letter clarifies the vast amount of information he had compiled on both the Stewart and Myers families. It also contains some valuable information about that undocumented fourteen-year span in Sallie's life.

After Henry Ferguson Stewart died, his maternal grandfather, Alexander McFarland, moved to Jamestown along with his wife and Alexander Stewart's widow, Lizzie. Henry wrote that Alexander "took charge of everything" for "there were no women's rights for him." He continued with, "He was probably justified, for the house was probably built with his money, and very probably in his name."[1] Living in that situation must have been difficult for Sallie, for Henry told his sons that "After grandfather's [John Stewart] death, June 28, 1870, probably with the substitution of Alex McFarland, for grandfather, as boss, conditions became so intolerable that mother decided to leave and come to her home."[2]

Sallie's father, Peter Myers, became ill that July, and Sallie visited her home in Gettysburg, staying there until her father died.[3] His death, combined with the situation in Jamestown, led Sallie to want to return home to her widowed mother and raise her son. Sallie's health was suffering as well, for Henry described her as probably having pulmonary tuberculosis. Caring for an ailing daughter-in-law and her small son placed a great burden on Grandmother Stewart.[4]

Having made the decision to return home, Sallie contacted Mr. David Wills, a Gettysburg attorney, and requested that he assume guardianship for young Henry. Mr. Wills agreed, and in late summer, 1871, Sallie and Henry returned to Gettysburg for good.

Sallie and son, Henry, c. 1880.
(ACHS)

Henry described David Wills with the following: "He was represented by many as a hard man—by some as unscrupulous—but if ever the God of the widow and the fatherless had a human representative on earth, it was David Wills."[5] Attorney Wills apparently faced a challenge trying to get money from Alexander McFarland for Henry's care, for Henry wrote that McFarland "took the stand that under grandfather's will the whole estate was grandmother's with the obligation to maintain me, and that if mother took me away, he would not pay her a cent."[6]

For the next thirteen years, Sallie worked as a dressmaker in Gettysburg to earn a living for herself and her son. Unable to return to teaching while raising a young child, dressmaking served as the means for her to be at home with Henry and still earn money. As Henry's letter indicates, "She had at times at least as high as four seamstresses working for her—and her clientele was large—but she worked hard and long hours—and her busiest months never netted as much as $20.00." Years later, Sallie would recall those years as the most difficult of her life when she told Henry, "I don't know how I got through them."[7] Faced with raising her son alone, she struggled to make ends meet in one of the few professions then open to women.

Despite her continuous struggle to earn a living, Sallie managed to send young Henry to private schools in an attempt to provide him with the best possible education. By 1884 Henry was enrolled in Hartwick Seminary, in preparation for entrance to Pennsylvania College.[8]

Tipton photograph of Henry A. Stewart with his mother, Sallie Myers Stewart, c. 1883. (ACHS)

Henry A. Stewart, taken to commemorate graduation from the University of Pennsylvania, May 1892. (ACHS)

Sallie resumed her active diary writing in 1884, the same year that she returned to teaching. Applying for recertification in the summer of 1881, Sallie received a three-year Professional Certificate. Pursuing a desire to educate black children, she sought work with the Freedman's Bureau in Virginia,[9] but returned to Gettysburg without obtaining a position. After her return, Sallie submitted her application to the Gettysburg Public School System, where she was appointed on August 11, 1884, as teacher of the Franklin Street School in Gettysburg, which served the black population of the town.[10] She wrote in her diary, "Commenced to teach today. 25 years ago today, I first began to teach. Today, my only child, a son taller than I went with me to the school house to see the beginning of my new work."[11] Henry wrote in 1931 that Sallie "labored 16 years there—long after she could have had a promotion to the more lucrative white schools—and did good work—being much loved by the colored people, young and old."[12]

That Sallie was "much loved" is easy to understand, for her involvement with the black population of Gettysburg extended far beyond the classroom. Her diary records activities at the African Methodist Episcopal Zion Church, where she took part in their religious celebrations, decorating the church with the children and attending their services. She also led her scholars in Decoration Day celebrations and parades out to Evergreen Cemetery, where they placed wreaths on soldiers' graves.

Sallie with students of the Franklin Street School. She taught, and also served as "janitress" of this school from 1884 to 1900. (ACHS photo)

265

Sallie advocated educational equality for the black children in Gettysburg. When integration into the white schools was finally established in 1898, Sallie wrote in her diary: "Colored children have been admitted to the high school," and described this event as "a piece of tardy justice," while additionally noting that integration caused a "great commotion" in the town of Gettysburg.[13]

Apparently, however, full integration occurred slowly and not without difficulty. The trouble surrounding the integration process must have created problems for Sallie, for in May 1900, she resigned from teaching at the Franklin Street School. Citing her frustration at integration efforts, she wrote in her diary:

> Finished the 16th year in the Colored School and it is the last. I notified the School Board some time ago that I would not be an applicant. The colored people are in a state of ferment over having admission to all the white schools and they will never get it except by appealing to the Court, but it has made me so much trouble that I feel that it is best for them & for me not to teach the school again. Until this year I enjoyed the work but I came near breaking down physically with hard work, annoyance and vexation.[14]

Sallie was granted a position in one of the grammar schools, but teaching there created its own problems. Apparently, her tenure in the Franklin Street School was not highly regarded by some of her new students, for Henry wrote, "Some of the older boys made her trouble continuously. They thought they were getting something inferior...her intense conscientiousness demanded that she stop with credit, rather than otherwise."[15] And so in November, Sallie decided to leave the profession for good. She explained her reasons as she wrote, "A few weeks ago I told the Board that if they could find a teacher for my school, I would like to be relieved. My school has not been pleasant, & I feel as though I could not stand the thought of teaching six months more. So, I have laid down the burden."[16] She continued, however, as substitute teacher for the borough until 1913, when she was 70 years old.[17]

Having "laid down the burden," Sallie was finally able to devote her energies toward more leisurely pursuits, like gardening, housework, and reading. Financial stability enabled her to enjoy life in ways she had previously thought impossible, for in 1891 Sallie finally received her widow's pension from the United States government, after eleven years of bureaucratic red tape and rejection.[18] Granted only $12 per month, the retroactive payment nonetheless meant a generous sum, and Sallie celebrated by purchasing two items "she had wanted from her girlhood...a black silk dress and gold watch."[19]

In February 1901 she wrote, "Now that I have leisure to read, I am enjoying Sir Walter Scott's stories." And as Henry later told his sons, this was the period of her life when she could do as she pleased, and she often told him, "Harry, I am glad I had my black bread first."[20]

Henry was by this time a grown man. Married in 1890 to Miss Jennie Battin from Virginia, an event noted in Sallie's diary with the words, "At last I have a daughter,"[21] Henry established his medical practice in Gettysburg, joining Dr. J.

W. C. O'Neal at his office on Baltimore Street.[22] On September 10, 1893, Henry and Jennie gave Sallie her first of four grandchildren, a boy named Henry Battin Stewart. Sallie helped Henry in his medical practice, keeping records, cleaning his office, and sometimes resuming her role of nurse, assisting with medical procedures.

Sallie spent the last two decades of her life pursuing other interests as well. She traveled often to Jamestown, Pennsylvania, to visit friends and to spend time at the grave of her beloved husband. Each fall, she noted in her diaries the anniversary of their wedding and his subsequent death with sadness, like the following entries found in September and October 1898: "It is 30 years since I took my last sad look at my husband's face before he was laid away forever from my mortal sight," and "31 years ago this morning I left my home the happy bride of the man I loved. I feel as though I would like to spend this day in the seclusion of my thoughts."

Pursuing a life of service, Sallie found fulfillment in her activities, and kept busy in local organizations like the Women's Relief Corps, the Civic Club, the Rebekkah Lodge, and the Ladies of the G.A.R. She became involved in the lyceum circuit, and helped to organize Chautauqua activities. In 1910 Sallie served as a census enumerator for Gettysburg.[23] She also took an active role in the Sons of Union Veterans, to which her son belonged, serving as his secretary and accompanying him to various encampments across the country. In 1901 she was elected a member in the National Association of Army Nurses of the Civil War. Organized after the Civil War by Dorothea Dix, the association gained momentum slowly, then became firmly re-organized in 1892 during the G.A.R. encampment in Washington, D.C.[24] Membership required documented proof that the candidate had served a period of three months, whether enlisted or volunteer, as a nurse during the Civil War. Upon receiving this news, she wrote in her diary, "This honor is conferred upon me because of my work among the wounded during and after the battle. I feel it is a very high honor indeed."[25] At the NAANCW Annual Convention in San Francisco in 1903, Sallie was elected national treasurer, the only non-enlisted nurse to hold a national office. She held that position until her death in 1922.[26] From 1901 to 1921 Sallie traveled to Boston, Atlantic City, Rochester, and other major cities nationwide, often alone, to attend their annual conventions.[27] Held in conjunction with the annual G.A.R. week, these conventions provided, among other things, opportunities for old friendships between soldiers and nurses to be renewed.

At the National Convention held at San Francisco in September 1912, Sallie had a reunion with William J. Sheriff, a soldier she had nursed during the Battle of Gettysburg, and with whom she had remained friends all those years since. The *Los Angeles Express* wrote an article about Sallie which carried the following headline: Woman Gettysburg Heroine Meets Veteran She Aided. The article described how, "Yesterday, Miss Myers, now Mrs. S.M. Stewart, met William J. Sheriff...of this city, one of the men to whom she ministered on that perilous day, to renew a friendship that has endured between the two since that July day almost half a century ago."[28]

1910 - present at Atlantic City.
" 1911" Rochester, N.Y:
" 1912 - Los Angeles.
" 1913, Chattanooga
" Detroit, 1914
" Washington, 1915
" Kansas City, 1916
" Boston, 1917
" Portland, Ore., 1918
" Columbus, Ohio, 1919
" Indianapolis, 1920
" Indianapolis, 1921

Mrs. Salome M. Stewart
NATIONAL TREASURER

Mrs. Stewart served under the maiden name of Miss Sallie Myers. She was a volunteer nurse. She resided at Gettysburg and during and after the battle cared for the wounded in her father's house, which was used as a hospital and also in the Roman Catholic and United Presbyterian Churches, where the first Division Corps Hospital was opened, and in Camp Letterman, the general hospital established east of the town. Her services of three months were all voluntary. She does not receive a pension. Her address is 228 Baltimore St., Gettysburg. She is the widow of the brother of a wounded soldier who died in her father's house. Her husband a Presbyterian minister died in 1868 of injuries received in the service. She was a teacher in the public Schools before the war, has taught for twenty-five years, and is now a substitute teacher in the Gettysburg schools.

Mrs. Stewart has been Treasurer of the National Association of Nurses of the Civil War for seven years. She was appointed one of the enumerators of the late census.

Page from commemoration booklet printed for National Association of Army Nurses of the Civil War, 1910 convention in Atlantic City, NJ. Notes on the page are written by Sallie Myers in 1921. Original booklet is on file at the Adams County Historical Society, Gettysburg, Pa.

With the passage of time, the NAANCW ceased to exist. With membership limited to those who served as Civil War nurses, the roster could only become smaller as, one by one, these honored women died. By 1915 there were only twenty-five members remaining, one of whom was Sallie Myers. The *Evening Star*, a Washington, D.C., newspaper, carried the following account of their annual convention held in that city:

> Like the G.A.R., the National Association of Army Nurses is one that cannot be recruited and soon must die out. This is one big reason why the other patriotic orders are vying with one another at this encampment to make the last visit here of the women who tended the wounded on the war-swept fields an occasion for an unstinted expression of the gratitude and affection of the Union in whose preservation they took such an important part.
>
> These war nurses will see their boys in blue, many of whom they saved from death fifty years ago, as they march along Pennsylvania Avenue tomorrow from the Peace Monument to the White House, from a stand built especially for their comfort....The veterans look upon the nurses as angels of mercy, and there is the strongest of bonds between the ex-soldiers and the fast-aging women who helped to lighten the weary burdens of the sick and wounded in the hospitals during the Civil War. They numbered at one time about 350, but their ranks have diminished almost to the vanishing point.[29]

Salome Myers Stewart and Allie Powers, c. 1910. (ACHS)

Sallie also pursued settlement work in Philadelphia for several years. Joining Cornelia Hancock, with whom she had worked as a nurse at Camp Letterman and became friends, she spent part of several winters at settlements in Philadelphia, engaged in social work and teaching.[30] While there, she continued her long friendship with Andrew Crooks, who escorted Sallie to lectures and social events in the city.

Other friendships remained important to Sallie, and the later years of her life brought visits from General Huidekoper, Jennie Jones (widow of Ben C. Jones) and William Sheriff, who at his death named Sallie one of the beneficiaries of his estate. She corresponded regularly with her friends, exchanging information on the Battle of Gettysburg, and other local items of interest. One letter written in 1913 to an unidentified person, and printed in the *Chattanooga* [Tennessee] *News*, is notable for its account on how Devil's Den was named. It survives as one of the few documents from Gettysburg history to "set the record straight," for the naming of Devil's Den has long been a topic for legend and debate. A portion of that letter is reprinted here:

> There is another wrong impression which I wish to correct, and that refers to the name "Devil's Den." Many persons have been told that the name was given to those immense rocks because of the fierce fighting there during the Battle of Gettysburg.
>
> My father's uncle, John Plank, was one of the early settlers of the County, and his farm included a part of the "Round Tops." As a child, I have heard him tell of the snakes which infested the country, and had their "den" among those huge rocks. Parties of men were organized to rid the neighborhood of these dangerous reptiles. One big old snake persistently eluded them. They could never kill or capture him, and they called him "The Devil." He finally disappeared, and it was supposed that he died in his "den." So, to Gettysburgers, that has always been "Devil's Den." This may or may not interest you. If it does, you are very welcome to it. If not, I presume you have a "waste-basket."[31]

Included at the bottom of this letter are these enigmatic words, "I was not an ardent admirer of Miss Wade." Why Sallie wrote that is unknown, for nowhere in her diaries or memoirs is there any other reference to Jennie Wade that might serve as explanation for that rather sharp statement. Sallie was friends with Jennie's sister, Georgia Wade McClellan, during their girlhood days in Gettysburg, and certainly knew Jennie before she was killed during the battle. Interestingly enough, that comment was not included in the *Chattanooga News* article.

In her later years, Sallie earned something of a reputation as a strong-willed woman, wont to have her way when the situation required it. Local stories tell that she ruled her family with an iron hand, a matriarch in every sense of the word. Sometimes she ruled others that way as well. One elderly resident of Gettysburg who died in 1992 remembered her as formidable, and recalled an incident that his father often related to him as a child.[32] According to the tale, there was an outbreak of spinal meningitis in Gettysburg in 1910 which seriously affected a number of children. Two weeks before the outbreak, there had been a reenactment, with an encampment at the Camp Letterman site. During this reenactment, a half dozen or so horses inexplicably dropped over dead. The town's leaders, unable to decide what must be done about the horses rotting and bloating in the hot sun, contacted men from Washington to visit Gettysburg and determine just why these animals had keeled over. In the meantime, the horses continued to rot, and then the spinal meningitis outbreak began. Sallie apparently decided that these decaying animals had something to do with the disease and confronted the Gettysburg men, saying, "To hell with the men from Washington! I want these horses moved out of here!" In short order, the horses were moved.[33]

Her stubborn will, evident in the above account, provided her strength through some difficult times which lay ahead. Sallie lived to see the outbreak of World War I, and said good-bye to her grandson Horace as he departed for France. Her youngest sister, Grace, died in 1918, before Sallie could make it to her deathbed. In her diary she sadly wrote, "I arrived after her death. Grace was my youngest sister, fourteen years my junior & when a baby & small child I had almost entire charge of her."[34]

When World War I ended and the news reached Gettysburg, Sallie was overjoyed. Her diary entry for November 11, 1918, contains these words: "The town is wild over the news 'It is over.'—A wonderful fantastic parade. Thank God." And just two years later, along with taking rides in her "coupe," digging up potato plants in her garden, attending granddaughter Margaret's graduation, and working with her local clubs, her diary contains this excited entry on July 31, 1920: "Registered for voting!!!" This woman who had struggled for years, made her own way in the world, and successfully maintained her independence in a man's world, voted for the first time at age 78.

Strong-willed and formidable she may have been, but invincible she was not. In January 1922, she wrote in her diary that she had gone to communion services at her church but "felt too bad & weak to stay for the whole service." On Thursday, January 12, her entry reads, "Usual work and a little washing, but spent most of the day doing personal writing." At the end of his typescripted manuscript, her son, Dr. Henry A. Stewart, typed the single word, "FINIS." In his letter to his sons dated 1931, Henry wrote, "With the dawn of January 17, 1922, came the end of an earthly life of usefulness, service, and devoted love." An article written about her in *The National Tribune* carried the following words: "One of God's good women went to her reward when Salome Myers Stewart closed her eyes on earthly things January 17." And at the Annual Convention of the National Association of Army Nurses of the Civil War in 1922 the few remaining "angels of mercy" carried her portrait on their badge.[35]

The inscription at the base of her tombstone in Evergreen Cemetery, Gettysburg, Pennsylvania, reads:

Daughter, sister & widow of a soldier
Faithful unto death
Above all
A mother

Grave of Salome Myers Stewart,
Evergreen Cemetery, Gettysburg, Pennsylvania.

EPILOGUE

In the years after Sallie died in 1922, the story of what she did during the Battle of Gettysburg and the impact she made on her time in history seemed to fade into the background as historians clamored to reconstruct the tremendous historical significance of Gettysburg in our nation's history. Some civilians of that time fared much better; their stories were instantly recognized and reproduced, assuring them of a proper place in Gettysburg history. Others, with stories just as fascinating and contributions just as significant, are still waiting for someone to unearth their stories and bring them to light.

The records are out there, somewhere, lying dormant for now, silent testimony to a time and place when unimaginable terror became, for awhile, common experience. There is an old adage, "If walls could speak, what stories they would tell." I was reminded of this as I wandered through the house on High Street where my great-great grandmother lived during the battle, stepped down into the cellar where so many wounded once lay, and stood there, many years later, trying to imagine the scenario of pain, fear, and deafening noise.

The Peter Myers house is modest, mostly unchanged since 1863, not greatly subjected to the whims of modernization. On its exterior wall, facing High Street, there is no bronze marker identifying it as a Civil War house, unlike many others that existed in the summer of 1863. This house is itself a metaphor for the untold stories of Gettysburg and a symbol of the story of Salome Myers Stewart.

Scattered throughout the Gettysburg area stand other traces of Sallie's story. From High Street, one can still walk to Cousin Carrie Sheads' house, to McPherson's Ridge, to the Seminary, and the spot near West Confederate Avenue where Alexander fell. One can still visit the Round Tops, Spangler's Woods, and Evergreen Cemetery where Sallie now rests. One can also walk to Hospital Woods, the site of Camp Letterman where Sallie tended "her boys" for many weeks. Many of these pieces of Sallie's story are preserved and protected for succeeding generations, cared for by the National Park Service or the town of Gettysburg. Others, like the Camp Letterman site, have tragically succumbed to the destructive forces of unplanned and wanton development.

Sallie's legacy of dedication and devotion to her soldiers, the community of Gettysburg, and her family exists in other, less tangible ways as well. Her photograph still hangs on the wall of the local G.A.R. hall as tribute to her contributions during that summer of 1863. The Gettysburg chapter, or "Tent," of the Daughters of Union Veterans of the Civil War, 1861-1865, is named the Salome Myers Stewart Tent in her honor. And her personal writings remain on record at the Adams County Historical Society, a small part of its vast collection of Adams County, Pennsylvania history.

Of her direct decendants, only a few lines remain. Her only son Henry fathered four children, Henry, Horace, Donald, and Margaret. Only grandson Henry had children, six in all, two of whom died in childhood. One of the remaining four is my mother, Jacqueline Stewart Sites. I am one of eleven great-great grandchildren of Salome Myers Stewart, and all eleven of us have produced only twelve great-great-great grandchildren. Only one of them carries the Stewart name.

The Henry B. Stewart (eldest grandson of Salome Myers Stewart) family, 1923. Back row: Joanna Elizabeth Izer Stewart, Henry Battin Stewart. Front row: Kathryn Izer Stewart, Mary Joanna Stewart, James Henry Stewart.

If my efforts have served to place Sallie Myers where she belongs in the continuing story of Gettysburg, or if, with this book, I have been able to give voice to the silent walls of the little house on High Street, then I am satisfied. I wrote this for Sallie, for my mother, my brothers, sister, and cousins, and for me. But most of all, I wrote it for the twelve who come after us and those unknown, yet to be counted, who will come after them.

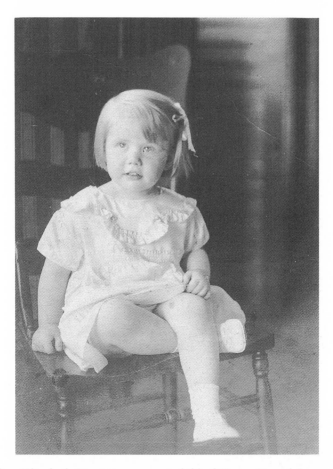

Jacqueline Elizabeth Stewart, youngest child of Henry B. and Joanna E. Izer Stewart, great-granddaughter of Salome Myers Stewart, age three. Photo taken 1937.

NOTES

In citing works in the notes, short titles have generally been used. Works frequently cited have been identified by the following abbreviations:

ACHS   Adams County Historical Society, Gettysburg, Pennsylvania
NARA   National Archives and Records Administration, Washington, D.C.
USAMHI U.S. Army Military History Institute, Carlisle Barracks, Carlisle, Pennsylvania

Chapter 1: The Early Years

1. Stewart, Henry A., letter to his sons, April 12, 1931, ACHS. The Stewart files contain the genealogy of both the Myers and Stewart families.
2. *Ibid.*, 8.
3. *Ibid.*
4. Stewart, Henry A., genealogy record, February 5, 1940, Sarah Rodgers personal collection, Fairfield, Pennsylvania.
5. *Ibid.*
6. Stewart, Salome Myers, Diary, 1862, ACHS. In the entry for March 25, Sallie notes her family's move to the home of Uncle Lewis Myers. Peter Myers is not included in census records for 1860, and tax records for Gettysburg Borough do not list Peter Myers as a property owner. At some point, the Peter Myers family lived in Wayne County, Indiana, for their son Jefferson's service records indicate that he was born there in 1840. By 1854, however, the family was back in Gettysburg, Sallie's composition book for that year notes her address as Gettysburg, Pennsylvania. Therefore, Peter Myers was probably just overlooked in the 1860 Census.
7. Stewart, Salome Myers, "Recollections of the Battle of Gettysburg," unpublished narrative written in 1897 and transcribed by Dr. Henry A. Stewart, in Stewart files, ACHS.
8. Stewart, Diary, 1860, Jacqueline S. Sites personal collection, Fairfield, Pennsylvania; Stewart, Diary, 1862, 1864, ACHS. Many references to these activities and Sallie's comments on church sermons exist throughout these diaries.
9. Stewart, Salome Myers, personal papers, ACHS. Her original certificate is among those papers.
10. Stewart, Henry A., letter to his sons.
11. *Ibid.*, 9.
12. Stewart, Salome Myers, personal papers, ACHS. The date of this note is unknown, but the original exists in the Stewart files.
13. Wert, J. Howard, "Old Time Notes of Adams County." A copy is in the Salome Myers Stewart personal papers, ACHS.
14. Stewart, Diary, 1860, entry for February 16.
15. *Ibid.* Although Sallie claims that Salome Troxell Sheads was the oldest inhabitant of Gettysburg at the time of her death, no documentation to verify this has been found.

16. *Ibid.*, entry for February 1.

17. Stewart, Diary, 1860; Stewart, Diary, 1862, 1864. Many references throughout the diaries produced this conclusion, especially Sallie's support for Abraham Lincoln's bid for the presidency.

18. See Robert L. Bloom, *History of Adams County, Pennsylvania, 1700-1990* (Gettysburg: Adams County Historical Society, 1992), 171-84, for a discussion of the political atmosphere in Adams County during this period.

19. Glatfelter, Charles H., "The Wide Awakes of Gettysburg: 1860," April 12, 1995, ACHS. *The Sentinel* for October 24, 1860, reported that the Wide Awakes were organized, and "ready to do good service in the contest of the 6th."

20. Stewart, Diary, 1860. Entries for October 19 and November 12 refer to Wide Awake activities, and the entry for November 15 refers to a torch-light procession.

21. Glatfelter.

22. This reference is an error found in Henry A. Stewart's transcriptions. The Zouaves home guard unit, formed in the spring of 1861, was led by the Rev. C.L.K. Sumwalt, assistant pastor of the Gettysburg Methodist Episcopal Church.

23. Stewart, Diary, 1860, entry for May 23.

24. Bloom, 187. Many of the men of Company E reenlisted after their three-month term expired, and became Company F of the 87th Pennsylvania Volunteers, serving for three years.

25. J. Jefferson Myers' service record, NARA. See also H. N. Minnigh, "History of Company K. 1st Inft. Penn's Reserves. 'The Boys Who Fought at Home'" (Duncansville, H.N. Minnigh "Homefront," 1891).

26. Peter A. Myers' service record, NARA. See also Bloom, 187.

27. Stewart, Diary. 1862.

28. Stewart, Diary, 1860, entry for March 31.

29. Moore, Frank, *Women of the War* (Hartford, Conn.: S.S. Scranton, 1866), 238.

30. Sheads family file, ACHS.

31. *Ibid.*, 244.

32. Stewart, Diary, 1862, entry for September 5.

33. "Cavalry to Winter Here," *The Compiler*, December 23, 1861.

34. Stewart, Salome Myers, personal papers, 1862, ACHS. Original note exists, but writer of the note is unknown.

35. Edwin W. Casey's service and pension records, NARA. Edwin Casey received a Certificate of Disability for Discharge on Sept. 24, 1862, for injuries incurred while stationed at the barracks in Gettysburg.

36. *The Compiler*, March 10, 1862.

37. Thomas E. Snyder family records, ACHS, Gettysburg.

38. Stewart, Diaries, 1860, 1862. Many references to Thomas E. Snyder's role in the Methodist church appear in these diaries.

39. Stewart, Diary, 1862; Thomas E. Snyder family records, ACHS. Snyder's file shows that instead of dying, he married and became the father of two daughters.

40. Stewart, Diary, 1862.

41. Stewart, Henry A., letter to his sons.

42. Peter A. Myers' service records, including muster rolls and certificate of discharge for disability, NARA.

43. *Ibid.*

44. Author unknown, copy in Stewart files, ACHS.

45. Company roster sheet, copy in author's personal collection, courtesy of Jacob M. Sheads, Gettysburg.

46. Stewart, Diary, 1862, entry for January 21.

47. *Ibid.*, June 13.

48. Bloom, 193.
49. Stewart, Diary, 1862, entry for October 27.
50. *Ibid.*, December 22.

Chapter 2: And the Battle Came Raging

1. J. Jefferson Myers service record, NARA. His certificate of disability lists the reason for discharge as chronic rheumatism.
2. Stewart, Diary, 1862, entry for January 2, from transcript by Henry A. Stewart, ACHS.
3. Johnson, Clifton, *Battleground Adventures* (Boston and New York, 1915), 176.
4. Bloom, 182-83.
5. *Ibid.*, 176.
6. "Gettysburg's Memories of its Terrible Fourth," *Philadelphia North American*, July 4, 1909. A copy is in the Stewart file, ACHS.
7. Johnson, 177.
8. Bloom, 172. Figures from the Federal Census show that the black population in Adams County, Pennsylvania, in 1860 was 474.
9. Stewart, Salome Myers, "Recollections...."
10. Stewart, Diary, 1863 (transcript), entry for June 21, ACHS.
11. In Sallie Myers' diaries, Eisenberg is spelled "Isenbert." A listing of Methodist ministers which appeared in an article in *The Compiler* titled "Methodism in Adams Co.," February 19, 1880, lists the spelling as Eisenberg. When quoting Sallie, her spelling is used throughout the book.
12. Stewart, Diary, 1863 (transcript), entry for June 21.
13. Johnson, 177.
14. Stewart, Diary, 1863 (transcript), entry for June 26.
15. *Ibid.*, June 29.
16. "Local Women Recall the Hectic Days of June/July 1863: Memories of the Battle of Gettysburg Recalled During 40th Anniversary of the Battle, July 1903," ACHS.
17. Myers, Susannah, "Some Battle Experiences as Remembered by a Young School Girl," *The Compiler*, April 24, 1907. A copy is on file at ACHS. Myers, 16 years old at the time of the battle, was a boarder at Carrie Sheads' Oak Ridge Seminary.
18. "Gettysburg's Memories of its Terrible Fourth," *Philadelphia North American*, July 4, 1909, A copy is in the Stewart files, ACHS.
19. Johnson, 177-178.
20. *Ibid.*
21. *Ibid.*
22. "How a Gettysburg Schoolteacher Spent Her Vacation in 1863," *San Francisco Sunday Call*, GAR Edition, August 16, 1903. A copy is in the Stewart files, ACHS.
23. Johnson, 178.
24. Myers, "Some Battle Experiences ...."
25. Johnson, 178.
26. *Ibid.*, p. 179.
27. Myers, "Some Battle Experiences ...."
28. "How a Gettysburg Schoolteacher...."
29. Johnson, 179.
30. "How a Gettysburg Schoolteacher...."
31. Henry F. Stewart's service and pension records, NARA.
32. Stewart, "Recollections ...."
33. Stewart, Diary, 1863 (transcript), entry for July 2.
34. "How a Gettysburg Schoolteacher...."

35. Stewart, Diary, 1863 (transcript), entry for July 3
36. *Ibid.*, July 4.
37. Henry A. Stewart genealogy records, ACHS. Sallie's references to the "Presbyterian churchyard" are confusing, and do not name a specific churchyard. In Henry A. Stewart's vast genealogy papers, positive identification of the Presbyterian church-yard (Robinson's Church), Allegheny County, Clinton, Pennsylvania, exists. Alexander lies there near his mother, Jane McFarland Stewart. Her gravestone carries the inscription, "buried with her chosen dead."
38. Stewart, Diary, 1863 (transcript), entry for July 6.
39. *Ibid.*, July 9.
40. Johnson, 180.
41. Coco, Gregory A., *A Vast Sea of Misery: A History and Guide to the Union and Confederate Field Hospitals at Gettysburg, July 1-November 20, 1863* (Gettysburg: Thomas Publications, 1988), 167.
42. Stewart, Salome Myers, personal papers, Stewart files, ACHS. One of Sallie's original passes (one of her "most prized possessions") exists in these files. Scott Hann of Mays Landing, New Jersey, has one of Sallie's original passes in his personal collection.
43. Stewart, Diary, 1863, (transcript) entry for July 25.
44. Coco, 172.
45. "How a Gettysburg Schoolteacher...."

Chapter 3: The Soldiers

1. Stewart, Diary, entry for July 1863.
2. "Oration by General H. S. Huidekoper at the Reunion of the Survivors of the 150th Regiment, Pennsylvania Volunteers," August 13, 1894, p. 7, Gregory A. Coco collection, USAMHI.
3. Huidekoper, Henry Shippen, "A Short Story of the First Day's Fight at Gettysburg," (Bicking Print, 1906), Robert L. Brake collection, USAMHI. Although Huidekoper states that he left the Myers home on July 9, Sallie records in her diary for 1863 that he left on July 6.
4. Dysinger, Doris (Special Collections/University Archives Assistant, Bucknell University) letter to Sarah Rodgers, April 27, 1994, and uncited newspaper obituary dated February 22, information in Alumni files, Bucknell University, Lewisburg, Pennsylvania.
5. *Ibid.*
6. Thomas Chamberlin service and pension records, NARA. See also Stewart, Diary, 1863 (transcript), entries for July 3 and 6.
7. Stewart, Diary, 1863 (transcript). Sallie's recorded date of departure for Chamberlin and Huidekoper conflicts with Huidekoper's later account, which states they left the Myers home on July 9.
8. Obituary of Brice X. Blair, *Huntingdon Monitor*, March 28, 1890, from Hann's personal collection.
9. Hann's personal collection.
10. Stewart, Diary, 1863, entry for July 8 (transcript).
11. *Ibid.*, July 24.
12. "How a Gettysburg Schoolteacher...."
13. *Ibid.*, p. 3. See also Stewart, Diary, 1864, entry for June 1.
14. Bates, Samuel P., *History of Pennsylvania Volunteers, 1861-5.* 5 volumes (Harrisburg, Pa.: 1870), 517.
15. Stewart, Diary, 1864, (transcript) entry for July 17.

16. "How a Gettysburg Schoolteacher...."
17. Coco, *A Vast Sea...*, 17. See also "How a Gettysburg Schoolteacher...."
18. "How a Gettysburg Schoolteacher...."
19. MacPherson, Byrle F., "Miss Alice Powers, Volunteer Nurse in Civil War, Taught Primary School for 30 Years," *The Gettysburg Times*, April 13, 1935.
20. James Fulton service and pension records, NARA.
21. Nesbit, John W., *General History of Company D, 149th Pennsylvania Volunteers and Personal Sketches of the Members 1862-1865* (Oakdale Printing, 1908), 15.
22. "How a Gettysburg Schoolteacher...."
23. Capt. James Ashworth, pension records, NARA. See also Stewart, Diary, 1863, entry for July 7 (transcript).
24. George F. Bates service and pension records, NARA. See also Stewart, Diary, July 1863 (transcript).
25. William Sheriff pension records, NARA. See also Stewart, Diary, 1863, entry for July 7 (transcript).
26. Stewart, Diary, July 1863 (transcript).
27. Amos P. Sweet lies buried in grave #37, Section C, Pennsylvania plot, Soldiers' National Cemetery, Gettysburg, Pennsylvania.
28. J. B. Young served as pastor of the Gettysburg Methodist Episcopal Church from 1871 to 1873. See the list of pastors included in "Methodism in Adams County," *The Compiler*, Feb. 19, 1890.
29. Stewart, Salome Myers, "Battle Experiences," *The Chattanooga Times*, Oct, 13, 1913. A copy is in the Stewart files, ACHS.
30. Mitchell, Mary H., *Hollywood Cemetery: The History of a Southern Shrine* (Virginia State Library, 1985), Appendix 2, 150.

Chapter 4: Two Brothers: Alexander and Henry Stewart

1. "How a Gettysburg Schoolteacher...."
2. Stewart, Henry A., letter to his sons.
3. *Ibid.*, 5.
4. *Ibid.*, 6.
5. Stewart, Henry A., genealogy papers, ACHS.
6. Stewart, Henry A., letter to his sons.
7. *Ibid.*
8. Nesbit, 1.
9. Ramsey, W. R., *History of the 150th Pennsylvania Regiment of the Bucktail Brigade*, Ramsey-Bassler collection, USAMHI.
10. Henry F. Stewart's service and pension records, NARA.
11. Bates, 612.
12. Stewart, Alexander M., letters, Stewart files, ACHS.
13. Matthews, Richard E., *The 149th Pennsylvania Volunteer Infantry Unit in the Civil War* (Jefferson, North Carolina, and London: McFarland & Company, Inc., 1994), 60-62.
14. Bates, 612.
15. Matthews, 60-62.
16. *Ibid.*, 67-79. See also Nesbit, 13-14. See also Bates, 612.
17. Alexander M. Stewart service records, NARA. See also Stewart, Diary, 1863, (transcript) entry for July 2.
18. Nesbit, 14.
19. *Ibid.*, 15.
20. *Ibid.*

21. *Ibid.*
22. *Ibid.*
23. "How a Gettysburg Schoolteacher...."
24. *Ibid.*
25. Stewart, Diary, 1864, entries for June 8-15.

Chapter 5: Wife, Widow, Mother

1. Stewart, Diary, 1864.
2. David Myers service record, NARA.
3. Sheads family files, ACHS.
4. Johnson, 181-182.
5. Stewart, Diary, 1864.
6. *Ibid.*, May 11.
7. Stewart, Salome Myers, personal papers, ACHS. Several original letters from Ben Jones are in those files.
8. Jones, Benjamin C., service and pension records, NARA.
9. *Ibid.*
10. Stewart, Diary, 1864.
11. *Ibid.*, March 12.
12. *Ibid.*, July 16.
13. Stewart, Diary, 1864, entry for January 13.
14. *Ibid.*, June 15.
15. Stewart, Diary, 1864. In her July 2 entry, she is referring to the incident when she narrowly escaped being shot by a minie ball which came in through the window, while she was tending Alexander Stewart.
16. Stewart, Diary, July 1864.
17. Stewart, Diary, 1864, entry for October 19.
18. Bloom, 178-184. In his discussion of wartime politics, Bloom notes that Abraham Lincoln did not carry Adams County in the election of 1864.
19. Stewart, Diary, 1864, entry for November 9.
20. Stewart, Salome Myers, personal papers, ACHS. Among these papers is her marriage certificate.
21. *Ibid.* The letter to Ada McMillan is among those papers.
22. "The Meeting Place of the First Synod of the West," *The Christian Union Herald*, October 7, 1926, 11.
23. Baptismal records of Jamestown Presbyterian Church, February 1869.

Chapter 6: The Later Years

1. Stewart, Henry A., letter to his sons.
2. *Ibid.*, 10.
3. *Ibid.*
4. *Ibid.*
5. *Ibid.*, 11.
6. *Ibid.*, 10.
7. *Ibid.*
8. *Ibid.*, 12.
9. *Ibid.*
10. From records on Franklin Street School, Betty Myers Collection, Gettysburg, Pennsylvania. See also Bloom, *History of Adams County...*, for his discussion on education and the segregated school system in Gettysburg.
11. Stewart, Diary, 1884, entry for August 12.

12. Stewart, Henry A., letter to his sons, 12.
13. Stewart, Diary, 1898, (transcript) entry for November 9.
14. Stewart, Diary, 1890, (transcript) entry for May 29.
15. Stewart, Henry A., letter to his sons.
16. Stewart, Diary, 1900, (transcript) entry for November 29.
17. Stewart, Henry A., letter to his sons.
18. Henry F. Stewart service and pension records, NARA.
19. Stewart, Henry A., letter to his sons.
20. *Ibid.*, 13.
21. Stewart, Diary, 1890, (transcript) entry for April 15.
22. Frassanito, William A., *The Gettysburg Bicentennial Album* (Gettysburg: The Gettysburg Bicentennial Committee, 1987). Frassanito identifies Dr. O'Neal's office as existing on the site of the Gettysburg Post Office. In 1995, the Adams County Public LIbrary is located in the old Post Office Building.
23. Stewart, Diary, 1890, (transcript)entry for April 15.
24. "Officers of National Association of Army Nurses," *The Evening Star*, Sept. 29, 1915, Washington, D.C.
25. Stewart, Diary, 1901 (transcript), ACHS.
26. Stewart, Diaries, 1901-1922 (transcript), ACHS. References to her re-election as treasurer for the NAANCW are a yearly occurrence in her diaries.
27. *Ibid.*
28. "Women Gettysburg Heroine Meets Veteran She Aided," *Los Angeles Express*, September 12, 1912, Los Angeles, California. A copy is in the Stewart files, ACHS.
29. *Ibid.*
30. Stewart, Diary, 1906, entries for February and March, ACHS.
31. "Reminiscences of Gettysburg," *The Chattanooga News*, October 30, 1913, Chattanooga, Tennessee. A copy is in the Stewart files, ACHS.
32. Pfeffer, Fred, personal interview by author, 1992.
33. *Ibid.*
34. Stewart, Diary, 1918, entry for October 4, 1918, ACHS.
35. Stewart, Henry A., letter to his sons.

SUGGESTED READINGS

Alleman, Tillie Pierce. *At Gettysburg: Or What a Girl Saw and Heard of the Battle*. New York: 1989.

Bates, Samuel P. *History of Pennsylvania Volunteers, 1861-5*. Harrisburg, Pa.: B. Singerly, 1870.

Bennett, Gerald R. *Days of Uncertainty and Dread: The Ordeal Endured by the Citizens of Gettysburg*. Littlestown: Gerald R. Bennett, 1995.

Bloom, Robert L. *History of Adams County, Pennsylvania, 1700-1990*. Gettysburg: Adams County Historical Society, 1992.

Broadhead, Sarah. *The Diary of a Lady of Gettysburg, Pennsylvania, From June 15 to July 15, 1863*. Hershey, Pa.: Reprinted by Gary T. Hawbaker.

Brodski, Bella, and Schenck, Celeste, eds. *Life/Lines: Theorizing Women's Autobiography*. Ithaca and London: Cornell University Press, 1988.

Burr, Virginia Ingraham, ed. *The Secret Eye: The Journal of Ella Gertrude Clanton Thomas, 1848-1889*. Chapel Hill: University of North Carolina Press, 1990.

Coco, Gregory A. *A Strange and Blighted Land*. Gettysburg: Thomas Publications, 1995.

Coco, Gregory A. *A Vast Sea of Misery: A History and Guide to the Union and Confederate Field Hospitals at Gettysburg, July 1-November 20, 1863*. Gettysburg: Thomas Publications, 1988.

Coco, Gregory A. *Killed in Action*. Gettysburg: Thomas Publications, 1992.

Conklin, E. F. *Women at Gettysburg: 1863*. Gettysburg: Thomas Publications, 1993.

Evans, Sara M. *Born for Liberty*. New York: The Free Press, 1989.

Frassanito, William A. *The Gettysburg Bicentennial Album*. Gettysburg: The Gettysburg Bicentennial Committee, 1987.

Frassanito, William A. *Gettysburg: A Journey in Time*. New York: Charles Scribner's Sons, 1975.

Frassanito, William A. *Early Photography at Gettysburg*. Gettysburg: Thomas Publications, 1995.

Matthews, Richard E. *The 149th Pennsylvania Volunteer Infantry Unit in the Civil War*. Jefferson, North Carolina, and London: McFarland & Company, Inc., 1994.

Nesbit, John W. *General History of Company D, 149th Pennsylvania Volunteers and Personal Sketches of the Members, 1862-1865*. Oakdale: Oakdale Printing, 1908.

Personal Narratives Group, eds. *Interpreting Women's Lives: Feminist Theory and Personal Narratives*. Bloomington and Indianapolis: Indiana University Press, 1989.

Shue, Richard S. *Morning at Willoughby Run*. Gettysburg: Thomas Publications, 1994.

Woodward, C. Vann, ed. *Mary Chesnut's Civil War*. New Haven and London: Yale University Press, 1981.

INDEX

Photo by John A. Marthers

Sarah Catherine (Sally) Sites Rodgers was born and raised in the Fairfield, Adams County, Pennsylvania, area and graduated from Fairfield High School in 1973. While raising her family of three children, she entered college and earned her B.A. from Mount Saint Mary's College, Emmitsburg, Maryland. Graduating magna cum laude in 1992, she was awarded numerous honors for excellence in education, original research, and academic achievement. Sally has worked for the Federal Communications Commission, the Migrant Child Development Program of L.I.U., and as a secondary schoolteacher in Frederick County, Maryland. She is presently the editor for Thomas Publications.